A GOVERNESS IN THE AGE OF JANE AUSTEN

1. A learned lady, as depicted in *Letters of the Late Alexander Pope Esq., to a Lady* (1769). *(Suffolk County Council)*

A Governess in the
Age of Jane Austen

The Journals and Letters
of Agnes Porter

Edited by Joanna Martin

THE HAMBLEDON PRESS

LONDON AND RIO GRANDE

Published by The Hambledon Press, 1998

102 Gloucester Avenue, London NW1 8HX (UK)
PO Box 162, Rio Grande, Ohio 45674 (USA)

ISBN 1 85285 164 3

A description of this book is available from
the British Library and from the Library of Congress

Typeset by Carnegie Publishing Ltd, Chatsworth Road, Lancaster

Printed on acid-free paper and bound in
Great Britain by Cambridge University Press

Contents

Illustrations

Text Illustrations

Illustration Acknowledgements

Most of the photographs were taken by Edward Martin. The author and
publisher are also grateful to the following for permission to reproduce illustrations: the National Portrait Gallery, London (I); Somerset County Council
(VI); Suffolk County Council (1); Somerset Archaeological and Natural History
Society (6).

In Memory of
My Father
Christopher Methuen-Campbell
1928–1998

Preface

I first met Agnes Porter twenty-five years ago in one of the attics of Penrice Castle, my family home. The house, a Georgian villa which stands on the Gower peninsula in South Wales, was built in the 1770s by Agnes's employer, my four-times-great grandfather Thomas Mansel Talbot, and it has never been sold. This means that nobody has ever thrown away the miscellaneous debris of family life, and I grew up surrounded by the books, sketches, photographs and other possessions of past inhabitants. I would open a drawer in the old nurseries and find a half-finished piece of sewing, which had been put away and forgotten almost two hundred years before. In the next drawer I might find a packet of tissue-paper, containing locks of hair from the heads of long-dead ancestors, or a bundle of music or embroidery patterns. In the attics I also found bundle after bundle of letters, and boxes full of old diaries and pocket books. Amongst these were the journals and letters of Agnes Porter. At first I read these mainly for the information that they gave about Penrice and the people who had lived there, but over the years I have come to realise that they have a wider value for students of the late Georgian period, and for anyone whose interests lie in the now-popular field of women's studies. Apart from a few short extracts which have been used in articles and an earlier book about Penrice,[1] none of this material has been published before. I am, therefore, particularly pleased to have this opportunity to introduce Agnes to a wider audience.

---

[1] Joanna Martin (ed.), *The Penrice Letters, 1768–1795* (Cardiff and Swansea, 1993).

Acknowledgements

My thanks are due first and foremost to my father, Christopher Methuen-Campbell, for allowing me to borrow and transcribe the family papers which form the basis of this book. The copyright of the original documents belongs to the Penrice Estate.

I have received help from the members of staff of numerous record offices and libraries. In particular, I should mention the archivists and librarians of the County Record Offices of Dorset, Gloucestershire, Norfolk, Somerset, Suffolk, West Glamorgan and Wiltshire; also the manuscripts department of the British Library, Cambridge University Library, the Edinburgh University Library, the Fox Talbot Museum at Lacock, the Guildhall Library, the National Library of Wales in Aberystwyth, the Public Record Office, the Royal Archives, the Scottish Record Office and Somerset Studies Library.

Amongst the many individuals who have given me assistance and advice, I am especially grateful to Richard Sinnett, a descendant of the the family of Agnes Porter's brother-in-law, who has shown me a number of Porter family mementoes, and has also given me invaluable information. I would also like to thank the following: Alan Bell (of the London Library), Rosemary Bigwood, Joy Cooke, Liz Davies, Charlotte Dent, Mary Dymond, Nesta Evans, Keith Harrington, the Hon. Charlotte Townshend, Roger Waine (Ilchester Estates) and Michael Wickes.

I am grateful to Martin Sheppard of the Hambledon Press for his enthusiastic help, and for his invaluable advice during the final stages of the preparation and editing of the text.

Last, but not least, I would like to thank my husband Edward Martin, who has lived with Agnes Porter for several years, and has helped me with the research and photography, besides acting as my chauffeur and companion on numerous expeditions in search of Agnes and her family and friends.

Editorial Note

The material has been arranged in chronological order, with the journals and letters combined. There is very little overlap between the two. I have retained the original spelling, but have modernised the use of punctuation and capital letters, both of which are erratic in the original documents. Some names are given in an abbreviated form in the documents: I have expanded these where it is possible to be certain of the identity of the person concerned.

I have, in general, used italics where words are underlined in the original documents. I have also added some italics for foreign words, and where the names of books are quoted.

There is a separate biographical index, with details of the people whom I have been able to identify with a reasonable degree of certainty. Another index gives details of some of the less well-known places mentioned in the text. I have also provided lists of the books owned or mentioned by Agnes Porter, and of the theatrical performances that she attended.

Any dates before 1752 may be presumed to be New Style.

Abbreviations

BL	British Library (Manuscripts Department)
DNB	*Dictionary of National Biography*
LA	Lacock Abbey
NLW	National Library of Wales, Aberystwyth
NRO	Norfolk Record Office
PRO	Public Record Office, London
WRO	Wiltshire Record Office

Introduction

Ann Agnes Porter was born in Edinburgh, a few years after the Jacobite rising of 1745.[1] For twenty years between 1784 and 1806, living in Somerset, Dorset and then South Wales, she was governess to the children and grandchildren of the second Earl of Ilchester. Agnes's first surviving journal was written in 1788, four years after she had joined Lord Ilchester's family, and a little over a year before the fall of the Bastille. Her last letter was written in January 1814. She died at Bruton in Somerset in the following month, just as twenty years of war between Britain and France were drawing to a close.

Jane Austen's *Pride and Prejudice* was published a year before Agnes Porter's death. There is no indication that Agnes ever read the novel, nor does she mention *Sense and Sensibility*, which was published two years earlier. But the society depicted in Jane Austen's novels was very much Agnes Porter's own world: a world of country houses and vicarages, of balls and card parties, and of visits to London and popular resort towns such as Bath and Malvern. It was a world that was peopled by gentlemen and aristocrats, by members of the clergy, army and navy officers and professional men, and by their wives, sisters and daughters. It is tantalising to realise that Jane Austen could even have met Agnes or her sister Fanny, as they had acquaintances in common.[2]

Agnes was an acute observer of the activities of the occupants of the great houses in which she lived. She also spent time in London, Edinburgh, Great Yarmouth, Swindon, Fairford and Bruton, and she wrote

---

[1] Her own family knew her as 'Nanny' or 'Nancy', but to everyone else she was Miss (or Mrs) Porter. Her pupils called her 'Po'. I shall refer to her as Agnes or Agnes Porter.

[2] Especially the Beaches of Netheravon, Wiltshire, and Williamstrip, Gloucestershire. See below pp. 30, 334 for the Porter-Beach connection. Jane Austen refers to the death of one of the Beach daughters in a letter dated 9 January 1796. See Deirdre Le Faye (ed.), *Jane Austen's Letters* (paperback edn, Oxford, 1997), p. 2. This must be Jane Hicks Beach, buried at Leyton, Essex, 7 January 1796.

about her life there and the people she met. Of particular interest are her accounts of the day to day lives and education of the daughters of the gentry and aristocracy in two very different households. Agnes also enjoyed travelling. Like Jane Austen, she was more interested in people than in places, and she has left entertaining descriptions of many of her fellow travellers. Her journeys included one from South Wales to Edinburgh and back, undertaken by stagecoach, without a companion, when she was in her early fifties. There are also vivid accounts of visits to the theatre and other sights in London.

Perhaps the most valuable aspect of Agnes Porter's own writings, however, is the insight that they give into the life and thoughts of an unmarried but employed gentlewoman in the late Georgian period. Agnes was, in many ways, the archetypal governess: the daughter of a clergyman who had no private income, she had to support herself and help her mother and sisters after her father's death. Her letters and diaries describe her own feelings of insecurity and worries about her possible fate if she could no longer work, and they also tell us a great deal about the ambiguity of her position within the society in which she lived, and her determination to defend and maintain her own status. In addition, she was a great self-improver, and her accounts of the books that she read, and her efforts to explore new subjects, give the reader an invaluable overview of the intellectual life of a well-read woman in the age of Jane Austen. She was interested in contemporary educational theories, and she read, and tried to put into practice, the precepts of some of the most widely-read educational writers of the day, including Maria Edgeworth and Hannah More. It must be admitted that Agnes's own occasional attempts at literary composition are pedestrian, but she certainly had a sense of humour and, even when life was difficult, she showed a determination to make the best of things, a lack of self-pity, and a genuine interest in and affection for the people with whom she lived.

Although Victorian governesses have been studied in some detail, much less attention has been paid to their predecessors in the eighteenth century and earlier.[3] It is, however, clear that female tutors had occasionally been employed since the middle ages, to educate the daughters of royal and noble families, and of the wealthiest members of the gentry. These governesses were often poor relations, who had

---

[3] For the nineteenth century, see Kathryn Hughes, *The Victorian Governess* (London and Rio Grande, Ohio, 1993). For earlier governesses, see Alice Renton, *Tyrant or Victim?* (London, 1991); and Bea Howe, *A Galaxy of Governesses* (London, 1954).

themselves received little formal education, and whose main value was as chaperons, rather than as teachers. This was true of one of the best-documented Tudor governesses, Mrs Hamblyn, who was employed to teach the daughters of Henry Sharington at Lacock Abbey in Wiltshire in the 1560s.[4] Nearly a century and a half later, around 1700, Lady Mary Wortley Montagu received 'the worst education in the world' from 'a good homespun governess' but was in fact largely self-educated, having taught herself from the books in her father's library.[5] The quality of governesses employed in even the greatest families improved little in the first half of the eighteenth century: in the 1730s George II installed Lady Deloraine as governess to his two daughters. She had evidently been chosen for her looks rather than her learning, as she soon became the King's mistress. There were a few exceptions: Elizabeth Elstob (1683–1756), who knew eight languages and became a renowned Anglo-Saxon scholar, avoided destitution by taking up a position as governess to the children of the Duke of Portland in the early 1740s. She remained with the family for the rest of her life, but was expected to teach her pupils little more than reading and writing, together with the basic principles of the Christian religion.

It was in the second half of the eighteenth century that private governesses gradually became more common, first in aristocratic households and then lower down the social scale until, in the nineteenth century, a governess became an essential status symbol in every genteel household. Agnes Porter is of particular interest because she was working at a time when only the wealthiest families employed private governesses. The only remotely comparable journal of a governess that has been published to date is that of Ellen Weeton (1776 to *c.* 1844) who worked mainly as a schoolmistress and was a private governess only for five years.[6]

The Documents

The letters and journals which make up the main part of this book have been handed down through the families of the descendants of Agnes Porter's favourite pupil, Lady Mary Talbot (*née* Fox Strangways). They are still in private hands.

---

[4] Coincidentally, Henry Sharington was an ancestor of Agnes's employer Thomas Mansel Talbot.

[5] Renton, *Tyrant or Victim?*, p. 23.

[6] Edward Hall (ed.), *Miss Weeton's Journal of a Governess* (new edn, Newton Abbot, Devon, 1969).

The journals are contained in three bound volumes, covering the years 1790–92 (with a few later entries), 1796–97, and 1802–5. There are also two volumes of letters. The first volume contains fifty-six letters from the years 1789–1810, and also includes a fragment of a diary for 1788. The second volume contains thirty-eight letters dated 1810 to 1814, with one letter of 1814 written by Agnes's friend Lucy Lloyd. The letters were probably collected and bound by Lady Mary Talbot's daughter Charlotte (later Traherne). Occasional notes and comments, mainly in pencil, have been added to the journals and letters by Lady Mary Talbot and Charlotte Traherne. In addition to the main collection, there is also one letter, written in 1813, which forms part of the Lacock Abbey collection at the Wiltshire Record Office. Most of the letters (seventy-five) were to Lady Mary Talbot, with two to her daughter Charlotte Talbot; fifteen to her sister Lady Harriot (later Frampton); and one to her nephew William Henry Fox Talbot.

There are numerous references to Agnes in contemporary letters and journals written by members of the Fox Strangways and Talbot families. None of these, however, gives us any useful information about Agnes's life and family. We do not know what she looked like, as no portrait has survived. She does say that she was plain in appearance.[7] For biographical information, we have to rely on references made in her journals and letters, usually in passing. Agnes says that she was born in Edinburgh, on 18 June, but the year of her birth is unknown. She presumably spoke with a Scots accent. The entry of her burial in the Bruton parish registers, in 1814, gives her age as 'about sixty'. Agnes does not give us her father's name or tell us where he came from, but she does say that he was a clergyman and she also names the Wiltshire parish where he was vicar. It is clear that her mother was a Scotswoman, and many of Mrs Porter's relations can be identified, but it has proved to be impossible to discover the mother's maiden name. Agnes does, however, give enough clues to make it possible to identify the majority of her friends and relations.

The Porter Family

Agnes Porter's father's family had been established in the east coast port of Great Yarmouth since at least the third quarter of the seventeenth century. The Porters and their relatives were merchants and professional men – people who, as a group, were able to increase their

---

[7] Journal, 25 October 1796.

prosperity and power during the course of the eighteenth century, until they became the dominant social and political force in provincial towns such as Yarmouth, rivalling the longer-established gentry families, whose manners they copied and whose sons and daughters they married.

In 1686 Agnes's great-grandfather, Francis Porter, married Elizabeth Jenkinson in St Nicholas's church, Great Yarmouth, one of the largest parish churches in England. Little is known about Francis Porter, though a deed of 1717 does tell us that he was a beer brewer,[8] and that he was one of the directors of the charitable Bluecoat School in Yarmouth. He died in March 1718, leaving several daughters and two sons, probably by different marriages. The older son, John Porter, was baptised at Yarmouth in 1692 and married Susan Pake, also in Yarmouth, in 1717. This John Porter, who was also a brewer, was Agnes's grandfather. He was admitted as a freeman of Yarmouth in 1720 – by purchase, rather than as a son of (or apprentice to) a freeman, which would seem to imply that his father was never a freeman. In 1724 John Porter was a trustee of the Bluecoat School. He and his wife both died in April 1729, leaving two children: a son called Francis, aged eleven, and a daughter Susanna, aged only two. Six other children, born between these two, had all died young.

Francis Porter, Agnes's father, was baptised at St Nicholas's church in February 1718. Daniel Defoe, who visited Great Yarmouth in the 1720s, described it as being 'for wealth, trade, and advantage of its situation, infinitely superior to Norwich': with a population of about 11,000 it was much smaller than Norwich with 30,000, but Defoe thought that Yarmouth was better built.[9] Great Yarmouth was at this time a prosperous port and market town, with an economy based mainly on the North Sea herring fishery. Yarmouth men also fished for cod and carried coal from Newcastle to London. The town's merchants exported cloth, made in Norwich and other nearby towns, to Holland, Portugal, Spain and the Mediterranean, and imported timber and naval stores from northern Europe for the local ship-building industry. In Francis Porter's day most people still lived in the Rows, an area of narrow courts and alley-ways dating back to medieval times, which had grown up on a sandbank at the mouth of the River Yare. During the

[8] NRO, Y/C10, Deeds of charity school, Great Yarmouth.

[9] P. N. Furbank, W. R. Owens and A. J. Coulson (eds), Daniel Defoe, *A Tour Through the Whole Island of Great Britain* (first published 1724–26; this edition London, 1991), pp. 25–30. It should be noted that there is some doubt as to whether Defoe actually visited every place described in the book, and precisely when the visits took place.

THE PORTER FAMILY

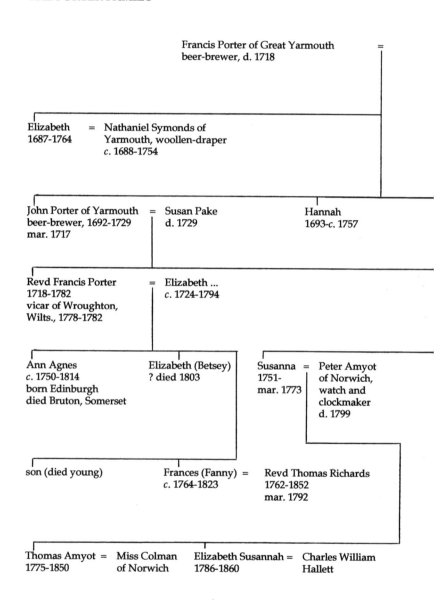

Francis Porter of Great Yarmouth
beer-brewer, d. 1718 =

Elizabeth   =   Nathaniel Symonds of
1687-1764   Yarmouth, woollen-draper
                     c. 1688-1754

John Porter of Yarmouth =   Susan Pake   Hannah
beer-brewer, 1692-1729   d. 1729   1693-c. 1757
mar. 1717

Revd Francis Porter   =   Elizabeth ...
1718-1782   c. 1724-1794
vicar of Wroughton,
Wilts., 1778-1782

Ann Agnes   Elizabeth (Betsey)   Susanna = Peter Amyot
c. 1750-1814   ? died 1803   1751-   of Norwich,
born Edinburgh   mar. 1773 watch and
died Bruton, Somerset   clockmaker
                                                       d. 1799

son (died young)   Frances (Fanny) =   Revd Thomas Richards
                     c. 1764-1823   1762-1852
                                         mar. 1792

Thomas Amyot = Miss Colman   Elizabeth Susannah = Charles William
1775-1850   of Norwich   1786-1860   Hallett

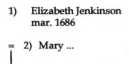

1) Elizabeth Jenkinson
    mar. 1686

= 2) Mary ...

Richard Porter
1702-c. 1774

Frances
1695-c. 1767

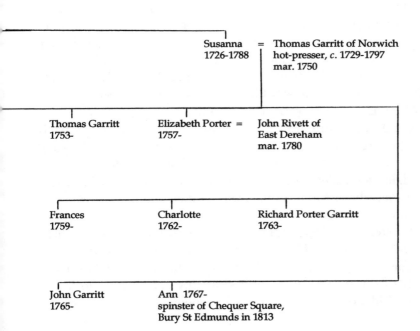

Susanna   = Thomas Garritt of Norwich
1726-1788   hot-presser, c. 1729-1797
                mar. 1750

Thomas Garritt   Elizabeth Porter =   John Rivett of
1753-   1757-   East Dereham
                                          mar. 1780

Frances   Charlotte   Richard Porter Garritt
1759-   1762-   1763-

John Garritt   Ann 1767-
1765-   spinster of Chequer Square,
                     Bury St Edmunds in 1813

eighteenth century the town was enlarged and gentrified, with the building of St George's church in 1714–16 and a new town hall in 1715. Defoe admired the town hall and the custom house. The houses of the Yarmouth merchants, he wrote, 'look like little palaces, rather than the dwelling-houses of private men'. In his day, however, Yarmouth was a sober place: he did not find 'abundance of revelling, or … assemblies, plays, and gaming meetings' there.

Of Francis Porter's early life we know nothing. He must have gone to school, but his name does not appear in the admissions registers of the Bluecoat School in Yarmouth. He and his sister probably went to live with relatives after their parents' early deaths. In October 1730, at the comparatively early age of twelve, Francis was apprenticed to his uncle Nathaniel Symonds, a woollen-draper and the husband of his father's older sister Elizabeth.[10] He must have served his full term of seven years, for in January 1739 he was granted the freedom of Great Yarmouth, for which he was qualified as the former apprentice of a freeman.[11]

Nothing is known of Francis Porter's movements during the next decade, but by the early 1750s he was in Edinburgh. By this time he had been ordained as an Anglican priest – Agnes records that her father performed the marriage ceremony for Dr Thomas Elliot and Helen, the daughter of Sir John Elphinstone, a marriage that took place in Edinburgh in 1751.[12] At about this time Francis Porter also married: his bride, whose first name was Elizabeth, and who had been born in about 1724, was a cousin of Dr Thomas Elliot.

Francis and Elizabeth Porter had at least four children, all probably born in Edinburgh. Ann Agnes, the eldest, was born between 1750 and 1752; there was a daughter called Elizabeth (known as Betsey), and a younger daughter called Frances (Fanny), born around 1762. There was also a son, whose name is unknown; he died young, but may have survived into his teens.

The Edinburgh into which Agnes Porter was born was the dark, dirty, polluted, labyrinthine Old Town, which huddled on the Castle Rock and stretched along the Royal Mile towards the palace of Holyrood. Expansion to the north was prevented at this period by a loch and marshland. Old Edinburgh was a city of tenements, of courts, closes,

---

[10] NRO, Y/C22/44, Records of Yarmouth apprentices, 1727–51.

[11] NRO, Y/C19/2, Yarmouth assembly book, 1737–50.

[12] Agnes calls him Sir James Elphinstone. I have so far failed to find any record of Francis Porter's ordination.

steps and wynds. Defoe commented on the 'throng'd' buildings, up to twelve storeys high, and on the 'stench and nastiness' amongst which the 50,000 or so inhabitants lived. He also found many well-built stone churches, houses and public buildings, and several 'very magnificent houses of the nobility' in the Canongate.[13] There was a constant bustle of traders and professional men and a lively intellectual life, centred on the churches, the law courts and the university. In all, it was an exciting, cosmopolitan, companionable city in which to grow up.

In 1757 Francis Porter inherited a sum of money from his aunt, Hannah Porter of Great Yarmouth.[14] A little over six years later, in 1764, he was a beneficiary under the will of another aunt, Elizabeth Symonds, also of Great Yarmouth.[15] In July 1765 Francis Porter, 'presbyter of the Church of England', was awarded the degree of Doctor of Divinity by the University of Edinburgh.[16] By this time, however, he seems to have left Edinburgh. He married several couples at St Luke's church in Chelsea between September 1763 and October 1764;[17] and the will of his last surviving aunt, Frances Porter, which was written in June 1765, describes him as 'The Revd Francis Porter of Chelsea'.[18] Frances Porter left property in Great Yarmouth to her nephew, in addition to shipping and shares in ships or vessels.

The Revd Francis Porter does not appear to have been attached to any particular parish at this time. He presumably belonged to that large group of clergymen who hired themselves out to take services wherever they could, hoping that they would eventually find a permanent position of some kind.[19] In the mid eighteenth century Chelsea was a pleasant riverside settlement, clustered around its old church on the north bank of the Thames and separated from London by marshes and heathland. Travellers were carried across the river by ferry until 1772, when the

---

[13] Furbank, Owens and Coulson (eds), *Tour Through the Whole Island of Great Britain*, pp. 310–19.
[14] NRO, NCC 260 Long, Will of Hannah Porter of Great Yarmouth, spinster, 1757.
[15] NRO, ANW 1764/18, Will of Elizabeth Symonds of Great Yarmouth, widow, 1764.
[16] *A Catalogue of the Graduates in the Faculties of Arts, Divinity and Law of the University of Edinburgh* (Edinburgh, 1858), p. 243. This appears to have been his only degree: he did not attend Oxford or Cambridge, nor was he awarded any other degree by any of the Scottish universities.
[17] Later known as Chelsea Old Church.
[18] NRO, NCC 313 Errington, Will of Frances Porter of Great Yarmouth, spinster, 1767.
[19] Irene Collins, *Jane Austen and the Clergy* (London and Rio Grande, Ohio, 1993), especially p. 21.

first bridge was completed. Around the village were the mansions of wealthy families, who favoured Chelsea as it was quiet and still almost rural, and as the air was thought to be healthier than that of central London. The grander houses were set amongst parks and gardens, including nursery gardens along the King's Road, the Ranelagh Pleasure Gardens,[20] and the Physic Garden. Within easy reach was London itself – the fastest growing city in Europe, a cultural magnet and an influential centre for the arts and polite taste.[21]

How long the Porters stayed in Chelsea is unknown, but they seem to have been in the London area until at least 1770, when Francis Porter performed his last marriage ceremony at St Luke's. In 1778 he finally gained a parish of his own, becoming the vicar of Wroughton, a large village near Swindon in Wiltshire.[22] He was presented to the living by John Hume, who was Bishop of Salisbury from 1766 to 1782. Obtaining a benefice at this period often depended on knowing, or being related to, the patron, but there is no obvious earlier connection between Porter and Hume. The years at Wroughton seem to have been happy and sociable – Agnes visited several friends from this period in later years. Francis Porter was only in Wiltshire for four years, however. He died on 24 March 1782 and was buried at Wroughton, where he is commemorated by a inscription on the floor of the nave, near the font.

Agnes Porter tells us virtually nothing about her childhood. There is no indication that she ever went to school, and it seems likely that she and her sisters were largely educated at home, perhaps with extra lessons in subjects such as music and dancing from local masters, as was a common practice at the time. Like her near-contemporary and fellow Scotswoman, the authoress Elizabeth Hamilton, she would have been instructed in 'writing, geography, and the use of the globes', together with dancing, French, drawing and music.[23] Neither Agnes nor Elizabeth Hamilton learned Latin, a fact which both regretted in later life. Both women were to a large extent self-educated, making use of the books that were available in the various houses where they lived. From a passing reference in 1798, it seems that Agnes and her sister Fanny spent some time in France, at Boulogne, during their youth. It is not clear if other members of their family were there too. Boulogne had a large English colony in the eighteenth century, and was known

---

[20] Open from 1742 to 1805.
[21] John Brewer, *The Pleasures of the Imagination* (London, 1997), p. xxv.
[22] The population in 1801 was 1100.
[23] Miss [Elizabeth Ogilvy] Benger, *Memoirs of the Late Mrs Elizabeth Hamilton* (London, 1818), p. 37.

as a refuge for debtors and other people who could not afford to live in their own country. It is also possible that the Porter girls were sent there expressly to learn French, as a knowledge of that language was considered essential for a well-educated young lady. In later life, Agnes's French was reasonably fluent. She also played the piano and harpsichord. She sang too, though we do not know if she had a good voice. The few sketches that have survived suggest, however, that she could not draw well. What she did have was a lively and enquiring mind. She retained her enthusiasm for learning throughout her adult life: her letters and journals record attempts to learn Italian, Latin and German, as well as details of the books that she read for entertainment and information.

Miss Ann Agnes Porter

Agnes Porter does not tell us exactly how or when she first became a governess. Her father does not appear to have been well off, and he probably found it difficult to support three unmarried daughters. From her diaries and letters it is obvious that Agnes was interested in men, and there is little doubt that she hoped to marry. But she was, as she herself admits, not pretty, and it is unlikely that her father could have provided much in the way of a dowry. Agnes's main asset were her brains. These were of limited help in the marriage-market at a time when women were expected to defer to men – and not, as Agnes certainly did, to show off their intelligence and extensive reading.

From references to some of her friends and acquaintances, it is clear that Agnes spent some time during her youth in London; she also writes of her 'juvenile days' at Yarmouth.[24] She certainly lived for some years with the Ramey family in Great Yarmouth. John Ramey (c. 1719–94) was one of the town's wealthiest and most prominent citizens. He was a contemporary of the Revd Francis Porter, and the two had probably known each other since childhood. Though Agnes's parents had never lived in Yarmouth after their marriage, Francis Porter had owned property there until at least 1771.[25] John Ramey and his wife Abigail (c. 1726–1811) had two surviving daughters, whom Agnes knew well and with whom she corresponded in later years. Both of the daughters were approximately the same age as Agnes, so she cannot have been

---

[24] Journal, 20 January 1805.
[25] NRO, Y/L1/8, Yarmouth Poor Rates. He had inherited some of it from his aunt Frances Porter. See above, p. 9.

their governess. She seems to have acted as a companion to Mrs Ramey. Agnes says that she was present at the wedding of Peter Upcher and Elizabeth Ramey, which took place in 1777, and she also says that she left the Rameys in 1782, presumably at the time of her father's death.

The Revd Francis Porter appears to have left little in the way of money or property to his wife when he died in 1782. Certainly not enough for her to live on, as Agnes supported her, at least in part, until her mother died in 1794. How much, if anything, the Rameys paid Agnes is unknown, but from 1782 onwards she needed to earn money to support herself and her mother. She went first, in 1782, to the Goddards, one of the leading gentry families of Swindon. Agnes does not tell us how she obtained this position, but at this period governesses were usually employed on the recommendation of a previous employer or mutual acquaintance. Wroughton, where Agnes's father was vicar, is only a couple of miles from Swindon, and if the Goddards did not know the Porters, they certainly had acquaintances in common, such as the Calleys and Codringtons. Ambrose Goddard of Swindon House, MP for Wiltshire from 1772 to 1806, and his wife Sarah, had at least six daughters, born in the 1770s and 1780s. Agnes kept in touch with the Goddards after she left in 1784. In 1797 she noted that she had visited Mrs Goddard and her six daughters in London.

Agnes stayed with the Goddards for less than two years, for in January 1784, when she was already in her early thirties, she took one of the most important steps of her life: she went to live at Redlynch, near Bruton in Somerset, as governess to the daughters of Henry Thomas Fox Strangways, second Earl of Ilchester, and his wife Mary Theresa. Once again, she must have obtained the position as a result of a personal recommendation. Lord Ilchester had a shooting-box at Maddington on Salisbury Plain, about thirty miles from Swindon, where the whole family went every autumn. Ambrose Goddard was a contemporary. Perhaps the two men met on hunting expeditions, or in London.

Agnes Porter and Lord Ilchester's Daughters

Lord Ilchester was the grandson of Sir Stephen Fox, Paymaster of the Guards to Charles II, who had amassed a vast fortune during more than forty years of service in the royal household. Sir Stephen's elder son, another Stephen, had played little part in public life but had been created Earl of Ilchester in 1756 – largely on the basis of the landed wealth that he had inherited from his father. The first Earl's younger brother, Henry Fox, had inherited much less, but as a notoriously corrupt Paymaster General of the Forces during the Seven Years War had acquired his own fortune and landed estate, being created Baron Holland in 1763. Lord Holland's younger son was the brilliant and colourful politician Charles James Fox. In taking the position of governess to Lord Ilchester's children, Agnes was therefore entering the household of one of the great Whig families of the day.

Lord Stavordale, as he then was (he became the second Earl of Ilchester on his father's death in 1776), had married an Irishwoman, Mary Theresa Grady, daughter of Standish and Mary Grady of Cappercullen, County Limerick, in 1772. By January 1784 Lord and Lady Ilchester had three daughters: Elizabeth Theresa, aged eleven; Mary Lucy, aged almost eight; and Harriot, aged five and a half. Another daughter, Charlotte Anne, was born in February 1784, shortly after Agnes Porter's arrival. There followed two more daughters: Louisa Emma in 1785 and Susanna Caroline in 1790, with one son, Henry Stephen, born in 1787. Although the Earl of Ilchester's main seat was Melbury, in Dorset, the children lived mostly at Redlynch until the dowager Lady Ilchester died in 1792.

The house at Redlynch had originally been built by Lord Ilchester's grandfather, Sir Stephen Fox, early in the eighteenth century. It had then been rebuilt and extended to accommodate the growing family of the first Earl and Countess of Ilchester about 1750. The alterations appear to have created two separate houses, standing a few yards apart but used in conjunction with each other. Redlynch was certainly unusual – George III, who visited the house in 1789, thought it 'extraordinary' – but the gardens and surroundings were beautiful. The children loved it.

It is clear from her diaries that Agnes was devoted to Lady Ilchester, who was a couple of years her junior. Lord Ilchester's choice of a bride had been an unconventional one: packed off to Ireland as a cornet in the First Regiment of Horse, probably in order to remove him from the temptations of the gaming-houses of London, he had fallen in love with the beautiful daughter of an obscure Irish gentleman, who was unable to produce much, if anything, in the way of a dowry. The marriage turned out happily, though Lord Ilchester was never an easy man to live with. His family, who had been distinctly dubious about his choice of a bride to begin with, had quickly been won over by Mary Theresa's unaffected charm and intelligence. In later years Lord Ilchester's sister, Lady Susan O'Brien, wrote of her sister-in-law:

> Though educated in another kingdom, and not with all the high accomplishments beginning to be common in this, such was her judgement,

THE FOX STRANGWAYS FAMILY

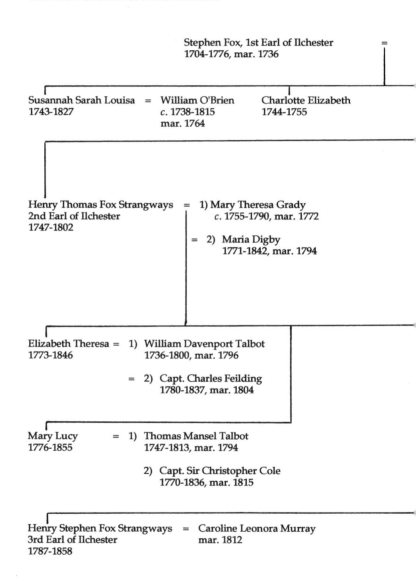

Stephen Fox, 1st Earl of Ilchester   =
1704-1776, mar. 1736

Susannah Sarah Louisa   =   William O'Brien   Charlotte Elizabeth
1743-1827   c. 1738-1815   1744-1755
                               mar. 1764

Henry Thomas Fox Strangways   =   1) Mary Theresa Grady
2nd Earl of Ilchester   c. 1755-1790, mar. 1772
1747-1802
                               =   2) Maria Digby
                                        1771-1842, mar. 1794

Elizabeth Theresa =   1) William Davenport Talbot
1773-1846   1736-1800, mar. 1796

                  =   2) Capt. Charles Feilding
                           1780-1837, mar. 1804

Mary Lucy   =   1) Thomas Mansel Talbot
1776-1855   1747-1813, mar. 1794

                       2) Capt. Sir Christopher Cole
                           1770-1836, mar. 1815

Henry Stephen Fox Strangways   =   Caroline Leonora Murray
3rd Earl of Ilchester   mar. 1812
1787-1858

Elizabeth Strangways Horner
1723-1792

Juliana Judith
1746-1749

Lucy   = Col. Stephen Digby
1748-1787   1742-1800
             mar. 1771

Christiana Caroline   = John Dyke Acland   Col. Stephen Strangways
Henrietta, 1750-1815   1747-1778   Digby Fox Strangways
                                      1751-1836

Frances Muriel   = Valentine Richard   Revd Charles   = Jane Haines
1755-1814   Quin, 1752-1824   Redlynch   mar. 1787
             mar. 1777   Fox Strangways   d. 1830
                          1761-1836

Stephen Standish Strangways   Harriot   = James Frampton
Fox Strangways 1777-1777   1778-1844   mar. 1799

Charlotte Anne   = Sir Charles Lemon   Louisa Emma = Henry Petty,
1784-1826   mar. 1810   1785-1851   3rd Marquess of
                                        Lansdowne,
                                        mar. 1808

Susanna Caroline
1790-1792

her manners and feelings, that no conversation could be more agreeable, or even more instructive, than hers was, and on all subjects, and in her company it was difficult not to improve. Her temper was quick and irritable, but subdued by her great judgement. She was the best of wives, often in very difficult situations: active and attentive to the care and improvement of her children ...[26]

Lady Ilchester's comparatively modest and informal background, and her obvious preference for life in the country with her children rather than the attractions of high society in London, probably made Agnes's life at Redlynch easier than it would have been with a mistress who had been born into an aristocratic and exclusive family.

Lady Ilchester was in poor health for much of her married life. She died in June 1790, six weeks after the birth of her sixth daughter. Two months later, on 13 August, Agnes began to keep a detailed diary: it is at this point that the series of her diaries and letters really starts, though there is one earlier letter and a fragment of a diary from 1788. For the next four years, until Lord Ilchester remarried in 1794, Agnes was to act in many ways as a mother to her pupils. She seems to have enjoyed the independence of her position, though her responsibilities were sometimes a burden.

Agnes Porter's references to Lord Ilchester are usually deferential. In 1790 she describes him as an 'excellent father to his children',[27] and in 1791 she says that he is 'kind, attentive, intelligent and delicate'.[28] A rather different impression emerges from a passing reference in a letter from Agnes's sister Frances Richards to Mrs Hicks Beach, written in 1793, when she writes that 'Lord Ilchester wishes not for grown-up daughters to inspect his conduct'.[29] Their letters indicate that Agnes's pupils were fond of their father. He often took them away on visits with him, instead of leaving them with their governess for most or all of the time. But other sources show that he could be difficult. His main interests were hunting and gambling – his daughter Elizabeth remembered in later years how he had 'spurned' her and one of her sisters 'brutally from him' when they ran up to embrace him as he returned early one morning from a night at the gaming-tables.[30] To some extent Lord Ilchester was conscious of his own faults: in a codicil to his will, written in 1791, he expressed his regret that his son 'will justly have

[26] Transcribed in Charlotte Traherne, 'Family Recollections' (MS).
[27] Journal, 22 October 1790.
[28] Journal, 18 February 1791.
[29] Letter, Frances Richards to Mrs Hicks Beach, 11 July 1793.
[30] C. R. M. Talbot, 'Characters of Some Members of My Family' (MS).

to accuse me for my follies, which will during his lifetime, I fear, much contract his income'.[31] His estates were, indeed, heavily burdened with debts when he died in 1802. Even his closest relatives found Lord Ilchester awkward to get on with: in later years his elder sister, Lady Susan O'Brien, remembered: 'My brother's reserve chill'd my heart out of all freedom, confidence and ease – yet he was good-natured'.[32] Lady Susan, one of the more extravert members of the Fox Strangways family, frequently commented on the extremely reserved natures of many of her relations.

During the two years after Lady Ilchester's death Agnes and her pupils lived mainly at Redlynch, though the two older girls spent an increasing amount of time elsewhere, either with their father or with aunts and cousins. Sometimes the whole family spent a few weeks at the family's main house at Melbury in Dorset, or at the dowager Lady Ilchester's summer home at Abbotsbury, on the Dorset coast. For approximately three months each year, between February and June during the height of the social season, the governess and all but the youngest children would usually move to Lord Ilchester's London house at 31 Old Burlington Street. Agnes enjoyed her visits to London, where she was able to visit and entertain old friends, and to go with them to the theatre.

The year 1792 saw several developments which were to have a profound effect on the course of the latter part of Agnes's life. In January Lord Ilchester's youngest child, Susan, died, and a week later Lord Ilchester, accompanied by his son Harry (Lord Stavordale) and his second daughter, Mary, left Redlynch for Wales, on the first stage of a journey to Ireland, where they were to visit Lord Ilchester's youngest sister, Lady Frances Quin, and his late wife's family, in County Limerick. They were to be away for eight months, during which time Agnes was to remain at Redlynch with the two youngest daughters, Charlotte and Louisa. In the meantime, Harriot remained at a boarding school in Weymouth, while the eldest daughter, Elizabeth, was presented at Court, and enjoyed her first London season, accompanied by her aunt Lady Harriot Acland.

Lord Ilchester returned with his son and daughter in September 1792, two months before the death of his mother, the dowager Lady Ilchester, who occupied the main family seat at Melbury. In the following year Agnes gained one pupil, Harriot, who left her school, and lost

---

[31] PRO, PROB 11/1384/908.
[32] BL, Add. MS 51359, Journal of Lady Susan O'Brien, 20 October 1812, fol. 134r.

another, when Mary in turn was presented at Court in the spring. In July the whole family left Redlynch, which had been Lord Ilchester's home since his marriage in 1772, and moved to Melbury, twelve miles north west of Dorchester. The house, with its remarkable tower, had been built by Lord Ilchester's ancestor Giles Strangways in the mid sixteenth century. It had subsequently been remodelled a century and a half later. Melbury was much larger and grander than Redlynch but appeared rather outdated by the 1790s. Lord Ilchester seems to have begun alterations to the house and grounds soon after his mother's death, but these were still unfinished when he himself died ten years later. His sister, Lady Susan O'Brien, did not approve of the changes, as she wrote in 1803:

> Hardly anything that used to give us pleasure remains. The shrubbery, the old grove, the flowers, the neatness, even nicety, of my mother's time, all gone. All appearance of grandeur, the old-fashioned grandeur, gone. The house, from striking everyone by its suite of rooms of different sizes, its fine old furniture so suitable for its stile, and its delightful green house at the end, now appears contracted and reduced, to look like a common gentleman's house.[33]

The year 1794 saw further changes. In February Lord Ilchester's second daughter, Mary, married Thomas Mansel Talbot of Penrice and Margam in Glamorgan. She was not quite eighteen years old, whilst he was a bachelor of forty-six and a contemporary of his bride's father. They had met two years previously, when Lord Ilchester and his children had stayed at Penrice on their way to Ireland. If Agnes had allowed herself to have a favourite pupil, she would certainly have chosen Mary. She was eventually to spend a number of years as governess to Thomas and Mary Talbot's children in Wales.

Back at Melbury, there were further developments. In August 1794 Lord Ilchester remarried: his second wife was a cousin, Maria Digby, who was twenty-four years his junior. The arrival of a new Lady Ilchester on the scene was greeted with a certain amount of dismay, not least by Agnes, whose position within the household at Melbury inevitably became less important. Nevertheless, life continued much as before during the next two years.

In April 1796 Lord Ilchester's eldest daughter, Elizabeth, married William Davenport Talbot, a cousin of Thomas Mansel Talbot. By this time the third daughter, Harriot, was spending less time in the school-

---

[33] BL, Add. MS 51359, fol. 68r.

room, so most of Agnes's time was spent with the two youngest girls, Charlotte and Louisa, and with their younger brother, Lord Stavordale. Agnes taught the latter to read and write, and to do simple sums, but from April 1796 a male tutor, the Revd Joseph Griffith, was also employed to teach the boy the Latin that he would need before he went away to school later in the same year.

In the autumn of 1796 Agnes was away from her pupils for six weeks, during which time she visited friends in Salisbury and London, and then spent a fortnight in Norfolk, where she first stayed with her old friend Elizabeth Upcher, in Great Yarmouth, and then visited relations in Norwich. A little over a month after Agnes's return to Melbury, early in November, she received the news that Mrs Upcher's husband had died suddenly. This was to prove to be another turning-point.

Agnes Porter's position within the Fox Strangways family had become much more difficult after Lord Ilchester's second marriage in 1794. The new Lady Ilchester was a friend and contemporary of Agnes's pupils, but she seems to have lost little time in making it clear that she wished to be mistress in her own household, no doubt resenting the presence of an older woman who, she felt, compared her unfavourably with her predecessor. Agnes was, as ever, discreet, but the occasional glimpse of her true feelings does emerge: in 1797 she wrote of Lord and Lady Ilchester's two-year-old son William that 'he is so sweet a child that at *last* he makes *even me* love him, *et c'est beaucoup dire*'.[34]

Agnes was not slow to make up her mind when, early in 1797, Elizabeth Upcher asked her to live with her in Norfolk. The final straw, it appears, was the information that Agnes would not have her own parlour, in which to entertain her friends, during the family's usual stay in London. Did Lord Ilchester understand Agnes's meaning when she thanked him for 'thirteen years' protection, and *several* years of happiness'?[35] She reflected afterwards in her journal that 'I had not said a single word more than I had resolved to do. I had not been induced by any little *female resentments* to hazard or compromise the tranquillity of a family I respected, though I looked upon myself as the victim of circumstances'. So, in September 1797, six months after handing in her notice, Agnes left Melbury and the Fox Strangways family. By the end of the year she was living with Elizabeth Upcher and her family in Great Yarmouth. As Mrs Upcher had offered her a hundred

---

[34] Letter, 9 July 1797.
[35] Journal, 28 March 1797.

pounds a year, with her 'affection, friendship and society',[36] Agnes must have hoped that this comfortable arrangement would last for many years.

Agnes Porter in Norfolk and South Wales

Great Yarmouth had changed a good deal between the 1720s, when Agnes Porter's father was a child, and the late 1790s, when Agnes lived there with Elizabeth Upcher. By 1801 the population was nearly 15,000. New public buildings had been added in the mid eighteenth century, and the sober fishing-port had transformed itself into a gentrified seaside resort, with a bathing-house, theatre and assembly rooms, together with numerous inns, catering for the needs of residents and visitors alike. Agnes clearly found the place rather dull, though she recognised that it had improved since her days with the Rameys. In January 1798 she told Harriot Fox Strangways that the 'young women here are beginning to emerge from the ignorance that universally prevailed some years back, yet the sciences and fine arts are by no means in an advanced state'.[37] The inhabitants were pious, led regular lives and did not believe in staying out late in the evenings. Agnes filled up her time with reading, going out for walks and visiting friends, and was happy to feel that Mrs Upcher enjoyed her company. In the event, she was not to be in Yarmouth for long.

No letters or journals written by Agnes between October 1798 and November 1800 have survived, but other contemporary sources make it possible to work out the course of events. Elizabeth Upcher died, apparently suddenly, in March 1799. She left Agnes £100 in her will.[38] Agnes was probably still with the Upchers when Elizabeth died but would have had to leave soon afterwards. Her feelings at this time are unknown, but she must certainly have been worried by the prospect of losing both her home and most of her income. In the end everything turned out well, for her former pupil Lady Mary and her husband Thomas Mansel Talbot asked Agnes to go and live with them at Penrice Castle as Mary's companion, and as governess to the growing family of Talbot children. Agnes was to stay at Penrice for the next six years.

Penrice Castle stands on the Gower peninsula in South Wales, an area approximately fifteen miles long and six miles wide, which lies to

---

[36] Journal, 16 April 1797.
[37] Letter, 16 January 1798.
[38] PRO, PROB 11/1323/323.

the west of Swansea. Gower, a popular holiday centre in the twentieth century, was remote and rarely visited by outsiders in the 1770s when Thomas Mansel Talbot decided to built himself a modern villa there, on land which had first been acquired by his de Penrice ancestors in the twelfth century. The owners of the estate had moved away from Gower in the mid sixteenth century, when Sir Rice Mansel, a descendant of the de Penrice family, had bought Margam Abbey and converted the abbey buildings into a mansion that was to be the family's main seat for the next two centuries. Thomas Mansel Talbot had inherited the Penrice and Margam estates in 1758 when he was ten years old. He had come of age in 1768 and had then spent several years travelling on the Continent, especially in Italy. By 1772, when he returned to Britain, he had both the money and the inclination to build himself a new house. He never seems to have liked the Mansels' house at Margam which was by this time rambling, inconvenient and neglected, having been little altered – and lived in only intermittently – since the death of the first Lord Mansel in 1723.

Impressed by the classical villas that he had seen in Italy, and filled with the contemporary enthusiasm for uncultivated, romantic scenery, Thomas had commissioned the Gloucestershire architect Anthony Keck to design a totally new house for him, below the walls of the de Penrices' thirteenth-century stone castle at Penrice, overlooking the Bristol Channel – a situation which Thomas described in 1773 as 'the most romantic spot in all the county'.[39] The house had been built and partly furnished during the 1770s, and a park, with a lake, woodland walks and gardens, had been planned and laid out at the same time under the direction of the landscape designer William Emes.

Thomas Mansel Talbot continued to travel during the 1780s, living at Penrice for only a part of the time. He was still a bachelor when Lord Ilchester and his son and daughter Mary stayed at Penrice on their way to Ireland in 1792. Thomas and Lord Ilchester were almost exactly the same age, having been contemporaries at Oxford. They had certainly known each other since 1783, being brought together by their mutual love of hunting: Thomas had spent a good deal of time during his bachelor years at Grateley in Hampshire, only fifteen miles from Maddington where Lord Ilchester and his family went every autumn.

Although Lord Ilchester probably only intended to spend a few days

---

[39] Letter, T. M. Talbot to William Beach, 3 January 1773. See Joanna Martin, *The Penrice Letters, 1768–1795* (Cardiff and Swansea, 1993), p. 83.

THE TALBOT FAMILY

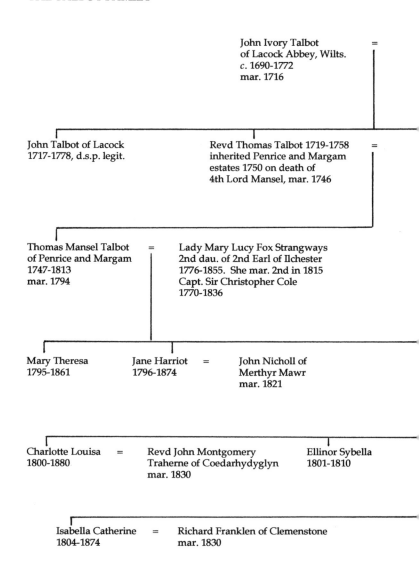

John Ivory Talbot   =
of Lacock Abbey, Wilts.
c. 1690-1772
mar. 1716

John Talbot of Lacock
1717-1778, d.s.p. legit.

Revd Thomas Talbot 1719-1758   =
inherited Penrice and Margam
estates 1750 on death of
4th Lord Mansel, mar. 1746

Thomas Mansel Talbot   =   Lady Mary Lucy Fox Strangways
of Penrice and Margam   2nd dau. of 2nd Earl of Ilchester
1747-1813   1776-1855. She mar. 2nd in 1815
mar. 1794   Capt. Sir Christopher Cole
                             1770-1836

Mary Theresa   Jane Harriot   =   John Nicholl of
1795-1861   1796-1874   Merthyr Mawr
                                    mar. 1821

Charlotte Louisa   =   Revd John Montgomery   Ellinor Sybella
1800-1880   Traherne of Coedarhydyglyn 1801-1810
                       mar. 1830

Isabella Catherine   =   Richard Franklen of Clemenstone
1804-1874   mar. 1830

Mary Mansel
1696-1735
dau. of Thomas, 1st Lord
Mansel of Margam, Glamorgan

Jane Beach   Martha   =   Revd William
1726-1768   d. 1790   Davenport
dau. of Thomas Beach of   mar. 1751   1725-1781
Fittleton and Keevil, Wilts.

Lady Elizabeth Theresa Fox Strangways   =   William Davenport Talbot
eldest dau. of 2nd Earl of Ilchester   1763-1800, inherited Lacock
1773-1846. She mar. 2nd in 1804   1778 on death of his uncle
Capt. Charles Feilding   John Talbot
1780-1837   mar. 1796

Christiana Barbara   William Henry Fox Talbot
1798-1808   of Lacock 1800-1877
                             photographer

Christopher Rice Mansel Talbot   =   Lady Charlotte Butler
1803-1890, mar. 1835   dau. of 1st Earl of Glengall

            Emma Thomasina   =   John Dillwyn Llewelyn
            1806-1881   of Penllergaer, mar. 1833

at Penrice, his stay there was prolonged by a broken carriage-spring and an attack of the gout – a painful complaint from which he suffered frequently. During the month that she spent in Wales, in January and February 1792, Lady Mary fell in love with Penrice – and her host fell in love with her. Mary was, however, only fifteen when she arrived at Penrice – she celebrated her sixteenth birthday during her stay there. She was still a schoolgirl and had not yet been presented at Court. She and her family inevitably had some doubts about the wisdom of marrying a man who was nearly thirty years older than she was. The marriage did not take place until 1 February 1794 – two years after the couple's first meeting. Even before Lord Ilchester and his daughter agreed to the match, however, Thomas embarked on a programme of redecoration and refurbishment at Penrice. The interior of the house was repainted and a number of rooms, which had been little used since the completion of the building over ten years earlier, were properly furnished for the first time.

At first Agnes's teaching duties at Penrice were light. When she arrived at Penrice, in the summer of 1799, the Talbots had three small daughters, of whom even the oldest was barely old enough to need a governess. In June 1799 Lady Elizabeth Talbot wrote to her sister Harriot, describing life at Penrice: 'Miss Porter reads to us part of every morning while we paint and work; the rest we drive or sail about in the bay, and sometimes dine and sometimes drink tea out'.[40] In a letter written at this time to Mrs Hicks Beach, in which he recorded his impressions of Agnes Porter, the Revd Sydney Smith also described Thomas and Mary Talbot and their home:

> I like your cousin Mr Talbot – he is good temper'd, unaffected and civil. I should think him too to be generous, hospitable, expensive[41] and passionate, fond of his wife and children to dotage. Lady Mary seems to be an amiable, valuable woman who uses her influence with her husband to the best purposes. She is shy, a little rural, for which I like her not the worse, and very handsome.[42]

Penrice was certainly isolated – the journey to Melbury took three days; and a trip to London generally involved five days of travelling. While few families living in western Glamorgan could match Thomas

[40] WRO, LA, unlisted, Letter, Lady Elizabeth Talbot to Lady Harriot Fox Strang-ways, 27 June 1799.
[41] Extravagant.
[42] See below, pp. 39–40.

Mansel Talbot's wealth or social position, the Talbots were nevertheless able to enjoy a reasonably lively social life.[43]

Swansea, the nearest town to Penrice, lies twelve miles away. Its population increased rapidly in the second half of the eighteenth century, to reach 6000 by 1801, but the town was still less than half the size of Yarmouth, and remained provincial and undeveloped in comparison with the other towns and cities with which Agnes was already familiar: London, Edinburgh and Norwich. Much of the increase in Swansea's population was the result of industrial development in the surrounding area, particularly the growth of coal-mining, iron-working and copper-smelting. Efforts were being made in the years immediately before and after 1800 to turn the town into a fashionable seaside resort, with the provision of bathing facilities, assembly rooms and a theatre. The juxtaposition of heavy industry and leisure facilities was somewhat incongruous: as Henry Skrine noted in 1798, 'all the resources of polished society are here at times to be found amidst the noise of manufactures and the buzz of incessant commerce'.[44] Most of the wealthier families lived to the west of the town, on the edge of Gower around Sketty and Singleton, within reach of Swansea but away from the commercial and industrial area, and with much-admired views across Swansea Bay. Amongst the Talbots' friends in this area were the Kings of Marino and the Calvert Joneses of Veranda. It was possible to get from Penrice to Swansea and back in a day, though the Talbots often stayed with friends for a night or two. Agnes visited Swansea from time to time with the Talbots and their children, and she spent a month at the bathing-house on the Burrows there with six Talbot children in November and December 1804. Agnes gives an account of the stay in her journal: numerous visitors kept her and the children occupied, but the position and facilities of the bathing-house clearly left a great deal to be desired.

By the time Agnes left Penrice in October 1806 there were eight children: seven girls and one boy. The eldest five were girls: Mary, born 1795; Jane, 1796; Christiana (Tina), 1798; Charlotte (Charry), 1800; and Ellinor, 1801. They had been followed by the only son, Christopher (Kit) in 1803, and then two more girls Isabella (Bella), 1804; and Emma, 1806. The Penrice Talbots were also joined, from time to time, by their

---

[43] See below, pp. 44–47, for further information on their social circle and Agnes Porter's place in local society.
[44] Henry Skrine, *Two Successive Tours Throughout the Whole of Wales* (London, 1798), p. 68.

cousin, William Henry Fox Talbot, born in 1800, who later became
famous as the inventor of the negative-positive system of photography.
At Penrice, teaching the elder children and helping to supervise the
younger ones was a full-time occupation for their governess.

Agnes Porter's health seems generally to have been good, though
she was incapacitated by a severe attack of gout for two months in the
summer and autumn of 1803. She was fit enough in 1805, when she
was in her early fifties, to undertake a journey by stagecoach to Edinburgh, where she spent three weeks visiting relations and old friends.
The Edinburgh that Agnes visited in 1805 was also a much-changed
city from the one in which she had been born. During the decades
after the Porters moved to Chelsea, the Nor' Loch, on the site of what
later became Princes Street Gardens, had been drained and the first
New Town had been built. In contrast to the ancient, dark, unplanned
buildings of the Old Town, the New Town was built to a regular,
classical design, centred on George Street, extending from Charlotte
Square at the west end to St Andrew Square in the east, with Queen
Street running to the north and Princes Street to the south. The new
houses were light, airy, spacious – and clean. Many of the city's wealthier
inhabitants moved into the New Town, leaving the Old Town to the
poor. Agnes's relation and old friend Elizabeth Keir was living in George
Street by 1805, when Agnes stayed with her. One could wish that Agnes
had commented in more detail on the transformation of Edinburgh
since her childhood days, though she did try to convince her dinner-
companions in London, on her way home, 'that the houses of the New
Town were beautiful; that the public edifices were grand; [and that]
the country was improving'.[45]

By the latter part of 1806, Agnes seems to have been finding that
full-time work as a governess to the Talbot children was too much for
her. In a letter written at this time, Lady Mary Talbot told Mrs Hicks
Beach 'Mrs Porter, who has been a comfort to us so long, thinks her
health unequal to the task of instructing so many little children, and
indeed means to retire to Fairford and spend the rest of her days in
peace and ease with her sister Mrs Richards'.[46]

So, in October 1806, Agnes left Penrice – though not for ever, as
she was to return several times to look after some of the children whilst
their parents were away. From 1806 until early in 1812 she lived in
Fairford, with her sister Fanny and brother-in-law Thomas Richards,

[45] Letter, 5 April 1805.
[46] Letter, Lady Mary Talbot to Mrs Hicks Beach, n.d. but must be 1806.

who had moved there in 1804, when Thomas had been appointed curate. Fairford was a small, well-built market town of Cotswold stone, with 1300 inhabitants and a magnificent late-medieval church. Life was busy, for Thomas Richards took his duties as curate seriously, and the household usually included two or three female pupils, including Thomas Richards's young niece Mary Morice.

The Last Years

From Fairford Agnes made several expeditions. Apart from three trips to Penrice, and one to Malvern with the Talbot children, she also stayed in London and at Scratby Hall in Norfolk. Between the autumn of 1809 and the spring of 1810 she spent nine months in Norfolk, with Elizabeth Upcher's sister, who was by this time the dowager Countess of Home. Lady Home may have considered employing Agnes as a companion, as her late sister had done, but Agnes was both lonely and bored in Norfolk. Scratby Hall is five miles from Yarmouth and Agnes found it a 'dreary spot'. The inhabitants were equally uninteresting. Even Yarmouth itself held few attractions: Agnes found few like-minded people with whom she could discuss literature. She missed her friends and was glad to leave Norfolk. She returned to Fairford in June 1810, after spending a few days in London.

Agnes eventually left Fairford in 1812. The reasons for this move are not entirely clear. A letter written towards the end of 1811 indicates that she found the town dull,[47] and in the following May she says that 'it is no longer convenient for my brother and sister to have me continue at their house as their inmate'. She may also have fallen out with Thomas Richards, for Lady Susan O'Brien – always a perceptive commentator – wrote in a letter at this time, following a visit from Agnes: 'Mr Richards, I find, was too strict for her – I suppose too Evangelical'.[48] Perhaps he did not approve of her favourite relaxations of playing cards and chatting with friends.

By the end of April 1812 Agnes was in Bruton in Somerset, where she was to be based for the remainder of her life. Bruton was near to Redlynch, where she had spent many of her happiest years, and she had friends there. Lady Susan O'Brien thought that she should be happy there:

---

[47] Letter, 22 October 1811.
[48] WRO, LA, unlisted, Letter, Lady Susan O'Brien to Lady Elizabeth Feilding, 19 July 1812.

Miss Porter ... is the most unalter'd creature that ever existed – her very compliments flow in the manner they have done since we first knew her, and have not diminish'd in number. She is much pleas'd with Bruton, which she finds full of good company and quite agreeable. I think it very likely that she will pass her time very pleasantly, as she is sociably and cheerfully inclined and will have her little card parties every night. As to learning, she will be a hundred miles above any body she will ever see, but she will be an oracle, and there is a gratification in being look'd up to, which perhaps none but those who have been look'd down upon, know. I am glad of her determination, as she will be within reach of us all, and is a very valuable friend on many occasions, and one who we all love and esteem.[49]

To begin with, Agnes stayed with her old friend Mrs Lloyd and her unmarried daughter Lucy, but by November 1813 she had moved into lodgings with the family of the Revd William Cosens, who was head-master of the King's School. Agnes was still in good health in the summer of 1813, when she visited Fairford and Penrice, and may also have travelled to London and Norfolk. Although she reported in November that she was 'very *tolerably* well, very *tolerably* comfortable',[50] she fell seriously ill towards the end of December, being unable to leave her room for four weeks. The winter of 1813–14 was a severe one, with hard frosts and heavy snowfalls in January. In the Bruton area the roads were blocked and a subscription was raised to subsidise coal supplies for the poor. At the end of January, in her last surviving letter, Agnes wrote that she had just been downstairs for the first time, but that she was 'pinched to a *thread-paper*'.[51] She died less than a month later. The final letter in this book was sent by Lucy Lloyd, who looked after Agnes in her final illness and ensured that Agnes's body was buried in the Lloyd family plot in Bruton churchyard. In her will, of which the final version was written in June 1813,[52] Agnes asked for her body to be watched for twenty-four hours after her death, with the face uncovered, and to be kept for six days before being buried. Was she remembering the story, recounted in her journal, of Sir Hugh Acland, who had been revived by several draughts of strong beer, some hours after he was supposed to have died?[53] Agnes also asked that her funeral should be 'as little expensive as possible'. She left two guineas each to

---

[49] Ibid.
[50] Letter, 6 November 1813.
[51] Letter, 26 January 1814.
[52] PRO, PROB 11/1560/530.
[53] Journal, 25 August 1791.

the nurse and servant who waited on her, and one guinea to each of five poor families in the parish. She left her personal possessions, including her books, manuscripts and letters, to her sister Fanny, and most of her money to be divided among Fanny and her cousins Susannah Amyot and Ann Garritt.

Family and Friends

In 1788, when the journals and letters begin, Agnes's close family consisted of her widowed mother, Elizabeth Porter, and two younger sisters, Elizabeth (Betsey) and Frances (Fanny). By 1791 Elizabeth Porter was living in Salisbury. She may well have gone there soon after her husband's death in 1782, as she would not have been able to stay in the vicarage at Wroughton. In common with many clergy widows at this period, she was not well off, having to be supported to a considerable extent by Agnes. By 1791 Mrs Porter was in poor health, suffering from 'excessive great weakness in all her limbs'. Occasional crises in Salisbury, due either to some deterioration in her mother's health or to the actions of her younger sister Betsey, called for visits from Agnes – she was there in January and April 1791, and again in November of the same year, when an alarming letter from Fanny gave Agnes a sleepless night, and sent her hurrying to Salisbury in a hired post-chaise. Another emergency, in July 1792, led to further visit, during which Agnes paid her mother's debts and found a nurse and a maid for her. There is no further reference to Mrs Porter from this date until 8 June 1794, when Agnes records her mother's death. Elizabeth Porter was buried with her husband at Wroughton.

Betsey, the middle daughter, seems to have lived mainly with her mother. She was clearly something of a problem to her family, and she and Agnes do not appear to have got on together particularly well. In June 1792 Betsey seemed at last to be making an effort to provide for herself when she obtained a situation as a governess to a young lady. But this lasted for only a month – by the beginning of August Betsey was back in Salisbury. Agnes does not mention Betsey again by name, though it is probable that some of the excised sections of the diaries concerned her. There is a reference to 'B——y's letter' in June 1797, and in August 1802 Agnes sent the Revd John Peele of Norwich, a relative by marriage, £5 for 'B——y' and mentions in her diary difficulties which 'I suppose will continue while she and I live'. Was Betsey living with friends or relatives in Norfolk by this date, or was she in an asylum of some kind? She may have died in 1803: a page of Agnes's journal for that year has been cut out following the words 'constant letters from my …', and the first entry on the next page, dated 7 October, includes the comment '*un triste jour*'.

Agnes Porter was closest to Fanny, the younger of her two sisters and approximately eight years her junior. Fanny was prettier than Agnes and probably more accomplished: Agnes wrote of her sister that 'she sings like a little syren, plays charmingly, draws with taste, and is most pleasing in conversation, having a talent for each person she converses with'.[54] Fanny, too, became a governess, and in the early 1790s seems to have been living with Michael and Henrietta Maria Hicks Beach at Netheravon in Wiltshire. It was no doubt through the Hicks Beach family that Fanny met her future husband, the Revd Thomas Richards, who was the curate at Hatherop in Gloucestershire, not far from one of the other Hicks Beach houses, Williamstrip Park. Michael Hicks Beach gave Fanny away when she married Thomas Richards at Netheravon in 1782. Agnes was evidently pleased for Fanny's sake that she had found a suitable husband, though there may perhaps be a slight note of jealousy in her comment in 1794 that 'just such another man, with ten years or more over his age, would make me a very happy woman'.[55]

After their marriage, Thomas and Fanny Richards lived at Hadley in Middlesex for a few years, and then, in 1797, moved to Knights-bridge. By 1802 they were in Swindon in Wiltshire, from where they moved in 1804 to Fairford, where Thomas Richards was curate until 1819. The couple had no children of their own, but their nephew and niece, James and Mary Morice (children of Thomas Richards' sister), lived with them for several years. Fanny also took in female pupils, probably in an attempt to supplement her husband's salary, since curates were almost invariably poorly paid. Agnes visited her sister and brother-in-law regularly, usually staying with them for several weeks at a time, and they also came to see her at Penrice. Towards the end of 1806, after leaving Penrice, Agnes went to live with the Richardses in Fairford, and was there, on and off, until the spring of 1812, when she went to Bruton in Somerset.

Fanny Richards, who died in 1823, was the main beneficiary of Agnes Porter's will. She and her husband had moved to Aberystwyth in 1819. Fanny was buried ten miles from there, at Llanddeiniol in Cardigan-shire, where Thomas Richards had inherited a small estate. Thomas Richard died in 1852 and was buried beside his wife.

---

[54] Journal, 3 September 1790.
[55] Letter, 22 July 1794.

Of Agnes Porter's other relations, she corresponded most regularly with Elizabeth Keir, a cousin of her mother, who lived in Edinburgh. Mrs Keir was probably about the same age as Agnes and they had known each other for many years. Agnes notes in 1805 that they had begun to write to each other when she was thirteen, which may have been when the Porter family left Edinburgh. They probably met again later in London, as Elizabeth's husband, Dr William Keir, was a physician at St Thomas's Hospital in the 1780s.[56] Agnes stayed at Mrs Keir's house in George Street when she visited Edinburgh in 1805, and she left her friend a legacy of £30 in her will. Agnes also had an aunt, Mrs MacLaurin – presumably a sister of her mother – who was living in Edinburgh in 1805. She does not appear to have corresponded with Mrs MacLaurin, who was in poor health by 1805 and had been reduced to poverty by her husband's behaviour. Agnes did what she could to help her aunt whilst she was in Edinburgh, and said that she would have stayed with her if she could have done so, but there is no further reference to Mrs MacLaurin or her husband in the journals and letters.

Agnes Porter also mentions some relations on her father's side. She saw them from time to time, and tried to help them on occasion, but she does not seem to have been particularly close to them. Her father had one surviving sister, Susannah, who had married Thomas Garritt of Norwich, a hot-presser, in 1750.[57] Susannah Garritt died in 1788, but in 1796 Agnes stayed with her daughter Susannah, the wife of Peter Amyot of Norwich. Agnes also knew Susannah Amyot's sisters, Charlotte and Ann, and her son, Thomas Amyot, who moved to London. When Agnes died she left a third of the residue of her estate each to Susannah Amyot and Ann Garritt who, with Fanny, were her closest surviving relatives.

Several friends are mentioned in the letters and journals – men and women with whom Agnes corresponded on a regular basis and whom she saw occasionally, usually during her visits to London. Some were relatives, and others had probably been friends of her parents. A number of Agnes's friends were involved in printing, publishing or the book-trade.

One old friend, whom Agnes had presumably met whilst she was

---

[56] In her will, written in 1834, Elizabeth Keir describes herself as 'relict of the deceased Dr William Keir of Wester Rhynd, physician in London', Scottish Record Office, SC70/1/53, pp. 223–28. Dr William Keir, MD (Edinburgh), physician at St Thomas's Hospital, London, is named as a subscriber on a book-list of 1783. See P. J. and R. V. Wallis, *Eighteenth-Century Medics* (Newcastle-upon-Tyne, 1988), p. 338.

[57] A hot-presser was involved in the production of high-quality, glazed cloth.

living in London, was Elizabeth Moser. Elizabeth was older than Agnes: she was born in London in around 1735, the daughter of Peter Liege, an eminent London surgeon of French Huguenot extraction. In 1780 she married Joseph Moser, 'artist, author and magistrate',[58] who was more than ten years her junior. Joseph, the son of a Swiss artist, was a cousin of the celebrated flower-painter Mary Moser. Mary was patronised by Queen Charlotte, who employed her to decorate a room at Frogmore. Joseph Moser had worked as an enamel painter in the 1770s and 1780s, and had exhibited at the Royal Academy, but after his marriage he 'devoted himself to literary pursuits'.[59] Agnes clearly thought that this had been an unwise decision. Her inability to conceal her opinion of Moser's literary efforts may have led to a gradual cooling in her relationship with the couple. In the 1790s she visited them quite often when she was in London, and in 1791 she refers to them as 'a genteel, sensible couple, and extremely polite to me'.[60] She also describes Mrs Moser as 'a woman of sense and politeness [who] possesses much polite literature'.[61] A year later, however, Mr Moser had become a poet, but was in Agnes's words 'no gainer by the change'. When he insisted on reading his works to his visitor, she found it difficult to keep awake. On this occasion she was evidently glad to escape from the Mosers' house.[62] In 1797, when she had not seen the Mosers for some time, Agnes found them 'rather formal' to begin with, though they gradually become more friendly.[63] Mr Moser was, however, depressed by the poor reviews of his latest literary effort. Agnes was not particularly sympathetic, commenting in her diary 'How happy and estimable he was in his own private character before he wished for *fame*'.[64] In Agnes's final reference to the couple, in June 1797, she says of Mrs Moser 'When I was very young I mistook her for a friend; find now that she was merely an acquaintance'.[65]

Agnes Porter eventually fell out with another long-standing friend, whom she refers to as Mr Green. He was the well-known London print merchant and mezzotint engraver Rupert Green who lived in Berners Street (off Oxford Street) in the 1790s. He helped Agnes to publish a

---

[58] DNB, xxxix, p. 178.
[59] Ibid.
[60] Journal, 30 January 1791.
[61] Journal, 13 February 1791.
[62] Journal, 18 January 1792.
[63] Journal, 30 April 1797.
[64] Journal, 19 May 1797.
[65] Journal, 4 June 1797.

book of children's stories in 1791. When Agnes sent him her 'tales' she noted in her journal, 'I am happy in friendship with several of the worthy among his sex, whose advice is frequently of the greatest benefit to me'.[66] By January 1792, however, everything had changed. Mr Green, whose late wife had been Agnes's friend, had set up house with a widow, Mary Charlewood. She called herself Mrs Green, but the two do not appear ever to have married. The new 'Mrs Green' was unfriendly towards Agnes, who commented: 'N.B. to give up that acquaintance for various reasons: friendship, no more than love, must be all on one side'.[67] The next, and final, reference to the Greens comes in 1812. By this time Valentine Green was in a sorry state: 'various speculations and expensive living' had bankrupted him in the late 1790s, and his son, who had also been ruined, had died in 1804.[68] From 1805 Green lived on £150 a year which he received as Keeper of the British Institution. In 1807 his 'wife's' daughter Harriet Charlewood had married James Innes-Ker, whose title to the Dukedom of Roxburghe was finally established in 1812, seven years after the death of the previous Duke. This sudden – and well-publicised – elevation of a connection of Valentine Green prompted Agnes to attempt to recover £100 which she had lent Mr Green to pay for the publication of her book. She therefore wrote to the Duchess of Roxburghe, explaining the situation. The Duke paid the £100, but Agnes then received an abusive letter from Mr Green himself, demanding that she should refund the money. She wrote sadly in a letter 'I never thought he could have been so cruel and ungrateful'.[69] Whether Mr Green really did owe her the money is unclear.

Agnes Porter's friendship with Dr Malcolm Macqueen was much closer and continued to the end of her life. In the late 1770s Macqueen had practised as a physician in Great Yarmouth, where his patients included John Ramey, at the time when Agnes was a member of the Ramey household.[70] It is clear that she saw him at one stage as a potential husband, though he was ultimately to disappoint her. In January 1791 she received a letter from an unnamed correspondent, who must have been Dr Macqueen, and noted in her journal that she had 'resolved to divest my mind of too tender an interest in the concerns of any male friend, and in fine not to be duped by the name of friendship to expect,

---

[66] Journal, 13 October 1790.
[67] Journal, 21 January 1792.
[68] James Greig (ed.), *The Farington Diary* (London, 1922–28), iii, p. 48.
[69] Letter, 22 September 1812.
[70] C. J. Palmer, *The Perlustration of Great Yarmouth* (Great Yarmouth, 1872), i, p. 370.

or entertain a sentiment beyond it'.[71] It soon becomes clear that the letter brought news of Macqueen's imminent marriage – and the end of Agnes's hopes where he was concerned. Later in the same month Dr Macqueen wrote to Agnes, describing his bride-to-be, Mariana Potter, as having 'an excellent understanding and an angelic disposition'. Equally importantly, she would inherit a large fortune when her father died.[72] On receiving this news Agnes decided to 'close our epistolary correspondence at his marriage, so sacred is that tye that in my opinion a woman of strict honour will not cultivate even a friendship with a married man unless she love the wife equally'. In the event, Agnes did not keep to her resolution, especially after Dr Macqueen had visited her in London and had assured her, 'You are her superior, and you will feel your self so the first instant' asking Agnes not to regard his bride-to-be 'with too critical an eye'.[73] Unfortunately for Agnes, her superiority did not make up for her lack of fortune. In later years Agnes saw the Macqueens from time to time when she was in London but – not surprisingly – she never seems to have been particularly friendly with Mrs Macqueen. It is possible to detect a note of *Schadenfreude* in an entry in her journal in 1805, following a visit from Dr Macqueen: 'His lady is, it seems, no friend to society, and neither makes her own acquaintances nor his welcome ... But he wished for riches – *et le voilà riche*. He told me with a sigh that wealth did not confer happiness'.[74] The last reference to Dr Macqueen is in a letter written in June 1813, eight months before Agnes's death, when she was planning to stay with him for a fortnight.[75]

Other friends and acquaintances included Mrs Pinnock, who lived in London. Her son was a clergyman, but she was evidently not well off, as Agnes gave her money from time to time. Mrs Pinnock is mentioned for the last time in 1805, when she was eighty-seven, but Agnes was still trying to help her son – who had four children and little money – two years later.[76] Agnes was always generous to those who appeared to be less fortunate than herself, in spite of the insecurity of her own financial position.

---

[71] Journal, 8 January 1791.
[72] Journal, 28 January 1791.
[73] Journal, 23 March 1791.
[74] Journal, 12 April 1805.
[75] Letter, 7 June 1813.
[76] Letter, 22 October 1807.

The Single Woman in Georgian Britain

The story of Agnes Porter's life illustrates many of the problems experienced by spinsters in the Georgian period – problems on which Agnes comments directly in her letters and journals. Few women in Georgian Britain chose to remain unmarried, at least if they belonged to the upper levels of society. Marriage enhanced a woman's status, as is underlined in Jane Austen's *Pride and Prejudice*, when Lydia Bennet asserts her right to take precedence over her elder, but unmarried, sisters, following her marriage to Mr Wickham.[77] She might not get on well with her husband, but a married woman would have a degree of independence: she could manage her own household, and if her husband died her marriage settlement would, in most cases, ensure that she had some control over her own money. A woman who never married would have to fend for herself, or remain dependent on the charity of her family. Whilst a husband could insist that his wife's marriage portion was handed over, an unmarried daughter or sister might find it difficult to persuade her family to give her anything more than a modest, and irregular, allowance. Agnes describes one such household in Great Yarmouth: 'We have an old lady who is quite extravagant and luxurious with regard to herself, yet refuses a grown-up daughter a little pocket-money, or the least independence in any[thing]'.[78]

Laurence Stone has shown that between 20 and 25 per cent of upper-class girls in the eighteenth century never married, compared with under 5 per cent in the Tudor period.[79] For Agnes Porter's generation, the proportion was roughly 25 per cent. It has been suggested that the daughters of parsons were particularly likely to remain spinsters: 'Anglican clergymen's families ... were large, and it would appear to have been normal to marry no more than a couple of daughters per generation (usually to other clergymen), leaving the rest to serve as housekeepers, governesses, ladies' companions or simply to stay at home to tend aged parents'.[80] In a period when there was a shortage of marriageable men, many a woman of Agnes's generation was condemned to spend her life like Miss Bates in Jane Austen's *Emma*. Miss Bates

---

[77] Jane Austen, *Pride and Prejudice* (Penguin Classics, 1972), p. 329.
[78] Letter, 20 December [1797].
[79] Laurence Stone, *The Family, Sex and Marriage in England, 1500–1800* (London, 1977), p. 380.
[80] Olwen Hufton, *The Prospect Before Her* (London, 1995), p. 253.

Enjoyed a most uncommon degree of popularity for a woman neither young, handsome, rich nor married. [Miss Bates] had never boasted either beauty or cleverness. Her youth had passed without distinction, and her middle of life was devoted to the care of a failing mother, and the endeavour to make a small income go as far as possible.[81]

Whilst a woman with either beauty or a large fortune could be reasonably certain of finding a husband at this period, and a woman who had both would be hotly pursued, one who, like Agnes, had neither, was likely to remain an old maid. Few women were as fortunate as Emma's former governess, 'poor Miss Taylor', whose husband had made enough money for him to be happy to marry a portionless woman.[82] Agnes did not, however, entirely give up hope. In 1792, a year after Malcolm Macqueen had disappointed her by marrying an heiress, she wrote to Lady Mary Fox Strangways, asking her to address her letters to *Mrs*, rather than *Miss* Porter, with the words: 'I know, my love, I am not yet an old woman, though I begin to be rather advanced in life for a Miss. Do not suppose that being styled *Mrs* will spoil my marriage – on the contrary, I may be mistaken for a little jolly widow and pop off when you least expect it'.[83] Four years later, Agnes enjoyed the company of a clergyman, Joseph Griffith, who was employed as a tutor for a few weeks before Lord Stavordale went away to school for the first time. Mr Griffith stayed at Melbury, and Agnes 'thought his conversation both sensible and agreeable'. Agnes was, however, worried when Lord and Lady Ilchester met her walking with Mr Griffith in the gardens, and she 'resolved to change my hours of walking, as it particularly behoved me to avoid any particularity or the least *seeming* indecorum'.[84] If there had been any hint of impropriety, she would have been out of a job immediately. Mr Griffith's name has been partly erased in some places, and a number of entries in the journal for 1796 have been cut out, so it does seem probable that Agnes's feelings towards him were more than those of a casual acquaintance. But Mr Griffith was to prove a sad disappointment, since it turned out that he was married – a fact that he had concealed from Lord Ilchester and everyone else at Melbury. Agnes continued to visit the Griffiths when she was in London, and in 1797 noted in her journal, with a certain degree of satisfaction,

---

[81] Jane Austen, *Emma* (Penguin Popular Classics, 1994), p. 17.
[82] Ibid., p. 13.
[83] Letter, 7 April 1792.
[84] Journal, 17–18 June 1796.

that 'Mrs Griffith seems sweet-tempered, but odd and nervous to a degree – at times almost to imbecility'.[85]

If, as in Agnes Porter's case, her family resources were insufficient, there were only a few ways in which she could support herself and remain a lady at the same time. Some girls became housekeepers or paid companions, and a few earned a living as artists or writers, but many turned to governessing. This was an occupation that could be followed by a lady without a total loss of status, and which would also give her a home. In such a situation a plain appearance was a positive advantage – especially if the lady of the house was responsible for choosing her children's instructress.

In the Porter family, all three daughters were involved in teaching to some extent. We know nothing about the girls' own education, but it seems unlikely, in the third quarter of the eighteenth century, that they had been educated specifically to become governesses. This certainly happened later on and there were many girls, like Jane Fairfax in Jane Austen's *Emma*, orphaned at an early age with a fortune of only 'a very few hundred pounds', who were 'brought up for educating others' so that they would be able to earn 'a respectable subsistence' for themselves when they grew up.[86] Entering a family as a governess did, at least, give a girl or woman a roof over her head and a modest income, though there was always the fear of what would happen if she lost her position or became too old or ill to work. Few, if any governesses, however, could hope to emulate Charlotte Brontë's Jane Eyre, and marry their employer – though many, no doubt, dreamed of doing so. They were far more likely to be seduced by their employer, or by another male inhabitant of the household, and then to be dismissed. The lack of provision for aged and infirm ex-governesses became acute in the first half of the nineteenth century, and this led to the foundation of the Governesses' Benevolent Institution in 1843.

Agnes Porter was only too conscious of the insecurity of her position – the prospect of a poverty-stricken old age clearly worried her. In 1791 she was upset by reports that Lord Ilchester's former housekeeper Mrs Hayes, whose death had just been reported, had been badly treated by some 'unworthy relations'. Agnes noted in her journal that 'I could not forbear partially and deeply reflecting on the ills that single women are exposed to, even at the hour of death, from being the property of no-one. My will is long since made, of what little I possess, and I hope

---

[85] Journal, 13 May 1797.
[86] Jane Austen, *Emma*, p. 123.

A Governess in the Age of Jane Austen

it will please Infinite Goodness that my last breath shall be received by
a tender and humane person, if not a friend'.[87] In her later years Agnes
wrote and rewrote her will several times, to take account of changing
circumstances and ensure that her savings were divided as she wished.
She was particularly concerned to ensure that Fanny would keep control
over her legacy if she predeceased her husband, for if Mr Richards
died intestate 'all he has would go to his sister's children, and what I
left might accidentally go from my own sister'.[88] It was with a trace of
wistfulness that Agnes wrote in her journal during her visit to Edinburgh: 'In Scotland an old relation is seldom ever left *solitary, whether
rich or poor* – a sense of domestic duty is very prevalent'.[89]

When compared with many of her contemporaries, Agnes was fortunate, for she was always able to maintain a reasonably comfortable
standard of living. Whilst she was employed, she would have received
her board and lodging in addition to her annual salary. During her
final years with Lord Ilchester's family she was probably earning a
hundred guineas (£105) a year. Mrs Upcher offered Agnes £100 a year,
and she also had an annuity of £30 a year from Lord Ilchester after
she left his household. However, problems arose after Lord Ilchester's
death in 1802. His will, which was proved at the end of 1802, had
actually been written in 1778, before the death of his first wife.[90] Lord
Ilchester had subsequently added numerous codicils over the years,
with many generous bequests to servants and former servants. One of
these codicils, dated 1791, mentioned Agnes, who was to receive her
salary for the rest of her life, if she 'continues in my family many years
longer with equal credit to herself (of which I do not doubt)'. Unfortunately for Agnes, it soon became clear that Lord Ilchester had left
personal debts which totalled almost £38,000, exceeding the value of
his personal estate by £6000.[91] There was, therefore, no money available
to pay the legacies mentioned in his will, and Agnes could not hope
to receive anything until the new, young Lord Ilchester came of age
in 1808. Agnes was so concerned by this state of affairs that she
abandoned her usual deferential approach to members of the family
and tackled her late employer's brother: 'I asked the Colonel what I
was to do in the interval, and added that should I from ill health be

[87] Journal, 26 May 1791.
[88] Journal, 16 November 1802.
[89] Journal, 16 March 1805.
[90] PRO, PROB 11/1384/908.
[91] Dorset RO, Fox Strangways, D124, box 241, 'Statement of the Late Earl of
Ilchester's Concerns'.

obliged to give up my profession and be reduced to want, I thought it would be a reflection on his noble family'. She added, darkly: 'He seemed to think what I said was *une façon de parler* – but he knows not me'.[92]

Fortunately for Agnes, she did not have to depend on the pension from Lord Ilchester alone. The Talbots paid her £100 a year from 1799 to 1806, whilst she was at Penrice Castle. This was comparatively generous: although the Edgeworths recommended that a governess in a wealthy family should have £300 a year,[93] the usual salary was much lower. Miss Elborough, governess at Penrice from 1806–7, was paid £50 a year, but another governess was employed at the same time. In Westmorland in 1809 Ellen Weeton was paid thirty guineas a year,[94] and it has been estimated that in the mid nineteenth century the average salary for a governess was between £20 and £45 a year, with an annual salary of as much as £100 being paid only to 'the "highly educated lady" who could find a position in a very well-to-do family'.[95]

When Agnes had to give up full-time work in 1806, the Talbots continued to pay her £30 a year. At this time her sister and brother-in-law were able to give her a home with them in Fairford. Payment of her annuity from Lord Ilchester began again in 1808, and this meant that she was at least adequately provided for. When she eventually left her sister and brother-in-law's house in Fairford 1812, she was able to live fairly comfortably in lodgings in Bruton – helped, from time to time, by gifts of money from the Talbots. When Agnes died in 1814 she left a total of approximately £2000.[96] Most of this was invested in 5 per cent Navy Stock, and would have produced a little under £100 a year. Towards the end of her life her annual income from all sources would therefore have been about £150.

Agnes Porter's Place in Georgian Society

In the autumn of 1799, when Agnes was living with the Talbots, the Revd Sydney Smith visited Penrice Castle. Smith, who was later to achieve fame as a preacher and essayist, and as the wittiest conversationalist of his day, was at this time an almost unknown curate and

[92] Journal, 26 August 1803.
[93] M. and R. L. Edgeworth, *Practical Education* (London, 1798), p. 549.
[94] Hall (ed.), *Miss Weeton's Journal of a Governess*, p. 205.
[95] M. Jean Peterson, 'The Victorian Governess: Status Incongruence in Family and Society', in M. Vicinus (ed.), *Suffer and Be Still* (Bloomington, Indiana, 1972), p. 8.
[96] PRO, PROB 11/1560/530.

tutor. He came to Penrice with his pupil Michael Hicks Beach, a cousin of Thomas Mansel Talbot, during a somewhat circuitous journey from the West Country to Edinburgh.[97] It is quite clear that Sydney Smith did not take to Agnes. The twenty-eight-year-old clergyman's description of her tells us at least as much about Smith's attitude to women as it does about Agnes herself, but his impressions are nevertheless illuminating.

Smith refers to Agnes in two letters, one to Mrs Hicks Beach and the other to her husband. In the first letter, written on 17 September 1799, he tells his employer:

> Miss Porter perhaps ought not exactly to be set up as a model of good breeding, judgment, beauty or talents. She is I daresay a very respectable woman, and may be a much more sensible woman than I think her, but I confess in my eyes she is a very ordinary article.[98]

In another letter, written a fortnight later, presumably in response to one disagreeing with his description of Agnes, Smith adds: 'I will not give up an atom of Miss Porter; instructed in books she may be, but infinitely vulgar she certainly is'.[99]

Sydney Smith may have thought that Agnes was vulgar, but few of her contemporaries would have doubted that she was entitled to call herself a lady. Her education, dress and manners indicated her social status even to those who knew nothing about her life and background: in 1789, when she was travelling by stagecoach from Wincanton to London, one of her travelling companions apparently referred to her as a 'gentlewoman', who 'seems a quiet, steady person'.[100] Gentility was, moreover, an indispensable qualification for her employment as a governess in the first place.

Agnes Porter's own relations, in both Norfolk and Scotland, belonged to a group of people, often referred to as the 'middling sort', that became increasingly numerous and influential in the course of the eighteenth century. They were moving from trade into the professions, and some of them were purchasing landed estates or marrying the sons

---

[97] It is not clear where their journey started: Smith was curate at Netheravon, Wiltshire, where the Beaches had a house, but they also had a house at Williamstrip, Gloucestershire.

[98] NLW, MS 11,981E, Letter from Sydney Smith to Mrs Hicks Beach, 17 September 1799. I am most grateful to Alan Bell for his help in locating this letter.

[99] Nowell C. Smith (ed.), *The Letters of Sydney Smith* (Oxford, 1953), i, pp. 47–48, Sydney Smith to Michael Hicks Beach, 2 October 1799.

[100] Letter, 21 December 1789.

and daughters of members of the lower levels of the landed gentry. The acquisition of wealth and leisure gave them importance as consumers: they joined libraries and purchased books; they patronised the theatres, concert-halls and art galleries; and they met together at balls and assemblies in London and the country towns.

Agnes's own paternal grandfather and great-grandfather had been brewers in Yarmouth; her father began life as a woollen-draper and then entered the church. One of Francis Porter's aunts married a woollen-draper, and his sister married a hot-presser. Other Porter connections went into the church, whilst Thomas Amyot, Agnes's cousin, became a wealthy man as a result of his work as a civil servant. On her mother's side, Agnes's Scottish relations seem to have belonged to a slightly higher social level than that occupied by the Porters in Norfolk. Although it is not clear exactly where Elizabeth Porter fits in, she was related to the Elliotts of Wolfelee in Roxburghshire. William Elliott, a lawyer, had bought the estate of Wolfelee in 1730. Other close relatives included the Ogilvies of Hartwoodmyres, Selkirkshire: Thomas Elliott Ogilvie, Agnes's mother's 'nearest relation', made enough money out of his employment in the Madras Civil Service to buy the Chesters estate in 1782. Elliott and Ogilvie relatives also included doctors, lawyers and army officers. In addition, there were connections with aristocratic families such as the Elphinstones and Carmichaels. When Agnes visited her relations in Edinburgh in 1805, she found it 'gratifying to my pride to see them move in so respectable a sphere',[101] though her mother's sister had come down in the world through 'her husband's carelessness and pride', which had been 'the cause of alienating both from their respective and respectable relations'.[102]

By moving from trade into the church, and by marrying a woman from a professional and landed background, Francis Porter had raised his own social status, together with that of his immediate family. He and his daughters used the status symbol of a coat of arms, though it is not clear if they were, strictly speaking, entitled to do so.[103] In a rural parish in particular, where members of the gentry and aristocracy were thin on the ground and it was often difficult to arrange social events,

---

[101] Journal, 13 March 1805.
[102] Journal, 12 March 1805.
[103] In 1796 Agnes noted in her journal that she had lost a seal with her father's arms on it (Journal, 13 October 1796). She later used a seal with the Porter arms of three bells on some of her letters, and silver with this crest has been handed down in the family. Similar arms were used by a number of different, and probably unrelated, families called Porter.

the clergy of the Church of England were, with the officers of the army and navy, 'considered eligible for neighbourhood society by virtue of their profession'.[104] So, when their father was vicar of Wroughton, Agnes and her sisters were invited to balls and parties by Mrs Calley of Burderop Park. It was probably through these Wiltshire connections that Agnes obtained her first position as a governess, with the Goddards of Swindon House.

Socialising with the landed gentry on long winter evenings in the country and making up sets for country dancing was one thing. Matrimony was quite another matter, and here the Porter sisters' lack of fortunes effectively eliminated them from competition in the higher levels of the marriage market. Neither Agnes nor her sister Betsey married: Agnes had hopes of Malcolm Macqueen, but he chose to marry an heiress instead. Fanny had at one time been 'tenderly loved', but her suitor had made 'a more worldly marriage' under the influence of 'interest, or prudence it is called'.[105] Fanny did marry, though not until she was thirty years old. Although her husband, the Revd Thomas Richards, had a small estate of his own in Wales, he and Fanny never seem to have been very well off – he never rose above being a curate, supplementing his salary by working as a schoolmaster, whilst Fanny took in female pupils.

A number of authors have drawn attention to the problems arising from a governess's ambiguous position within the household of her employers.[106] In order to be considered suitable as a companion and tutor to well-born young ladies, a governess had herself to be a lady, but she was also an employee. Since she was neither a servant nor a member of the family, her happiness depended to a large extent on the goodwill – or otherwise – of the parents of the children entrusted to her care. In order to maintain her position within the household, the governess had also to keep her distance from even the upper servants.

During the period covered by the journals and letters, Agnes Porter was employed in two closely-related households. Her position within these two households was quite different. An examination of her experiences underlines the extent to which a governess's situation varied according to the circumstances of the family with which she lived.

---

[104] Collins, *Jane Austen and the Clergy*, p. 108.
[105] Journal, 17 January 1791. Agnes refers only to 'my sister', but Fanny seems to be the more likely of the two.
[106] See, in particular, Peterson in Vicinus, *Suffer and Be Still*, pp. 3–19; and Hughes, *The Victorian Governess*, especially pp. 85–116.

We know little of Agnes's relationship with the second Countess of Ilchester, who died in 1790, six years after Agnes joined the family at Redlynch. Lord Ilchester appears in the journals and diaries as a somewhat distant figure, who seems to have allowed Agnes a good deal of independence. She had a room of her own at Redlynch (nineteenth-century governesses often had to sleep with their pupils), and also expected to have a bedroom to herself, with the use of a parlour where she could entertain friends, during the family's visits to London. Although most of the day was spent with her pupils, maids were available to dress them, give them their meals, and put them to bed – and also to wait on Agnes herself. She had a certain amount of free time, usually in the evenings, and could receive visitors such as her sister Fanny, who spent six days at Redlynch in September 1790. Occasional trips away, especially visits to her mother, were also permitted. If Lord Ilchester was away, friends and relatives often dined with Agnes and her pupils. When the master of the household was at home, however, the governess's position was more clearly defined. As Agnes wrote in her journal: 'When Lord Ilchester is from home I spend the evenings with his daughters; when he is at home I pass them alone'.[107] Life in the depths of the country was, indeed, often lonely. Agnes occasionally felt the lack of a 'rational companion' and regretted 'the unavoidable lack of society in my situation'.[108] In the absence of adult members of the family, the only other occupants of Redlynch were the servants, and of these the housekeeper was the only one whose social status even approached that of the governess.

Agnes Porter's situation at Penrice Castle was rather different from that at Redlynch and Melbury. She had known Lady Mary Talbot since the latter was seven years old; she had 'tried to supply ... a mother's love' to Mary and her brother and sisters, and had acted as their companion and confidante. Although Agnes always refers to Lord Ilchester's daughters as *Lady* Mary or *Lady* Elizabeth, her relationship with them was on a more equal level than had been possible with Lord and Lady Ilchester. Penrice Castle was much smaller than Melbury or Redlynch, and life there, with a house full of children, was much less formal. In 1804 the traveller Benjamin Malkin noted that Penrice was 'scarcely large enough' for the Talbot family;[109] and when John Llewelyn

---

[107] Journal, 2 December 1790.
[108] Journal, 4 August 1791.
[109] B. H. Malkin, *The Scenery, Antiquities and Biography of South Wales* (London, 1807), ii, pp. 491–92.

of Penllergaer paid a visit in February 1806 he had to sleep in a bed in the housekeeper's room 'for want of a better'.[110] Although Agnes had her own room, it would have been difficult for her to spend as much time apart from her employers as she had done in Lord and Lady Ilchester's household, and it is clear that she lived with the family for most of the time. In 1806 Mary Talbot told Mrs Beach that Agnes 'always breakfast, dines and sups with us and is our companion in the evening, but in the mornings we of course follow our different avocations'.[111]

Penrice was geographically isolated, and a long way from Mary's family and the friends and acquaintances of her youth. Henry Skrine, who toured Wales in 1798, wondered why Thomas Talbot had deserted 'the noble seat of Margam, in the midst of a populous and plentiful country' to 'form a fairy palace in a dreary and desolate wild, far from the usual haunts of man, and near the extremity of a bleak peninsula'.[112] A year later, Sydney Smith commented 'Penrice is a pretty place enough in a wretched country – the flower garden is delightful, but for any communication with the human species a man may as well live on Lundy Island as at Penrice'.[113] So, in addition her role as governess to the Talbot children, Agnes was valued as a companion for their mother, one who knew most of the same people, and shared many of the same interests.

Thomas Mansel Talbot was the greatest resident landowner in the western half of Glamorgan at the end of the eighteenth century. His gross annual income of approximately £8000 to £10,000 was probably rivalled only by that of the industrialist John Morris of Clasemont and Sketty Park.[114] Talbot and Morris knew each other, but they never seem to have been particularly friendly. If they had socialised only with families from the same level of society, the Talbots' life at Penrice would have been very lonely indeed. In fact, neither Thomas nor Mary Talbot was interested in moving in the grandest social circles, and both disliked London intensely. Thomas had never taken much part in public life and, unlike most of his predecessors as owners of the Penrice and

---

[110] Pocket book of T. M. Talbot, 18 February 1806. Talbot does not say where the housekeeper slept.

[111] Letter, Lady Mary Talbot to Mrs Hicks Beach, 24 June ?1806. See also Agnes's Journal, 24 March 1804, for details of how she spent her time at Penrice.

[112] Skrine, *Two Successive Tours*, pp. 69–70.

[113] NLW, MS 11981E.

[114] From 1806 he was Sir John Morris. The Morrises moved from Clasemont to Sketty Park in 1806 to escape the pollution from their own copper-works.

5. Penrice Castle, Glamorgan, the home of the Talbot family,
by Thomas Rothwell, 1792 *(Private Collection)*

Margam estates (and also his son), had never been Member of Parliament for Glamorgan. As early as 1787, he had written that 'the very retir'd life I have for some years past led, has made it somewhat disagreeable to me to wait on great people, and I feel it's a thing that gains on a man most incredibly'.[115] Most of his closest friends before his marriage were clergymen or, in Glamorgan, local gentlemen whose estates were considerably smaller than his own.

Amongst the Glamorgan friends who are mentioned most frequently by Agnes, and also by Thomas and Mary Talbot, were the incumbents at Margam and Oxwich. Dr John Hunt, whom Thomas presented to the living of Margam in 1794, had been a contemporary at Oxford and a hunting companion in the West Country before moving to Glamorgan. Hunt and his wife were regular visitors to Penrice. In return, the Talbots often stayed with them at Tynycaeau near Margam,

---

[115] Martin, *Penrice Letters*, p. 100.

where Thomas had built a new rectory for his friend. He had also built a rectory for another old friend, the Revd John Collins, whom he had presented to the living of Oxwich in 1772. Collins had married in 1781, and the youngest of his ten children were the same age as the eldest Talbot daughters. The rectory at Oxwich was within easy walking distance of Penrice Castle, and visits from one house to the other were made on an almost daily basis when the Talbots were at home. Also nearby were the Revd James Edwards of Reynoldston and his wife who, like the Hunts, had no children of their own, but enjoyed the company of the young Talbots. Swansea friends included Edward King of Marino, a Customs official, whom Thomas Talbot had known since the 1780s. Amongst the local gentry families who visited Penrice, and upon whom the Talbots called from time to time, were the Lucases at Stouthall and the Llewelyns of Penllergaer, neither of whose wealth or standing rivalled that of the Talbots.

Many members of the Talbots' circle thus belonged to the same level of society as Agnes and her own relations and friends. This could cause problems, and some embarrassment, as acquaintances did not always know how to treat a governess. Agnes describes one particularly revealing episode, which took place at Margam in 1802: when she rose to leave, at the end of a visit to Dr and Mrs Hunt, another visitor, Mrs Pryce, offered to help Agnes with her cloak.[116] Mr Pryce, however, 'made her a sign of disapprobation'. This incident, according to Agnes 'dwelt on my mind more, perhaps, than it merited'. The next day Mr Pryce was more polite, but Agnes responded with 'a very reserved, silent curtesy'. She then helped Mrs Pryce with her cloak, with a quotation from Laurence Sterne: 'Hail the small courtesies of life, for smooth do they make the road of it'. Then, 'I looked up at Mr Pryce – he cast his eyes down – I had *my* revenge'.[117] This may seem petty, until one remembers how importance the maintenance of her status as a gentlewoman was to Agnes Porter.

Occasionally, the behaviour of the Talbots' friends and acquaintances gave Agnes reason to feel superior to them. After her visit to Edinburgh in 1805 she stayed for a few nights with Mr and Mrs Joseph Green, whom she had met at Penrice as they had rented Fairyhill, a house in Gower, for a few years. Mr Green's occupation is unknown; he may have been in business, and he certainly does not seem to have owned a substantial estate of his own. At dinner with the Greens, Agnes's fellow

---

[116] Probably Jane (*née* Birt), wife of John Price (q.v.).
[117] Journal, 21 October 1802.

guests took pleasure in making fun of the Scots. Agnes noted in her journal, 'Mr Green himself a pleasing man, but his *rich* visiters intolerably vulgar'.[118] From time to time, too, she commented somewhat disparagingly on the Collinses of Oxwich rectory and their attitude towards the education of their children.[119]

Women and Education in the Georgian Period

Sydney Smith's description of Agnes Porter as 'infinitely vulgar' tells us a good deal more about contemporary attitudes to educated women than it does about Agnes's own appearance or behaviour. Learned women were, as a rule, mocked or despised, rather than admired. Ideas of gentility and propriety dictated that girls should, first and foremost, be brought up to be good wives and mothers. If they were intelligent and enjoyed reading and studying, this might be permitted, but only if there was enough time left over from their household duties. What was absolutely not the 'done thing' in polite society was for women to show off their learning and suggest that they might be more knowledgeable than their male companions. This is where Agnes offended against contemporary ideas of how a gentlewoman should behave, as is indicated (unconsciously) by her own description of a gathering in the London house of her friends Mr and Mrs Williams: 'I was in great spirits and enjoyed the evening very much. A Miss D-s seemed to envy me a little for engrossing a good deal of the gentlemen's attention. She, pretty and insipid, was but little noticed – myself, plain, but chatty and tolerably agreeable in conversation had in fact all the beaux present about me'.[120] The men might have enjoyed an evening in Agnes's company, but they were more likely to propose marriage to the insipid Miss D-s. Agnes could rarely resist showing off her extensive reading or correcting her companions – male or female – if she disagreed with them. In her defence, it must be said that any addition to the limited social circle at Penrice would have been welcome, and Agnes must have enjoyed the chance to discuss books and the outside world with a well-educated man such as Sydney Smith.

Throughout the Georgian period girls were brought up, above all, to be good wives and mothers. In an era when the schooling of boys was firmly grounded in the teaching of Greek and Latin, many commentators doubted that women could be educated in the same way:

---

[118] Journal, 5 April 1805.
[119] Letters, 20–22 May and 6 June 1811.
[120] Journal, 25 October 1796.

'The female mind, being deficient in rational powers, was unfit for the necessary mental effort required to study the classics'.[121] Girls' minds were too weak to stand up to hours of concentrated study, and too much learning would make them unfeminine – and unmarriageable. Nor was a rigorous academic training necessary for girls, 'since their sphere of activity was firmly circumscribed within the kitchen, sickroom and nursery, where skills of a manual and practical nature were all that was required'.[122]

Attitudes to female education were changing during the eighteenth and early nineteenth centuries, but writers in the late Georgian age were, in general, no more sympathetic towards blue-stockings than their predecessors had been. Before the beginning of the eighteenth century, the emphasis was on moral and religious instruction, and the acquisition of the practical skills that would be needed by the mistress of a household: some cookery, the making of simple medicines and, above all, needlework. Reading and writing were also useful, together with simple arithmetic and the keeping of household accounts. In farming households, and the families of merchants and tradesmen, wives and daughters might still be expected to take an active part in looking after the dairy and poultry, or running the shop or business. Girls should be brought up to be 'humble, modest, moderate, good housewives, discreetly frugal, without high expectations which will otherwise render them discontented'.[123] The girls of aristocratic and gentry families, who had more free time, would also be expected to acquire some of the less obviously useful accomplishments, such as singing, playing a musical instrument and dancing, together with a brief acquaintance with a foreign language – usually French.

Girls were often educated at home, by older members of their family, perhaps with the help of masters to teach music, dancing or French. From the middle of the seventeenth century onwards, however, many girls, of both the middle and upper classes, were sent to school, either as boarders or as day-girls. The standard of teaching at these schools was often abysmal, but at least the girls were kept busy and – it was hoped – out of the way of unwelcome suitors. Social education was

---

[121] Patricia Phillips, *The Scientific Lady: A Social History of Women's Scientific Interests, 1520–1918* (London, 1990), p. 12.

[122] Ibid.

[123] John Evelyn to his grandson, 1704, quoted in L. A. Pollock, 'Teach Her to Live under Obedience: The Making of Women in the Upper Ranks of Early Modern England', *Continuity and Change*, 4 (1989), p. 242.

more important than academic training – but neither was provided very effectively in the majority of girls' schools.

The main development in female education during the first half of the eighteenth century seems to have been an growing emphasis on ornamental accomplishments, and a neglect of practical instruction. Women spent less and less time working in the family business, sewing and embroidering, or taking an active part in the management of their household, and more time learning how to walk and dance elegantly, and how to sing, draw, play the harpsichord and read and write French. They also had more time to read books and write letters, but many seem to have spent a large part of their leisure time chatting and playing cards. As more and more girls learned French and had lessons in music and drawing, however, the social value of these accomplishments decreased. As the Edgeworths wrote in 1798: '[Accomplishments] are now so common that they cannot be considered as the distinguishing characteristic of even a gentlewoman's education'.[124]

At the end of the eighteenth century there was a discernible movement against the overemphasis on accomplishments, and towards the provision of more in the way of moral education and intellectual stimulation for girls – even though the aim was to produce well-mannered, lively and intelligent companions for their husbands and children, rather than women who enjoyed learning for its own sake. The opinion of the middle-aged hatter, whom Agnes met during her journey by stagecoach from the West Country to London in 1789, was probably fairly typical of the period: 'He thought women could never be taught too much, as knowledge would qualify them to be proper companions for their husbands and, at the same time, would, by teaching them their duty, make them humble'. Perhaps surprisingly, the young glover who took part in the same conversation expressed a more old-fashioned point of view: 'Provided a women can make a good pudding, cast an account, and keep her house neat, I think she may make a wife to please any reasonable man'. In her account of this journey, Agnes mocks the 'Miss from Sherbourne school' who provides a classic example of a girl who had received a fashionable education and was, in theory, accomplished, but had acquired little in the way of common sense or useful knowledge – the girl claimed that she would not give up the accomplishment of speaking French 'for the world', but soon showed herself to be unable to understand a simple French phrase.[125]

---

[124] Edgeworth, *Practical Education*, p. 529.
[125] Letter, 21 December 1789.

The Education of the Daughters of the Fox Strangways and Talbot Families

The educational experiences of successive generations of the Fox Strangways and Talbot families underline the changes that were taking place during the Georgian period. In the middle of the eighteenth century it was still quite usual for the daughters of aristocratic families to be sent away to school. The daughters and granddaughters of these women were, however, much more likely to be educated privately, at home. Boarding schools became less exclusive, and fell increasingly out of favour with the higher levels of society.

The first Countess of Ilchester, Elizabeth Strangways Horner, who was born in 1723, apparently received little in the way of a formal education. Her parents separated when she was a child and during her early years she was dragged around the fashionable towns and cities of Europe by her mother, who was by this time the mistress of Henry Fox (who became the first Lord Holland in 1763). According to one of her own daughters, Elizabeth received 'the education usual at that time – reading, writing and the principles of religion'.[126] In 1736, at the age of thirteen, she was married to Stephen Fox, the elder brother of her mother's lover, though Elizabeth and her husband did not live together until 1739, when she was sixteen. The first Countess does not appear to have paid a great deal of attention to the education of her own daughters, of whom four survived to adulthood. Lady Ilchester spent a good deal of her time in London. As a result 'the daughters were great part of their time with the housekeeper, and went to visit their mother at her toilet in a formal sort of way'.[127] Moreover, though education was by this time 'much advanced', 'she thought the same she had received was sufficient for them'. The eldest daughter, Lady Susan, who was born in 1743, was often with her mother in London. Whilst she was there she does seem to have had some lessons with the authoress Madame Le Prince de Beaumont, a French refugee who spent many years as a governess in private families.[128] Her published works included *Le magasin des enfants*, which was 'practically a treatise on education, perhaps the first of such modern treatises',[129] and included a character (Lady Sincère), who was supposedly based on Lady Susan Fox Strangways herself. As a result of

---

[126] Account of 'The Four Countesses of Ilchester', written 1817 by Lady Susan O'Brien and included in Charlotte Traherne's 'Family Recollections'.

[127] Charlotte Traherne, 'Family Recollections'.

[128] She was in England *c*. 1750 to 1762.

[129] Charlotte Traherne, 'Family Recollections'.

these lessons, Lady Susan became 'a very good French scholar, and a most agreeable converser'. It is clear from her later letters and journals that she was highly intelligent, though (in the words of a younger relative) 'her principles and education ... had been neglected'.[130] Lady Susan seems to have read a good deal, though much of her education was gained when she was an adult. Lady Ilchester does not seem to have been particularly good at watching over her strong-willed eldest daughter, who eloped in 1764 with William O'Brien, an actor whom she had met when they both took part in amateur theatricals at Holland House. At least two of Lady Susan's younger sisters, Lucy (born 1748), and Frances (Fanny) (born 1755), were sent to Mrs Shields's fashionable boarding school in Queen Square, Bath, where they were contemporaries of Fanny Burney, whose father, Charles Burney, taught there in the 1760s.[131] It seems likely that the other daughter, Harriot (born 1750), was there too. Nothing is known of the education that they received, but the emphasis is likely to have been on the acquisition of social skills rather than intellectual attainment.

In the next generation, the two eldest daughters of the second Earl and Countess of Ilchester never went away to school. In 1787 Harriot, the third daughter, was sent, at the age of about nine, to a school in Weymouth, apparently because she had an injured or deformed knee and it was hoped that sea-bathing would be beneficial. She remained in Weymouth, on and off, for about six years. At first she was at a school run by 'poor dear gouty Mrs Morris',[132] but in 1791 she was moved to Mrs Hepburn's school. Harriot's letters from Weymouth indicate that contemporary doubts about girls' schools were only too well-founded – the girls had lessons in French, music and drawing, but much of their time seems to have been spent gossiping and playing games. The teachers did not always set a very good example: in an undated letter Harriot reported that Mrs Hepburn's husband 'has gone so far as even to have beat (in a slight degree) his wife in one of his passions'.[133] Her sisters' governess clearly had a low opinion of the standard of Harriot's schooling. In December 1790, when Harriot was at Redlynch for a while, Agnes noted in her journal 'My dear Lady Harriot good and

---

[130] Harriot Georgiana Mundy (ed.), *The Journal of Mary Frampton* (London, 1885), pp. 18–20.

[131] Joyce Hemlow et al. (eds), *The Journal and Letters of Fanny Burney* (Oxford, 1972–84), iv, p. 254.

[132] Letter, Lady Susan O'Brien to Lady Mary Fox Strangways, 21 March 1791.

[133] Letter, Lady Harriot Fox Strangways to Lady Mary Fox Strangways, *c*. 1791.

amiable. I hope I shall enable her to make up for her school-days' indolence, and consequently small progress'.[134]

When Agnes Porter left Melbury in 1797 she was not immediately replaced. Harriot's younger sister, Charlotte (aged thirteen or fourteen) was sent to Mrs Devis's fashionable girls' school in Queen Square, Bloomsbury, which was known as the 'Young Ladies' Eton'. Although the girls were taught French, history, geography and other academic subjects, the main emphasis at the school was on manners and deportment.[135] It is not clear what arrangements were made for the further schooling of the youngest surviving daughter, Louisa, and she may also have been sent away to school for a while, to be 'finished'.

By the early nineteenth century, the situation was rather different. None of the Talbot girls was sent away to school – in spite of the difficulty of finding suitable governesses, and of persuading them to stay in such a remote place as Penrice. The Talbots doted on their children and wanted to have them with them as much as possible. Thomas Talbot also clearly had a low opinion of girls' schools, as he indicated in 1796 in a letter to Mrs Hicks Beach, who had asked if Lady Mary knew of a suitable governess for her daughters:

> I can't here refrain from giving my opinion that they [the Hicks Beach girls] should not go to any school: the sweet engaging and delicate manner they have been hitherto bred up in might possibly suffer from bad example ... As to schools for girls, it is as unserviceable and dangerous as keeping boys at home: the one is liable to be run away with by the dancing master, and the other fall in love with the kitchen maid etc.[136]

Governesses in the Eighteenth Century

As girls' boarding schools fell out of favour in the second half of the eighteenth century, the number of governesses in private households increased. Mary Wollstonecraft, the writer, became a private governess in 1778, and Selina Trimmer was engaged to teach the daughters of the Duchess of Devonshire in 1786. Agnes Porter and her sister Fanny both started teaching in the 1780s. Agnes's first employers, the Goddards in Swindon, were untitled, but they belonged to the higher ranks

[134] Journal, 16 December 1790.
[135] Mary Cathcart Borer, *Willingly to School* (London, 1976), pp. 185–88.
[136] Letter, T. M. Talbot to Henrietta Maria Hicks Beach, 7 February 1796.

I. Henry Thomas, second Earl of Ilchester (1747–1802) by Thomas Beach (1778). *(Private Collection)*

II. Mary Theresa, second Countess of Ilchester (*c.* 1755–90) with her daughter Elizabeth, by Thomas Beach (1777). *(Private Collection)*

III. Thomas Mansel Talbot (1747–1813), miniature, artist unknown (1806). *(Private Collection)*

IV. Lady Mary Talbot (1776–1855) and (?) her son Christopher, miniature, artist unknown (1806). *(Private Collection)*

IX. The Revd Thomas Richards (1762–1852), Agnes Porter's brother-in-law, miniature by A. Charles (c. 1795). *(Private Collection)*

X. Frances Richards, *née* Porter (c. 1764–1823), sister of Agnes Porter, miniature by A. Charles. *(Private Collection)*

XI. Agnes Porter's trunk, with her initials on the lid.

of the gentry, as did Thomas Mansel Talbot's cousins, the Hicks Beaches, who were employing governesses from the 1790s.

The change came about in part as a result of an alteration in parents' attitudes towards their children. A greater concern for their daughters' religious and moral welfare, combined with a newly-found delight in domesticity and the company of children demonstrated by some members of the aristocracy (most famously, Georgiana, Duchess of Devonshire), was to make many parents wary of sending their daughters away to boarding-school. Ideas about girls' education were, moreover, changing again in the last decades of the eighteenth century, with a reaction against ornamental accomplishments and more emphasis on moral training and useful learning – though the intellectual content was still somewhat limited. For most parents employing a governess, a ladylike manner was more important than obvious intelligence. Agnes was probably unusual in that she actually enjoyed teaching, and she was certainly better educated than many of her contemporaries, whose function might still be closer to that of child-minder than that of tutor.

The rising demand for private governesses towards the end of the eighteenth century coincided with an increase in the numbers of girls and women who, for various reasons, needed to find employment. To some extent, as has already been indicated, this resulted from the fact that many girls from respectable backgrounds could not hope to inherit enough money to live on, and were never able to find a husband who could support them. At the same time, one consequence of the French Revolution in 1789 was the presence in Britain in the 1790s and early 1800s of numerous well-born and educated, but indigent, French ladies. Since a knowledge of French was essential for a sophisticated young lady at this period, many of these *émigrées* found positions as governesses. In a letter written in 1796, Thomas Mansel Talbot commented: 'I suppose that at this time there is a greater choice of French governesses than ever was known, and possibly of the highest rank, good sense and respectability'.[137]

The latter part of the eighteenth century should, perhaps, be seen as a transitional phase, during which the wealthiest families resorted to private governesses or boarding schools, or a combination of both, for the education of their daughters. Jane Austen and her sister Cassandra were sent away to school (in the 1780s): the Austens were Anglican clergy, who 'hovered at the gentry's lower fringes',[138] though

---

[137] Letter, T. M. Talbot to Michael Hicks Beach, 7 February 1796.
[138] Park Honan, *Jane Austen: Her Life* (London, 1987), pp. 29–30.

they had some grand relations. Jane Austen was well acquainted with both governesses and their employers, and it is possible to detect some traces of contemporary developments in her work. She does not give a governess to the Bennet girls in *Pride and Prejudice* (first published in 1813, but partly written in the 1790s) – but their father, with £2000 a year, belongs only to the middling ranks of the gentry. At the same time, Lady Catherine de Bourgh, who is much richer and grander than the Bennets, employs a governess to teach her sickly daughter. Sir Thomas Bertram of Mansfield Park, who is a baronet, with 'a handsome house and large income', also employs 'a governess, with proper masters' to educate his daughters.[139] *Mansfield Park* and *Emma* were both written in the second decade of the nineteenth century, and governesses also feature in the latter book. Miss Taylor had become governess to Emma Woodhouse and her sister when Emma was five years old. The Woodhouses, were 'first in consequence' in Hartfield,[140] and were thus precisely the kind of family that might have been expected to engage a governess at this date, especially as Mrs Woodhouse had died when Emma was a small child.

Agnes Porter and her Pupils

The changing attitude to girls' education in the latter part of the eighteenth century may be seen in the Fox Strangways family. The second Countess of Ilchester, Mary Theresa Grady, took a great deal more interest in her children and their upbringing than her mother-in-law had done. Because of her dislike of fashionable London society, she and her children spent much of their time in the 1770s and 1780s in the country, at Redlynch in Somerset. For families living in the depths of the countryside, there was only a limited amount of scope for supplementing the education that could be provided by friends and relations with lessons from specialist masters, as the latter were mainly to be found in London and the larger provincial towns. Mary Theresa may also have felt that her own education was deficient – her father was a gentleman, but not a particularly wealthy one, and she had been 'educated in another Kingdom [Ireland], and not with all the high accomplishments beginning to be common in this'.[141] Unlike the first Countess, she was religious, and had 'a heart stored with good

---

[139] Jane Austen, *Mansfield Park*, pp. 41, 56.
[140] Jane Austen, *Emma*, p. 7.
[141] Lady Susan O'Brien in Charlotte Traherne, 'Family Recollections'.

6. Redlynch, Somerset, the home of Agnes Porter and her pupils until 1793:
'Redlinch House, 1851, used now as a farm house' by W.W. Wheatley.
(Somerset Archaeological and Natural History Society)

principles, and an understanding to direct the use of them'. Pregnant
and in poor health, as she was for much of her married life, she felt
the need for an experienced and sympathetic teacher to supervise and
educate her children whilst they were at home.

Agnes Porter was not the first governess to be employed to teach the
children of the second Earl and Countess of Ilchester. Little is known
of her predecessor, apart from the fact that she had proved to be 'very
untrustworthy'. In later years Lady Mary Talbot (*née* Fox Strangways)
remembered little of this woman, apart from the fact that she had taken
Lady Mary to see the glassworks in Bristol without permission, when
Lady Ilchester was ill at Clifton.[142] From the beginning, it was clear
that Agnes was different: according to Charlotte Traherne 'my mother
[Lady Mary Talbot] used to described herself as a very naughty, sulky
child when Miss Porter came, and with her sweet good sense and
discernment of character used to charm her out of her obstinacy'.[143]
Her pupils gave Agnes the affectionate nickname 'Po' and she was 'Po'
to the children of the next generation as well.

---

[142] Charlotte Traherne, 'Family Recollections'.
[143] Ibid.

Whilst Agnes was with Lord Ilchester's family, at Redlynch and later at Melbury, the composition of the group of pupils in the schoolroom altered from time to time, as the older girls 'came out' and entered society, whilst the younger ones started their first lessons. In March 1788, when the first, fragmentary, journal opens, Agnes had two pupils for most of the time: the eldest daughter, Elizabeth, aged fourteen, and her sister Mary, who was twelve. Their sister Harriot spent most of the year at her boarding-school in Weymouth, though she joined her elder sisters for lessons from time to time when she was at home. By 1790 much of Agnes's time was spent with the younger girls, Charlotte and Louisa (aged six and five), whilst Elizabeth and Mary were spending less and less time in the school-room, as they were often away on visits, with their father or with other members of the family. Lessons finally came to an end for the older girls when they were presented at Court: Elizabeth in 1792 and Mary in 1793, followed by Harriot in 1797.

Agnes taught her younger pupils to read and write. The girls also studied history, geography, classics (in translation), the French language, and French and English literature. In August 1790 one morning was spent 'Relating passages from ancient and modern history', and in the afternoon of the same day 'We entertained ourselves with a play of Shakespeare's: *Richard II*'.[144] Shakespeare was very popular, though Agnes would probably have used Thomas Bowdler's *Family Shakespeare* had it been available at this date.[145] In 1790 she noted: 'In the afternoon read *King Lear* to Lady Mary. N.B. never to read that play any more, it is absolutely too much'.[146] Moral education was not neglected: the children read the Bible and other improving works, and on Sundays Agnes listened to her pupils as they said their prayers and recited the catechism. Although needlework was less important than it had been fifty or a hundred years earlier, the girls were still taught sewing and embroidery. Agnes was with the younger girls for much of the day, even after their lessons had finished: on one afternoon 'we made a party to the lodge, where we drank tea with much glee';[147] whilst on another day, when the weather was bad, Agnes 'made a party' with her pupils at the game 'puss in the corner'.[148]

The girls' academic education was usually Agnes's responsibility, but

---

[144] Journal, 21 August 1790.
[145] Thomas Bowdler's expurgated (or 'bowdlerised') edition of Shakespeare's plays was first published in 1818.
[146] Journal, 19 November 1790.
[147] Journal, 7 September 1790.
[148] Journal, 30 July 1791.

specialist, invariably male, masters were employed from time to time, especially when the family was in London. In 1791, when Agnes was with Lord Ilchester's daughters in London, she noted: 'At home all day with my pupils and their various masters. What a pleasure it is to me to see them daily improve in person, manners and elegant accomplishments'.[149] A writing-master is mentioned in 1791, but most of the masters instructed the girls in the social skills that they would need when they entered adult society. Every well-born girl at this period was expected to play a musical instrument: Agnes was at least able to supervise the girls while they practised, but in 1788 Elizabeth also had music lessons in London from M. 'Helmandel'. Dancing and deportment were equally important, and in 1788 a Frenchman, M. Chapui, was employed as a dancing-master. During a stay in London, in March and April 1796, Lord Ilchester's younger daughters 'made great progress with their masters in music, drawing and dancing'. Agnes, in the meantime, 'supervised as well as I was able, and made them practise in the intervals'. At the same time Lord Stavordale, the only boy, spent two hours a day learning Latin. Agnes, showing her usual desire for self-improvement, was able to sit in on some of the lessons, and 'got all the declensions pretty perfect'.[150]

No specific training was available for governesses before the end of the eighteenth century, though Agnes had no doubt gained some experience from helping to teach her younger brother and sisters. To a considerable extent, she must have developed her teaching methods through practice, but she was also interested in contemporary educational theories. In 1791 Mrs Digby gave Agnes a copy of *Leçons d'une gouvernante à ses élèves* by the well-known and prolific French authoress Madame de Genlis, whom her oldest two pupils met at Stourhead at this time. Madame de Genlis had been influenced by her fellow-countryman Jean-Jacques Rousseau, who had emphasised the necessity of devising a plan of education which would suit each individual child, and which would bring out its own innate talents and abilities. Despite the radicalism of his ideas on education and society, Rousseau was deeply traditional in his attitude to women, believing that they were naturally inferior, and that girls should be educated only to be useful and pleasing companions for members of the opposite sex. Madame de Genlis therefore laid great emphasis on accomplishments, particularly those connected with the performance of music.

---

[149] Journal, 5 February 1791.
[150] Journal, 24 April 1796.

The writings of Madame de Genlis were still extremely popular at the end of the eighteenth century, and many of her books are in the library at Penrice. Yet her ideas on education were beginning to look somewhat old-fashioned by this time. Agnes and Mary Talbot also read and discussed the works of other, more up-to-date theorists, most of whom expressed their doubts concerning the value of ornamental accomplishments. They also questioned the usefulness of learning, by heart, lessons which often consisted mainly of long lists. In Jane Austen's *Mansfield Park* Maria and Julia Bertram could 'repeat the chronological order of the kings of England, with the dates of their accession, and most of the principal events of their reigns', together with 'the Roman emperors as low as Severus; besides a great deal of the Heathen Mythology, and all the Metals, Semi-Metals, Planets, and distinguished philosophers'.[151] Jane Austen evidently did not feel that the two Bertram girls could be described as well-educated. Agnes would no doubt have agreed.

One of the most influential of the writers on education in the latter part of the eighteenth century was the Evangelical Hannah More who, though deeply conservative in her emphasis on propriety, did at least believe that women should be given a more rigorous academic education. As early as 1786 Agnes copied the following paragraph from Hannah More's writings into her extract book:

> A lady may speak a little French and Italian, repeat passages in a theatrical tone, play and sing, have her dressing room hung with her own drawings, her person covered with her own tambour work, and may notwithstanding have been very badly educated. Though well-bred women should learn these, yet the end of a good education is not that they may become dancers, singers, players or painters, but to make them good daughters, good wives, good Christians.[152]

Hannah More's book *Strictures on the Modern System of Female Education* was first published in 1779; Lady Mary Talbot acquired a copy of the fourth edition in 1799. More's popularity continued: in November 1809 Agnes was reading *Hints for the Education of a Princess*, and she had also read, and liked, *Coelebs in Search of a Wife* by the same author. Hannah More was in favour of an improved system of education for women, as they would then be better equipped to influence the people around them – including their husbands and children – and make them better

---

[151] Jane Austen, *Mansfield Park*, pp. 54–55.
[152] From Hannah More, *Essays on Various Subjects, Principally Designed for Young Ladies* (Cork, 1778), pp. 84–85.

people. Together with her contemporary, the poet William Cowper,[153] she advocated a life of quiet domesticity, preferably in the countryside, where it was easier for the individual to concentrate on the development of his or her relationship with God. The sentiments of William Cowper and Hannah More were echoed by both Agnes and Lady Mary Talbot – and no doubt helped to reinforce the latter's natural reluctance to involve herself in smart society life in London, and her preference for spending her time with her husband and children in the house and garden at Penrice. Mary's own letters and diaries show an enduring search for self-improvement, combined with frequent self-examination with regard to her own feelings and dealings with other people.

Another extremely popular author at this time was Maria Edgeworth. In June 1802 Agnes noted in her journal that she was reading *Practical Education* by Maria and her father Richard Lovell Edgeworth, published four years earlier,[154] She comments that 'Between theory at night and practice all day, I should do *something*'.[155] The Edgeworths were also influenced by Rousseau, in that they believed that children were reasonable human beings, whose natural gifts might be brought out by education, but they were rather more interested in the needs of girls than Rousseau had been. Both boys and girls should be taught by example, and should be reasoned with, rather than punished. Girls should, however, be taught to be more restrained than boys, 'because they are likely to meet with more restraint in society', and because 'much of the effect of their [girls'] powers of reasoning, and of their wit, when they grow up will depend on the gentleness and good-humour with which they conduct themselves'.[156]

For both boys and girls, the Edgeworths stressed the importance of fresh air and exercise, and practical work. Children were to be encouraged to use their hands, and to play with toys that 'afford trials of dexterity and activity', such as 'tops, kites, hoops, balls, battledores and shuttlecocks, nine-pins and cup and ball'. They could be taught chemistry and mineralogy, and they might also study living plants and fossils. Gardening was a particularly suitable occupation for children, as it combined academic study with fresh air and exercise. In later years the Edgeworths were criticised for their emphasis on practical education at

---

[153] Cowper was one of Agnes Porter's favourite poets. See below, p. 69. See also Leonore Davidoff and Catherine Hall, *Family Fortunes* (London, 1987), pp. 162–72, for the influence of Cowper and More at this time.

[154] The book is still at Penrice.

[155] Journal, 7 June 1802.

[156] Edgeworth, *Practical Education*, pp. 167–68.

the expense of the cultivation of a child's mind and imagination, but they did give female pupils an alternative to endless hours of sewing or practising the harpsichord.

The Edgeworths laid great emphasis on the importance of setting good examples for children, and of avoiding bad company. In particular, they stressed the undesirability of leaving children too much in the company of servants, from whom they would pick up 'vulgar' manners. 'If children pass one hour in a day with servants', they wrote, 'it will be vain to attempt their education'.[157] The children's mother, or a governess, should be present whilst the children were being dressed, and children should never be sent out to walk with servants. This was an additional reason for a family to employ a governess, who would be expected to supervise the daughters for much of the day, not only at lesson time.

In 1807 Agnes recommended the educational writings of Elizabeth Hamilton to her former pupil Lady Harriot Frampton, commenting that Miss Hamilton 'shews a method of bringing the faculties to perfection', and that 'I think Lady Mary's practice keeps pace with Miss Hamilton's theory'.[158] Miss Hamilton followed Hannah More in stressing the importance of moral education, although she admitted that it was unrealistic to expect that children should be totally isolated from servants. Although she was hostile to ideas about the equality of the sexes, believing that women should be taught to value virtue above all, and should not try to emulate men in public life or educational attainments, she believed that boys and girls should be educated together during their earliest years, in order to avoid 'the pride and arrogance which boys acquire from early ideas of inherent superiority' due to 'the trifling accomplishments to which the girls are devoted [which] they despise as irrational'.[159] From a later letter it is clear that Henrietta Maria Hicks Beach was also an admirer of Miss Hamilton's works.[160]

Henrietta Maria, the mother of Sydney Smith's pupils Michael and William Hicks Beach, had three daughters who were older than the Talbot children; Lady Mary Talbot consulted her regularly on educational matters. In the late 1790s the Beaches employed a Mrs (or Miss) Williams as a governess for their daughters. She must be the Mrs Williams who was recommended by Sydney Smith in a letter written in 1797 as being 'extreemly good tempered and perfectly well bred'.[161] Henrietta

---

[157] Edgeworth, *Practical Education*, p. 126.
[158] Letter, 24 August 1807.
[159] Elizabeth Hamilton, *Letters on Education* (Dublin, 1801), pp. 190–91.
[160] Letter, 13 August [1810].
[161] Smith, *The Letters of Sydney Smith*, i, pp. 8–9.

Maria Hicks Beach gave a copy of Mrs Williams's manuscript 'Plan on which I should wish my daughters to be educated' to the Talbots. This is interesting, as it summarises contemporary ideas on how girls should be educated within these wealthy households, which were comparatively enlightened, though still essentially conservative. As might be expected, Mrs Williams laid particular emphasis on religious and moral training. She believed that girls should have religion 'so interwoven in their hearts and souls as to prevent their ever being contaminated by any bad examples they may meet with, or led astray by any of the prevailing errors or follies of the times'. Their minds should be well-informed: they should learn history, geography, botany, natural history and astronomy, as well as being 'perfectly mistresses of ... the historical and natural history of their own country and its antiquities'. They should be well acquainted with the best authors in the English and French languages; they should be excellent accountants, should be able to organise their own household, and should have 'some notion of the value of landed or funded property, repairs of estates and expences of building'. They should also be able to manage without servants and make their own clothes if necessary. Such a programme could have left little time for other occupations, but the girls were also to be 'well acquainted with the rudiments of drawing and musick', and they should be able to sing and dance. To this catalogue of the qualities of the ideal woman, Lady Mary Talbot added a few words of her own: 'God, hear the prayer of an anxious mother: "Let my children be perfect Christians"'.

Theories about the aims and practice of female education were certainly plentiful at this period. Even Sydney Smith wrote an article on the subject, published in the *Edinburgh Review* a decade after his meeting with Agnes Porter.[162] In this, he showed himself to be more enlightened than many of his contemporaries. He refuted the commonly-held theory that men had a greater capacity for learning than women and recommended that more attention should be paid to the education of girls. In particular, he noted that 'It is said, that the effect of knowledge is to make women pedantic and affected; and that nothing can be more offensive than to see a woman stepping out of the natural modesty of her sex, to make an ostentatious display of her literary attainments' – as Agnes had no doubt tried to do, when they met at Penrice. But in the *Edinburgh Review* Smith argued that learned women would cease to

---

[162] Sydney Smith's article on female education was first published in the *Edinburgh Review* in 1810. See *The Works of the Revd Sydney Smith* (3 vols, 2nd edn, London, 1840), i, pp. 200–20.

appear affected if there were more of them: 'Diffuse knowledge generally among women, and you will at once cure the conceit which
knowledge occasions while it is rare'. Sentiments such as these alone
did not, however, bring better schooling for girls, and there was little
change until the latter part of the nineteenth century.

It is interesting to note that neither Agnes nor Lady Mary Talbot ever
appears to have read anything written by Mary Wollstonecraft, whose
radical *Thoughts on the Education of Daughters* and *Vindication of the Rights
of Women* were published in 1787 and 1792 respectively. Both Agnes
and Lady Mary would doubtless have been shocked by Wollstonecraft's
belief that girls could, and indeed should, be educated to the same level
as boys. They may have regretted the fact that so little importance was
attached to the education of girls beyond the most basic level, and
wished that they had more opportunities for self-improvement, but
neither expressed any doubts that the main aim of educating girls was
that they should become dutiful Christian daughters and mothers. The
books that they read – by conservative authors such as Hannah More,
John Moir and Thomas Gisborne – reinforced this attitude, which was
shared by the vast majority of their friends and relations.[163]

What was the practical effect of this intensive study of educational
manuals by Agnes Porter and Lady Mary Talbot? How did the education
of the Talbot girls differ from that of their mother and her sisters?
The Talbots spent most of their time in the country at Penrice, where
life was much more informal than it had been at Redlynch and Melbury.
They rarely went to London, so the scope for employing specialist
masters to give an extra gloss of sophistication to the girls' various
accomplishments was limited, though dancing and music masters did
travel out from Swansea to Penrice in the early years of the nineteenth
century. The children at Penrice benefited greatly, however, from the
fact that their mother was able and willing to give them a good deal
of her time – and she, like Agnes, continued to educate herself in a
wide variety of subjects long after she had left the school-room. Learning
lists of words does not appear to have been an important part of the
curriculum: the children were encouraged to ask questions and discuss
the subjects that they were studying. An indication of Agnes's teaching
methods is given in a letter written in 1810, when she says that 'Miss

---

[163] In addition to the works of Hannah More, the library at Penrice includes *Female
Education: or An Address to Mothers on the Education of Daughters* by John Moir (London,
new edition, n.d. but with inscription 'Mary L. Talbot 1799'); and *An Enquiry into the
Duties of the Female Sex* by Thomas Gisborne (7th edn, London, 1806, with bookplate
Thomas Mansel Talbot).

Jane finds herself forced to lend her attention, as I frequently ask her the impertinent questions of "Who was this person? What was his motive? How did it succeed?" And so on'.[164]

Agnes was mainly interested in literature, history and languages. With her, the Talbot children learned reading, writing and arithmetic, with some French and a little Italian, and they also studied stories from the classical authors, together with history and geography. When Agnes left Penrice in 1806, Lady Mary asked Mrs Hicks Beach to enquire for a replacement governess, who should be 'a religious and well-educated woman' and should be able to teach 'French and English grammatically and the fundamental part of musick'.[165] To these traditional areas of study, Lady Mary Talbot, in common with many women of her generation, added a wide range of scientific subjects, including natural philosophy, geometry, chemistry and natural history. In 1794 her wedding presents from her husband had included books on birds, fish, insects, butterflies, fish, shells, ferns, grasses and flowers. Many of these books were beautifully illustrated and must have helped to stimulate the interests of the Talbot children. Lady Mary was devoted to her garden, spending many hours studying horticultural books and plant catalogues, and also doing much practical work in the gardens herself. The Talbot children helped their mother in the garden and collected wild flowers, fungi and mosses, which they then tried to find in the books in the library at Penrice. They made frequent expeditions to the Gower beaches, from which they returned loaded with shells and pebbles, to be sorted, washed, drawn and identified. They also began to collect geological specimens, fossils and flints, some of which were found on Chesil Beach during visits to Lord Ilchester's house at Abbotsbury in Dorset. They studied astronomy too, and their letters include many references to their sightings of comets and eclipses of the sun and moon. William Henry Fox Talbot, the first cousin of the Penrice Talbots, often joined them during their lessons and expeditions. It seems probable that the foundations for his life-long passion for botany and horticulture – with his interest in astronomy, chemistry and other scientific subjects – were laid during his long holidays in Gower.[166]

It is clear from Agnes Porter's writings, and also from other contem-

---

[164] Letter, 4 September 1810.

[165] Letter, Lady Mary Talbot to Henrietta Maria Hicks Beach, n.d. [probably early 1806].

[166] For further information on Fox Talbot's connections with Penrice, see Joanna Martin, *Henry and the Fairy Palace: Fox Talbot and Glamorgan* (Aberystwyth, 1993).

porary letters and diaries, that the Edgeworths' strictures about keeping children away from servants could not always be followed in real life. Although the children spent a great deal of time with Agnes or with their mother, there are frequent references to them being dressed and put to bed, given their meals and taken for walks by their maids. Indeed, C. R. M. Talbot recalled, in later years, that he had been afraid of his mother when he was a child, and had looked upon his nurse as 'my only friend in the world'.[167] The memorial inscription in Penrice churchyard to Sukey, the children's nurse for nearly thirty years, bears witness to the affection that the Talbots felt for several of their servants. Nevertheless, the Talbots obviously did worry about leaving their children with servants: in 1806, when Agnes had said that she wished to leave Penrice, Lady Mary told Mrs Hicks Beach that she was considering engaging two governesses, so that the sub-governess could supervise the children when the superior governess was otherwise occupied 'to prevent their ever being with servants'.[168]

The Talbot girls were better educated than many of their contemporaries. By no means all mothers were as intelligent or as diligent as Mary Talbot, and many governesses showed little aptitude or enthusiasm for teaching. There were, limits, however, and too great a devotion to learning was still not encouraged. Charlotte, the fourth daughter, seems to have been the cleverest, and in later life she studied heraldry, genealogy, architecture and local history, but as a child she was discouraged from being too bookish. In 1809, when Charlotte was nine, Agnes commented 'I hope [she] makes merry at dancing, playing, dolls etc. If she reads too much she will be called a book-worm – that will never do'.[169] It must have been galling for girls such as Charlotte when their younger brothers, whom they had helped to educate during their earliest years, returned from boarding-school to patronise them and show off their knowledge of Greek and Latin, which were not generally thought to be suitable subjects for girls, and which few governesses were able to teach.

Living in the countryside for most of the time as they did, the Talbot girls would have appeared unsophisticated to many contemporaries of the same social class. People who met them commented on their naturalness, which their mother and Agnes encouraged: in a letter to Lady Mary Talbot, written in 1810 Agnes wrote, 'You know how much I prefer,

---

[167] C. R. M. Talbot, 'Characters of Some Members of My Family'.
[168] Letter, Lady Mary Talbot to Mrs Hicks Beach, 24 June [1806].
[169] Letter, 17 September 1809.

7. The orangery at Penrice by Emma Talbot, *c.* 1830. *(Private Collection)*

8. The rock pool in the pleasure gardens at Penrice by Emma Talbot, *c.* 1830. The figure glimpsed through the doorway is probably Lady Mary Talbot, who was fond of wearing a Welsh *whittle* or cape (of flannel) when gardening. *(Private Collection)*

9. Penrice Castle from the north-west by Emma Talbot, *c.* 1830. *(Private Collection)*

in children's culture, the want of a pruning knife to the barrenness of fruits'.[170] In the same year George Eden (later Earl of Auckland), a friend of the Talbots, wrote from London to say that he had seen Lady Mary's sister, Lady Elizabeth Feilding, together with the oldest of the Talbot children, Mary, who was also staying in London. Lady Elizabeth had asked George Eden if he knew of a dancing master who would 'teach Miss Talbot how to enter a room in the most graceful manner'. Eden commented 'I am sadly afraid that they are going to spoil all that you, nature and Penrice had between you brought to great perfection'.[171]

It may have been partly as a result of their rural upbringing, combined with their mother's reluctance to attend society gatherings in London, that none of the girls made a spectacularly good marriage. The four who found husbands married into local gentry families in Glamorgan: Nicholl of Merthyr Mawr, Traherne of Coedarhydyglyn, Franklen of Clemenstone and Dillwyn Llewelyn of Penllergaer. All were perfectly respectable, and some gained titles during the course of the nineteenth century, but none was as wealthy or as well connected as the Talbots. Only one of Thomas and Mary Talbot's children married into the aristocracy: the son, Christopher, married Lady Charlotte Butler, daughter of an Irish peer, the first Earl of Glengall. The origins of Lady Charlotte's father were, however, somewhat unusual: it was said that his mother had been a beggar-woman in the town of Cahir in County Tipperary, who been deserted by her husband. The husband had eventually died in the East Indies in 1788, unaware that he had just succeeded a distant cousin to become the eleventh Baron Cahir.

Free Time

Agnes was a sociable woman. Many of her happiest hours were spent paying visits, chatting with friends and playing cards. She was a pious Christian and went to church regularly, but – in common with most other members of 'polite society' at the time – she was also a keen theatre-goer.[172] Agnes was fortunate enough to be able to visit the London theatres reasonably frequently during one of the golden ages of their history. She saw actors and actresses whose names are still remembered, including John Kemble, Dora Jordan and Sarah Siddons, and she probably also saw David Garrick. Her vivid descriptions of her theatre

---

[170] Letter, 13 August 1810.

[171] Letter, George Eden to Lady Mary Talbot, 12 March 1810.

[172] Brewer, *The Pleasures of the Imagination*, p. 71.

visits are among the most enjoyable passages in her journals. But these visits to London, and occasional weeks spent with friends and relatives in other parts of the country were the exceptions: infrequent interruptions in an otherwise lonely existence. It is not surprising that Agnes included several quotations from Alexander Pope's 'Ode on Solitude' in her letters and journals – she must have known the poem by heart.

It is difficult for us, living at the end of the twentieth century, with all the wonders of modern travel and telecommunications at our disposal, to imagine what it must have been like to live in an isolated country house in Britain in the decades before and after 1800, with only children and servants for company. But this is how Agnes spent much of her life. Her only communications with the outside world were through letters, occasional newspapers and conversation with visitors. During the long hours that she spent alone in her room, her entertainments were writing letters, reading and other solitary occupations, such as sewing and playing the harpsichord. Nevertheless, she was more fortunate than many of her contemporaries: visitors did come fairly frequently to both Redlynch and Penrice; she was able to go away from time to time, either to visit her own family or to accompany her pupils when they went to London or elsewhere; and she usually had a well-stocked country-house library at her disposal. At Redlynch there was even a 'servants' library', to which Agnes decided to give a copy of the improving text *The Whole Duty of Man* in 1790. Agnes could afford to buy books from time to time, though the choice of books to purchase was limited outside London – she records her dismay in 1809 at being unable to find any French or Italian books in Great Yarmouth.[173] Agnes was also given books by her friends and former pupils. Many of her contemporaries, who had to rely on the provincial circulating and subscription libraries for their books, were much less well provided with reading material. Agnes did not need to make use of the libraries in Swansea, but she does record the gift of her copy of *Walker's Dictionary* to the new Glamorgan subscription library there in 1804.[174]

Reading was a means both of passing the time and of self-instruction. Like her contemporary Anna Larpent, Agnes clearly aspired to 'a refinement which can only be felt in the pure pleasure of intellectual pursuits'.[175] Agnes occasionally makes a distinction between books read for pleasure and for educational reasons. In 1790 she was reading *The*

---

[173] Letter, 25 November 1809.
[174] Journal, 18 April 1804.
[175] Brewer, *The Pleasures of the Imagination*, p. 57.

Whole Duty of Man 'a most excellent instruction', but she also describes how 'I treated myself with Tasso and an hour of *Ormond's Life*'. She also read Gaudentio di Lucca 'to amuse me'. Later in the same year she was still reading *The Whole Duty of Man*, for improvement, together with *Gil Blas* for entertainment. In 1794 she enjoyed the works of Marie Jeanne Riccoboni and, for her 'more serious reading', the *Life of Gustavus Adolphus* by Walter Harte. In 1804, when staying with Fanny and Thomas Richards in Swindon, Agnes noted in her journal, 'I have read since I was here Dr Lyttleton *On the Articles* and the Bishop of London's lectures. Our amusing reading was *The Infernal Quixote*'. Agnes and her friends and correspondents enjoyed discussing the books that they had read, and reading aloud was also popular: it was a more sociable occupation than solitary study, and meant that the listeners could get on with other work, such as sewing. In 1804, at Penrice, Agnes noted that Thomas Talbot had read Carl Philipp Moritz's *Travels in England* to the company one evening, and later in the same year he read 'an act of a new play called *Almahide*'.[176]

Agnes Porter's choice of reading material was varied, but probably quite typical for her time. She read sermons – both those of her father (apparently unpublished) and those of well-known preachers, including Hugh Blair and John Moir. Improving works, apart from *The Whole Duty of Man*, included Luigi Cornaro's *Discourses on a Sober and Temperate Life*. As has already been seen, Agnes was interested in educational theories: she read books by the Edgeworths, Elizabeth Hamilton, Hannah More and Sarah Trimmer. She also tried to study Italian, German, and geometry. For pleasure she read historical works, particularly the lives of famous men such as Gustavus Adolphus, the Duke of Ormond, and Frederick the Great. She also read periodicals, including the *Spectator* and *Annual Register*. Travel literature is only occasionally mentioned, and she does not seem to have read many books on geography or natural history – unlike a number of her pupils, especially Lady Mary Talbot, for whom botany and horticulture became a life-long passion.

Works of fiction, both prose and verse, make up at least 50 per cent of the list of books owned or mentioned by Agnes. Although contemporary commentators condemned novel-reading as frivolous and uninstructive,[177] Agnes enjoyed a large number of such books, in addition to more elevated works. She knew *Evelina* by Fanny Burney and she owned a copy of *The Romance of the Forest* by Ann Radcliffe.

---

[176] See pp. 353–58 for full details of these and other books mentioned by Agnes.
[177] John Brewer, *The Pleasures of the Imagination*, pp. 193–94.

She read novels by female authors such as Charlotte Smith, Elizabeth Hamilton and Jane West, also enjoying French authors, including Claris de Florian, Le Sage, Marivaux and de Genlis. Agnes also liked poetry. Amongst the poems she mentions as having read are *The Village* by George Crabbe, *The Farmer's Boy* by Robert Bloomfield and *Marmion* by Sir Walter Scott. She was fond of Petrarch, Tasso and Ossian. Her favourite poets included Alexander Pope, William Shenstone and, in particular, William Cowper – 'the most beloved writer of the period', reputed to be Jane Austen's favourite author.[178]

In addition to reading, Agnes also enjoyed writing. For a gentlewoman of her day, letter-writing was an important occupation: it helped to fill in the long hours spent alone in her room, and receiving letters reduced the inevitable feelings of isolation. Exchanging letters was an essential means of maintaining and reinforcing friendships, of discussing and passing on gossip about mutual acquaintances, and of finding out what was going on in the outside world. Agnes corresponded regularly with several relations, old friends and, in later years, her former pupils. She had very definite ideas on the purpose of letter-writing and tried to convey these to her pupils: 'A letter to a friend seems to me simply this: giving them an hour of your company, notwithstanding whatever distance separates you. To do this is to convey your thoughts to them while you are writing ...'[179] Sending letters was expensive in the days before the penny post: the cost was usually paid by the recipient, but letters sent to or by peers and Members of Parliament went free under certain conditions. Whilst she was in Lord Ilchester's household Agnes would have been able to obtain from her employer franked, post-dated covers for her letters, which meant that she did not have to worry that she might be imposing an unwelcome expense on her many correspondents. In later years Agnes was sometimes able to obtain covers from acquaintances: two letters sent from Fairford in 1806 and 1807 are endorsed 'Free, W. Windham',[180] and a letter from Malvern in 1810 has a cover signed by Charles Lemon.[181]

Agnes was familiar with the works of Joseph Addison, who recommended the keeping of a journal as a means of self-examination,

---

[178] Davidoff and Hall, *Family Fortunes*, pp. 157–58.

[179] Letter, 12 March 1793.

[180] Agnes's cousin Thomas Amyot was private secretary to William Windham, the war and colonial minister.

[181] Charles Lemon was MP for Penryn in Cornwall, 1807–12 and 1830–31 (he also held other Cornish seats, 1831–57). He married Agnes's former pupil Charlotte Fox Strangways in 1810.

through which the writer might achieve good taste and refinement.[182] Writing her own journal was certainly important to Agnes. In it she recorded day to day events, and also her thoughts and hopes, together with details of the plays that she had seen, her journeys – often by stagecoach – and the books she was reading. Although she cannot have expected that her journals would ever be published, they were read by the families of her pupils during her lifetime. In 1812 she sent Lady Mary Talbot a parcel of letters, together with two volumes of her own journals, with the comment that they 'will perhaps amuse you, and are peculiar in the circumstance of adverting to the education of both the *mother* and her *children*'.[183] Unfortunately, the expectation that her journals would be read by other people led Agnes to delete some words (though some of these deletions can be deciphered), and to cut out some sections or whole pages. The entries which have been lost seem to have included material that Agnes felt to be too personal, painful or revealing: it is interesting that the name of the Revd Joseph Griffith has been crossed out (presumably after Agnes discovered that he was married). It seems likely that some entries relating to her sister Betsey have also been removed.

Writing, both in poetry and prose, was a popular occupation among educated women at this time, when an increasing amount of their work was being published. Agnes certainly had some literary pretensions too. The journals include a number of poems written by her, and there are also some references to a children's book that she wrote, which was published in 1791 with the help of her friend Valentine Green. This book, *Triumphs of Reason Examplified in Seven Tales, and Affectionately Dedicated to the Juvenile Part of the Fair Sex by the Author*, was published anonymously, and probably in a fairly small edition: I have so far been unable to locate a copy. The exact basis on which it was published is unclear: Agnes appears to have contributed something towards the costs and it seems most unlikely that she actually made a profit from the publication.

The Wider World: Court Connections, Politics and Patronage

Outside the largely domestic world inhabited by Agnes Porter and portrayed in the novels of Jane Austen, the decades on either side of the turn of the eighteenth century were also the age of the French

---

[182] John Brewer, *The Pleasures of the Imagination*, pp. 107–8.
[183] Letter, 7 November 1812.

Revolution and wars against Napoleon; of rebellion in Ireland; of Fox and Pitt; of the Prince of Wales and the madness of King George III. Many of these aspects of contemporary society are touched on, if only in passing, in Agnes Porter's letters and journals.

Lord Ilchester's main interests were hunting and gambling. He took little part in public life, though he did attend the House of Lords from time to time. He held no post in the royal household, unlike his Digby relatives. His cousin and brother-in-law Colonel Stephen Digby was a vice-chamberlain to Queen Charlotte from 1783 to 1792 – it was probably because of this that the King and Queen, with three of the Princesses, visited Redlynch on their way from Weymouth to Longleat in 1789. The visit was not a total success: it rained all morning, so the royal family was unable to see the gardens and park, though they 'showed themselves very graciously at the windows' to the crowds of local people waiting outside.[184] Agnes was presumably at Redlynch during this visit, though she does not refer to this occasion. Colonel Digby was also Deputy Ranger, and then Ranger and Keeper, of Richmond Park from 1792 to 1800. Other members of the Digby family also had positions at Court: Julia, daughter of William Digby, Dean of Durham, was a maid of honour to Queen Charlotte from 1789 until she married in 1794, and was a woman of the bedchamber to the Queen from 1805; Admiral Robert Digby was a groom of the bedchamber in 1792; and Lord Ilchester's second wife, Maria Digby, was a favourite lady of the bedchamber to Queen Charlotte from 1804 until the Queen's death in 1818, apart from a period from 1814 to 1816 during which she was 'lent' to Princess Charlotte. Alicia Campbell, an old friend of Lord Ilchester and his family, was another friend at Court. She was appointed sub-governess to Princess Charlotte, the daughter of the Prince of Wales, in 1805, and became Keeper of the Privy Purse to the Princess when she married in 1816. Mrs Campbell was still with the Princess when she died in childbirth in the following year.

There were connections with the House of Commons too, most notably with Lord Ilchester's much more famous cousin, the Whig leader Charles James Fox. Fox spent three days at Redlynch in January 1791. Agnes does not say what she thought about him, but it is clear, from a letter written shortly after the visit by Lady Susan O'Brien, that the inhabitants of Redlynch were all Foxites: when a visiting footman declared, when drinking a toast, 'May the Fox fall into a Pitt', the

---

[184] Charlotte Traherne, 'Family Recollections'.

servants of Lord Ilchester 'exclaim'd "You had better hold your tongue, we are every one Foxes and we won't have such things said here"'.[185]

At a time when advancement in the church, the army and in the other professions depended to a great extent on knowing the right people, families such as the Foxes and the Talbots were important sources of patronage for their relations, friends and acquaintances. Both Lord Ilchester and Thomas Mansel Talbot were patrons of several church livings, and both would have received a constant stream of letters from men looking for advancement or employment. In South Wales, John Hunt and John Collins held the livings of Margam and Oxwich as a result of the patronage of their old friend. As a favoured member of a wealthy household, Agnes was expected to play her part in promoting the interests of her own friends and family. The letters and journals include several references to her attempts to fulfil these obligations: in 1790 she wrote to her cousin Mrs Amyot 'concerning a young woman whom I hope to place in a comfortable situation through my sister';[186] and eight years later she was hoping to obtain a position for Mrs Amyot's sister Ann Garritt as governess to one of the Digby girls. Agnes's greatest achievement came when she asked Lady Ilchester to use her influence to help Dr James Keir, the son of her old friend Elizabeth Keir: this seems to have been accomplished with the assistance of Sir Walter Farquhar, a fashionable doctor who was consulted both by the Fox Strangways family and by the Prince of Wales. Probably less successful was Agnes's request, in 1802, again through Lady Ilchester, that she herself should be considered as a recipient of St Catharine's Bounty. Later, in 1810, Agnes hoped that two of her former pupils, Lady Mary Talbot and Lady Harriot Frampton, would help to find new pupils for her sister Fanny.[187]

The French Revolution

The fall of the Bastille in July 1789, with the years of revolution and European war which followed, formed a background to the lives of Agnes and the people among whom she lived during the period covered by the journals and letters. In common with most other members of the Whig Opposition, who felt that the overthrow of the excessive and

---

[185] Lady Susan O'Brien to Lady Mary Fox Strangways, 15 February 1791.

[186] Journal, 25 December 1790.

[187] Journal, 23 May 1802, 7 November 1802, and Letter, 12 June 1810. I have been unable to identify St Catharine's Bounty, but it may have been a charity which helped unmarried women.

arbitrary power of the *ancien régime* was justified, Charles James Fox welcomed the French Revolution to begin with, calling it 'The greatest event ... that ever happened in the world'.[188] This initial euphoria turned to dismay and then horror as the full implications of events taking place in France became apparent.

It has been observed that Jane Austen rarely comments directly on the Revolution and its after effects.[189] While this also applies to Agnes Porter, Agnes had friends in France, and she describes several encounters with *émigrés* who were living in Great Britain. The most notable of these was the famous authoress Madame de Genlis, whom Agnes's pupils met at Stourhead. Agnes encountered several French priests, including M. Panyer, the chaplain to the nuns at Amesbury, with M. Marêt and M. Boisvy, whom she met in Salisbury. Agnes was clearly fascinated by these men, whom she described as 'as agreeable men as I ever knew – all of them insinuating to a degree'.[190] As the daughter of an Anglican clergyman, and a pious churchwoman herself, she was somewhat suspicious of Roman Catholics. Agnes also met other refugees from France in her sister's house in 1798, including M. de Vevrotte, the former President of the Parlement of Dijon, who was accompanied by 'a female Laplander'. The precise status of the Laplander within the Vevrotte household was the subject of much contemporary speculation.

After 1793, when the French king, Louis XVI was executed and Britain entered the European war against France, the inhabitants of the coastal counties of southern England were in constant fear of invasion by French troops. A noticeable feature of the period during which Agnes wrote her journal and letters was the presence, particularly along the south coast, and in ports such as Great Yarmouth and Swansea, of large numbers of men connected with the army and navy. Two of Jane Austen's brothers were naval officers, and she used her knowledge of their world to develop characters such as Fanny Price's brother William in *Mansfield Park*, and Admiral Croft and Captains Wentworth, Harville and Benwick in *Persuasion*. Several of Agnes's friends and acquaintances were in the regular army or navy, and others were involved with one or other of the numerous Volunteer regiments which were raised at this time. Lord Ilchester's daughters were by no means immune to the charms of such men. William Davenport Talbot, the first husband of Agnes's oldest pupil Elizabeth, was a junior officer in

---

[188] Quoted in Eric J. Evans, *The Forging of the Modern State* (London, 1996), p. 61.

[189] R. W. Chapman in Le Faye (ed.), *Jane Austen's Letters*, p. ix.

[190] Journal, 7 November 1796.

the regular army before his marriage, and then served in the Wiltshire Supplementary Militia until 1799. Elizabeth's second husband, Charles Feilding, was a Captain in the Royal Navy, who retired from active service in 1809, though he was still on half pay when he died (as a Rear-Admiral) in 1837. Lady Mary Talbot also chose a naval officer as her second husband: in 1815, two years after Thomas Talbot's death, she married the recently-retired hero of the capture of the Banda Islands, Captain Sir Christopher Cole. A Cornishman of comparatively humble origins, he was quite clearly the real love of her life.

In February 1794 Lady Susan O'Brien wrote from Melbury to tell Lady Mary Talbot that 'An invasion is really so much and so universally talk'd of that one hardly knows what to think', and said that she might flee to Wales 'on a poney' if the French landed at Weymouth.[191] In January 1797, when she was with the Digbys at Minterne, Lady Susan noted in her journal: 'Nothing talk'd of but military preparations, invasion and deffence. The situation of the country but too alarming'.[192] Shortly after this, in February 1797, a French force numbering 1400 did indeed land near Fishguard, just fifty miles from Penrice Castle. Agnes was not there at the time, but Thomas and Mary Talbot were at home with their two small daughters. The French ships had been seen from Gower before they reached Pembrokeshire: as Mary wrote to her sister Harriot, 'We had reason to be in a fright, for tho' they landed in Fiscard Bay in Pembrokeshire, as we did not know how many there were of them we thought we should have their company'.[193] Thomas Mansel Talbot was offered the command of the Glamorgan-shire Provisional Cavalry in 1798, but refused it. How useful they would have been if the French had landed again is debatable: in March 1798 Talbot described a muster, at which:

> The horses, from being weak, and many only just taken up after so wet a winter as we have had, made a most wretched appearance, and ... the troopers from this part of the county run races over Britton Ferry sands, lam'd or threw down most of their horses, and are return'd home quite unfit for service ... I hear the people about Cowbridge and Cardiff sent poneys; one man had a mangy horse and was not suffer'd to come near the others.[194]

Thomas Mansel Talbot nevertheless held the rank of Lieutenant-

[191] Letter, Lady Susan O'Brien to Lady Mary Talbot, 18 February 1794.
[192] BL, Add. MS 51359, 'Journal of Lady Susan O'Brien', 1770–1813.
[193] Letter, Lady Mary Talbot to Lady Harriot Fox Strangways, 26 February 1797.
[194] Letter, T. M. Talbot to Michael Hicks Beach, 19 March 1798.

Colonel of the voluntary Glamorganshire Rangers; he also contributed £500 a year to a local fund for the defence of Swansea and Gower during the period of the war.

There were further worries, resulting from disturbances in Ireland as well as France. In 1798, during Wolfe Tone's rebellion, Agnes's friends Mr and Mrs Simpson, fled from Dublin to North Wales, and from time to time she also heard news of her former pupils' Grady relatives in County Limerick and other parts of southern Ireland. In the summer of 1803 Fanny asked Agnes to leave Penrice immediately, and come to live in Swindon, as she was afraid that the French might land in Wales again. Agnes was, however, sanguine. She told Fanny, 'When I leave my dear Lady Mary I would not do it at a time of apprehended calamity – having shared in her good things, I would not leave her in trouble'.[195]

Two years later, after the battle of Trafalgar in 1805, fears that Britain would be invaded again could be laid aside, at least for the time being. Agnes did not live to hear of the final defeat of Napoleon at Waterloo in 1815, but by the time of her death, early in 1814, the French forces were in retreat throughout Europe and peace negotiations had begun.

Agnes was not forgotten by her pupils and their descendants, who continued to read and enjoy her letters and journals – a letter written in 1921, and tucked into one of the journals, shows that they were still being passed around the family over a century after Agnes's death. Though it has proved impossible to find a copy of Agnes's book of children's stories, there can be little doubt that she would have been delighted to think that her thoughts and recollections, written down during long hours spent alone in her chamber, might eventually reach a wider audience.

---

[195] Journal, 14 August 1803.

The Journals and Letters
of Agnes Porter

1788

This first fragment of a journal dates from 1788, when Agnes Porter had been governess to Lord Ilchester's daughters for four years. The family lived mainly at Redlynch, but during the winter and spring Lord and Lady Ilchester would take some of their children to stay in their London house, 31 Old Burlington Street. Whilst they were there, masters would be employed to teach the girls subjects such as French, drawing, music and dancing. They also went to art galleries and theatres, attended concerts, and visited friends and relations. Agnes was able to meet old friends and go with them to the theatre in London.

13 March Thursday: rose at half past six, past an hour and a half in my chamber, then went to the harpsichord till nine. A lively breakfast with my three dear friends, after which Lady Elizabeth and I together prepared very assiduously for Monsieur Helmandel:[1] he was very well pleased with the lessons practised. Afterwards I spent two hours with Lady Mary and Harriot at French, English and music, then half an hour of *Numa*[2] to our mutual satisfaction. Went in the evening with Mrs Matthews to the play, intending to see the heroine of the theatre Mrs Siddons,[3] but the house was so full there was no possibility of entering any where, and several hundreds of people were obliged to return. To console myself, went to Covent Garden Theatre – it was also crouded, and we could gain admittance no where but in the two-shilling gallery. Had a very tolerable seat, except in one circumstance: a sailor on the bench before me being extremely fat, and not finding his form broad enough, sat farther back and reposed himself on my knees all the spectacle. It was in vain for me to suppose what an honest, good creature he might be – I found him a great *fardeau* [burden] – he kindly offered me his rum bottle to enable me the better to go through the

---

[1] Probably Nicolas Joseph Hüllmandel (1751–1823).
[2] J. P. Claris de Florian, *The Adventures of Numa Pompilius* (1788).
[3] Sarah Siddons (1755–1831).

fatigues of the evening, but neither my companion nor self took any advantage of his liberality. The play *The Belle's Stratagem* – Miss Pope the Belle. She danced a most elegant minuet and did some of the scenes very well, but on the whole the English actors are very inferior to the French – they know not how to fill the stage; they are not enough *dégagés*. A Garrick, a Pritchard or a Siddons are exceptions.[4] On the whole, spent an agreeable evening, and got to bed by twelve.

14 March Friday: rose at seven, as usual. An hour in my room, and as usual another at the harpsichord. We prepared for Mr Parsons, whose hour with us always glides away imperceptibly. We then studied two hours, after which we took a little touch of *Numa*. My two dear children did their verbs and then walked out. At five I retired upstairs, read two hours of history, half an hour in my prayer-book, and went to bed at nine.

15 March Saturday: rose at half past six. The morning as usual. After breakfast extremely busy with Lady Elizabeth, at her music, then French. N.B. she writes French already much better than some French women. My two young ladies had their music master and did both very well – Lady Harriot in particular. She is a nice lady at her music, but I wish she would not give into the vocal part of it quite so much when she is above stairs – but no more on this subject. When their music master was gone we said catechism, and then Monsieur Chapui made his appearance, through whose appearance I hope my dear Lady Mary will, in time, become a pupil of the Graces. I returned to my room at five; drank tea; wrote an hour; read two hours; and gave half an hour to reflection, without which a judicious writer has observed that life cannot be properly conducted, either for time or for eternity. Thus ends my week's journal, March 15th, 1788. Agnes Porter, Old Burlington Street, No. 31, London.

---

[4] *The Belle's Stratagem* by Hannah Cowley was first performed (at Covent Garden) in 1780. Miss Pope was the actress Jane Pope (1742–1818). David Garrick (1717–79) and Hannah Pritchard (1711–68) were both well-known actors.

1789

Agnes's first surviving letter dates from December 1789, when she travelled by stagecoach from Wincanton (near Redlynch) to London, and then on to Norfolk, to visit friends and relations.

1. Letter from Agnes Porter, Norwich, to Lady Mary Fox Strangways, 21 December 1789

You desired me, my dear Lady Mary, to give you all the particulars of my journey and the company I met with on the road.* That my memory may not play me false in such very important occurences, I shall obey your injunctions now. From Wincanton I set out with a young glover, a middle-aged hatter, and an old grocer, with the addition of a Miss from Sherbourne school who, as soon as we were seated, informed us where she had been educated, and assured us that Sherbourne was the very first place in the world for female accomplishments. The hatter said he should then place his own daughter there, for he thought women could never be taught too much, as knowledge would qualify them to be proper companions for their husbands and, at the same time would, by teaching them their duty, make them humble. 'If they want to learn their duty, let them read the Bible' said my neighbour the grocer'. 'Law, Sir, will the Bible teach us to talk French as well and as fast as English – will it shew us how to sing and play on the harpsichord, or to *walk in the first position*? Though a very good book, yet it can't do all that for us.' 'And no matter for that' said the glover 'provided a woman can make a good pudding, cast an account, and keep her house neat, I thinks she may make a wife to please any reasonable man. But howsomdever, Miss, as you say you larnt music, suppose we have a song from you?' The young woman immediately

---

* For information about and details of people, places, books and plays mentioned in the text, where there is no specific note, see below, pp. 333–58.

began one – sang it in a very particular style, and when it was over said to me: '*Shinty vue* [*chantez-vous* – do you sing], *Madame?*' I told her that I should understand her better if she spoke English. 'La, Ma'am, how I pity you! What, not speak French? I would not give up that accomplishment for the world – well, it certainly is your misfortune, Ma'am.' 'As to misfortune' said the grocer 'I do not see much in it – this gentlewoman here seems a quiet, steady person, and most likely is kind and obliging to her husband and careful to keep her children, if she has any, right and light, which I think if she does so is better than to *parly franchee* as you call it, or such like. As for my part, I think a woman can talk quite enough in her mother tongue, and has no need to dun folks with a noise in more languages than one, as they have words enough and to spare in plain English.' The hatter and Miss were shocked at such assertions; the glover coincided with the old man, and their arguments I thought amusing on each side of the parties. When the young woman and I were by ourselves I told her in French that, as I supposed our fellow travellers did not understand that language, I thought it better to decline the pleasure of answering her in French. She looked a little serious, and replied in English 'Ma'am, I am not so far in the French phrases'!

When arrived in London, I found good Jemima well, who took great care of A. P. for that evening and the next day at dinner. Mr Williams saw me to the stage at six in the evening and left me with three fellow travellers, who accompanied me to Norwich. They were very agreeable men – a captain of a *[word illegible]* Indiaman, a Yarmouth merchant, and a lawyer, who were so obliging as [to] take all the trouble of the journey off my hands as much as possible. They regulated the windows during the night at my pleasure.

Have I not fulfilled my promise to my dear Lady Mary? In return, let me beg of her to be punctual to medicine, to collar, and a little hundred more, etc., etc., to present my grateful respects to Lord and Lady Ilchester, love to my dearest Lady Elizabeth, and believe me her very affectionate Agnes Porter.

Pray, a kiss to the sweet Ladies Charlotte and Louisa. Farewell, my love.

1790

Lady Ilchester died in June 1790, six weeks after the birth of her sixth daughter. Two months later Agnes began to keep a journal, which covers the period to September 1792, with a few later entries. In August 1790 Agnes and her pupils were at Redlynch, where they stayed until January 1791.

Journal, 1790

13 August We spent the day as usual.

14 August Lord Ilchester went to Melbury. The young ladies and I spent the evening together: we walked, read, and had a little musick.

15 August To church. At my return read half an hour in the *Duty of Man*.[1] After dinner I finished my *Irish History* by Coxe.[2] Colonel Strangways drank tea with his nieces and me, after which we took a beautiful walk. At our return we read some extracts and spent the evening very pleasantly.

16 August We spent the day as usual, divided between our studies and rural amusements.

17 August My dear Lady Charlotte not at all well – rather feverish. Sent for Mr Sampson. He said it proceeded from a cold, advised her to be quite still, and to take a few draughts at stated times. I nursed the darling child – reflected at night on my situation which (though a single woman) was attended with all the anxieties of a mother.

18 August My darling a deal better – my spirits rose in consequence. The others all well. At night I treated myself with Tasso[3] and an hour of *Ormond's Life*.[4]

---

[1] *The Whole Duty of Man … With Private Devotions* (various editions).

[2] Sir Richard Coxe, *Hibernia Anglicana: or the History of Ireland* (1689).

[3] Torquato Tasso (1544–95). Numerous editions of his works were published in the seventeenth and eighteenth centuries.

[4] Thomas Carle, *The History of the Life of James, Duke of Ormond* (1736).

19 August Miss Julia Digby[5] breakfasted at Redlynch. She is a most amiable young lady and resembles her charming family. As maid of honour to the Queen she is obliged to attend St James' at this undue season of the year when London must be dreadfully hot and unpleasant. The dinner and tea past most agreeably. I had the pleasure of contemplating youth, beauty and innocence: the lovely cousins were happy in this meeting. At night we conversed about Madame Genlis, whom Miss Julia Digby had often met at Spa.[6] She did not think her at all agreeable in society, and was much disappointed in her.

20 August Lady Elizabeth lost her agreeable guest. We spent the day, however, very well and pleasingly.

21 August We spent the morning in relating passages from ancient and modern history. Mr Charles Digby dined with us. In the afternoon we entertained ourselves with a play of Shakespeare's: *Richard II*.

22 August Read before breakfast in the Duty of Man. To church. After it I wrote a few letters to some dear absent friends. We then walked, read, chatted etc. My dear Lady Charlotte is almost quite well again – may I be truly thankful!

23 August Mr Sampson tells me dear Lady Charlotte will recover her looks in a few days. This gave me spirits to enter into a little chat with him – he is a very well-informed, intelligent person. A vial of salts laying accidentally on the table, he told us of what it was made: the soot of the Egyptian ovens where their chickens are hatched. A great quantity of the common kind of hartshorn is [not?] made from *hartshorn* or any other such substance. Wood soot will also make it, but the real is of a yellow tinge, the mock like water.[7]

24 August We spent the day as usual in our various studies: Shakespeare furnished us with evening entertainment.

25 August Had a letter from my dear sister Fanny. She proposes coming to see me next week – *quel plaisir!* We spent the day with chearfulness in the pursuit of my dear pupils' improvements.

26 August The day as usual. I had a letter from my friend Mr Green: his son is married – how happy it would have made his poor mother to witness that day.

---

[5] Elizabeth Juliana Digby (died 1807).

[6] Stéphanie Felicité, Madame de Genlis (1746–1830), a well-known authoress.

[7] Smelling salts were made from salt of hartshorn (carbonate of ammonia).

27 August I rose at six. Read an hour in *Ormonde's Life*. Walked out before breakfast, then our studies and a play of Shakespeare's.

28 August My dear pupils all well, happy and amiable. My study is that every thing concerning their education, health etc. should be conducted as nearly as possible the same as it was under their blessed mother's direction. May she prove their model, as in all their concerns I have aimed at making her mine.

29 August At church. Before I went I read in my *Duty of Man*. N.B. to give it to the maids – a most excellent instruction it is.

30 August I rose early, wrote a long letter to my dear mother, then breakfast and studies. Lord Ilchester returned, to the great joy of all his children. In the evening I wrote to Mr Simson to wish him joy on his son's birth; to Mr Green to congratulate him on his son's marriage. I then repaired to my forte piano, play'd an hour, and to bed.

31 August Went to Wincanton in the hopes of meeting my sister. Did not – was much disappointed, but endeavoured to spend the day as usual. At night rather melancholy; thought of some unpleasant circumstances and saw them in their worst light; endeavoured to raise my mind to a better way of thinking, and in great measure succeeded. Read an hour in *Gaudentio di Lucca* to amuse me.[8] To bed by eleven.

1 September My sister Fanny arrived about twelve, to my great joy. She looked well, in good spirits. I was happy in her company. Lord Ilchester and the young ladies all goodness to her on my account. I have continual and encreasing reasons for gratitude in my present situation – God make me thankful!

2 September Made holiday with my dear Fanny. We walked, we chatted, we almost danced with pleasure. In the evening she sang and played and opened her future prospects without reserve.

3 September I carried my sister to Stourhead. We spent a most delightful day together, wandering in those charming scenes for several hours. We then had a snug little dinner, and home by nine at night. In the evening we had a long and interesting discourse. Besides the tie of nature binding me to her, she is a most agreeable young woman – she sings like a little syren, plays charmingly, draws with taste, and is most pleasing in conversation, having a talent for each person she converses with.

4 September At home with my dear pupils and sister. Colonel Strang-

---

[8] *The Memoirs of Signor Gaudentio di Lucca* (1737).

ways dined with us, so did Mr Whitick.[9] The latter seemed kindly partial to my dear Fanny.

5 September Not at church, Lady Elizabeth not being quite well. Did not chuse to leave her. My dear Fanny and I enjoyed ourselves in the evening together.

6 September My dear Fanny was obliged to leave me. We parted with regret, yet I was grateful for the pleasure I had enjoyed. Saw her to the stage, and so we parted.

7 September My dear pupils and I spent the morning at our studies. After dinner we made a party to the lodge, where we drank tea with much glee. The simplicity of the apartment and the novelty of every thing around us gave much pleasure to my young friends. A party is not made there above once in a year. My pleasure was dampened from the recollection of the past time when the charming mother graced the rural fête – but so it must be.

8 September Passed the day very agreeably with my dear pupils – have the satisfaction to see them improve daily, and the comfort to think I am useful to them. A letter from Mr G-n;[10] I believe he is one of my very good friends.

9 September We spent the day as usual – all my dear pupils well, I thank God. I long now to see my dear Lady Charlotte, who has been absent with her papa and brother these five days. In the evening we had music and reading.

10 September Spent the day in our usual studies.

11 September In the morning our historical game, which is a source both of amusement and of literary improvement to us. Lord Ilchester and Lady Charlotte returned – both well, thank God.

12 September At church. In the afternoon a long walk; at night I read in the *Duty of Man*. To bed early.

13 September A letter from my dear Miss Mitchell informed me of her marriage to Mr Alexander of the twelfth of last month. I rejoiced to hear that so amiable and worthy a woman is now settled for life, and has a friend and protector – yet it breaks into my future prospect of spending my evening of life with her. No matter – it is for her advantage she should not, and that friendship deserves not the name which loses not its own partial views in the larger prospect of another's happiness.

---

[9] The Revd Walter Wightwick (*c.* 1728–1807).

[10] Sic. Probably Green, but could be Gordon.

14 September I wrote to my dear Mrs Alexander and to Mr Green. At night I read the *Duke of Ormonde's Life*.

15 September My two elder pupils paid a visit to Mrs C. Digby. In the evening I read an hour in *Tacite*,[11] wrote an hour, visited my children in bed, and then went to rest myself. Thank God, my mind very easy: 'Study and ease together mix'd'.[12]

16 September With my dear pupils: they drew while I read to them. We took the book alternately. My dear little loves are all well – they have the best of fathers, who is contented in my care of them. In the evening I settled some accounts, and wrote to my dear mother and to my friend Mr Gordon, then I studied a little German. It seems a very harsh language to a beginner. Said my prayers, read my Bible, and to bed by half past ten.

17 September Our studies as usual. In the evening took a charming walk with my dear Lady Elizabeth.

18 September Had a letter from my sister Fanny. She will reach home to morrow. Our historical amusement in the morning. In the afternoon music and a play of Shakespeare's.

19 September Rose at seven, had a letter from my dear Miss Owen, went to church. On my return answered Miss Owen's letter: she writes me that all the people are *en militaire* and that the very postilions wear swords. She finds the town of Boulogne much improved as to buildings etc. After dinner I read in the *Duty of Man* and in the *Duke of Ormonde's Life*. At night I read a number of letters from absent friends, and then to bed early.

20 September The day past agreeably with my dear pupils.

21 September Accompanied my dear Lady Elizabeth to Bruton church, where she was confirmed by Dr Moss, Bishop of Bath and Wells. May a blessing be on this, as on every act of her life! All the dear little ones rejoiced to see us return. A happy afternoon together. At night I dipt into the *Duke of Ormonde's Life*, studied a little German, said my prayers and went to bed early. At church, some poor country girls were so intimidated by the Bishop's order to hold their heads close while he confirmed them that they never changed the position till the whole was over.

22 September Spent the day as usual with my dear pupils. At night I

---

[11] A. N. Amelot de la Houssaie, *The Annals and History of Tacitus* (1692).
[12] Alexander Pope, *Ode on Solitude*, line 13.

wrote to Monsieur L'Abbé de Cléry to thank him for his attentions to my dear Miss Owen.

23 September Our studies as usual. In the afternoon Sully's *Memoirs* and a play of Shakespeare.[13] At night I read a beautiful poem on the nature of flowers and plants, an hour's music, and to bed early.

24 September A very happy day with my young friends. A pleasant walk in the evening, and saw the sun set in splendid majesty: its long beams of 'levelled light' were beautiful to behold. Vivid purple, serene blue and burning gold compleated the glorious scenery. I do not like Pope's somewhere giving the moon a preference over that bright luminary – poetry should adorn, not controvert, the truth.

25 September The day as usual. Our historical annecdotes afforded us much amusement. I had letters from the agreeable Mrs Moser, my friend Mr Wilkes, and from Lady Susan O'Brien.

26 September To church. In the afternoon I wrote to Mrs Moser and Miss Sanxay. In the evening I read in the *Duty of Man,* reperused a number of letters, and to bed by ten.

27 September Rose at seven; read my Bible etc. till eight; walked till nine; with my young pupils till one; walked till two; dinner at three; with my dear young friends till five; walked till six. Met old Betty Silverthorne, asked her for her daughter, told me she was in a very far-off country – on requesting the name of this foreign land, she told me: 'They do call it Kent, Ma'am'. Poor, good Betty has resided in her village ever since her birth these seventy-eight years. Gave her a trifle with much pleasure. In the evening an hour with my little darlings. When they left me I wrote some letters, studied a little German, read a little Italian, and went soon to bed, thank God in the utmost tranquility of mind.

28 September Rose soon and wrote to my dear mother and sister Fanny. With my dear pupils as usual. Mr Whitick dined with us.

29 September Lord Ilchester and the two elder ladies went to Abbotsbury. I spent the day in much tranquility with my dear little pupils. At night I transcribed one of my little tales, which amused me a good deal.

30 September I spent the day as usual with my little friends. It is to me a delightful employment to watch over their health and improvement. When inclination coincides with duty we ought to esteem

---

[13] Maximilian de Béthune, Duc de Sully, *Memoirs* (*c.* 1640).

ourselves happy. At night I wrote to my friend Mr Green – sent him my fairy tale.

1 October Studied and walked out with my dear pupils. The weather remarkably fine. It was said of Hershel[14] that he foretold our summer would this year be in September and October. The weather has indeed been extraordinarily pleasant, and Redlynch appears in all its verdure.

2 October Lady Harriot Acland with her daughter and niece spent the day at Redlynch. Some years since, when all that charming woman has gone through in America is read, it may be imagined that she was a strong, bold-spirited, masculine woman, but on the contrary, gentleness and the sweetest female delicacy of manner and person form her characteristics and description. She is rather under the middle stature, has the most delicate complection and the sweetest mild blue eyes, with a countenance full of benevolence, the prettiest little hands in the world, and a mouth adorned by smiles. Such in her person is the celebrated Lady Harriot Acland, and to the honour of our age celebrated for her virtues and conjugal affection.[15] Her daughter is very pretty indeed, and has but to follow her mother's example to be very good.

3 October At church. After church, Lady Harriot and I took a long walk together, spent the afternoon in her charming conversation.

4 October Lady Harriot and the two young ladies proceeded on their journey to Lymyngton. In the evening I transcribed my tales, had an agreeable letter from my eldest pupil, Lady Elizabeth.

5 October With my dear little pupils as usual. Had a letter from Mr Green – he likes my fairy tale and advises me to publish them [sic] and put a little money in my purse by so doing. I wrote to my dear mother and to Fanny.

6 October The day as usual.

7 October With my dear pupils all the morning. In the afternoon I worked hard at my tales.

8 October We did our little studies, after which I wrote to my dear Lady Elizabeth and Mary.

9 October Gave my children a little treat – we dined in another room and played all together very comfortably. Thank God, the youngest is a thriving child: dear memorial of her charming mother!

10 October At church. When we returned, read in the *Duty of Man*. N.B. to give it to the servants' library – it is so excellent a book.

---

[14] The astronomer William Herschel (1738–1822).

[15] See below, p. 333, for Lady Harriot Acland.

11 October As usual the morning. At night I finished transcribing my tales.

12 October I wrote to several friends, then spent the day as usual.

13 October Sent the tales to my friend Mr Green – desired him to act for me in them as he thought best. I am happy in a friendship with several of the worthy among his sex, whose advice is frequently of the greatest benefit to me.

14 October With my pupils as usual. Mr Pearson, a distant relation of the dowager Lady's, dined with the young ladies and me. I spent the afternoon very agreeably in his company – he is a clergyman, whose life began in adversity. He was menaced by perpetual dependance, but gained the heart of an amiable woman with a large fortune, with whom he is now happily settled. We expatiated together on the virtues and charms of the ever dear Lady Ilchester.

15 October Spent the day as usual. At night I read in *Tacite* – a most agreeable translation by Amblot de la Houssay. The political and critical notes are extremely entertaining.

16 October As usual. I wrote to my dear pupils at Abbotsbury.

17 October At church, and wrote to my sister Frances.

18 October I spent the morning with my dear charge, then walked out. Past by Meillar Eton's cottage – advised her to allow her daughter, a girl of sixteen, one penny out of the money paid her for knitting a pair of stockings, to encourage the poor girl to industry. I began the little fund, but fear the mother will not continue it. At night I wrought hard at my needle.

19 October Had a gay letter from my dear Lady Elizabeth – in rhyme. Answered it at night:

> My dear Lady Elizabeth –
> I received your epistle with so much surprize,
> That, believe me, I scarcely could credit my eyes.
> And have you the conscience to complain of A. P.,
> Who has scribbled you letters to the number of three,
> She sent a narration of *les jeux brutiques* [the Bruton games],
> Inform'd you your sisters had never been sick,
> She told you fair Acland had writ you a letter,
> In the name of caprice, how could I do better?
> I think of you early, I dream of you late,
> I enjoy your amusements, yet envy your fate.
> You wander at pleasure round Abbotsbury towers,
> Where old Father Time never reckons his hours.
> You pick up smooth pebbles, as careless you go,

And admire the bright waves, as they dash to and fro,
Then seated by night, in that dear drawing room,
You number the stars and converse with the moon.
When objects like those, so truly sublime,
Have engaged your attention a suitable time,
You turn to the table where your grandmama sits,
And form a snug party at commerce[16] or whist,
Where ease and good humour enliven the game,
And, victor or vanquished, the pleasure's the same.
I've many an annecdote longs for your ear,
But all shall be hush till Eliza appear.
Your *bocage* deserted, your A. P. forlorn,
And things lie unseen till Eliza return.

20 October After our studies, we enjoyed the fine weather in the shrubbery. It was quite delightful. At night I read the *Duke of Ormond's Life* and admired at intervals the moon from my closet window. She was surrounded by thick clouds, from which she emerged with enchanting brightness. To my mind this gave the image of a virtuous soul that was breaking loose from the mists of mortality.

21 October The day as usual. My dear pupils all well, I thank God.

22 October Had a letter from my dear Lord Ilchester which encreased the sentiments of gratitude I owed him. Excellent father to his children! Honourable and sincere in all his conduct! His goodness, and my dear Lady Ilchester's to me must ever be written on my heart. All my pupils well, and as lovely as the rose-buds 'just opening to the view'.[17]

23 October The day as usual.

24 October At church. Read in the *Duty of Man* – an excellent book. Walked out. In the evening, wrote to my dear mother and sister Fanny.

25 October Mr C. Digby dined with the little ladies and me. After dinner we walked out. He told me an annecdote of Lord Bathurst – Pope's Bathurst – that in speaking to a gentleman of his acquaintance on the follies of youth, he made this observation 'In youth the absence of pleasure is pain, in old age the absence of pain is pleasure'. What shall we say of the space between?

26 October The day with my dear pupils. At night I read the first volume of the *Prince of Abyssinia* – sweet book.[18] As I was preparing for bed, I was thankful that I had spent a day free from pain and misfortune,

---

[16] A card-game.

[17] Probably from the poem *William and Margaret* by David Mallet.

[18] Samuel Johnson, *The Prince of Abissinia: A Tale* (1759).

and had an easy, comfortable couch to repose on. I softly added to myself: 'True happiness is gratitude to God'.

27 October With my pupils. At night I wrote to Lord Ilchester.

28 October Spent the day as usual. Met poor Betty Silverthorne – she observed that the weather began to grow poor for folks that had no firing. Poor woman: at seventy-eight [to] want the comfort of a fire! N.B. to send her wood. Spent the evening, as usual, alone, but very agreeably – read and wrote from Shenstone, one of my favorite authors.[19] Read his *Ode to Memory* – drew parallels from it that were pleasing, though mournful, yet might with Ossian[20] say 'My soul was brightened with song', and I remembered the friends of my youth, and the still dearer father 'whose every word to me was melody, whose every glance was love'.

29 October Purchased a small provision of wood for poor Betty Silver-thorne. Spent the day as usual with my beloved children.

30 October The morning at our studies. In the evening I entertained myself with *Gil Blas* – who would suppose that such a man's daughter as Le Sage should die in an alms house in Boulogne?[21] But this was really the case: the English used to make the poor old woman presents.

31 October At church. At my return finished reading the *Duty of Man*, and then made it a present to the maid that waits on me. In the evening I wrote to my dear mother, and to Lady Mary.

1 November Spent the day as usual with my pupils. Had a letter from Mrs Quin, the favorite sister of my ever dear Lady Ilchester. It breathed the tenderest sentiments for the family, and expressed the most interesting confidence in my care and love for the dear motherless children.

2 November The morning with my dear children. In the evening studied Tasso. N. B. a French lady once told me 'Que le Tasse étoit un poème charmant, mais que *La Jerusaléme délivrée* valoit encore beaucoup mieux'.[22] Ignorance in any respect is a misfortune, but pretended knowledge is a folly both mean and odious.

3 November With my darlings all day. When they were gone to rest, I wrote to Lady Susan O'Brien and to my much beloved and esteemed

---

[19] William Shenstone (1714–63). Poems published 1737 and later.
[20] The poems of 'Ossian' were written by James Macpherson (1736–96).
[21] Alain René Le Sage, *Histoire de Gil Blas de Santillane* (several editions in the 1720s).
[22] *La Gerusalemme liberata*, a poem by Torquato Tasso.

Miss Owen – I apply to her a line I have read somewhere: 'Nor changed to *please*, but *pleased* because the same'.

4 November Had a letter from my dear Fanny, who has received my little present safe. Spent the day with my dear young pupils as usual. Walked in the shrubbery, thought much of their ever dear mother. O! How often as I walk past her favourite shrubs or flowers do I impulsively repeat: 'Sweet lady! Dear and excellent woman!' It is impossible in my situation that I can forget her, neither would I. I fear I begin to love the amiable little Charlotte too much – N.B. to watch over myself that I do not give way to improper partialities, to endeavor to love them equally, that I may perform my duties as I ought.

5 November Sent my dear mother her money, which God Almighty give his blessing to, both in the use and enjoyment! Spent the day with my darling children.

6 November As usual. At night I read in the *Duke of Ormonde's Life* and studied Tasso.

7 November At church. Walked with my dear pupils, told them little scripture histories. At night I read and wrote to some dear friends: Dr Macqueen, Mr Peele, Mrs Keir etc. N.B. told the latter that a friend thought her novel of *Interesting Memoirs* one of the few that merited criticism. If she encourage me, I will tell her the few exceptions I find to that charming performance (under another's character).[23]

8 November I heard from my dear Fanny – her affairs not fully settled. I thought a deal concerning it and grew very pensive, so had recourse to *Gil Blas* for amusement.

9 November With my dear pupils as usual.

10 November As usual spent the day in much tranquillity. My dear Lady Elizabeth and Mary returned, to my great satisfaction, with their father.

12 November Had much discourse with my dear young friends, and great pleasure in their society.

13 November Spent the day at our studies etc.

14 November At church. Took a long walk with my dear pupils. At night I read and wrote.

15 November Spent the morning at our studies as usual. In the afternoon Lady Mary gave me an account of her amusements at Abbotsbury.

---

[23] This must refer to Susannah Harvey Keir's book *Interesting Memoirs: By a Lady* (2nd edn, Edinburgh, 1785).

N.B. Dame Ford there still alive, but at ninety-two complains that the infirmities of her age are *beginning* to lay hold of her – she says that about thirty years ago, when she was a *young* woman she never felt an ail. Dear old creature! She acts in the treble capacity of tooth-drawer, midwife and apothecary to the parish of Abbotsbury. The people there are very long-lived indeed.

16 November My dear Lady Elizabeth's birthday. Invited to sup with them on the occasion. Spent an agreeable day – seven years I have now seen in revolution, and the pretty child of ten years of age shoot up into the fine woman of seventeen. What is the florist's pride or pleasure compared to this! The family, with Colonel Strangways and Mr Whitick, formed the party.

17 November The morning as usual. At night I read *Ormond's Life* and *Gil Blas*.

18 November Wrote to my dear mother. The day at our studies, *à l'ordinaire*.

19 November The morning as usual. In the afternoon read *King Lear* to Lady Mary. N.B. never to read that play any more, it is absolutely too much. At night Lady Harriot Acland and her daughter arrived, to the joy of their friends at Redlynch.

20 November The morning as usual. Had half an hour's conversation with Lady Harriot. At night I finished my dear *Gil Blas* – I was sorry to take my leave of him. How poor was Voltaire's praise of that delightful work only to say 'Il y a du naturel' – a work which abounds in the liveliest pictures of human life, and [is] replete with humour, truth and morality. Yes, morality.

21 November It was very bad weather. Did not go to church: read a sermon of my dearest father's. To me they have a peculiar unction – a father's sentiments and hand. May the advice ingraft into my heart, that we may meet again in the regions of *immortality!* In the afternoon I wrote some letters; at night I read. To bed at eleven.

22 November Heard that my dear Miss Owen was returned to England – wrote to her. Mr and Mrs L. Damer spent a day at Redlynch. Speaking of Barinton introduced the subject of robbers: Mr Damer said he was robbed lately, but had time to conceal his watch before the highwayman advanced. He gave his purse immediately, but on being asked for his watch he made answer he wore none. 'Upon your honour?' said the highwayman. 'Upon my honour', replied Mr Damer, 'but you may search me if you please'. 'No Sir, the honour of a gentleman is sacred' said the sentimental highwayman, and so took his leave with a most graceful bow. Lady Harriot and the rest of the Redlynch visitors proceeded on their journey.

23 November The day as usual with my dear pupils. At night I entertained myself with the *Duke of Ormond's Life*.

24 November A letter from Miss Owen, another from Mr Green. They both gave me great pleasure – no person ever was happier in the favours of friendship than I am. The day as usual.

25 November With my dear pupils. At night I wrote to Lady Home and to my dear Mrs Alexander. I claimed a particular and minute account from the latter of her present situation. I told her with truth that though her marriage had lessened my solicitude concerning her, nothing could abate my attachment. *The Duke of Ormond* an hour. To bed at eleven.

26 November The day happily with my dear young friends. Gave Betty Silverthorne a nice pair of spectacles. She had complained that her eyes at seventy-nine began to fail her at her prayer book of a Sunday evening. As she had never worn spectacles, [I] flatter myself it will be a renewal of sight to her.

27 November The day as usual. At night Tasso and the *Microcosm*, an ingenious work of some young Etonians.[24] It will do lasting credit to that learned seminary, at least in my opinion, who am charmed with this publication.

28 November At church. Had a letter from a dear friend. The letter extraordinary, the friend unaccountable: too aspiring for happiness, too restless for contentment, yet noble, generous, good. This letter dwelt on my mind. To turn my ideas into a smoother channel, read a sermon of my dearest father's. Finished the first volume of *Ormond*, said my prayers, and went to bed.

29 November The morning as usual with my pupils. The evening in music and reading.

30 November Had a letter from my friend Mr G—n. Extremely obliging and agreeable the contents. Wrote immediately to thank him. The day with my pupils. At night I answered Dr Macqueen's letter according to my ideas of true friendship. Heard also from my dear Miss Owen – amiable woman, happy be her fate!

1 December Spent the day agreeably with my dear pupils, who daily improve both to the eye and heart. What a pleasure it is to spend one's

---

[24] *The Microcosm: A Periodical Work by Gregory Griffin of the College of Eton* (1787). It was written by George Canning and others.

days encircled by beauty, youth and innocence. This is my present position among my blooming pupils. At night Tasso and Dryden.

2 December The day as usual. Heard of Miss Fielding's fan. Admired its simple elegance. The design: His Majesty's picture with a wreath of flowers, under it these words: 'He is well, and millions are happy'. At night we chatted, danced, sang, and spent the evening agreeably. When Lord Ilchester is from home I spend the evenings with his daughters; when he is at home I pass them alone.

3 December Wrote a long letter to my dear Miss Owen. The day as usual, at night we read a play of Shakespeare.

4 December The morning at our studies. I had a letter from Mrs Upcher – N.B. burnt. The day as usual.

5 December At church, then read a sermon of my dearest father's.

6 December Mrs Damer spent the day at Redlynch. Had the pleasure to hear her play – she is one of the finest *lady* performers in England. It was a high luxury to me to hear her charming fingers run over the keys with the most rapid execution.

7 December Our studies as usual. At night I wrote to my Yarmouth friends, then took half an hour of Ossian. Delighted with it: 'A sun beam to the soul'.

8 December All my lovely pupils well. Spent the day very pleasingly, the evening in music and reading.

9 December A letter from my sister Fanny. Filled with thoughtfulness: 'Ma in ogni clima, Via piu si stima, Del conquistare, Il conservare [in all circumstances, it is more important to keep than to conquer]'. Wrote to her; thought of her; and dreamt of her.

10 December The day as usual, all my dear pupils well, thank God. At night the *Duke of Ormonde's Life* with half an hour of Ossian.

11 December Lady Harriot Strangways returned to be under my care for a few weeks, after three years' absence on account of her health.[25]

12 December My two elder pupils went to their father at Melbury. I remain here with the other four and Miss T. Wightwick. To church, then a *dear* sermon at home. Heard my children [say] their catechism etc. Walked with them, and to bed early.

---

[25] Harriot had been sent to a boarding school in Weymouth in 1787. She had a bad knee, and it was thought that sea-bathing would be beneficial.

13 December As usual. In the evening read Ricoboni's *Lady Catesby* – it is beautifully written.[26]

14 December The day as usual with my young friends. My time at present passes with serenity and contentment. Such are valuable days, yet they make no figure in a *journal*. Wrote to Mrs Alexander and Miss Owen and Doctor Macqueen.

15 December As usual.

16 December My dear Lady Harriot good and amiable. I hope I shall enable her to make up for her school-days' indolence, and consequently small progress.

17 December The day with my pupils. At night I read and wrote transcripts from Ossian. I love that poet more than ever – he is sublime, yet tender.

18 December The day as usual.

19 December At church. A sermon at home; in the evening Tasso.

20 December Lord Ilchester and his two daughters returned home.

21 December Lady Harriot Acland and her daughter arrived at Red-lynch. My dear pupils all well.

22 December The day as usual. At night I indulged myself with Ossian.

23 December Very pensive all day, bordering a little on ill-humour. Perceived this, which encreased my self-dissatisfaction. At night took myself to task – found it all originated in disappointment at not receiving a letter from a particular correspondent. Very angry with myself for this weakness; resolved to shake it off and grow perfectly good-humoured the next day.

24 December Kept my resolution. With my pupils – all past agreeably. · At night a letter from my dear sister Fanny more satisfactory than the last. Read a sermon, and to bed.

25 December Christmas Day. With my dear pupils at church. Accompanied my eldest to the altar; thought of her dear and charming mother; endeavoured to turn my thoughts into another and more proper channel, and not to regret her whose happiness was secured. This day twelvemonth we visited the house of God together – little did I then think that we so soon should lose the ornament of her family and sex. When returned from church, read a sermon of Mr Moir's – an excellent

---

[26] M. -J. Riccoboni, *Lettres de Mildady Juliette Catesby, à Milady Henriette Campley, son amie* (1759).

one.[27] At night wrote to Mrs Amyot concerning a young woman whom I hope to place in a comfortable situation through my sister.

26 December Sunday – at church.

27 December Spent the day as usual.

28 December With my dear pupils. Took an agreeable walk with Lady Susan O'Brien. She gave me a comical annecdote of the Indian customs – a lady of quality who was very fond of dancing gave a ball to some English company, and danced herself. An Indian chief then present begged she would not for his entertainment descend to an exercise so unbecoming to her rank as dancing, and offered to send for some dancing women that he kept and paid for that purpose, as he was shocked to see her ladyship so far demean herself. At night I wrote to several dear friends, and read in the *Duke of Ormonde*.

29 December Spent the day agreeably in my usual occupations. A letter from Fanny – answered it. To bed at eleven.

30 December The day as usual. A long discourse with Lady Harriot Acland concerning my dear young friends. That charming lady is sincerely interested in their welfare.

31 December As usual. Thank God no particular misfortune nor care.

---

[27] John Moir, *Sermons on Some of the Most Useful and Interesting Subjects in Religion and Life* (1784).

1791

On 19 January 1791 Agnes went to Salisbury, where she spent a few days with her mother and sisters. Three days later she travelled by coach to London, where she was joined in early February by Lord Ilchester and his daughters. They stayed in London until the end of April 1791. On 28 April Agnes returned to Salisbury by stagecoach and then on 3 May she joined her pupils at Redlynch. They spent most of the rest of 1791 at Redlynch, with short visits to Melbury and Abbotsbury. In November Agnes spent a week in Salisbury with her mother, who was unwell.

Journal, 1791

1 January The day as usual. At night rather pensive – recollected the kind friends with whom I had spent the first day of last year with some regret of their society. N.B. to remember what Dr Moore observes: 'One great source of vexation arises from our indulging too much indifference for the blessings we possess'.[1] N.B. to avoid this folly. Wrote to my dear mother.

2 January Not at church – Lady Charlotte not quite well. Invited by the dowager Lady Ilchester to dine with her – could not go. At night my darling better. Had the pleasure of Mrs Churchyard's company to tea – a very sensible, worthy person. At night I read a sermon; wrote in my journal; prayers and bed.

3 January The day as usual with my pupils. Had a letter from my good friend Mr Green – my tales are now in the press. Much obliged to him for taking so much trouble – he proves the sincerity of his friendship by his actions, not professions. At night read in *Tacite* – a delightful book, and the comments and notes (added to it in Amelot de la Houssaye's translation) make it historically instructive in the events

---

[1] The quotation is probably from Dr John Moore (1729–1802), the physician, novelist and friend of Smollett.

of more modern times. Wrote to my mother and sisters, as to the Revd Mr Gordon. N.B. Mr Charles Fox arrived at Redlynch.

4 January Lady Harriot Acland and I were employed in a very melancholy manner: taking an inventory of the late, ever dear, Lady Ilchester's jewels etc. for the use of her children. At night the unpleasing impressions remained in full force: a pensive evening, a troubled night.

5 January Mr Fox left Redlynch after breakfast. I past the morning with Lady Harriot in the same manner. As we came to miniature pictures of her father, the late Earl of Ilchester, and of her sister the late Lady Lucy Digby, 'Alas!' said the amiable lady 'I have here memorandums of almost all my friends'. N.B. my mind was stronger than yesterday – Lady Harriot suffered more. At night I wrote to some friends and read in Tasso, so at eleven to bed.

6 January Twelfth Day: a day of jubilee to the younger part of my pupils. Told my two little darlings at night a fairy tale. My sweet little Louisa said 'I do love fairies, Miss Porter, they can do so much good'. When they were gone I wrote a seventh tale in addition; sent it to Mr Green. N.B. Mr Fox said there were some things in Mr Burke's pamphlet *On the Revolution* which he could not understand.[2] To critics be it left to decide whether that implied a reflection on the writer or reader. My dear Lady Charlotte not well – a bad eye.

7 January In the morning with Lady Harriot Acland. It was a dismal employment – she wept and said she had experienced every visissitude of woe. I advised her to look forward to her blooming daughter and future tender ties. This amiable lady alluded to the death of her husband, father, three children, and sister, with the dear Lady Ilchester, whom she loved *as a sister!* But *who* did not love *her?*

8 January In the morning with Lady Harriot Acland. Had a letter [from Dr McQueen] which I long have wished to receive. It on the whole vexed and disappointed me: an emblem of all earthly expectations. Resolved to divest my mind of too tender an interest in the concerns of any male friend, and in fine not to be duped by the name of friendship to expect, or to entertain, a sentiment beyond it.

9 January Answered the letter. Was satisfied with it: to be on my guard against a too tender friendship. We may be sure it errs when it occasions uneasiness. True and unmixed friendship is designed as a balm on life.

[2] This refers to Edmund Burke's famous book *Reflections on the Revolution in France*, which was published in November 1790. Burke was one of the first, and most influential, critics of the French Revolution.

Very bad weather – did not go to church. Read two sermons, then an hour in *Tacite* – then wrote in my journal. A letter from good Mrs Hayes; Mrs Churchyard in the afternoon.

10 January Spent the day with my dear pupils. Had a letter from Mrs Upcher – memorandum to burn it, at her own desire. At night the *Duke of Ormonde's Life* and Tasso.

11 January A letter from Mr Green. The tales advance owing to his friendly interference. He boasts of his influence with the *Devil* in the proof being sent to me so soon – corrected it, thought it read tolerably well in print. Perhaps *l'amour propre y trouvoit sa part*. With my pupils as usual.

12 January Wrote to Mr Green. Studied with my pupils. Mr O'Brien favoured us with half an hour of his company – he was observing what a favourite Mr Charles Fox was with all foreign ministers: he was an adept in their languages and understood their various characters. Mr O'Brien, making him one day a morning visit, was struck with the sight of a very fine picture in an Asiatic habit and a scymeter in his hand. He asked whose – Mr Fox made reply 'You know General Potomki is said to be of no family and is solicitous to be thought of an ancient one – I accidentally heard of that picture: a Potomki who was noble above two hundred years ago – and have purchased it for a present for the Russian favorite'.[3] N.B. Mr O'Brien recommended Cooper's poem of *The Task*.[4] N.B. to read it soon.

14 January I wrote to Dr Macqueen, Mr G-n and my sister Fanny. Spent the day as usual. Gave Edie a shilling for her poor old father – perhaps it may encrease her filial duty when she sees a stranger consider him. Read Tasso, and to bed at eleven.

15 January The day with my dear pupils, who are all well. Mrs Churchyard drank tea with me – she is an amiable and worthy person. I wrote to my dear mother.

16 January At church. In the afternoon read two sermons, some letters, and went early to bed.

17 January A letter from Mrs Keir. It informed me of the death of a gentleman with whom our family had been intimately connected, and who once so tenderly loved my sister. Interest, or prudence it is called, taught him to make a more worldly marriage, but we knew his amiable

[3] Prince Grigori Alexandrovitch Potemkin (1736–91), the best-known favourite of Catherine the Great.
[4] William Cowper (1731–1800). His poem *The Task* was first published in 1785.

qualities and still esteemed him. Though we had none of us seen him for twelve years, yet the hearing of his death threw a pensive, gentle sort of melancholy over my mind 'The remembrance of past times came like the evening sun upon my soul'. He has left a widow with eight children – perhaps my sister's fate may in the event be happier than if he had married her. We are short-sighted creatures – desire and regret alike preclude the enjoyment of the present.

18 January Spent the day with my beloved pupils; an hour or two engaged with Lady Harriot Acland. At night prepared for my little journey.

19 January Breakfasted with my young friends. Lord Ilchester had the goodness to send me to Wincanton, where I took the stage to Salisbury. My travelling companions were a young lawyer and a very agreeable young gentlewoman. He entertained us with the account of the apparition which appeared to Pliny in a house he had at a low price on account of its being haunted. Did not recollect the story, so asked whether it was the elder or younger Pliny. He told me 'the younger', and added 'Madam, you must be a great Latinist to be acquainted with Pliny'. I have known several classical scholars fall into similar mistakes from not being equally versed in English writings and translations. I remember a learned gentleman's entertaining a well-bred female company with the history of Andronicus the slave, lion etc., for want of having read our favourite *Spectator*. The young lady told me she was going to live in London with her brother and gave me her address, entreating my future acquaintance. The first time I ever met with a traveller of so much hospitality. N.B. when in London to get a friend to enquire her character and to indulge myself with her acquaintance if it proves an agreeable one. Arrived at night at my dear mother's. Supped with her and Betsey – shared my mother's bed, whose dear arm was *[some words erased]* – great indulgence. She is tolerable, I thank God, but at sixty-six, in a weak habit, infirmities will intrude. She has no pain, but excessive great weakness in all her limbs. Dear woman! Heaven bless her and smooth the eve of life!

20 January Fanny added her dear little person to our family party. We spent the day together – she looked quite amiable: rather thinner than when at Redlynch, but it becomes her to be so. We had various family subjects to discuss.

21 January Spent an hour in the morning early by my sister Fanny's bedside. She shewed me a letter from a particular friend of hers which gave me a good deal of light into a worthy character. Trust she will yet be happy in the tenderest friendship of a person of real merit, and whose attachment for her seems of a steady nature. We also conversed about our dear mother and Betsey's present views. Fanny was in the evening with her Syrencott friends, I with my mother and Betsey.

22 January Took the post coach at five in the morning for London. Three gentlemen were my fellow travellers, who each of them acknowledged having been drunk the evening before. N.B. not quite sober then. They slept, and I reflected on several interesting subjects. Arrived in town safe, very fatigued – to bed by ten.

23 January A letter from Mr Green, and another from Mrs Williams, of invitation for Tuesday and Wednesday. Did not go to church – rather fatigued. Wrote to Fanny and Redlynch. Spent the day quite quiet and alone – no-one in the house with me but an old woman. Asked her if she was a wife or widow: made me answer she was as *yet* a maid, and never intended to change her condition from foolish love-motives; whenever she married she would do it with prudence. *Bon çela!* At sixty-five. The answer was worth a crown. At night I read my prayers; an hour in Tacitus; wrote my journal; and went to bed at ten.

24 January Mrs Colonel Digby did me the honour to invite me to dinner, but I staid at home with some faint chance of seeing a dear friend. As the time was uncertain, chose to wait at home all the day. Worked, read, and did all in my power to spend it tolerably. Colonel Digby lent me *The Village*[5] to read – had recourse to it for amusement, as Dr Macqueen did not arrive.

25 January Spent the day at Mr Green's. His son has got a beautiful young wife, about eighteen. Extremely elegant – she has her school friend on a visit with her, a very amiable lady, married also. It seems a most happy family now in all respects. My friend, the father, received me with much cordiality. My tales go on swimmingly – he takes all the trouble on himself. Past the day very agreeably.

26 January Wrote to Dr Macqueen. Drank tea and supt at Mr Williams', spent the evening with whist and good humour. To bed by twelve.

27 January Went to Cheapside in the morning; at night at home. Knitted and read Tasso. Had a note from Mr Green with some proof paper to correct. Overlookt and returned it – told Mr Green in my answer that the *Devil* was the main instrument of our present correspondence.

28 January Had a letter from Dr Macqueen. He is on the point of

---

[5] George Crabbe's poem *The Village* was first published in 1783.

matrimony with a lady of fortune and who, by his description, possesses, beside, 'an excellent understanding and an angelic disposition'. May they be happy together, and he prove as good a husband as he has been a sincere and constant friend. Ruminated half an hour on this subject: I determined to close our epistolary correspondence at his marriage, so sacred is that tye that in my opinion a woman of strict honour will not cultivate even a friendship with a married man, unless she love the wife equally, and is known, esteemed and beloved by her as much.

29 January Answered Dr Macqueen's letter. N.B. wrote in a gay, chearful style. Expressed my contentment at his happy 'prospects', but told him I should transfer my epistolary favours to some forlorn bachelor, as he had been, 'ainse faites place, Monsieur le Bienheureux, à quelque pauvre misérable'. Read Tasso. Lady H. Acland did me the honor of a visit.

30 January At church at St James. Dr Parker preached – a very old gentleman with a weak, low voice. Did not hear the half of what he said, which entirely broke the connection. N.B. he told a lady I know that he wondered St James' church should be so thin, for he preached every Sunday himself. She longed to tell him that was the very reason. Drank tea with Mr and Mrs Moser, spent the evening most agreeably in their company: a genteel, sensible couple, and extremely polite to me.

31 January My dear Mrs Pinnock spent the day with me. We gave a loose to friendly confidence. She told me that tomorrow her friend Miss French changes her name, attended with some very particular circumstances. Spent the day most agreeably.

1 February Walked out in the morning. At night three of my dear pupils arrived, to my great joy. The dear little ones were so delighted to see me again – how sweet it is to be loved by innocence! Pretty creatures, they entwine around one's heart. I gave them some London ribbonds, we then made *pincushions* and were quite happy.

2 February Spent the day agreeably with my three dear pupils. Mr Farqhuar [Farquhar] came to see Lady Harriot's knee – she is well, I thank God, in every other respect. My dear Miss Owen paid me a *[word illegible]* visit.

3 February Lord Ilchester and my other two dear pupils arrived with dear little Lord Stavordale. My pretty little Susan is left behind with her nurse. My two eldest pupils' joy at seeing me, and mine at our meeting, was very great. Poor Lord Ilchester was extremely melancholy

– he misses his beloved wife in every place he goes to, still more at home, which her society endeared. They spent the day with Lady Harriot Acland, I with the younger part of the family at home.

4 February Spent the day happily with my dear young friends. Called on my dear Miss Owen – she is going to Durham with an amiable family and one pupil only. May she be as happy as she is good!

5 February At home all day with my pupils and their various masters. What a pleasure it is to me to see them daily improve in person, manners and elegant accomplishments.

6 February At church at St Martin's.[6] An excellent discourse from Doctor Hamilton: 'O! Give me understanding in the way of godliness'. An animated preacher, and charming subject, with the organ delightful. After church dined and spent the afternoon with Mrs Williams, her husband and brother. She and I talked much of our prospect in the lottery, as we have a sixteenth between us. Said we would give five guineas to the poor in case we had a prize. N.B. to give half a guinea in charity in case it proves a blank, by way of consolation and making amends for the money thrown away on the share of the ticket. Mr Williams perfectly good-humor'd as usual. Mr T. Williams talked a good deal – told me the story of Mareschale Saxe and the haunted house. Madame Bonne relates the story without naming the personage it happened to.

7 February Mrs Williams drank tea and supt with me. She is an amiable woman, discreet and sensible. She admired my dear children; we spent the evening very agreeably.

8 February Heard an extraordinary story of General Gunning's daughter and the Marquis of Blandford; another of Lord Faulconberg and his new lady Miss Cheshyre that was. N.B. to write them in my memory – too long for a journal. My dear pupils all well and amiable. Tuesday – the day as usual.

9 February Wednesday. Wrote to my mother and sister Fanny. The day as usual with my pupils.

10 February Thursday. Walked a great deal. At night studied Tasso and read in the *Duke of Ormonde's Life* – my dear children all well.

11 February Wrote to Mr Green to enquire after the process of my little tales. The day as usual.

12 February Mr Green called on me and brought my manuscript and the proof with him. We talked half an hour of his and my domestic

---

6 Probably St Martin-in-the-Fields.

concerns: he asked my opinion of a point that concerned himself, answered him with the sincerity and freedom of a friend. He has been the most generous of fathers – may he never repent of it. His concern in my affairs, too, has been most obliging.

13 February Not at church – it rained all the morning. Drank tea with the agreeable Mr and Mrs Moser. Spent a charming evening: our conversation fell on history and the manners of modern times. Mrs Moser is a woman of sense and politeness, she possesses much polite literature. I believe I have their good wishes.

14 February The day with my pupils. The time I spend endeavouring to improve them makes but a small figure in my journal book. I trust it will turn out to their and to my benefit in the Book of Life, where all actions, thoughts and designs are registered by an unerring and gracious hand. Amen.

15 February With my pupils all day. At night I amused myself with writing extracts from several books I had perus'd, wrote in my journal, read *Marianne*,[7] played on the piano forte, and to bed by eleven. Wrote to Dr Macqueen.

16 February Spent the day as usual with my pupils and their masters. At night read in the *Life of the Duke of Ormonde*.

17 February My good friend Mrs Pinnock spent the day with me. She told me some very extraordinary particulars of her friend Miss French, now Mrs Heale – it grieved me to hear this worthy woman say that she had no friend in the world but this lady and myself. If she has but one friend beside me, it is incumbent on me to assist her the more for that reason. Revolved on future methods etc. for that purpose. At night, Tasso.

18 February With my dear pupils. Spent the day as usual; supt by invitation with Lord Ilchester and his two elder daughters. Situated as they are, what happiness it is that they have a father like Lord Ilchester! Kind, attentive, intelligent and delicate.

19 February Went in the morning to see the Shakespeare Gallery.[8] Most pleased with Opie's, Northcote's, and Hamilton's performances. Fuseli's pencil appears to me great in witches, fairies and other beings

[7] P. C. de Chamblain de Marivaux, *La vie de Marianne* (*c.* 1735).

[8] Alderman John Boydell's Shakespeare Gallery was in Pall Mall. It contained illustrations of scenes from Shakespeare's plays, specially commissioned from the best-known artists of the day. The gallery was opened *c.* 1789, its contents being dispersed after Boydell's death in 1804.

of the imagination, but his other figures want substance – have all an aerial cast unsuited to the nature they represent. A most delightful Puck by Sir Joshua Reynolds: the little merry mischievous fairy express[es] in a smile his roguish and amusing character. A Juliet by Opie appeared to me extremely interesting – Paris is mourning over her as she lay, supposed dead on her intended marriage day. Her mother is wringing her hands with finely-depicted anguish, while the father hides his face. The latter circumstance too trite – at least it so appeared to me. Many others were highly entertaining. At my return, received the last proof of my tales. Sent the title page (*Triumphs of Reason examplified in Seven Tales, and affectionately dedicated to the Juvenile Part of the Fair Sex by the Author*); returned them to Mr R. Green.[9] Spent the evening at Mrs Williams'. After supper we enjoyed ourselves in a social conversation. Some odd characters were mentioned, and it now occurs to me that I represented some circumstances concerning them in too free and satirical a manner. Never to commit the like fault again, but always to remember that mirth degenerates into censoriousness when good nature pays for the entertainment. It was very wrong indeed.

20 February Not at church. Read my prayer-book, and an hour in *Ormonde's Life*. Wrote in my journal, spent the evening at home with my pupils.

21 February In the evening went with Lady Elizabeth an-airing to Hyde Park. It is there one sees London in perfection: splendid equipages, beautiful women, fine men and spirited horses form altogether a delightful spectacle. In the evening I wrote to my mother and sisters, read Tasso, and went early to bed.

22 February The day with my pupils.

23 February As usual.

24 February The young ladies from home, so I took a long walk. At night I read Miss Helen Williams' poems, recommended to me by Mrs Moser – liked them very much.

25 February Spent the day with my pupils; the evening at Mr Williams'. An agreeable clergyman and I beat man and wife at whist. The brother betted on my side. Disappointed by an accident of the carriage; lay there all night. Dear Mrs Williams treated me with the utmost hospitality.

---

[9] Mr R. Green was Rupert Green, the son of Agnes's friend Valentine Green, who was helping her to publish her book. Searches at both Melbury and Penrice Castle have failed to produce a copy of this book.

26 February A letter from Dr Macqueen – extraordinary, as all his are: 'Generous, noble, good, but never to be understood'. At night I found myself very ill – a bad cold was changed into a fever. During the night revolved many serious thoughts in my mind, recommended myself to God with entire resignation to his will.

27 February Mr Farquhar was sent for to bleed me. He said it should have been done the night before. The perspiration, he believed, would effect a cure without bleeding. He sent me medicines.

28 February Much better, though very weak. Attended my dear pupils. Mr Green paid me a morning visit and brought me the first book printed of my little tales. N.B. to inform no other person I wrote them till I see how they take: miscarriages always awkward – should they fail or be much criticised, I shall lay snug. My friend Mr Green likes them, but friends are not the best judges. Lord Stavordale's birth day – four years. Little did we think, in our joy at his birth, that in less than four years he would have no mother.

1 March Read my little book over. Made out the *errati* [sic] which I sent to Mr Green to forward to the booksellers. Lord Ilchester carried his daughter Harriot to Weymouth for the benefit of bathing: the accident in her knee will deprive her family of her for some years to come. God Almighty preserve her from a white swelling! Her health in all other respects is excellent, her spirits charming.

2 March With my dear pupils. Endeavoured to entertain them as well as I could in their father's absence. Spent the day very happily.

3 March Lady Harriot Acland paid her nieces a visit. Had a long and kind conversation with me. She is one of the best and most amiable persons in the world, so everyone thinks that knows her.

4 March The day as usual – all well, thank God.

5 March At our studies, then an-airing to St James' Park. The day charming, the walk pleasant, and my pupils returned as blooming as roses and as gay as larks from their promenade.

6 March At Mr Moser's. Spent an agreeable evening with them – the conversation never languished. Mrs Moser pleases without being solicitous about it; Mr Moser has with all his favourites an earnest desire to please and qualities to succeed in it.

7 March At the play with Mr Williams at the Little Theatre, Haymarket – *The Busy Body*. Very badly performed – Lewis was the only good actor. The entertainment was written by one of the actors, Mr Fennel: *The Advertisement* – a string of *equivoques* straining to be witty and *double* *entendres* spoilt the piece.[10] An amiable young gentleman that sat in the next box to us exclaimed 'E troppo, molto troppo', but very few men had his delicacy – they all seemed much pleased with every petty instance of would-be wit and real bad taste. Supt with Mrs Williams and her husband and brother.

8 March With my dear pupils as usual.

9 March As usual, all well.

10 March After our studies went out an-airing with my dear young friends.

11 March Mr Nichols the writing-master told us a particular instance of a young woman's change of fortune through a lottery ticket. On her father's dying in debt (a merchant) she resolved to go to service. The lady she went to advised her to aspire to a superior place than her family offered, and promised to mention her to several persons of fashion. The young woman left her, much comforted by her goodness, and passing by a lottery office she thought she would lay out a guinea or so to give herself another sort of chance at the same time. She bought a (sixteenth) share of a ticket, which the next day proved a great prize and brought her twelve hundred pounds. She immediately lodged it in in the bank and went to board in a merchant's family till she had settled her future plan of life. In a few weeks, a man of fortune who visited in the family saw her and loved her. They were soon married, and she now rides in her own coach and proves a woman of good sense and much merit.

12 March With my dear young friends as usual. Happy in each other.

13 March At church. A very good discourse: 'And the poor had the gospel preached unto them'. I drank tea at Mrs Godard's at her invitation. Returned at eight, read the psalms, and to bed by ten.

14 March The day with my dear pupils.

15 March Drank tea at Mrs Williams'. A deal of easy chat and a hand at whist. N.B. all her castles of the air and mine vanished into smoke as our share in 16,205 is a [blank].[11]

16 March Sent half a guinea to a person in distress as I said I would do in case of a blank, so my share in the ticket has done some good. Spent the day with my dear pupils, who are the best and sweetest young

---

[10] The plays performed at the Little Theatre, Haymarket, on this night were *The Busy Body* by Susannah Centlivre and *The Advertisement*, a farce by James Fennel. The performers included William Thomas Lewis (*c.* 1748–1811).

[11] A blank was a lottery ticket which did not gain a prize.

people in the world. Received a letter from Dr Macqueen, who appears to me to be on the verge of matrimony. The lady will in all probability have fortune – may she also possess every amiable quality and every agreeable qualification.

17 March A note from Mr Green with six books of my tales. They are quite compleated and will soon be published. I shall rest anonymous, as only Mr Green knows who wrote them: I hope they will produce young readers some amusement, and me a little money. I spent the day with my pupils, the evening at the forte piano.

18 March Colonel Strangways breakfasted with his nieces and me, after which I wrote to Lord Ilchester, then our studies as usual.

19 March The day with my dear pupils.

20 March The morning with my young friends, the afternoon at Mr Moser's.

21 March We took a walk in St James' Park, then attended our various masters. Mrs Williams spent the evening with me at chat and cribbage; her husband came to supper and to take care of his dear little wife home.

22 March As usual with my pupils. At night I read a play of Johnson's, recommended by Mr Moser and an excellent performance: *Volpone*.[12]

23 March Was invited by Lady Elizabeth to join their promenade. Found an unusual repugnance in going out, so asked her to call on her aunt in my stead. I staid at home with my two dear little children. Just as we had dined, a smart vis-à-vis[13] stopt at the door and a gentleman enquiring for me was shewn into the parlor, when – behold – who should I see but Dr Macqueen! He spent an hour with me, during which he acquainted me with his intended marriage and every circumstance concerning it. The lady, he says, has an excellent understanding, with an angelic disposition: a woman of rank, with a very large fortune in reversion if her father does not marry again, who has been a widower twenty-two years. My friend was full of his bright prospects, talked much of the lady's disinterested love and the offers she had refused for his sake. He added these remarkable words: 'My dear Miss Porter, you are her superior, and you will feel your self so the first instant, but for my sake search her not with too critical an eye'. He proposed her waiting on me, which I declined. He then asked me if I would visit her, I answered I would when she was Mrs Macqueen, as soon as they both

---

[12] Ben Jonson, *Volpone* (1607).
[13] A type of light carriage, in which the seats faced each other.

pleased. After the most tender professions of friendship he left me to ruminate on all I had heard. I drest myself and went to Mrs Williams', where I spent the evening. A very agreeable clergyman was one of our party.

24 March With my pupils.

25 March As usual.

26 March Spent the day with my dear young friends. At night amused myself with the piano forte. A letter from my dear Miss Owen.

27 March At church. A good sermon very badly delivered. Tried to fix my attention to the discourse. In speaking of a false shame, the preacher observed that though men were ashamed to be caught at their religious duties – to be constant frequenters of divine worship – yet, said he, they are not ashamed to fill the temples of dissipation or sacrifice at the altar of folly, nay, refined in viciousness, they even pervert their nature – the men by effeminacy, the women by boldness. Returned to my two darlings, heard them their catechism, told them a tale. Had the pleasure to see them quite happy. In the evening I wrote to Dr Macqueen; my journal; and to bed by eleven.

28 March Went to Mrs Williams'. Disappointed in a box ticket, so resolved to venture to the pit under her husband's care. We accordingly went – suffered great hardships from the heat and bruises – the air so bad the lamps were extinguished where we stood. In utter darkness for some minutes; the heat and press inexpressibly fatiguing; we panted for breath; lost Mrs Williams, but she happily met with a Welsh gentleman of her husband's acquaintance who took care of her. My hair fell down and got intangled between men's shoulders and elbows – was afraid of being scalped. Suffered extreme torture, but at last we got in. I rejoiced that we had escaped with our lives and limbs, but resolved never more to get into a similar predicament. Saw the charming Siddons in Desdemona – she was all elegance and sensibility. Kemble was a most interesting Othello; Bensley a tolerable Iago.[14] The entertainment on the whole was delightful. We returned to Mr Williams' house with ease and safety, there we chatted over the perils and pleasures of our enterprize.

---

[14] Shakespeare's *Othello* was performed at Drury Lane on this night. The actors included Sarah Siddons (1755–1831), her brother John Philip Kemble (1757–1823) and Robert Bensley (*c.* 1738–1817). The 'entertainment' was *The Deaf Lover*, a farce by Frederick Pilon.

29 March With my dear pupils. A most kind letter from Mrs Quin, my ever dear Lady Ilchester's sister.

30 March Lord Ilchester returned. He left his daughter Lady Harriot well and happy at Weymouth.

31 March With my dear pupils: our studies as usual.

1 April I drank tea and supt at Mr Williams'. A nice old lady there whom I liked much – Mrs Pryce; a pretty Miss Davies, and an affected Mr -. He put me in mind of Evelina's Mr Smith[15] for conceit and vulgarity. My kind friends were exceedingly obliging to me as usual.

2 April I wrote to Mrs Quin.

3 April At church – St Martin's. A very good discourse from Dr Hamilton, on prayer. In the afternoon at Mr Moser's: spent an agreeable evening in their society – they are most pleasing people, and I really believe very partial to me, at least, I flatter myself that my regard is returned.

4 April With my pupils as usual. Their studies go on well – they are good, and I am happy.

5 April A letter from my amiable Miss Owen. The day with my elder pupils, as my dear little ones went in the morning to Hawley to stay a week with Mrs William Digby *[next page mostly cut away]*.

10 April ... being industrious people all the week, enjoyed this little party of pleasure with a glee that the sons and daughters of dissipation can never experience. Returned to their house and a comfortable dinner. An agreeable young clergyman was of our party; a young citizen and his pretty sweetheart. Heard the merchant ... *[part cut away]* ... to supper. La Chevalière d'Eon made one of the subjects of conversation: she, poor woman, is soon to have an auction of all her furniture and books, as the National Assembly has deprived her of her annuity. The Prince of Wales sent her a present of a hundred pounds.[16]

11 April I wrote to Mrs Alexander, then spent the evening in our usual studies. At dinner with my young friends, Lord Ilchester and Miss Caroline Digby.[17] Called on Mrs Goddard in the evening, walked, wrote to Fanny, played an hour on the forte piano, read Tasso, and to bed by eleven.

---

[15] This refers to *Evelina* by Fanny Burney (1778).

[16] The 'Chevalière' d'Eon was actually a man: Charles Geneviève d'Eon de Beaumont (1728–1810), who always wore women's clothes during the latter part of his life. Contemporaries were unsure of his true sex.

[17] Frances Caroline Digby.

12 April Another most agreeable letter from my dear Miss Owen. Spent the day with my pupils, dined with them and Lord Ilchester. The discourse turned on Mrs and Miss Gunning's foreign expedition and the death of the amiable Lady St Asaph. Lady Elizabeth repeated a conversation she heard a few days before Lady St Asaph died: 'O! My dear Mrs—, I hope Lady St Asaph will not die before next Wednesday, as I shall be in utter despair if she does'. Mrs –: 'Pray don't make yourself so wretched, my dear Lady –: I dare say Lady St Asaph is not in such a *hurry* to *die,* but what she would willingly oblige you and defer it a few days longer. But what makes you so solicitous that she should survive next Wednesday?' Lady –: 'Because, my dear creature, next Wednesday is my ball day, and if she dies before or on Wednesday, I shall lose the company of two of my beaux – her husband and brother – and at any rate my ball will be rather thin of beaux. Won't it be shockingly cross?' The other assented, which finished this tender-hearted dialogue.

13 April Wrote ... *[rest cut away]*.

15 April A letter from the Countess of Home. My pupils and I spent the day pleasantly.

16 April As usual.

17 April At church, heard Dr Hamilton. Drank tea at Mr and Mrs Moser's – took my leave. Mrs Moser said she was sorry, Mr Moser looked ... *[rest of page cut away]*. We spent the evening agreeably, yet my spirits were far from high. They expressed both of them an obliging concern in my happiness – I am ever obliged to them for it. Since this time twelvemonth I have [been] through a great deal of trouble, but there are sun-shines and storms in the moral as in the natural world. Let us enjoy the first, with due gratitude to the Divine Disposer, and take shelter from all the latter under the 'healing shadow of His wings'.

18 April Spent the evening with Mrs Williams, very chearfully. I did not leave them till twelve. When I mentioned taking leave she would not hear of it, but desired we might talk of that another day.

19 April With my dear pupils. Settled with half a dozen of their masters. N.B. went to the bank.

20 April As usual.

21 April I spent the day with Mrs Pinnock. Carried her to a tavern, where we had a snug and comfortable dinner. She entrusted me with all her affairs; had the satisfaction to be useful to her; and as my abilities encrease am determined to be more and more so. In the square, observed a poor, meagre old woman: she did not beg, yet had every appearance of poverty. Ventured to offer her a trifle: 'God bless you, Madam, and thank you' replied the poor woman 'for nothing can be poorer than I!' The tones of her voice were eloquent, and how I came to give no more I cannot conceive. When I turned back to follow her she was quite out of sight. Poor meek soul!

22 April Good Friday. A very rainy day – afraid to go out. Read the service to my pupils, and then spent a few hours *toute seule*.

23 April The day with my pupils.

24 April Easter Day. Went to St Martin's, where I attended the duties of the sacred day. Drank tea and supped with my good friends the Williams'. We went in the evening to the Orphan Asylum [the Foundling Hospital in Guilford Street]: the music good, the entertainment delightful. To see so many innocent creatures preserved from poverty and ruin is a sight the most affecting. Their united voices give a pleasure superior even to harmony, and raise the heart in gratitude to that great and good being who has 'placed us in a world of sun and shade, where those that bloom shall shelter those who fade'.[18] An agreeable, social supper at Mr Williams'. Took my leave of them with regret.

25 April Went an-airing and a-shopping with my pupils. Called on the way on Mr Green to repeat my thanks and bid him farewel. On his side have passed real obligations towards me; on mine have been shewn the tender attentions of friendship. Query – which is most obliged?

26 April Settled with my pupils' remaining masters, and some other little affairs, prior to my leaving London.

27 April Walked about, shopping, and prepared for my journey.

28 April Rose at four, set off in the five o'clock stage for Sarum. A very ... *[rest cut away]*.

29 April All the morning with my dear mother. Endeavoured to chear her spirits; was her handmaid in dressing and settled many little conveniencies for her comfort. Had I an independency, how happy should I be to attend on her, but fortune forbids such satisfaction, as I could not give her my company without lessening her provisions and comforts. In the evening walked out with Betsey: our opinions quite different, but I ... *[rest cut away]*.

1 May The morning with my dear parent. In the afternoon went to St Thomas' church with my sister. It was a pleasure to me to hear her voice join in the church service with much devotion, and in the psalms

[18] S. J. Pratt, *Sympathy*, book ii, lines 241–42.

with great taste. The sermon was good, the preacher insipid: no breach of charity to suppose it was not his own. Spent the evening with my mother and sister.

2 May With my dear mother all day.

3 May Rose at three. Left my dear mother with several melancholy ideas – endeavoured to recover my serenity of mind, and to reflect that I left her under the guardian care of Providence, whose mercies she had ever confided in, and whose dispensations she had always revered. Arrived at Redlynch: found my two darling little girls there before me and the dear little infant rather better. Went to bed early, much tired.

4 May With my dear little people.

5 May Settled my apartment to my liking. The country delightful, my room chearful. Every conveniency and, even, elegance of life – how thankful should I be!

6 May My elder pupils returned with their father and brother. Our meeting always gives us pleasure, however short the absence.

7 May We walked about and enjoyed the rural beauties of Redlynch.

8 May At church. Walked to Bruton in the afternoon to see Mrs and Miss Lloyds.

9 May With my pupils at our studies.

10 May Our studies. I wrote to my dear mother and sister Fanny.

11 May Company at dinner. My elder pupil, Lady Elizabeth, did the honours of the table with much gracefulness. A letter from Fanny.

12 May My younger pupils and I dined at Dishcove with their grand-mama Lady Ilchester. Spent the day very agreeably.

13 May With my pupils as usual. At night read over a parcel of letters from my dearest father and brother. Went to bed pensive.

14 May With my pupils. Our studies successful – played at our old historic game. My thought was Cesar's robe when killed; Lady Elizabeth's Mahomet's shoulder of mutton which had announced itself poisoned; Lady Mary's the pigeon which was killed by a hawk and dropt some blood on Bernini's bust of Charles I.

15 May At church. In the afternoon read one of Moir's sermons. A walk in the evening, read some letters, and to bed by eleven.

16 May The day with my pupils. Mr Whitwick dined with us; at night I finished Tasso and wrote to some absent friends.

17 May With my dear pupils. At breakfast Mr Whitwick quoted the words 'painful pre-eminence' as Milton's. I thought they were Addison's: Mr Whitwick laid me a pot of coffee that I would not find them in all

Addison. At night I read *Cato* and found the quotation – had a charming entertainment in the reperusal of this beautiful piece, where real grandeur of mind is so justly and perfectly delineated.[19]

18 May Company at Redlynch with Mr and Mrs Charles Digby – spent the day agreeably. In the evening a charming walk, an hour's music etc.

19 May With my pupils as usual. All well, I thank God – charming creatures all. In the evening I began Ariosto.[20]

20 May Wrote to Mrs Upcher. Mentioned our friend Dr Macqueen's intended marriage as a happy event – so I hope it will prove to both parties. With my pupils the usual time. At night a long and pleasing walk in Redlynch grove – enjoyed it much. The birds serenaded me, and every breeze was impregnated by the balmy odours of the shrubbery. Every object delighted my eye, while contentment possessed my breast – reflected on the large share I was blessed with of earthly enjoyments: 'Rural pleasure, friendship, books, ease, and alternate *study* – useful life', health and chearfulness. Went to bed in a desirable frame of mind. N.B. to endeavour to maintain and cherish such grateful sentiments.

21 May The day with my pupils. At evening a walk with my dear Lady Elizabeth. Endeavoured to reconcile her to her amiable young friend's marriage – she feared their mutual regard would be diminished by this change of life. Friendship in very youthful minds is a passion; in maturer life it is a principle, but always a source of pleasure to the tender heart.

22 May At church. At my return read one of Moir's sermons which are very good. In the evening a charming walk – to bed early.

23 May Heard that poor Mrs Hayes, Lord Ilchester's late good housekeeper, was very ill at Bath. Very sorry indeed to hear it – wished to put off the engagement at Mr Whitwick's and to go to see her, poor woman, at Bath, but this was not convenient. Went with Mrs C. Digby and two of my pupils to Somerton – a very sweet spot and the environs charming, but my spirits rather low all day. Mr Whitwick did all in his power to make our visit agreeable: on the whole it was so.

24 May Wrote to Bath to enquire after good Mrs Hayes – fear I shall have melancholy accounts of her.

25 May A letter brought into my room before six in the morning, when in bed. Asked if it was Bath – if it was sealed with black? On

---

[19] Joseph Addison, *Cato: A Tragedy* (1713).
[20] Ludovico Ariosto (1474–1533). *Orlando furioso* was one of his most popular works.

being answered in the affirmative, was certain poor Mrs Hayes was dead. Too true! She died at five o'clock yesterday morning – poor dear woman, I felt the blank of one that loved me. Some sighs and tears were due both to her and to myself. Employed the day at our usual studies.

26 May Had information which laid open some very bad treatment of poor Mrs Hayes by some unworthy relations. Deeply affected at this account – beside, I could not forbear partially and deeply reflecting on the ills that single women are exposed to, even at the hour of death, from being the property of no-one. My will is long since made, of what little I possess, and I hope it will please Infinite Goodness that my last breath shall be received by a tender and humane person, if not a friend – but His holy will be done. We have such frequent mementos of mortality that it behoves us to stand as prepared as possible.

27 May With my dear pupils. At night read a little in Ariosto and the *Russian History*.[21]

28 May Our historical game. Lady Elizabeth extremely clever at it, as at every thing else – she is a charming young lady indeed. Heart, head and person all combine in her favour. They are all delightful young people – I am happy in them.

29 May At church. In the afternoon wrote to my mother, sister and some other friends. A sweet walk at night.

30 May Company at dinner. An agreeable day – with my pupils as usual.

31 May The day with my dear young friends. At night we went to see a machine for moving grown trees of Lord Ilchester's invention. It succeeded perfectly well: as it rose with a large mass of earth, and the tree in the middle of it, Lord Ilchester said he 'felt his heart rise with it'. It was a beautiful sight, and every spectator, to the number of above twenty, enjoyed it much. Supt at night with Lord Ilchester and the young ladies: spent the evening very agreeably.

1 June Wednesday. The day at our studies as usual; at night I enjoyed a sweet walk. The dowager Lady Ilchester drank tea at Redlynch, had the goodness to send and invite me. Afterwards a charming walk, which I enjoyed much: half an hour in a grove, the setting sun gilding the branches of the trees with intermingling light – beautiful. The birds added their charming concert and, to compleat its harmony, I heard

---

[21] The *Russian History* was probably *The History of Peter the Great, Emperor of Russia* by Alexander Gordon (1755). See also below, 20 July 1791.

it with a peaceful and contented breast. When I returned, read half an hour in Cowper's poems, my Bible, and to bed.

2 June The day with my pupils. Wrote to poor Mrs Hayes's sister, told her my opinion without disguise, and that I hoped never to set eyes on one of them: inhumanity merits the most open contempt from every one. At night I wrote to dear Mrs Upcher – treated Dr Macqueen's marriage as an event to be wished for – may it prove so in all the consequences.

3 June The day as usual. At night, a walk and Ariosto.

4 June At our studies. The evening, walked out: charming weather, beautiful country, chearful house, worthy family – what blessings I enjoy!

5 June Rose early, took my morning rounds – all my dear pupils well. Read a sermon, went to church. In the afternoon, took a walk to see the good Miss Lloyds and their mother at Bruton: a charming walk, the tea was ambrosial after it – a dish of good humour, beside.

6 June At our studies as usual.

7 June The day as usual. At night I wrote to my mother and sisters.

8 June The day agreeably with my young pupils. At present I enjoy all the charms of the country – Redlynch is so beautiful that wherever one turns the sight, it is delighted. At night I studied Ariosto, and then wrote to Mrs Williams and Mrs Moser.

9 June The day as usual.

10 June At our studies, which passed our time in the most pleasing manner.

11 June Our historical game – it afforded us much amusement.

12 June At church. I afterwards read a sermon of Moir's, then wrote to some dear friends, a walk and to bed early.

13 June With my dear pupils. They are good, and I am happy. N.B. Miss Caroline Digby married to Mr Neave.

14 June As usual.

15 June With my young friends. At night I wrote several letters.

16 June Read over a parcel of letters written years ago, with various and mingled sentiments. With my pupils.

17 June As usual.

18 June Our studies, walks etc. Our dear Lady Harriot returned home. N.B. my birth day.

19 June Lady Elizabeth and I stayed the Holy Communion – thought of her who is now a blessed saint in heaven, with whom I used to attend this holy institution. Dear lady – blessed woman! Read a sermon; spent some time in very serious reflection; a walk and to bed early.

20 June With my dear pupils. Wrote to my mother and Fanny.

21 June A letter from Miss Grant, which informed me of Dr Macqueen's marriage.

22 June Wrote to him on this event.

23 June With my dear pupils. Mrs T. and a very talkative lady dined with us. In my evening walk, considered if I were the husband of this lady, whether I would wish to be of a loquacious or silent nature.

24 June Captain Goldsborough and Mr H—r dined with us. In the evening, walked out to see a tree mov'd by Lord Ilchester's new invented machine. It was beautiful to see the tree glide along – they carried beside it above three tons of earth. We supped all together.

25 June The day with my pupils as usual.

26 June At church. On my return, read a charming sermon of Moir's on the subject of Balaam and his ass. The Miss Lloyds drank tea with me. I walked about with them, and we joined in admiring the beauties of Redlynch. Good girls, not for admiring Redlynch, but for their prudent, worthy conduct.

27 June As usual.

28 June A letter from my dear Miss Owen, which gave me some very serious reflections on her account.

29 June Wrote to Miss Owen a very long letter: told her my mind with all the freedom and earnestness of friendship.

30 June With my dear pupils. Wrote to several friends.

1 July As usual.

2 July *A l'ordinaire avec mes chères élèves.*

3 July At church.

4 July Lord Ilchester and Lord Stavordale went to Melbury. I spent the day with my beloved pupils.

5 July With my young friends as usual. All well, good and happy.

6 July With my pupils at our various studies: history, French and English, music and geography supply us with occupation, and amusement too. At night I studied Ariosto, and wrote a letter to Mamselle Baillie, an old French acquaintance, to enquire after her welfare. Many a happy day have we spent together in France.

7 July With my pupils all day.

8 July Lady Harriot Acland and her daughter arrived at Redlynch, which gave my dear young friends great joy. They have now a maternal and sisterly friend added to their society.

9 July Our historical game. Lady Elizabeth's thought: the silver roof of St Dennis's church, taken down and converted into money for the poor by Clovis II; Lady Mary's the gunpowder of the famous plot; Miss Acland's the garland decreed to Pausanius for killing Phillip; Lady Harriot Strangways – Elisha's staff, which he threw into the river; mine the poisoned feather with which Zenophon tickled Emperor Claudius's throat.

10 July At church. Lord Ilchester returned to see his sister. At night I read a sermon of Moir's.

11 July My dear Lady Harriot Strangways returned with her father to Weymouth for the benefit of sea bathing.

12 July With my pupils. A letter from Dr Macqueen in answer to my congratulatory one – he was married on the 8 of June 1791. At night I studied Ariosto and wrote a few lines on Lord Ilchester's new invented machine:

> Tho' now extinct in ancient lore,
> And elves and goblins now no more
> Diversify the scene;
> I shall a wondrous tale rehearse
> Till now untouch'd in prose or verse,
> Which past on Redlynch Green.
>
> A beach, with leafy honours crown'd,
> Who, firm and tranquil, grac'd the ground
> Perhaps a fifty years,
> Burst on a sudden from its place
> And, moving with attractive grace,
> Full in our sight appears.
>
> It rose to a majestic height
> Inspir'd spectators with delight,
> Then calmly glid along;
> Conquer'd both high and sloping ground,
> Compass'd a noble circuit round,
> Then stood, the pride of song.
>
> Some say, a dryade there confin'd,
> Who wish'd a newer spot to find,
> This novel flight perform'd;
> But, first addressing Redlynch chief,
> Of him she ask'd a prompt relief,
> And meaner influence scorn'd.

How they this curious transit wrought,
Outsoars the pow'r of common thought,
The secret to display.
But well 'tis seen o'er Redlynch place,
Tho' Ilchester may plant each grace,
'Tis *genius* leads the way.

13 July With my dear pupils.

14 July As usual.

15 July Wrote to my mother.

16 July A letter from Miss Baillie, who was married about two months ago to Monsieur Caboche du Fossé, an advocate of Parliament when kings were respected, but since the Revolution he is retired to a country seat and lives with much privacy. N.B. my acquaintances are marrying very fast off my hands. They will leave me in the lurch, I believe – *n'importe, je serai toujours heureuse en dépit du celibat.*

17 July At church. Colonel Strangways dined with us. In the evening a pleasant walk, a sermon and to bed.

18 July Wrote to Fanny and had a letter from Mr Wilkes – now in London.

19 July Lord Ilchester, his sister and two elder daughters went to Melbury. I remained with my three little darlings.

20 July With my children all the morning. They performed their little studies very prettily, after which walking and a tale for their amusement followed of course. In the evening, placed myself in my own room opposite theirs. Entertained myself an hour with the *Life of Peter the Great,* then Ariosto. Wrote to my dear mother, and to bed by eleven.

21 July My lovely little girls well and happy. As it rained, we had 'puss in the corner' instead of a walk. Dear little Lady Susan grows much stronger, and every morning pays me a visit for the pleasure of thumping an old spinet in my room with her dear little hands. She will not go past my room door till she has had this satisfaction, and must have a book before her when she plays, to imitate her sisters. At night I received a letter from Mrs Moser – answered it. Looked in upon my dear children, as I constantly do the last thing before I go to bed. All well, thank God.

22 July Little studies and a nice walk. Redlynch is in great beauty at present, and is daily improving. In the evening I amused myself with the harpsichord and pen, Ariosto etc.

23 July All well and happy. Drank tea at the lodge.

24 July At church with my two darlings. After dinner, Lady Charlotte desired I would tell some story out of the Bible: this is made one of our her highest treats, and she begged I would promise to let her read the Bible herself. I said it was too great an honour yet: I would see what I could do when she is eight years old, if she behaved extremely well till then. I had large promises – sweet innocent!

25 July My little loves as usual. At night Lady Charlotte, in order [to] protract the moment of going to bed, wrote me a letter – her own diction and spelling, as follows: 'Dear Po, I love you very much, and I will be good (Po, how do you spell "would"?' 'W.O.U.L.D.'). 'My dear little *Po,* I would have you to know that I *will* be good – C.S.' Spent the evening in writing, and to bed at eleven.

26 July Very agreeable letters from *mes élèves* at Melbury. Answered them immediately. All my children well.

27 July A letter from my worthy friends Mr Peele and Mrs Pinnock – each turned of seventy, yet a lively letter.

28 July With my dear children as usual.

29 July Health of body; peace of mind; quiet by day. N.B. to write one day's journal particularly.

30 July Rose at seven. Bolted my door till I had said my prayers, then opened it, and in rushed my two children. A thousand things have they to say to Po after a night's separation. Heard them say their prayers. N.B. very short, but explained to them. Lady Louisa read me a hymn of Watts – a very favourite author with them both. 'O, beautiful!' cries the sweet Charlotte upon hearing 'How doth the little busy bee!'[22] Recollected how I used to despise these for their bad poetry: esteem them now for their goodness and condescension, thus happily as we advance in life, we get to prefer the useful to the fine, in every thing. Saw my darlings at eight o'clock, happily seated over their milk and bread, then left [them] with their maid and took a turn round the shrubbery. Breakfasted at nine, my loves by my side at play with their dolls. Told them if they played very prettily I would certainly allow of their reading and writing a little afterwards as a reward. They soon claimed my promise and performed their little studies very prettily. N.B. the grand punishment for any misconduct is not to allow them to do their studies. They returned to their play and I practised the harpsichord till twelve, then we walked out in the shrubbery. The weather very rough and cold – made my loves take exercise. We were

---

[22] The first line of the poem *Against Idleness and Mischief* by Isaac Watts (1674–1748).

out till two. Sent them to dress and read an hour in *Peter the Great* – the hour slipt away imperceptibly as I contemplated the life of that astonishing personage. Dined at three, spoke French all the time at table. After dinner told them a tale, then our little studies, then they played while I was at work an hour. The weather very bad, so I made a party with them at 'puss in the corner', found my own spirits rise as I endeavoured to amuse my darlings. Sent them with their maid at seven to supper. I then studied an hour in Ariosto, at eight I heard them say their prayers and saw them in bed. Returned to my own tranquil but solitary apartment. Sat and recollected some absent friends, some departed – repeated with energy these lines: 'Absent or dead, still let a friend be dear! A sigh the absent claims, the dead a tear'.[23] Endeavoured to shake off the too pensive mood; revolved the many blessings I enjoyed; supt on water gruel *par préférence;* read an hour in *The Correspondents* – delicious little work – felt, I think, all its simple beauties.[24] Said my prayers, and to bed at eleven. A pretty exact sample of my time as it now passes.

31 July At church. Wrote to Mrs Alexander, Miss Mitchell that was. Read in Moir's sermons. To bed early: the weather extraordinarily bad – wind and rain, quite a storm but, as my honest countrymen say: 'Be it but fair weather within doors, and all is well'.

1 August With my dear little children, spent the day as usual.

2 August Ditto.

3 August The same.

4 August A letter from Mrs Williams, in which she envies my enjoyment of the verdant shades and cooling streams of the country. In answer I observed that I indeed possessed these, but where was the rational companion to remark their beauties to? When I had sent my letter, reflected seriously on my own sentiments and feared I was too sensible to the unavoidable want of society in my situation. Resolved to turn my attention more to its various blessings than to its one defect, lest I should prove ungrateful to the Supreme Disposer.

5 August With my beloved children. In the evening wrote to my dear Miss Owen.

6 August Mr C. Digby dined with his little cousins and me.

7 August At church. Miss Lloyd drank tea with me: a very good young

---

[23] Alexander Pope, *Epistle to Robert, Earl of Oxford*, lines 13–14.
[24] *The Correspondents: An Original Novel in a Series of Letters* (1775) may have been written by Miss Berry.

woman, she is industrious, dutiful to her mother and contented with her allotment in life – one of the first of virtues.

8 August My two elder pupils returned – their satisfaction at seeing me was great, but I received them a little coolly, because during the three weeks' absence they only had written once. They have not now their dear mother to remind them of any attention due to me, but I can assert myself when there is occasion for it, and would do so as much for their advantage as my own. We drank tea and supt together.

9 August We spent the morning in an agreeable manner: Hume and *Anne of Austria*[25] supplied us with entertainment. A little music and drawing were the interludes. In the evening a charming walk, and an easy chat after supper.

10 August The day past profitably (I hope) and agreeably.

11 August Lord Ilchester and his sister Lady Harriot Acland returned to Redlynch with Admiral and Mrs Digby.[26]

12 August A large company at Redlynch to dinner. At night I wrote to several friends, my dear mother, etc.

13 August A long conversation with the amiable Lady Harriot Acland. Spent the day with my pupils, the evening alone. Read Ariosto and wrote several letters, and closed my year's journal from August 13th 1790 to this day August 13th 1791. Agnes Porter, Redlynch.

20 August Lord Ilchester – Mr Campbell – living of Eisley in Cricklade etc., etc.

25 August Mr Sampson told me an extraordinary annecdote concerning the Acland family: a young gentleman about fourteen, the only male branch remain[ing of] it, fell dangerously ill, and died on the fifth day of the disease. As the family was now extinct, the grief of the friends and connections was great. The funeral was to be very magnificent, and the corpse was attended by some female relations. When they were fatigued, the upper servants took their turn to watch, and these again employed some menials to supply their place. One night that it was the coachman's turn to sit up, he took with him two of the stable boys and a large tankard of strong beer. When they had drunk enough to make them very chearful, one of them proposed giving Master a sup too – they poured a large horn-full down the body, and every time the tankard or horn went round they repeated this ceremony,

---

[25] Probably David Hume, *The History of England* (1754). There were several books about Anne of Austria.

[26] Admiral Robert Digby and his wife Eleanor.

the coachman observing that poor Master used to love a sup of good liquor as well as the best of them. They soon thought they heard a sigh proceed from the body, they drew nearer and perceived it to move. They examined the face and found it was red. Upon this, they alarmed the family, had him removed from the *table* to a warm bed and, proper assistance being had, this young gentleman was restored to life, married and had a numerous family, from whom descend the present various branches of the Acland family, into which Lady Harriot Strangways, Lord Ilchester's sister, married: the same lady so justly celebrated for her conjugal affection. I am told that at Sir Thomas Acland's they still shew the table where the youth was laid, and the tradition is carefully preserved in the family ...[27]

15 September Read Cornaro *Essay on Health* – resolved to become his disciple in temperance.[28] The less excess committed, the less shall I have to reform.

1 October Lady Mary Strangways, conversing with a person about a lady of their acquaintance once: the person, as an excuse for her partiality, exclaimed 'But she has so much beauty!' 'What is beauty?' rejoined Lady Mary, with a tone of utter contempt. N.B. she herself in the full possession of youth and beauty, and the most lovely bloom that ever adorned sixteen. A gentlemen, asserting some particular in the East Indies with great warmth, the other enquired if he had ever been there. 'No, Sir' he replied, 'but I had a cousin that was once very near going.'

2 October A letter from my dear Mrs Upcher, pressing me to make her a visit at Yarmouth. To do it if possible, either soon or next spring. If I can do it soon, I shall gratify my impatience of seeing so good a friend; if I cannot go before spring, shall be able to perform the journey with more economy, being then in London. To console ourselves through life, we have only, as the French call it 'Savoir tirer profit de tout'.

4 October Met with a pretty annecdote in the news paper: a young gentleman, reading *Zaïre* [29] to an amiable young lady, read these words with such expression 'Je t'aimerai toujours' that she cried out 'Will you?'

17 October We went to Melbury. Passed three days there in an agreeable manner, and then on October 21st proceeded to Abbotsbury. A

---

[27] This story, which appeared in the *Gentleman's Magazine*, was told about Sir Hugh Acland, 6th Baronet of Killerton (1696–1728). See Anne Acland, *A Devon Family* (London and Chichester, 1981), pp. 13–14.

[28] Luigi Cornaro, *Discourses on a Sober and Temperate Life* (*c.* 1627).

[29] A play by Voltaire (1733).

snug party: Lord Ilchester, his seven children, *et moi*. Great amusement in pebble-hunting – the sea prospect very grand, and seen from the drawing-room window as if we had been on board a ship. The poor people there are mostly fishermen, and have lineally resided there ever since Cruel Harry. When they assemble in the morning for the purpose of fishing, they all kneel down and one of them prays aloud that God would bless them with encrease. Then one of the most experienced fishermen casts his net, crying 'In the name of God, amen'. At night they publicly assemble at prayers in like manner. Many proofs of the ancient magnificence of the abbots remaining in the ruins of Abbots-bury: Henry VIII utterly despoiled them of all they possessed, of which a pair of antique massy candlesticks now remain at Abbotsbury Castle, given to an ancestor of the Strangways family. A chapel yet remains, dedicated to St Catherine, romanticly situated on the brow of a hill. Hither the nymphs annually repair to apply for the saint's patronage on the subject of matrimony. Lady Susan O'Brien and Mr O'Brien spent a few days at Abbotsbury, so did Mr and Mrs Jenkyns. My dear pupils and I spent our time very agreeably – the bathing was of service to them all. Lady Harriot Strangways rather gets better as to her knee – in every other respect she is quite well.

15 November The three little ones and I went to Melbury. On the 18th we returned to dear Redlynch, happy to see home.

19 November An alarming letter from my sister Elizabeth concerning my poor dear mother. Very much afflicted at its contents – designed going by Monday's stage to see her – a very restless night.

20 November Rose early, and determined not to lose an hour, but to hire a post chaise. A very melancholy journey – endeavoured to prepare my mind for the worst. Found my dear mother at her tea, attended only by a little girl – N.B. my sister Elizabeth from home on a tea visit. Comforted my dear mother; watched by her side all night; resolved to procure her a nurse; revolved every circumstance concerning it.

21 November Rose early; went out to several places; heard of a person as nurse who had an excellent character – lived fifteen years in her last place. Went after her – hired her. To give her good wages – liked her appearance. Returned to my dear mother, took care of her the rest of the day – she is weak but, thank God, in no pain. Had a sleepless night, but my dear mother had a very good one.

22 November Some serious discourse with Betsey, but all in vain. Were not a parent's welfare concerned, I would take the poet's advice: 'Disgust conceal'd is oftimes prudence, when the defect is radical and past a cure'. Passion, inconsideration, and ignorance of self are dreadful evils, but with God nothing is impossible. Wrote to my dear Fanny to prevent her needlessly hurrying to Sarum. Sat with my dear mother all the day. Mrs Peniston drank tea with us – her conversation extremely agreeable.

23 November With my dear mother as usual. Introduced her new maid, Mrs Betty, to her – they appeared to like each other much. In the afternoon my mother's spirits so much better that we chatted and sang Scots songs together.

24 November Sat by my dear mother all day – better, thank God. Mrs Betty came home: my mother much pleased at the thought of having a steady, clever person about her. We were very comfortable in her little apartment.

25 November I called in the morning on Fanny's worthy friend Mrs Dyke. She gave me a pleasing character of Mr Richards. Returned to my dear mother, who was low at the thought of my leaving her. Dear woman! Were I independent, I would never leave her, or were only my own interest concerned – but alas! She possesses the comforts of life only at the price of my absence from her. Told her I would see her soon again. At parting she turned from me to hide her tears – tears which drew drops of blood from my heart. I hope they are not ominous, but never was she so concerned at parting from me. Slept at the inn a couple of hours.

26 November Rose at three; went by the stage at four. Company: a lethargic old gentleman, an insane young one, an officer, a fine lady, and a pretty country girl. At breakfast the officer shewed me the Duchess of York's print: a very fine woman, if like it. I was observing that our last Duchess of York was, I thought, Clarendon's daughter. 'Excuse me, Madam' said the young gentleman 'there have been fifty Duchesses of York since that time.' He then took out a ten-pound note and began twisting it as a servant would do a paper to light a candle with. His brother-in-law, the officer, could not prevail with him to put it up properly. 'Sir, will you allow me to do it for you?' said I. He put it into my hand immediately. I folded and presented it to him: receiving it with a sweet smile, he said it *was* a ten-pound note, *now* ten guineas. Poor youth! He was an affecting and an interesting object. His brother told me that he had had an excellent understanding, and that his present melancholy situation was owing to a fever about two years ago; that he had eloped from them a year since, and was not discovered till a few days ago; that he had in that interval been plundered of his money and led into many excesses. When the country girl handed the tea kettle, he flew to take it from her and, gently pressing her hand, said: 'It is the prophanation, Madam'. Poor young gentleman – how melancholy! His brother said that the physicians gave hopes of him if

he could be but kept quiet. O, how I wished his recovery – poor youth!
The lethargic gentleman told me he had slept almost a week. The
captain gave several amusing annecdotes. At the gates met Lord Ilchester – asked him if he excused my elopement. He said I should have
flown to my mother, and acted quite properly in having no hesitation
on the subject. Found my beloved pupils all well.

27 November To church. Reflected that I had done all I could for
my dear mother, so determined to make myself as easy as possible. A
letter from dear Fanny. In the evening I wrote to my mother and to
Mrs Peniston, then in my journal. Read, said my prayers, and went
early to bed.

29 November Sir Richard Hoare, Mr Earle and the celebrated Mr
Coxe, who published his *Travels into Various Countries of Europe* spent
the day at Redlynch.[30] N.B. Mr Coxe an agreeable man, about fifty.
Does not quite answer one's ideas of him, in conversation, as a writer.
I chanced to sit between him and Mr Earle – we chatted away pleasantly.

30 November Lady Harriot Acland came to Redlynch.

6 December Finished the *Life of Petrarch*. Shed tears at his death –
amiable man! Pure and benign spirit! What joy must there be in meeting
with such as thine in the regions of immortality! N.B. to read his works
among my first Italian studies.

27 December My pupils were invited to a ball at Sir Richard Hoare's
to meet Madame de Genlis and her pupil Adèle – Mademoiselle, the
Duke of Orléans' daughter. I spent the evening with the Colonel and
Mrs Stephen Digby.

28 December Lord Ilchester returned to Redlynch. He said Madame
Genlis made Lady Elizabeth compliments of her pronunciation of the
French, and the day went off most agreeably. Beside Mademoiselle,
there were Pamela *et* Harriot, two more pupils of Madame Genlis. I
spent the evening with Mr and Mrs Stephen Digby – she had the
goodness to make me a present of *Les Leçons de Madame de Genlis* – a
charming book, which does the highest honour to its author.[31]

---

[30] William Coxe (1747–1828). His *Travels* in Poland, Russia, Sweden, Denmark and
Switzerland were published between 1784 and 1790.

[31] Later note: 'N.B. Pamela is since married to Lord Edward Fitzgerald'. Contemporaries believed that Pamela was the illegitimate daughter of Madame de Genlis
and the Duke of Orléans. In December 1792 Pamela married the Irish republican
leader, Lord Edward Fitzgerald, who was related by marriage to the Fox Strangways
family. Mademoiselle d'Orléans was Adèle, the legitimate daughter of the Duke of
Orléans; Harriot was Henriette de Sercey, a niece of Madame de Genlis.

30 December   Mademoiselle Orléans very little, but extremely pretty; Pamela beautiful; Harriot agreeable; Madame Genlis lively, entertaining.

1792

The events of 1792 were ultimately to have an important effect on the course of the latter part of Agnes Porter's life. On 7 January Lord Ilchester's youngest daughter, Susan, died aged twenty months. Five days later Agnes left Redlynch for London, taking with her Elizabeth Fox Strangways, who was to be presented at Court, together with her cousin Kitty Acland, later that spring. On 13 January Lord Ilchester, with his son Harry (Lord Stavordale) and daughter Mary, set off on a journey to County Limerick, in the west of Ireland, where they were to visit Lord Ilchester's youngest sister, Lady Frances Quin, and also the Gradys, the family of his late wife. The party travelled via South Wales, where they spent a month staying with Lord Ilchester's old friend and contemporary, Thomas Mansel Talbot of Penrice and Margam, who was to marry Lady Mary two years later. During Lord Ilchester's absence, which lasted until mid September, Agnes and her two youngest pupils, Charlotte and Louisa, spent most of the time at Redlynch, though they were all at Melbury for a few days in May, and Agnes was summoned to Salisbury, to see her mother, in July. Agnes was, however, unable to attend the wedding of her sister Fanny, which took place at Netheravon in Wiltshire in March. On 14 November, two months after her son's return from Ireland, the dowager Countess of Ilchester died.

Journal, 1792

7 January We had the misfortune to lose our dear little child Lady Susan Strangways. She died after fifteen days' illness, at five in the morning, Saturday January 7, 1792, aged one year and eight months. I watched her almost constantly, that is eighteen hours of the twenty-four. Much affected at her loss – God preserve the other six to be a blessing to themselves and to all that know them! Amen.

12 January Went with my dear Lady Elizabeth to London.

15 January At my dear Mrs Williams'. Had the pleasure to meet Mr Williams of Wroughton there – spent the day most happily. Lord

Ilchester and Lord Stavordale and Lady Mary set off for Wales and Ireland on the 13th.

16 January At Mr Green's. All is changed there: the lady of the house – and every thing. Thought more of what I missed than what I saw. Mr Green very pensive.

17 January At home with dear Mrs Williams.

18 January At Mr and Mrs Moser's. N.B. he is become a poet – no gainer by the change. Both kind to me, but read me his works all the day – it was a dull one. I grew heavy, was afraid I should sleep. Glad to return to Mrs Williams, who is 'blest with good nature and with sober sense'.

19 January Went to St Albans about business for Fanny – did not succeed.

20 January At Mr Williams'. My dear Fanny arrived at London. She introduced her friend, the Revd Mr Richards – a very amiable man.

21 January Spent the day with my dear Fanny and her *Caro Amante* – we walked; we rode, and made purchases, spending the day most happily. Mr Green and I ended the book affair at Mr Hookham's. Young Mrs Green denied herself to me; Mr Green appeared serious, nay even embarassed. At parting he was quite melancholy. N.B. to give up that acquaintance for various reasons: friendship, no more than love, must be all on one side.

22 January My dear Fanny and Mr Richards took leave of me. I set out for Sarum.

23 January With my dear mother. Settled her affairs: paid nurse; restocked the little purse, and tried to amuse my dear parent. Talked to Betsey with earnestness – time will shew to what effect.

26 January Returned to my darling children at Redlynch – our joy was mutual at meeting. Pretty creatures! How engaging to the heart they are. We will revolve into our studies tomorrow – I flatter myself, with the usual success.

8 March A letter from the amiable Mrs Quin to inform me that Lord Ilchester, Lady Mary and Lord Stavordale were arrived safe in Ireland. Lord Ilchester had been detained some weeks in Wales by the gout. I thank God he is now recovered. My dear children well.

2. Letter from Agnes Porter, Redlynch, to Lady Harriot Fox Strangways, Mrs Hepbourn's Boarding School, Weymouth, 16 March 1792

My Dear Lady Harriot,

I received both your letters yesterday, and am much obliged to you for them. That from Melbury had been put into a wrong post, which occasioned an encrease of postage and great delay in its reaching Redlynch.

Your aunt, Lady Susan, wrote me word of your *terrible accident*, as I must term a fall to a person in your situation. I hope in God it will make you more careful for the future. My dear love, consider that the comfort of your future life depends in great measure on your circumspection now.

Your friends arrived safe and well at Cappercullen on the 28th of February. Your sister Mary is beloved by all that know her on both sides of the channel. Your sister Eliza is quite well and, I make no doubt, is much admired in the great world for her goodness, elegance, and polite accomplishments. Your darling sisters here are in perfect health and the best little children you ever knew. Lady Charlotte just now left her doll to ask me 'who now had the keeping of the pitch-pipe of Gracchus the Orator?' This will shew you that she has much observation in her studies, and indeed history delights her above every thing. Louisa is a pretty little work-woman; her great entertainment in point of literature is a fairy tale.

I wished you to have mentioned my book to Mrs Hepbourn as a school publication, which has met with much encouragement from several of the first female seminaries. As far as you, my dear Lady Harriot, you shall have one when we meet – you must not talk of pecuniaries to your old friend A. P. Your father will settle the expence – he has bespoken ten copies, and you shall be reckoned as one. You shall have it with your friends when I am so happy as to see you at Redlynch. Your sisters talk of you with impatience.

My love to good Molly, and believe me sincerely yours, A. Porter.

You must remember, when your father permits of your paying home a visit, to bring every music book – my *spec.* among the rest. I hope you read half an hour every day in your own apartment.

Journal, 1792

29 March Thursday: my sister Fanny was married to the Revd Mr Richards – happy may they be! By this event I gain a brother, and my

dear sister, I hope, an affectionate and faithful husband for life – A. P,
April 6, 1792.

7 April Received a letter from Mrs Williams, which informed me of
the death of her brother-in-law's wife at Wroughton. He had been
married but four years, and had lost his first child. She, poor woman,
died the fifth day after the birth of the second. I never saw her, but
her husband's situation affected me much. 'Dear Sir, I pray God to
bless and comfort you – I am, with the greatest sympathy, your sincere
friend, A. Porter.' Condolance can never be too brief, where the affliction is sincere.

3. Letter from Agnes Porter, Redlynch, to Lady Mary Fox Strang-ways, Cappercullen, County Limerick, Ireland, 7 April 1792

My Dearest Lady Mary,
I received your kind letter of no date, and thank you for it. You are a
happy young lady to have such friends as you describe, who remind
you of every thing proper to pay attention to. I have no fear of your
ever failing in essentials, but life is justly observed to be made up of
little things, therefore it becomes highly necessary to pay a constant
regard to them. Blessings on your Uncle Tom,[1] as you call him, for
making your dear little head his province – take care of *that* and all
will go well. It makes me happy to find you use proper exercise and
keep good hours – I shall expect to see you rosey as a carnation and
straight as the poplar when next we meet. It is three months since I
saw my dear Lady Mary – I do not think I have been so long parted
from you these eight years. I do, my dear love, write to your sister
Harriot, as you seem to wish I should but, except when I once sent her
a good hearty scold, I never could draw a letter from her in return.

Your sisters here are perfectly well, and [as] sweet children as ever
were seen – they both of them have a true love for society. I had the
Miss Lloyds here lately to dinner, and that same day Mr Sampson was
detained by Mrs Fye's illness, so when my loves saw five or six covers
instead of our usual three their eyes absolutely sparkled with pleasure.
'So, Po' cried Lady Charlotte 'to day we have company. Pray remember
that we have a card table at night.' I accordingly promised we should
be quite grand and have every thing she could wish, so after tea the
Miss Lloyds formed our party at commerce, and had they been duchesses my two darling children could not have done more to make

---

[1] The Revd Thomas Grady.

themselves quite agreeable. Yesterday they were both engaged in a serious conversation about their father's love for them: 'But you know, Charlotte,' said Louisa 'my father loves Harry the best of us all – for, Charlotte, you know he has but *one Harry*.' As I perceived she looked rather pensive at this conclusion, I asked her how many Louisas her papa had? How many Lilys? How many Maries, Charlottes etc., and assured her as he had but one of each of these dear children he loved them all equally, or according to their goodness. I believe I shall carry Lady Charlotte to London for a day or two on account of her teeth, as Lady Harriot Acland says we had better make our minds easy by going to the 'fountain head' at once. I only wait to hear from Mr Masterman, as our Bath jaunt left me literally with but two shillings and sixpence in my pocket.

When you direct to me, pray write *Mrs* Porter. I know, my love, I am not yet an old woman, though I begin to be rather too advanced in life for a Miss. Do not suppose that being styled *Mrs* will spoil my marriage – on the contrary, I may be mistaken for a little jolly widow and pop off when you least expect it. My dear Fanny changed her name on the 29th of last month. Mr Beach did her the honour to officiate as father: they invited me, but my going was out of the question. At the same time Mr and Mrs Upcher asked me to see them; Lady Home sent me an invitation to Hirsel; and Dr Macqueen's lady to Norwich. The Lord forgive me, Salmon thought they were crazy – but when Lord Ilchester returns he will perhaps have the goodness to let me go to the friends who invited me last October.

My dear pupils and I go on extremely well. Our studies are a pleasure to us all, and air and exercise are properly attended to. They send their love to all with you; they look charmingly – they never were better, I thank God.

I shall have the pleasure to write to dear Mrs Quin next time, and, with the most respectful compliments to your father, Mr and Mrs Grady and all the family, am my dearest Lady Mary's ever affectionate Agnes Porter.

Journal, 1792

10 May My dear little pupils and I were sent for to Melbury. We spent some time there very agreeably with their grandmama and Lady Susan and Mr O'Bryan. We returned home on the 22nd – found a letter from poor Mr Williams.

June Considering the uncertainty of this mortal life, I made my will.

Having reason to think that my brother-in-law would not chuse, for some very good reasons, to interfere in our family affairs, I, with the Revd Mr Williams' leave, appointed him my executor in case my dear mother survives me. He will take care of her affairs, being the most material part of my legacy.

16 June A letter from Dr Macqueen, to acquaint me with his wife's safe delivery of a very fine boy the first of this month.

17 June A letter from Mrs Quin, my dear Lady Ilchester's sister. She is soon again to change her name, to Gumbleton. May she be happy as she deserves is my sincere wish. Also a most kind letter from my sister Fanny, with an affectionate postscript from Mr Richards. My dear Mrs Pinnock is now on a visit at their house, which gives me sincere pleasure. I am happy in that marriage, which God Almighty prosper!

30 June Had a letter from my sister Betsey to inform me that she has got a situation as governess to a young lady. What a satisfaction will it be to me if she continues there long enough to make it of permanent advantage to her. I pray God it may turn out to her real benefit. How happy should I be to have both my sisters well provided for their life – Fanny in her good husband's care, Betsey by her own industry and prudence.

2 July A letter from my dear Lady Mary in the morning. Spent the day, as usual, in endeavouring to make my pretty pupils as happy as I could, and at the same time improve them. I walked out with them after dinner; at night I spent some hours alone in my own apartment as usual, but with a degree of pleasure which the mind cannot always experience. I revolved the many blessings of my present situation; the goodness of the family; their friendship for me; the beauty and merit of my pupils, etc. I enjoyed the sweetness of the evening, the lovely landscape my window presented me with. *Le Bos* in my hand,[2] and a rose on my table, compleated the gratification of the tranquil hour. May I ever be grateful for all the various bounties of Providence – A. P., July 2nd, 1792.

3 July A most unpleasant letter from Sarum concerning my dear mother: she not pleased with her daughter Elizabeth's conduct – sad vexations for me: my mother low-spirited; has private debts which make her uneasy; not well and wishes to see me. Considered the contents a little while, and then wrote that I would fly to her and make quite easy

---

[2] Sic. I cannot identify Le Bos. Does Agnes mean the influential French critic, the Abbé Jean Baptiste Dubos (1670–1742)?

in every circumstance, if in my power: 'When a parent suffers, the anguish is too native'.

9 July Set off for Salisbury to my poor dear mother. Staid four days, had one of the heaviest strokes of affliction I ever felt;[3] paid my dear mother's debts; made her as easy as I could; laid in some nourishing, comfortable things, and left her a good nurse and tidy little active maid to wait on her. Returned to Redlynch on the 14th.

14 July A kind letter from my brother and sister Richards. They are much incensed at Betsey – N.B. to behave to that person as if I felt no resentment at her conduct; to assist her when ever I can; to reproach her as little as possible.

1 August Betsey returned to Sarum – a sad affair!

4. Letter from Agnes Porter, [Redlynch], to Lady Mary Fox Strangways, County Limerick, Ireland, 5 August 1792

My Dear Lady Mary,

I was in hopes there would not be time for you to receive any more letters in Ireland, but Mr Masterman acquaints me that you will have this, he is pretty certain, as he does not hear of your intending to set out as yet.

You may be sure that we, the poor little *wie* [wee] *three* at Redlynch, begin to long exceedingly to see you again. Lady Charlotte wishes you to write instantly and to name the exact day we may expect you home. Lady Louisa sends her love to *every body* and hopes they will not forget the Irish chest of drawers, and begs it may be packed up so carefully as to receive no damage in the way. They are now at my side, the happiest, dearest little creatures in the world. Your sister Lady Elizabeth gave them half a crown each and your aunt gave us permission to use her carriage for the purpose of spending this same great sum, so the other day we set off in great state for the famous town of Bruton, where we were delivered of the burdens of riches, and they are now wheeling a coach and man on horseback round the tapestry. We are to have tea and a plate of gooseberries as soon as this letter is written, and after tea we are to enjoy our selves in the beautiful shrubbery.

We have had rather a rainy season, but today it is uncommonly fine, and Redlynch appears in great perfection. The Miss Lloyds came to see me the other day: they exclaimed that it was a heaven upon earth

---

[3] Note by Lady Mary Talbot: 'This was her sister's unnatural conduct to her mother'.

– how could the family have the *heart* to leave it! In short, it was quite a paradise, and my darlings were the angels, you may be sure. They had a cousin one day with them – a pretty, slender, girl of sixteen, and my little friends were transported at seeing her. I really believe she put them a little in mind of their sister or you. How rejoiced they will be to see you again! And you, my dear Lady Mary, will I know be always kind to them – their tender years require indulgence and even patience from their sisters, which I make no doubt they will always meet from you who love them, both for their own sake and your dear father's.

I hope you had my last safe. I wrote to Mrs Gumbleton last week, but should not have written to you again had it not been for Mr Masterman. Your sister and cousin[4] were a day here, but the London hours, being transported to Redlynch, occasioned my seeing but little of them. They breakfasted at past twelve o'clock – they looked exceeding well. I hear that Lady Ilchester and all the family at Melbury are in good health.

My mother is better, as I hear. My brother and sister Fanny are quite well – if they come to Wiltshire, as I have some hopes, I have taken the liberty to ask them to come and see Redlynch. I have had a great deal of family trouble and cares on my mind: I was ready to cry out what did it avail me to be a *singleton* in this world if I have as much anxiety as other people who are married. Some persons, and several particulars, would require my personal attendance, but I put *all* off till your return. Do not suppose that the grievances I allude to affect my being equally interested in my dear pupils – their studies, amusements and little excursions go on all the same.

With best respects to Lord Ilchester, and love to the dear Harry I am, my dear Lady Mary, ever affectionately yours, A. Porter.

Journal, 1792

16 August Carried my two dear children to Stourhead. They were much delighted with their afternoon: we looked at the pictures and had a pleasant couple of hours as could possibly be.

5. Letter from Agnes Porter, Redlynch, to Lady Mary Fox Strangways, County Limerick, Ireland, 18 August 1792

My Dear Lady Mary,
We received your kind letter yesterday, which made your sisters and

---

[4] Note in another hand: 'Lady E. Strangways and Kitty Acland'.

Po very happy. To hear that Lord Ilchester is quite recovered, and that you and the dear Harry are well gives me greater satisfaction than I am able to express.

Your little tent parties must be pleasing indeed, and no doubt the salmon brought from the water to the *cook* must be eaten with peculiar relish, as well as in its highest perfection, when you recollect who caught it. How I should have delighted to see your dinner *champêtre*, and how truly amusing must the rural entertainments prove which you so agreeably describe. Such ribbands as your uncle bestows give more satisfaction than the *garter* and are received with as much emulation. I cannot say the *grinning* party would be so desirable a sight – I hope your dear little boy does not practise such hideous contorsions. Pray give his two sisters' love to him, and tell him Po is much obliged to him for not forgetting her, and that she shall love him as long as she lives.

Our weather here has been very fine too – the shrubbery is quite charming; the balsams are very fine and add much beauty to the alcove. Your sisters and I have lately taken a little airing by way of variety in your aunt's carriage – she has got a phaeton, so left the chariot here with a permission to make use of it.[5] We went yesterday to Stourhead and had a refreshing dish of tea with good Mrs Lloyd. The young ladies were entertained in the drawing room where Master Hoare's portrait is, and gained Mrs Lloyd's heart by both in one moment declaring that it was the prettiest picture of all in the house. She shewed them all, and when she came to Cleopatra's picture Lady Charlotte gravely enquired if the man standing by her was not Octavius Caesar. 'You pretty angel, do you read all day?' exclaimed Mrs Lloyd 'to know such *antique* matters at your age.' When we came to the picture or landscape of Venice, I bade Lady Charlotte look at that city built on the sea – she named it instantly, and kept up her credit through the whole. Your pretty Pet was much entertained, you may be certain, and they both made such pertinent enquiries concerning every thing they saw as gave great pleasure to our conductress. She promised that Master Hoare should have the honour of waiting on the young ladies soon, and all the way home Lady Charlotte gave me her instructions concerning this said visit. 'When Master Hoare comes, Po, I shall walk out with him into the garden and shew him every thing myself – and, you know, there will be no occasion for you to walk close with us – you can just drop a little behind, you know, and amuse Louisa.' 'Indeed!' cries the dear Louisa 'I shall amuse myself, and Master Hoare too.' 'No, my

---

[5] The aunt referred to is Lady Harriot Acland.

love, that won't be pretty, for as I am the eldest it is for me to amuse the company and do the honors of the house. I shall make tea and you, Louisa, may hand the bread and butter.' They are perfectly well, and very good, sweet children. Lady Charlotte makes some progress in *les belles lettres*, and Lady Louisa adds to these the art of sewing: she has just now finished a present for you, of her own work except a very little of my assistance – you are not to know what.

I hope your sister Lady Elizabeth writes often to you – you will soon have it in your power to be of much use and improvement to each other. You, my love, must endeavour to acquire a little of her elegance and easy turn of conversation, while I hope she will resemble you in a love of home and a talent for domestic happiness – a very great one in the œconomy of human life. You will very soon, my dear Lady Mary, cease to be my pupil, but I trust you will never cease to regard me in the light of a most sincere and tender friend and that, in that character, you will permit me at times in the absence of your female relations to hint my opinions on subjects which may concern your conduct or happiness. I know the goodness of your understanding, but at your age the advice of a more experienced person is sometimes of real utility.

I hope you keep up your *good morning customs* and I pray God Almighty to bless and preserve my beloved and amiable young friend, and hope I shall soon have the joy to see her dear little *pawky eyne*.[6] Sisha[7] is quite well and much obliged to you – as for me, I am your ever affectionate Agnes Porter.

Journal, 1792

22 August Finished *Ariosto*.
19 September Thank God, my dear Lady Mary, Lord Ilchester and Lord Stavordale arrived safe from Ireland after an absence of eight months.
November Lady Dowager Ilchester died.[8]

---

[6] Artful/shrewd eyes.
[7] 'Sisha' was a pet-name for Agnes's sister Frances Richards.
[8] She died on 14 November 1792.

1793

In late 1792 or early 1793 Lord Ilchester's third daughter, Harriot, left Weymouth, where she had been at school since 1787, and joined her sisters in the school-room at Redlynch. In April or May 1793 the whole family, including Agnes, went to London, where Lady Mary Fox Strangways was presented at Court. They probably left London for Redlynch in June, and in the following month moved to Melbury, which then became the main residence of Lord Ilchester and his family.

6. Letter from Agnes Porter, [Redlynch], to Lady Mary Fox Strangways, Melbury, 8 March 1793

My Dear Lady Mary,

I am happy to hear you are well, and have now great hopes that Lord Ilchester will escape the fit of the gout this season and that the late symptoms are quite vanished. I dare say, my dear love, you spend your time very agreeably – you have your work and Watson[1] for a rainy morning within doors, and when the morning invites you abroad you have delightful walks in and round Melbury, then at table a beloved and tender father's company. These are great blessings, and I do not pity *you* for being from Redlynch, but *ourselves* in being deprived of such dear society.

Your sister's rash is entirely gone off and she is to day in perfect health. As to her spirits, she is chearful, which is I think all that can reasonably be expected in her present solitude. Lady Charlotte is quite well, but not so studiously disposed as she used to be: having discovered in me a great inclination to give her a large portion of my time and attention in her sister Louisa's absence, she sometimes thinks proper to draw back and is never so heartily disposed to engross me as when

---

[1] Later note: *'History of Philip II'*. This was Robert Watson, *The History of the Reign of Philip II, King of Spain* (1777).

she sees me at any particular study deeply engaged with her sister Harriot. You know the dear little whimsical love as well as I do, but we go on very well on the whole. Lady Harriot is quite amiable in every respect – I have the greatest reason to be satisfied with her industry and excellent qualities.

I need not recommend to you your *morning practice* here: I am well assured that my dear Lady Mary is steady in her first duty, *upon principle,* where-ever she is. With such a determined resolution the world will have no temptations that will ever have power either to shake your morality or bewilder your reason.

May God Almighty ever bless and keep you and *all* you love! I am, my dear Lady Mary's true and affectionate friend, Agnes Porter.

7. Letter from Agnes Porter, [Redlynch], to Lady Mary Fox Strangways, Melbury, 12 March 1793

My Dear Lady Mary,

Thank you for your nice little notes which always give me pleasure, but I think you are rather mistaken in your idea of letter-writing, so I shall in this leisure half-hour give you my opinion on that subject, and when we meet we will compare our sentiments together.

A letter to a friend seems to me simply this: giving them an hour of your company, notwithstanding whatever distance separates you. To do this is to convey your thoughts to them while you are writing. It little signifies what scenes surround you or what company you see – no, it is *yourself* your friend requires, and extraneous circumstances have no farther weight than as they affect and interest *you*. It is what you do; what you think; what you hope, fear, expect or wish, that forms matter for a friendly correspondence and, if you are in a state of perfect tranquillity, the calm transcripts of a serene mind must give delight to the eye of friendship. So write me as short letters as you please, but no more tell me that 'the place affords no subjects'.

We really begin to flatter ourselves that you will return this week – do not contradict our hopes, we beseech you. You will be much pleased with your three sisters' good looks, and dear Lady Harriot's improvements. Last night our amusement was reading your *Jean de Calais*. Lady Elizabeth had never chanced to read it, and Lady Harriot's pleasure and mine was to observe the effects which the various incidents had upon her. The ghost was introduced with becoming solemnity, and Lady Harriot and I plumed ourselves not a little.

Je vous ai promis une lettre pour aujord'hui, ma chère Ladi Marie;

c'est avec bien de plaisir que je vous tiens parole. Toute la famille à Redlynch se porte au parfait: on se promène; on fait la lecture; on travaille un peu; enfin on s'amuse aussi bien qu'il est possible de le faire pendant votre absence. Ainsi, hâtez votre retour, ma chère amie, pour nous combler de plaisir. Votre soeur Charlotte vous fait mille amitiés; elle dessine une petite ferme à mon côté, et m'interrompt de tems en tems pour me demander si le dessin n'est pas des plus jolis: 'C'est une maison pour vous, ma chère Po, quand vous serez bien vieille'. C'est un charmant bijou que votre soeur Lady Charlotte, ainsi que la petite Louise.

Je viens de lire un livre dont je suis très contente: il me paroît fort bien écrit, et rempli de bon morale – ce sont des lettres entre une bonne mère et sa fille nouvellement mariée. La jeune dame se trouve dans les circonstances les plus affligeantes, et en même tems les plus délicates; la mère lui donne des bons conseils dont il s'ensuivent des conséquences les plus heureuses. Je n'ai pu avoir qu'un tome de cet ouvrage intéressant, mais quand nous serons à Londres je vous en procurerai la lecture.

Auriez vous bien la complaisance de faire acheminer mes lettres ci incluses; faites mes respects les plus distingués à Milor votre père; embrassez les chers enfans de ma part, et pensez quelque fois, ma chère Lady Mary, à votre très sincère amie, Agnes Porter.

[I promised you a letter today, my dear Lady Mary. It is with great pleasure that I keep my promise. All members of the family at Redlynch are well: we walk, we read, we work a little, altogether we are as happy as it is possible to be whilst you are away. So come back soon, my dear friend, and we will be delighted. Your sister Charlotte sends you a thousand remembrances: she is drawing a little farm beside me, and interrupts me from time to time to ask if her drawing is not very pretty: 'It is a house for you, my dear Po, when you are very old'. Your sister Lady Charlotte is a charming jewel, and so is little Louisa.

I have just read a book which pleased me very much. I thought it very well written, and full of good morality: these are the letters between a good mother and her recently-married daughter.[2] The young lady finds herself in circumstances which are most afflicting and, at the same time, most delicate: her mother gives her good advice, which produces the happiest consequences. I have only been able to obtain one volume

---

[2] Note in another hand: '*Madame de Montier* by Madame Le Prince de Beaumont, 2 volumes'. This was J. M. Le Prince de Beaumont, *Letters of Madame du Montier* (1756).

of this interesting work, but you will be able to read it when we are in London.

Please have the goodness to forward the letters which I am including; give my respects to My Lord your father; embrace the dear children for me; and think sometimes, my dear Lady Mary, of your very sincere friend, Agnes Porter.]

Journal, 1793

9 July Lord Ilchester and his family removed to Melbury, Dorsetshire.

18 July Lady Mary and Harriot were confirmed by Dr Madan, Bishop of Bristol. I accompanied them for that purpose to Sherbourne church. Mem. the Bishop a very venerable and a very agreeable gentleman.

21 July Closed this journal – Agnes Porter.

1794

The year 1794 saw further changes. In February Lord Ilchester's second daughter, Mary, married Thomas Mansel Talbot and left Melbury for Wales. Agnes's mother died in June, and in August Lord Ilchester remarried. The new Lady Ilchester was a cousin, Maria Digby, who was twenty-four years her husband's junior.

Journal, 1794

1 February Lady Mary Strangways was married at Melbury chapel to Mansel Talbot Esquire.
8 June I lost my dear mother, A. P.

8. Letter from Agnes Porter, Melbury, to Lady Mary Talbot, Penrice Castle, 22 July 1794

I did not intend my last as anything more than a 'How da ye?' I have to thank you for your great kindness in giving an invitation to Sisha who, whether she can avail herself of it or not, must feel extremely obliged to my dear Lady Mary. Mr Richards' excursion into Wales concerns business, and as he is one of those rare old-fashioned husbands who love their wives' society, he takes his Fanny with him. [During] the week he was with me at Sarum he wrote to her *[word missing]* times, and exclaiming on the age it appeared to him since he had left her, I bade him pack up his alls and be gone, which he very soon did. But happy was I to think that in that instance I had so uncomplaisant a brother-in-law: indeed, just such another man with ten years or more over his age would make me a very happy woman, but God alone knows in which station we shall best act our parts and work out our own eternal happiness, and well it is for us all that His wise and gracious will should be accomplished in all things.

When I go to Town I will, if you give me leave, purchase and select some amusing French books for your perusal. You know, you never were very fond of the studying that language, and had I not called *Gil Blas* to our assistance, I doubt much whether you would ever have read it at all, as with a very excellent understanding there is a *little something* that prevents your making a great progress in any pursuit unless where your own inclination prompts your efforts and gives your natural good abilities fair play. I am glad, however, that you have an opportunity of speaking French, which is the most pleasing method of acquiring it. I love the amiable among that nation very much indeed: there is a certain pleasing *badinage* in their conversation which makes one almost forget the cares of life, while their minute attentions look so like benevolence that they charm the heart and tend, as Sterne expresses it, to strew the path of common life with 'rose-buds of delight'. I hope yours abound with full-blown flowers, to bring forth in due time the fruits of happiness and joy. Take care of your precious health! 'Audace si, ma cautamente audace [audacious, yes, but cautiously audacious]' – excuse this little touch of pedantry, if you should so style it. I hate, in general, letters made up of scraps of different tongues, and seldom fall into it – at least, I flatter myself so.

Your darlings here are all quite well. Lady Louisa has recovered her rosey cheeks; Lord Stavordale is quite stout; Lady Charlotte is in perfect health, and has been very good for a whole long week; Lady Harriot is always so, and grows very handsome in her person, and pleasing in her manners. She says you owe her two letters – pray do not tell her that I have mentioned it, for the dear little Pussey is a little touchy at times, with all her good sense and good qualities. The dear Harry is not yet gone [to] school, but I believe he soon will. Mr and Mrs Cha ...[1] came here to day – they have been very attentive [to me] and the children, so has Lady Susan. [We are] better off in point of neighbour-hood here than [we used] to be at Redlynch in your father's absence. He is still at Worthing, Steyning, Sussex, but I think you may now direct to me as *usual* under a frank to your father. He is quite well, so is Lady Elizabeth. *Squire Twig's Adventures* do not come out till next winter, and not then by subscription, but the same writer has lately published some light summer reading in a couple of volumes called the *Turkish Tales* – I have a set for you, if you have no objection, at six shillings.[2]

---

[1] Page torn, but must be Mr and Mrs Charles Strangways or Digby.

[2] The author was Agnes's friend Joseph Moser. The books to which Agnes refers are *The Adventures of Timothy Twig Esq. in a Series of Political Epistles* (1794) and *Turkish Tales* (1794).

The children all unite in love to their dear Mary – Lady Harriot begs you will write to her. We have had very sultry weather here for a week past, and a storm last Friday, but it did no harm to the inhabitants and has beautifully refreshed the earth. God bless you, my dear Lady Mary, is the *prayer* of your ever affectionate Ann Agnes Porter.

9. Letter from Agnes Porter, Melbury, to Lady Mary Talbot, Penrice Castle, 1 August 1794

I hope my dear Lady Mary is perfectly well. I have the pleasure to inform you that all at Melbury are in good health – your little sisters were made very happy indeed by your last kind letters, and I can assure you they are full of love for their dear sister Mary, but regretted the epistles were so small, as each dear little *billet doux* cost tenpence – half a crown the three. We grudge no money but what goes in to our king's treasury, so be pleased to send them another time larger, viz. better, bargains.

Your father is in hopes of soon returning home; dear Harry's going to school is postponed till then. Lady Elizabeth is at times but poorly – she weakens her stomach by non-sustenance. I do not hear from, but sometimes of, her. Your sister Harriot is at present quite happy in Miss Syndercombe's company, who appears to be an agreeable, artless girl. They are at present walking through the lower suite of apartments, the two little ones in their train, listening to a most wonderful story, in which the mama desired her children to sit down on a great stone and not to eat a bit for three days and three nights. The composition is Lady Harriot's, and great is the attention paid to it by the happy auditors. Lord Stavordale is gone with Cavenagh on a fishing expedition, and Po is established at the writing table to chat with one who is often in her memory, and always in her heart. Your aunt Lady Harriot is at Tunbridge, and I hear Miss Kitty is better. Lady Susan O'Brien sent for your sister and me to spend a day at Stinsford: the company beside themselves was a Mr Floyder and Mr Davis – we spent an agreeable day. We were last Wednesday at Maiden Newton,[3] so you see we no longer shall deserve the name of recluse. Mrs Strangways is as pretty as ever. They seem very happy with their three nice little *tits*. So much for excentric news, now for a little in the domestic way: you must know that Hymen intends to light his torch in honour of several swains and nymphs in the family – Mr Dibble and a Miss Wallace of Evershot;

---

[3] Home of Lord Ilchester's younger brother, Charles Redlynch Fox Strangways.

Mr Smyth and a Miss Somebody at Abbotsbury; Nanny and Mr Greaves; Susan and a bricklayer at Wroughton. All these intend soon to follow the example set them by the *head* of the family.

I have not heard from my Fanny for some time, but I hope and believe she is well, and also *sa chère moitié*. My good friend Mrs Pinnock is charmingly, but I wish I could persuade her to live at her son's, as I think at the age of seventy-seven it is hazardous to be at one's own care only. I hope when my affairs are settled, which will happen in a few months, to be able to add a little annual encrease to this dear woman's income. It is not worth living to be useful only to one's self, and alas! I have now only myself to care for – I mean as to pecuniaries, but I have many to think of in other respects. Take care of your dear health and do not (I charge you) walk eight miles – it is suicide – never do it again. I visited your room to day: my heart sunk within me – the stool stood in the closet exactly in the spot I had last seen you sit on it. I removed it with a deep sigh, and was obliged to leave the room. I do not think I shall ever go into it again without your own sweet self.

Farewel my dearest Lady Mary – *Dieu vous bénisse*, A. P.

Journal, 1794

28 August Lord Ilchester married Miss Maria Digby.

10. Letter from Agnes Porter, Abbotsbury, to Lady Mary Talbot, [Penrice Castle], 11 September 1794

I have given my darling here half a holiday, that I might converse this afternoon (in spite of distance) with my dear Lady Mary, and it is to be in folio as you see. After telling you that they are all well, I shall begin with what seems to me the most important point alluded to in your dear letter, namely Lord Ilchester's marriage. During our stay in Town I had never heard a syllable of the matter, and never dreamt of such a thing. I was called to Sarum on my dear mother's account, and after a melancholy fortnight arrived at Melbury in such a disposition of mind as to suppose nothing could affect, or rouze me from, the torpor of spirits I was in. However, I was mistaken, and was still to feel myself all alive to any thing that concerned you or yours. Mrs Fye came running up to my room on afternoon in a hurry, with a 'Madam, Madam, what will you give me for news, and a marriage too? Who do you think is on the point of marriage? It is My Lord himself, I promise

you – but law! How pale you do grow – you ben't sick, be ye?' I said I
was but poorly. She then bade me guess – in a faint voice I said 'Miss
Maud' – 'No'. I then guessed Miss Digby, as these were the only young
ladies Lord Ilchester had any acquaintance with. This was the manner,
my dear Lady Mary, in which I first heard this important event, and I
did not recover for some days. When Lord Ilchester came to Melbury
he acquainted me himself with his intention. He endeavoured to put
a good face on, but I saw he was much affected – he said he had been
a happy man in that state before, and he hoped to be happy again;
that he had endeavoured to act the part of a good parent to his dear
children; and he had reason to believe that they in return would wish
to see the evening of his days set in peace and comfort; that the
daughters who was of the most consequence to his domestic happiness
was already settled; the elder might likewise leave him soon, and her
stay became quite precarious; that the third, though a charming girl,
was too young and too thoughtless to be his companion; and that he
foresaw he should be desolate and solitary soon if he did not again
enter the married state, but so determined was he never to vex his
children in so important a point, that he had offered to Lady Elizabeth,
if she disapproved of this affair, to give up all thoughts of it and never
mention it to Miss Digby, though in that case he must suffer, as his
heart was engaged by the many virtues and good qualities he had
discovered in that young lady. Afterwards, when he paid his addresses
in form, she would give no decisive answer till she had consulted both
his single daughters, and if they had a dislike to the connection nothing
on earth should move her to complaisance. This was the more noble
in her, as by that time Lord Ilchester's constant attentions and endeavours to please had succeeded in engaging her affections. Lord Ilchester
became miserable at the uncertainty that might occur, and I believe
Lady Elizabeth had very serious subjects for alarm, both as to her
father's happiness, and even his health and life, had he been finally
disappointed. You know, my dear love, you were not present to see
how things went on gradually, nor what reason your sisters had to be
reconciled to, and even to forward, this event. Poor Lady Harriot has
suffered, I believe, a great deal, and her conduct has been superior to
her years.

I do not wonder at the feelings of your dear heart, I can safely assert
that I have sympathized with you in them all, and have shed many a
tear, not 'that *this* came, but that the *other* went' – an angel on earth
could only put me in mind that I had lost her – sacred be her memory
for ever! And if from her blessed state she casts an eye upon mortality,

she will rejoice that her Henry meets with a helping hand in the decline of life, for no jealousy can disturb the mansions of the blest. I would have you, my sweet love, revive in your own dear breast every tender feeling for your remaining parent – believe me, he was much to be pitied after he lost you. Had he married any one whatever, however beneath him, yet in giving her his name he would give her a title to respect, particularly from his own children. His choice is universally approved of, and were you to see her unaffected sweetness, her unassuming manners, you would hold out your generous hand to encourage her. She was void of ambition or pride; she loved your father and wished to make him as happy as she could; by her own good will no one should call her any thing but *Maria*; and if you send her a few lines calling her, as you please *Maria* or *Cousin*, merely to signify that you wish her happy in her new state, I believe it would give her great pleasure, as well as your father. But this I speak merely from conjecture, and to shew my extreme confidence in you. I know you have better advice at your *right hand* than any Po can give.

What pleasure it gives me to hear you are well and happy – long may it be so! Lady Elizabeth is better, but has been very poorly on the starving plan, and owing to it. However, Mr Farqhuar has convinced her of the necessity of some mortal sustenance and she is getting on well again, and it expected home in about a fortnight. She will still have the same rooms she had – your cousin would not suffer any change. Lady Harriot is charmingly in her health. Her spirits have not been quite so good of late – she reminds me of what another *dear soul* was for about a year before *she married* – but this one, you know, has not yet got out of my magic spell, so I rouze her and make her study, driving out, if I can, the idea of any *agreeable modern* by the consideration of a Cesar, a Cato or an Alexander. These are gentry, by the bye, that she has a great predilection for, and they are of great use to us at times, but she is a pretty, sweet soul, and deserves all your tenderness and sisterly approbation. Lady Charlotte grows amazingly tall, strong and handsome. She begins to love work a little, such as netting and making dolls' caps, which I am very glad of, as it helps sometimes to keep her quiet. As to your *Petty,* she is still the same pretty good little creature, and at times extremely humorous. Someone said something to Lady Harriot about Cupid – 'Phoo' replied she 'stupid.' 'What' said Louisa 'do you call Cupid stupid? Not so stupid but what he can shoot through your little heart Harriot, and then call him stupid if you can.' Indeed, they are both so clever that Lady Susan said very gravely to me the other day 'Do, pray, Miss Porter, do your best to keep these children back a little'. Lady Susan is quite well, so is the *Caro Sposo;* Mr and Mrs Charles Strangways are quite well – she looks every hour to lay down, and does not go abroad any more. Colonel Strangways is also very well – he was at Melbury lately.

Lady Harriot Acland is at Pixton. Miss Acland had the goodness to send me Riccoboni's entire works, eight volumes elegantly bound: some I like, and some I do not. Her *Lady Catesby* is a charming character, and represents the passion of love in the utmost delicacy and tenderness; her *Fanny Butlerd* is a naughty woman, and a bold voluptuary, yet Riccoboni tries to make a heroine of her.[4] It is surprizing how the same person could represent or approve of two such different characters. My more serious reading has been the *Life of Gustavus Adolphus* by a Mr Harte. It is very interesting – he was indeed a great hero, and a most excellent man.[5]

---

[4] M. J. Riccoboni, *Lettres de Mistriss Fanni Butlerd à Milord Charles Alfred, duc de Caitombridge* (1759).

[5] Walter Harte, *The History of the Life of Gustavus Adolphus, King of Sweden* (1759).

1795

No journal has survived from 1795, and there is just one letter which appears to have been written in this year. Agnes and her pupils probably spent most of the year at Melbury.

11. Letter from Agnes Porter [London], to Lady Harriot Fox Strangways [Melbury], n. d. Probably 1795

My Dear Lady Harriot,

Owing to various disappointments and little disagreeable accidents, I did not leave Sarum till yesterday morning. I had no travelling companion but a poor country girl who was seated on the outside, but owing to the inclemency of the weather I invited her to come and share the coach with me. Indeed, I owed her something for the amusement I had enjoyed in a dialogue between herself, her mother at parting, and the coachman: 'God bless you Mr Coachman, do you take care of she, she is but a young thing' said the mother. 'Never fear, Mistress, young things do very well in London.' 'I knows my direction where to be sent in London' interrupted Rose 'every one there must know my mistress, as how she is sister to Mrs Sharp the grocer at Sarum.' 'What is her direction?' 'She lives' replied Rose 'in Dan Street, St Inns, Sow-how.' '*Sowhow?*' said Mr Coachy 'why you may as well tell me '*Bow-wow*' – good luck and I be to take care of a gell who knows no more than a blind mare what house she is to go to.' As the coachman pretended entire ignorance, I offered my service as interpreter, and read the curious scroll of her mother's writing, supposing it to mean 'Dean Street, St Ann's, Soho'. As in the course of our journey I found I should derive no great information from my fellow traveller, I bethought me as the next good, what advantage I could be of to her, and undertook to make her pronounce her direction to her new home in the English language. I made her repeat it every five minutes and she, being a pretty apt scholar, got it tolerably well in the short space of *eighteen hours,* only making a small mistake in *Soho,* at times calling it *So So,* and at others *Heigh ho.* This was indeed the strain I ended in myself after all my labours, mental and corporeal.

Betty Palmer met me, and happy was I to enter Old Burlington House. Dr Macqueen, Miss Owen, Mrs Pinnock and Mrs Moser had been to see me *the day before I arrived.* I must now return their civilities which, with affairs of some consequence to me, will employ me in Town till near next Thursday. I then proceed to Hadley, but thought it too long to defer writing to my dear Lady Harriot, to whom I am a most sincere, though sometimes a tormenting, friend, Ann Agnes Porter.

My respects, love, kind wishes etc. properly distributed, if you please. A thousand kisses to *Lady Ilchester's three good children.*

1796

From March to June 1796 Agnes and her pupils were in London, where Lady Elizabeth Fox Strangways married William Davenport Talbot in mid April. In September Agnes left Melbury on an excursion which took her first to Salisbury, and then to London. She then went on to Norfolk, staying in Yarmouth and then London again. At the end of October she left London for Salisbury, and at the beginning of November she returned to her pupils at Melbury.

Journal, 1796

7 March The three dear children and I left Melbury.

10 March Arrived in London.

11 March I went to Hadley; had the pleasure to find my dear sister and Mr Richards quite well.

12 March Happy in their society

13 March The same – thank God, quite well and quite happy.

14 March (Monday). Returned to London.

15 March Dear Miss Owen spent the evening with me. She gave me such an account of her prospects as afforded me the greatest satisfaction.

16 March Dr Macqueen drank tea and sat with me till ten o'clock. I am happy to have two such friends as Miss Owen and Dr Macqueen – equally respectable for virtue and abilities.

17 March I staid at home and wrote letters.

18 March I drank tea with good Mrs Pinnock who, at the age of seventy-eight, possesses chearfulness and, under the pressure of narrow circumstances, preserves an unfailing resignation and peace of mind.

19 March At home.

20 March At church. Heard an excellent sermon, the subject 'Do good to all men' – a young clergyman preached. 'It is when we do good to others', said he, 'that we do most effectual good to ourselves.' The poor little charity girls enforced the sermon by a hymn, and I contributed my *mite* with pleasure. I then drank tea with Mr and Mrs Moser – they were both well, and kind to me as usual. Mr Moser read me a letter from Mr Burke complimenting him on his last literary performance – on his urging this *plaudit*, I observed that *Plato alone* made an audience.

21 March Monday. At home with my dear pupils till twelve o'clock. I then waited on Lady Harriot Acland and sat an hour with her. Had the pleasure of seeing Miss Acland and her *fiancé* Lord Porchester. The marriage is to take place next month – both are young, amiable and rich.

22 March My dear Mrs Pinnock spent the day with me. She chatted, she sang, and played at 'I love my love' with my children as if she had been but sixteen years of age.

23 March The morning from eight to three o'clock at our various studies. In the afternoon I walked into the City and was measured for a mourning ring for my worthy Mrs Franklin. I drank tea at Mrs Williams' with a large party – N.B. a lady there from the country seemed to think the most marvellous circumstance in London was her having dined one day at *four* o'clock.

24 March With my pupils – their various masters are much pleased with their diligence and daily improvements.

25 March Good Friday. At St James Piccadily Dr Gibson preached 'Do this in remembrance of me'. A good sermon; an excellent reader; and the most melodious clerk I ever heard – I would go a mile to hear him say 'Amen'. My dear children went to the Chapel Royal with Lady Ilchester. Lady Charlotte heard the Queen say 'Who are these pretty children?' – their Majesties, with the two elder princesses, were present.[1] Lady Louisa was rather hurt at the Queen's laughing and speaking at church – 'Indeed Po', said the sweet child 'it was not quite pretty in Her Majesty was it?' Spent the evening alone.

24 July Resumed my journal after a very long chasm in it of four months, but in London had not time to write and cannot now recollect the daily occurences, but will endeavour to note *events*:

[17 April] My dear Lady Elizabeth was married to Mr Talbot,[2] cousin to her brother-in-law. At two the company assembled in the drawing room – present, her father, Lady Ilchester, Lady Harriot Acland, Miss Acland, her sister Harriot, the children and my self – Mr Charles Strangways, her uncle, performed the ceremony. Her father gave her

---

[1] King George III, Queen Charlotte, and the Princesses Charlotte and Augusta.
[2] William Davenport Talbot.

away; her voice trembled, but she did her best – did not articulate the word 'obey', but behaved on the whole very prettily – was dressed in a green riding habit, black hat and feather; a long white veil fell down over her face. After the ceremony her father embraced her – dear man! – with tears. Lady Harriot Acland's eyes glistened – she thought of the *tender mother*, gone for ever – the same thought occupied me during the solemnity, and lay heavy at my heart. All present wished them joy, and drank their health. The bridegroom looked quite happy; the bride was sweetly serene. In a quarter of an hour the happy pair set off for Bath – they went to dear Mrs Gumbleton's, where they spent a fortnight in her company, after which they went to Wales, and Mrs Gumbleton to Ireland.

[24 April] Miss Acland was married to Lord Porchester. I had a note in a day or two after from Lady Harriot Acland, sending me in a present from Lady Porchester all Metastasio's works.[3] During my stay in London I visited my friends Dr and Mrs Macqueen, Mr and Mrs Moser, and Mrs Pinnock. I went twice to the play; went also to the Shakespeare Gallery – poets etc. I went several times to my dear sister's at Hadley, where I never failed to enjoy in her and Mr Richards' society the greatest pleasure – 'The flow of soul'. During our stay at London my dear pupils made a great progress with their masters in music, drawing and dancing. I superintended as well as I was able, and made them practise in the intervals. The Revd Mr Griffith attended Lord Stavordale two hours every day for his Latin – by often sitting with them I got all the declensions pretty perfect.

10 June Lord Ilchester desired me to ask Mr Griffith if he would give Lord Stavordale a few weeks of his time in the country previous to his being sent to school, which he promised to do, if he could in the mean time provide for his two churches.

12 June I spent with my dear brother and sister – they are to continue another year (if it please God) at Hadley.

13 June I dined with Dr, Mr and Mrs Williams. In the evening he saw me to the mail, where I found Mr Griffith, who told me he would wait upon Lord Ilchester the week after. I travelled all night, reached Melbury the next day – found Lord Ilchester, his son and daughter Harriot there before me. They met me in the hall, and my dear pupils rejoiced to see me as if I had been abroad a twelvemonth. I visited my

---

[3] The poet and dramatist Pietro Antonio Domenico Bonaventura Metastasio (numerous editions of his works, 1730s and later).

room, books and pictures with pleasure; settled myself quite at home in a few hours.

16 June Lady Ilchester and the rest of the family arrived.

20 June [sic] Mr Griffith arrived at Melbury – his pupil rejoiced to see him – he admired the beauties of the place, and seemed much pleased with his reception.

17 June I walked out – Mr Griffith joined me in my walk – I thought his conversation both sensible and agreeable.

18 June In the evening I was again joined by Mr Griffith. Met Lord and Lady Ilchester, who smiled at our *tête-à-tête*. N.B. I resolved to change my hours of walking, as it particularly behoved me to avoid any particularity, or the least *seeming* indecorum.

24 June About [this date] Lady Harriot Acland with Lord and Lady Porchester came to spend a few days at Melbury. When I went up to the sweet young lady, and said I had the honour to wish her *ladyship* joy, she snatched hold of my hand and said 'My dear Mrs Porter, I cannot bear this ceremony from you – call me not *ladyship*, I beseech you'. She then gave me a kind salute and, taking my arm, walked round the pleasure-grounds with me. Few heiresses marry so well as Miss Acland has done, but *she* had a *Lady Harriot Acland* for her mother.

25 June I had a long and *unreserved* conversation with Lady Harriot Acland.

10 July About [this date] the family went to Sherbourne leaving the three younger children, Mr Griffith and I to keep house. I invited them all to tea – after tea I played drafts with Mr Griffith. I made the children stay [to] supper with us – they left us at half past nine. I then desired a servant to bring my candle at ten – till then, Mr Griffith and I chatted together. Our discourse turned upon Lavater – Mr Griffith told me he himself was so far a physiognomist that he had seldom been mistaken in his first ideas upon character. He promised me that next winter he would shew me a curious book written previous to Lavater's upon that subject.[4] The servant then appeared and I wished him good night, as I generally sup in my own room. He thanked me for my company with an air as if he felt it both a favour and a gratification.

12 July Lord Digby spent the day at Melbury – he politely invited Mr Griffith to visit him, and regretted his not having accompanied the rest of the party to Sherbourne Castle.

---

[4] Johann Caspar Lavater (numerous works on religion, education and physiognomy, 1770s and later).

14 July About [this date] poor Lord Digby fell from his phaeton and broke his leg. It was set immediately and he was so composed, and did so well under this misfortune, that he would not allow his sister to put off her marriage, which took place as intended upon the 18th or 19th. Since my return I went every week to Lower Melbury as usual, but changed the day, not liking to go the same day as I did when Mr and Mrs Field were of the party – they are gone to live in Wiltshire. My dear Miss Owen was married last month to the Re ... *[five pages torn out here].*

... July Studied with Lady Harriot and the three children till half past two – our studies French, English and arithmetick, with a little work. Dressed for dinner; Mr Charles Strangways dined with us – he asked me *en badinant* how I did since Mr Griffith's departure – I laughed and answered 'As well as could be expected'. We had an agreeable party at dinner – Lady Harriot, her uncle, myself and the dear children. The rest of the family were gone to visit Lord Digby. I drank tea with Mr and Mrs Jenkins – we had a party at commerce. Returned at nine, read an hour in *Paul et Virginie*,[5] wrote my journal, said my prayers, and to bed.

25 July Tuesday: rose at seven; heard my dear children read as usual – etc; walked out with them half an hour. After breakfast our studies till two o'clock – Lady Harriot not with me. My dear younger pupils read and wrote French; read and wrote English; did a sum; wrote a copy, and practised music. Colonel Strangways dined at Melbury. After dinner Lady Harriot told me she intended practising music – I replied she was right to do so; I thought her finger had lost a good deal since she had left London. She then told me she should *not* practise – rather a strange decision upon my remark. But her Ladyship is sometimes a little odd in *small* matters, *mais bonne et charmante quant à l'essentiel.* After dinner my dear Lady Louisa was with me two hours – work and history formed our amusements. Mrs Strangways drank tea with us. We had a dance after tea – my partner Colonel Strangways. Danced till I could dance no more; came up to my apartment; read half an hour in *Paul et Virginie* – wrote my journal; said my prayers, and went to bed.

26 July Wednesday: rose at seven, read, and heard my pupils say their prayers. Lord Stavordale was cross and did not read well – I was much displeased with him, and took no notice of him at breakfast. After it I went out to walk; in my return it rained; I saw my dear little Lord

---

[5] J. H. B. de Saint-Pierre, *Paul et Virginie* (1788).

Stavordale running to meet me with a *parapluie* in his hand, with which he covered me and said 'My dear *Po*, I won't be *cross* another morning'. Sweet boy! Long may you retain such feelings! We studied from eleven till near three. Lady Harriot did a great deal – clever and good. My dear children were very diligent – for their reward I read to them an hour in *Les Journées Amusantes*, which they understood as if it had been English.[6] After dinner I made them study and write English. At six we all walked out – I met in the pleasure grounds Lady Ilchester and Lady Susan O'Brien. They were admiring a rose in Lady Ilchester's hand – Mr O'Brien said 'Give me that rose, to please my nose'. His lady accused him of barbarous doggrel – I said he should have wished to die of a rose in aromatic pain or some such pretty thing! 'It is all mighty pretty' replied he 'but we must descend to common life at last.' Lady Ilchester gave me the rose, saying 'Will you add it to your bouquet Miss Porter?' I certainly have received presents of greater value from Lady Ilchester, but never one that obliged me so much as this rose – I put it in water immediately. We drank tea at seven; after tea Lady Susan read a few charades and rebusses.[7] N.B. she liked one of my making:

> Though I upon the earth be found
> No latitude can mark the ground;
> Yet I allure by hopes of gain
> The bright-ey'd nymph and daring swain
> And what I hope will more surprize
> No parallel can match my size.

(The Equator)

After tea I returned to my own apartment: it was too dark to read; it was too early to have light, so I sat and ruminated. I leaned my head against my dear mother's little cane, which hangs at my bed-head, and I thought of her – I recollected how often we had enjoyed the close of day together. I could recollect even the beams of moon-light upon her serene beloved face. That was too much: 'I shall see her again' I exclaimed 'in the light of immortality!' A sigh, a tear of consolation eased my heart. I supt, but did not encline to write my journal.

28 July Thursday: did not rise till near eight. My three dear children said their prayers. Lord Stavordale took great pains in his reading; Lady Harriot also came and read in the Bible and *Spectator*. N.B. she is such an enemy to dry rules that she never leaves a mark in either,

---

[6] M. A. Poisson de Gomez, *Les journées amusantes* (1722).

[7] Puzzles.

so about five minutes are generally spent in finding the places. To do this as our first sum in the rule of three: at five minutes per day, how much per annum? After breakfast, as it rained, my pupils did not go out but worked half an hour with their aunt, while I wrote my yesterday's journal. I then practised the piano forte half an hour. Our studies as usual till half past two; my two younger pupils and I by ourselves at dinner – settled it to be very kind to each other to make amends for the absent. After dinner music, and writing English. At six we drank tea and then walked out till eight. At night I studied Italian half an hour, and then read *Werter* – was so much engaged in his *Sorrows* that I finished the book.[8] It was too late to write my journal – prayers and bed.

29 July Friday: rose at half past seven, heard my three dear children read their Bible and say their prayers – Lady Harriot also with me. When they were gone I read half an hour in my Italian Bible – mem. – in three chapters had to look but for three words. From ten till two at our studies: writing, work, French and English, with a little musick and arithmetick. Walked from two till past three – settled it in my mind that if I lived and was well I would go to Yarmouth next October. Considered that life was short, and delays hazardous; reflected upon the pleasure my dear Mrs Upcher would have in seeing me – a glimpse of my sister and other friends *en passant*. At three dressed for dinner. Lady Harriot brought me a packet from Lady Mary Talbot containing a letter, and a handkerchief of her own dear handy-work for me [and] three purses for the children: Lord Stavordale had his, but Lady Charlotte and Louisa [are] to wait another week for their presents, as there must be a deal of good conduct to merit their sister's gifts. We all dined at four – N.B. Lord Ilchester drank a glass of strong beer because I advised him to it after his fatiguing walks. Lady Ilchester, Lady Susan O'Brien and Lady Harriot all gay and agreeable. In the afternoon I played an hour. Tea at seven. In the evening had a pleasing half hour's chat with my dear Lady Harriot – we kissed and parted – only for the night, I hope. Retired to my own apartment, read an Italian play, *Alessandro*, an essay of Montaigne, wrote my journal and went to bed.[9]

30 July Saturday: rose at seven. My dear children as usual – studies the same. After dinner read *Le Malade Imaginaire* to Lady Harriot – she loves Molière. After tea Mr O'Brien objected to a note of mine in *Johnson's*

---

[8] Johann Wolfgang von Goethe, *The Sorrows of Werter* (English translation, 1779).
[9] P. A. Rolli, *Alessandro* (1726); and Michel de Montaigne (many editions of his essays published in the sixteenth century and later).

Works, where I had found fault with Lord Goer's styling Johnson 'poor man' twice in a recommendatory letter[10] ... *[page torn out here]* ... 'He was a great favourite of mine.' 'And of mine too' replied His Lordship, 'for I think him a sensible, worthy, well-informed man.' This was a great deal for Lord Ilchester to say, who never lightly or indiscriminately praises – nor ever but with sincerity. I read Montaigne and to bed.

1 August Monday: rose at seven. My dear children as usual. Studies till two in the afternoon; Lady Harriot practised and played charmingly – a sweet finger and, to say the truth, a sweet lady: lively without affectation or levity; sensible and accomplished without pedantry; with ease and good humour in her countenance, and as fine a bloom as ever adorned eighteen in her cheek. At night there was a ball – six couple: Lady Ilchester and Mr Davis; Lady Harriot and her Uncle O'Brien; Mrs Charles Strangways and Lord Stavordale; Lady Charlotte, Louisa and two Miss Haines. Lady Susan O'Brien and I conversed together and looked at the dances. I then went to my room and wrote my journal – so concludes this week's diary 'In health of body and peace of mind'[11] – *Dieu merci* – Ann Agnes Porter, August 1st, 1796.

13 August I mentioned to Lord and Lady Ilchester my wish of visiting Yarmouth next October. Lord Ilchester said he would be much obliged to me if I would suit my journey to the time of his sending Lord Stavordale to Town, that he might go with me – he should wish him to be some days under Mr Griffith's[12] care before he went to school, and would like that gentleman to carry him to his new seminary and point out his proper form. I consented to this scheme, and should be happy to be useful to my dear friend Lord Stavordale.

14 August At church some time before service began. I thought of my departed friends, and each of them past in succession through my memory – my Reverend father; my tender mother; my dear brother; the charming Lady Ilchester, and many more all pressed upon my heart. I was not afterwards the less devout, at least I hope so.

15 August Monday: drank tea at Mr Jenkins' – my dear children both with me. We returned by moon light, which was delightful – the rest of the family was at Lord Paulet's.[13]

---

[10] J. B. de Molière, *Le malade imaginaire* (numerous editions of this play, 1670s on). Many collected editions of the works of Samuel Johnson were published in the 1780s and later.

[11] Alexander Pope, *Ode on Solitude*, line 11.

[12] Name partly erased.

[13] This was probably Castle Hill House at Buckland Newton, Dorset.

16 August Tuesday: the day as usual. At night I read over my journal touching my departed friends – wrote in *this*.

17 August Wednesday: the day as usual. Mr and Mrs Jenkins dined with us; Lady Sheffield and Mr Sheffield drank tea. Mr Sheffield seems to me a man of great observation – I make no doubt he sees into characters he is conversant with. In the evening I read good old Montaigne; studied Italian; wrote my journal and to bed at ten.

18 August Thursday: my dear Mrs Moore – Miss Lloyd that was – paid me a visit in her way to Weymouth. She was with her husband, and both of them seemed quite happy. I shewed them the house and gardens of Melbury, which they admired very much. The day as usual, at night I read *Adriano*[14] and Montaigne.

19 August Friday: Lady Charlotte Whynfield (late Digby)[15] dined at Melbury, as did Sir John and Lady Sheffield, Mr Sheffield, Mr Whynfield and *[gap]*. I hope her husband has more merit than beauty, else *tant pis pour Milady*. We drank tea in the pleasure-ground. Our studies as usual – N.B. a letter from dear Lady Mary Talbot to promise a visit here in two weeks time.

20 August Saturday: the day as usual – pretty Miss Syndercombe, Lady Harriot's friend has ... *[page torn out here]* ... characters not bad in essentials – deplored the baseness of the person these letters concerned and had to write to a lawyer, my brother-in-law, and Mrs Peniston. I must comfort myself in the reflection that whatever inconveniency may occur, it will be unmerited from that unhappy person.

28 August Lord and Lady Ilchester went to London with dear Lord Stavordale, who is to be a week under Mr Griffith's tuition and then sent to school. At church much more composed in mind than I was last Sunday. Real misfortunes make us exert our *strength* – little vexations we yield to, but it is wrong.

29 August We drank tea at Lady Sheffield's.[16]

2 September We spent the day at the amiable Mrs Strangways'.[17] By her desire we set out early and got there to breakfast – my dear pupils had a happy day, and I a most pleasant one – one of the prettiest young women that can be, with her agreeable husband and four cherubs,

---

[14] James Hurdis, *Adriano or the First of June: A Poem* (1790).

[15] Lady Charlotte Wingfield.

[16] Pencil note in another hand: 'Her house near Melbury, Woolcombe, now pulled down'.

[17] Pencil note in another hand: 'Maiden Newton'.

make a delightful spectacle – this sweet woman, now only six and twenty, has been married these ten years, and makes an admirable mistress of a family, which I mean to include every tender part.

3 September My dear Lady Mary Talbot, her husband and child arrived safe at Melbury. It was an affecting scene: a pleasure chastised by tears – at least mingled with them. Her dutiful and affectionate heart paid the tribute due to her excellent mother's memory – in time we became composed and enjoyed the pleasure of being with each other. Her child is a fine creature, about a year old. Another will soon follow – I hope a *son*.

4 September A happy day with my dear Lady Mary. Her child is a fine little rosy girl, full of life and spirit. 'My dear Po' said Lady Mary 'what shall I do with my baby? For *mother and child* are both' ...[18] At church – a nice evening. We spent several days most agreeably.

9 September Friday: Lord and Lady Ilchester returned: a good account of dear Lord Stavordale. Mr Griffith[19] is to visit him once in the month, which will be both a pleasure and advantage to the dear boy.

10 September Drank tea at Mr Jenkins'.[20] Returned with Lord Ilchester and Mr Talbot in an open carriage – was seized with cold.

11 September In bed all day – had a good deal of fever. Kept my bed five days – suffered much from fever, pain and weakness. Bad nights, bad days, but endeavoured to keep myself as quiet as I could. Recollected what Rousseau says: 'La prière d'un malade, c'est la patience'. Lady Mary visited me every day, so did Lady Harriot. My dear little Louisa never failed bringing me a nosegay every day of mignionette. I had Mr Mellier, their surgeon, to attend me, and every possible care was taken – it pleased God to restore me to health.

17 September I sat up all day. My dear Lady Mary returned with her husband to Wales – they took with them Lady Harriot.

18 September Lord and Lady Ilchester, with the three children, went to Abbotsbury. I preferred staying a few days here, and then to prosecute my journey. Lady Ilchester told me all the beds were pulled down in Burlington Street. Rather in trouble where I should lie the first night I reached London – it would be too late and hazardous to go to Hadley; Mrs Williams was in Wiltshire, her husband also from home, so I could not go there. Mrs Macqueen was in Bedfordshire, so I could not with

---

[18] Sic.

[19] Crossed out.

[20] Pencil note: 'Lower Melbury'.

propriety go to the Doctor's. Mr and Mrs Moser have no spare bed, so I cannot go there. Dear Mrs Pinnock is in lodgings where they lock up at ten every night, so I could not go there. Mrs Welsh at Kensington. Resolved at last to stop at Sarum at good Mrs Peniston's till I heard that Mrs Williams was returned, or till I should hear from my brother-in-law.

19 September Monday: treated myself with reading a play of Shakespeare in the new grand edition. My eyes almost dazzled with the whiteness of the paper and the beauty of the type. Had a visit from Mr Jenkins – shewed him Shakespeare and some of the prints – he was much pleased with them. Mrs Jenkins was at Weymouth. Mr Jenkins had been at the Review – six thousand fine men reviewed by Her Majesty – a grand sight. Mr Jenkins after the Review was in company at night – one toasted the Prince of Wales, another said 'With all my heart, and may he never want a kind father!' Another toast was 'A good heart to ourselves, with a better to our enemies'.

20 September Rose at eight; said my prayers; read in my Italian Bible. After breakfast another of Shakespeare's plays – recollected an elegant stanza or two in *The Correspondents*:

> O! Master of the female heart,
> To whom its every string is known,
> What rapt'rous joy must thou impart
> To her who once possest thy own.
>
> Ye virgins pluck the freshest bays,
> Ye matrons deck his honour'd bier,
> Ye mothers teach your sons his praise,
> Ye widows drop the silent tear.

In the evening I read the elegant little work this is taken from. Had a kind letter from Lord Ilchester, and another friendly visit from Mr Jenkins – I grow stronger and better every day.

21 September Wednesday: the morning as usual. Wrote to Fanny and Mrs Williams. Sent and ordered a post chaise to take me to morrow at eight o'clock to Dorchester. At night I wrote to dear little Lady Louisa, had an obliging note from Lady Ilchester to enquire after my health – answered it. Supt on gruel at eight, and then wrote my journal thus far. Hope to return and resume it, if it please God, in health and spirits – Ann Agnes Porter, Melbury House, September 21st, 1796.

[4 November] Returned home to Melbury House. Shall endeavour to recollect my travels: I spent a few days with Mrs Peniston at Sarum, had agreeable company in two emigrant priests Monsieur Marest *et*

Monsieur Boisvy. Had a letter from Mr Thomas Williams, desiring me to make his brother and sister's house my home adding that he had ordered every thing comfortable for my reception – wrote him a letter of thanks, but said I would defer my visit till his brother and sister were returned. A letter at the same time from my brother, advising me not to venture to Barnet in the evening, but to lay at *such* a place which he recommended in London.

24 September Reached London about four in the afternoon, having travelled all night. Went to bed directly and slept *fourteen* hours. The next day, Sunday, went to Dr Macqueen's. Spent the day with him – we talked over past events, remembered our Yarmouth friends and had a charming day. When he went out to visit a patient he left me *Massillon* as I was too much fatigued to go to church. I read a sermon of this French preacher's on the Last Judgement – a most excellent one.[21] The Doctor returned to tea, which I made for him. He shewed me his lady's *oratoire* – said if only seven persons were admitted to heaven, she would be one of them. He said he was as happy, he believed, as most people – there must always be some deficiency. He saw me to my lodging.

26 September Monday: I did all my country friends' commissions for them.

27 September Tuesday: I went to the bank and bought some stock. Had to wait some time for my agent. Heard two clerks abusing the late Lord Mansfield – the one said he was, like all the rest of the nobility, absolutely good for nothing; the other replied he must except Lord Exeter, who was so good a man that an attorney would not reside within twenty miles round him.

28 September Wednesday: went to Hadley. Happy with my dear brother and sister – spent ten days with them delightfully. We worked and chatted in the morning; walked after dinner; musick and cards after tea ... *[page torn out here].*

[October] ... coach stopt. I soon afterwards found my self in my dear Mrs Upcher's arms. She ordered me some refreshment, and saw me put to bed, where I slept above twelve hours.

9 October Sunday: called upon dear Mrs Ramey, went to chapel with my friends.

10 October The day with Mrs Upcher at home: the old extraordinary discourse – wonderful delusion!

---

[21] J. B. de Massillon, *Sermons* (*c.* 1750).

11 October Called upon my relation Miss Church.

12 October At Mrs Ramey's. A nice party at whist – supper and all chearful.

13 October On wanting to seal a letter, found that I had lost from my watch a seal with my dear father's arms, and another trinket given me by Lady Elizabeth. Wrote to my sister and my dear pupils.

14 October Mr Upcher made me a present of two very handsome seals, which I shall always value greatly.

15 October A party at Mrs Upcher's – cards, tea and supper. My dear Mrs Ramey looked exceedingly well – she has an agreeable companion in Miss Dade, a very elegant[22] young woman.

16 October Sunday: at chapel – Mr Dade preached.

17 October Monday: spent the day at Mrs Joseph Ramey's – cards and musick made out the evening.

18 October Spent the day at Miss Church's – she was lively and agreeable; her good mother wonderfully well for her age – near ninety. She played cards, chatted, and ate a hearty supper.

19 October At Mrs Ramey's. We were all very happy – when I took leave of her I felt a pang at my heart – she kist me affectionately, and said she hoped my next visit would be to her.

20 October Thursday: I left Yarmouth. My dear Mrs Upcher and self much affected – she looked through the window at me while I continued in sight. Upon looking back I saw her dear face as fixed there – *parting* is a bad affair. Arrived at Norwich, at my cousin Amyot's. A pleasant family: a sensible husband, ingenious son, and pretty little daughter. She herself would be a charming woman were there not a *dash* of *worldliness* in her, which shades her qualities. My dear cousin Charlotte[23] met me at her sister's.

21 October Friday: Mr Peele called on me, and I drank tea at his house in the afternoon.

22 October At Mrs Dunham's. Went also to see a French lady's pictures – *herself* the most interesting of all: beauty elegance and sensibility adorned her lovely person – she and her husband lost an estate of £4000 per annum. She draws portraits and he lets a chaise.

23 October Sunday: at Mrs Amyot's. In the afternoon her youngest sister, Miss Anne Garritt, a charming young woman, and myself took

---

[22] 'Fine' crossed out.
[23] Garritt.

our places to London. Travelled all night – reached it safe the next day about noon. I saw my cousin to her friend's house and then repaired to Mrs Williams, whom I found with her family quite well.

25 October Tuesday: a card party at Mrs Williams'. Two tables – I was in great spirits and enjoyed the evening very much. A Miss D-s seemed to envy me a little for engrossing a good deal of the gentlemen's attention. She, pretty and insipid, was but little noticed – myself, plain, but chatty and tolerably agreeable in conversation had in fact all the beaux present about me. Her old uncle was in the number and the most polite of all.

26 October Wednesday: Mr Griffiths called upon me to invite me to tea. I went and spent the evening very agreeably – his wife is a very pretty brunette. She told me she had been married fourteen years; she complained of nervous disorders and seemed a great valetudinarian. We played whist – they kept me to supper, and when Mr Williams' servant came they sent him back as Mr Griffiths said he would take care of me home. He rallied a little on the subject of the Melbury ladies' curiosity to discover whether he was a married man or not, and his own resolution not to satisfy it. To that his wife said 'But Lord Ilchester must know as you wrote letters to me frequently'. 'Did not you observe' returned he 'that your letters came to you all directed under a cover to our friend *[name illegible]*?' 'That really looked' replied Mrs Griffiths 'as if you wished to conceal your marriage – what could be your inducement?' He said no more on the subject and our game at whist went on, after which a very nice little supper. At twelve o'clock a coach was at the door and Mr Griffiths saw me to Mr Williams'.

27 October Thursday: at Dr and Mrs Macqueen's – an agreeable evening.

28 October Friday: expected my dear Fanny, but was disappointed.

29 October Saturday: at Drury Lane: the exquisite Siddons in the *Grecian Daughter* – she was great indeed. The *Scotch Ghost* was the entertainment.[24]

30 October Sunday: in the evening set out for Sarum.

31 October Monday: arrived at dear Mrs Peniston.

1 November Tuesday: a party at Mrs Peniston's. She told me some particulars of her family – her great-grandfather was a Sir John Davis.

---

[24] The plays performed at Drury Lane on this night were *The Grecian Daughter*, by Arthur Murphy, and *The Scotch Ghost, or Little Fanny's Love*, a ballet by Giacomo Gentili.

2 November Wednesay: Monsieur Panyer, chaplain to the *nuns* at Amesbury, dined at Mrs Peniston's. A Mr Edgeworth, confessor to the late King of France, had been to visit Monsieur Panyer, and gave him the following affecting particulars, which he repeated to me, with tears.[25] He had been dismissed by the King when every other comfort was taken from him – and no mass allowed to be celebrated. He remained in retirement and disguise for some time – only the King knowing of his retreat – when at last after some months he received an order from the Convention to attend their summons. When he appeared at their tribunal he perceived about ten or twelve in close consultation who had the air of self-condemned criminals. He was asked if his name was Edgeworth? Upon answering 'It was' they told him they had given Louis Capet permission to see him and might then depart with the Deputy who was going to carry his *arrête* of death for the next day. A *fiacre*[26] was in waiting, which carried them to the prison. During the way the Deputy wept and deplored his own unhappy fate in being the fated messenger of death to the best of kings. When they reached the prison the Deputy went to the King alone to announce the fatal sentence. Mr Edgeworth looked round him with terror and dismay: the monsters he beheld looked like demons from Hell, ready to execute all evil with greediness. In a few minutes the messenger returned and told him to go up to the prison. When he saw his royal, but unfortunate, master he lost all command of himself and, embracing the King's knees, he exclaimed: 'O! Sire, I ought to comfort you, but alas I have none for myself'. The King raised and embraced him. 'I am accustomed to calamity' he said, 'and prepared for the worst that can befall me, but to see a faithful subject is too, *too* much.' He then leaned his head upon Mr Edgeworth's breast and burst into tears. In a few minutes he recovered his composure, and said his most ardent desire was to have mass performed the next morning, that he might have the comfort to leave the world with decency and composure by the confession of his faith and a communion with his God. Mr Edgeworth offered to procure him this consolation. He flew back to the Convention, and told them the *King* wished to hear mass before he died. They demurred upon this request and said it would not be convenient: there was no priest; there were no requisites; besides their number was insufficient then

---

[25] The Abbé Edgeworth's account of the death of the French king is included in Gaston de Beaucourt, *Captivité et derniers moments de Louis XVI: récits originaux et documents officiels* (Paris, 1892), ii.

[26] A hackney coach or cab.

present to form a Convention. Mr Edgeworth replied that he summoned
them in the King's name to call a Convention and to give an answer
to his request. This was done, and they all repeated it would be
inconvenient as there was no *priest*. Mr Edgeworth then said he himself
was a priest, and would undertake the office – a reluctant consent was
at last given, and Mr Edgeworth returned to the King, who expressed
the utmost satisfaction on finding his request granted. 'Six long weeks'
he said, since he had been with-held from the altar – 'but I shall now'
said he 'depart this life with decorum and with peace.' 'God' he added
'is my comforter, my enemies cannot take his peace from me.' Just
then a soldier, or rather goaler, entered and said 'Louis Capet the
Convention have given your wife and family permission to take leave
of you'. Such a scene then followed as surpassed the powers of description. Mr Edgeworth did not attempt it, but leant his head on the table
and wept. The same guard came and told the royal mourners they
must part immediately. The King was quite overcome for some time
and repeatedly said 'Ah! Quel malheur d'être tant aimé – bénissez-les,
mon Dieu – bénissez-les à jamais.' He then wiped his tears and recovered
his serenity. Mr Edgeworth no more saw him either depressed or
agitated; he was all calmness and fortitude; he read his last will to Mr
Edgeworth twice over – his voice never faultered; he laid down on his
palliasse and slept most profoundly for six hours; he rose at eight and
went through the service of the mass with the utmost alacrity and
satisfaction. 'I die innocent' he said 'my just judge and heavenly father
will make me happy.' At ten a jailer entered abruptly: 'I understand
you and' said the King 'I come'. 'Will you, my friend, accompany me?'
he said to Edgeworth. 'O Sire, I am ready to die with you.' The King
went out with his hat in his hand but, perceiving all those without side
of the apartment had their hats on, he put his own on, and past them
with an air of firmness and dignity. At the door a fiacre was ready, with
a messenger from the Convention, who was stepping in first when the
King stopt him and said: 'Que je passe le prévenir, moi.' This messenger
was seating himself on the King's side in the fiacre, but the King placed
Mr Edgeworth, saying 'C'est lui qui est ma partie'. They were two hours
in arriving – the King read in his prayer book alternately with Mr
Edgeworth in a firm voice. When they reached the place and they
offered to tie his hands he resisted and said 'C'est trop', but on Mr
Edgeworth's reminding him how acceptable the humiliation would be
in the eyes of God, and cited[27] his Saviour's example, he held both his

---

[27] Sic.

hands out and suffered them to be tied. When on the scaffold the trumpets and drums sounded according to their orders. The King bowed as desiring leave to speak; every instrument ceased – all was silence and attention; the King said: 'I die innocent – I forgive my enemies and pray God to avert his vengeance for my blood, and to bless my people'. He took two turns on the scaffold and then prepared himself for death. Mr Edgeworth was kneeling by him and, in the excess of feeling, had lost all recollection till he was roused by the words *'The head of a traitor'* and, looking up, saw his sovereign's head streaming over him in the monster's hand. He instinctively fled and got safe to England, where he is known for his talents and admired for his fidelity. When he told his master that the clergy had been received and sheltered in England: 'Ah, la genereuse nation!' said the King 'la genereuse nation!' This narrative caused many a tear to flow – I never was more affected by another's distress. Monsieur Panyer spent the day with us, and invited us to see the convent at Amesbury.

3 November Thursday: Monsieur Boisvy read me an hour in Bossuet, and Monsieur Marêt gave me the pope's *Oration of Louis XVI* to read.[28] I did not like it, it was bigotted and, drawing a parallel between the French king and Mary Stewart, said they both died martyrs to their faith by the hands of *heathens*. I thought the English nation merited a softer appellation. When Monsieur Marest asked my opinion of the piece I said 'Il écrit en pape'. 'C'est vrai' me repondit-il – 'il écrit en pape, et en père de tous les *fidèles*'. An agreeable evening, but left them at nine of the clock and travelled all night. Reached Melbury about eight in the morning, went directly to bed, slept some hours. When I awaked, heard that the family were returned from Abbotsbury. Dined with Lord and Lady Ilchester and my dear pupils – both grown and looked *charmingly*. My own apartment and my own books appeared delightful.

7 November A very polite letter from both my French priests in return to my compliments. They with Monsieur Panyer were as agreeable men as I ever knew – all of them insinuating to a degree. Very different, yet all pleasing: Boisvy was pensive and profound; Monsieur Marest was gay and sweet-tempered, extremely handsome and full of vivacity; Monsieur Panyer was benevolent and courteous, with a flow of words that seemed in his *narrative* to be as much the effusions of humanity

---

[28] Bishop Jacques Bénigne Bossuet (1627–1704) (numerous works, especially sermons, published, 1680s and later). Pius VI was pope from 1775 to 1799.

as power of eloquence – they were all interesting. Monsieur Boisvy's morals were severely pure – he said all novels were destructive to virtue, and that when a youth *Télémaque* had done him more injury than he could bear to reflect upon.[29] They all of them seemed good and pious men, and I hope will yet have the joy to return to their country and friends. Mr Edgeworth received a letter of thanks from Louis XVIII, written by his own hand. N.B. his plan of a telegraph was much approved of by the Duke of York.

13 November My dear Lady Mary Talbot was safely delivered of her second daughter.[30]

21 November Dear Lord Stavordale came home for the holidays.

12. Letter from Agnes Porter, [Melbury], to Lady Mary Talbot, [Penrice Castle], 2 December 1796

I congratulate you, my dear Lady Mary, on the birth of your daughter, and wish she may prove a blessing to her parents and an ornament to society. I thank God for your happy recovery, and with the compliments of the season I wish you every felicity and enjoyment of life.

Your father has had the gout, but not near so bad as it was last year – he is now almost well again. Your sister are both in perfect health, yet Louisa is very thin, which sometimes gains her the name of 'little *hatchet*-face beauty'. Lady Charlotte is tall, stout and fair. They are both dear, good girls on the whole, and so entirely free from all personal vanity as to suppose any civility paid to their exterior mere mockery and badinage. Their understanding is now so much improved that I can fix them to subjects of morality, or pure reasoning, for half an hour at a time. Charlotte will sometimes exclaim 'Po, that is not at all entertaining', but in a few minutes she will lend an attentive ear. As to the dear Louisa, she is all diligence whatever be the subject in question. It will always be hers 'with dignity to stoop, with caution rise'. I believe I am making a half rhyme on the occasion – but no matter, you will comprehend *it* and *me*.

I hope you will not think of going out for a *fortnight* to come. The weather here is extremely sharp, and I cannot suppose it milder with you. Be cautious, my dearest love – *hâtez-vous lentement*, and consider your precious health. The mother of a family should be of consequence

---

[29] This probably refers to François Salignac de la Mothe Fénelon's book, *Les avantures de Télémaque, fils d'Ulysse* (1699).

[30] Jane Harriot Talbot, born 13 November 1796.

in her own eyes – self-preservation becomes one of her chief duties. But I need not *preach* to you, for I am persuaded that your good heart will always dictate what is right, and your good sense accomplish it.

Give a kiss to your pretty elves for me, take good care of *their mama*, and tell her I am her affectionate and sincere A. Agnes Porter.

Journal, 1796

8 December My dear friend Mrs Upcher lost her worthy husband. He died, after a three days' illness, from cold. This melancholy news was sent me by Miss Dade and Dr Macqueen.

13 December I wrote a line to my poor afflicted friend. Very low myself – much affected at the loss of so good a man.

20 December I wrote to Mrs Ramey.

27 December An answer from her. Mrs Upcher composed and resigned.

1797

In February 1797 an old friend, Elizabeth Upcher of Great Yarmouth, whose husband and son had recently died, asked Agnes to live with her. At the end of March Agnes told Lord Ilchester that she wished to leave his family, and gave six months' notice. From early April until mid June Agnes was, as usual, in London with her pupils. In June she returned to Melbury, and probably stayed there until her notice expired at the end of September. By the end of December she was in Yarmouth.

Journal, 1797

6 January Lady Elizabeth and Mr Talbot, with Lady Harriot, returned safe from Wales.

11 January A letter from my dear Mrs Upcher.

15 January I wrote her a long one. Lady Harriot Acland paid me a visit: I mentioned my brother to her – hope it may prove useful.

16 January I finished my journal up to this day, January 16th, 1797 – Ann Agnes Porter.

29 January Sunday: my dear Mrs Upcher lost her son Ramey Upcher, of the small-pox. I ruminated upon this melancholy event, thought it not at all improbable that my friend might wish to have me live with her – I knew myself to be her favourite female friend, and she was by circumstances now left almost destitute of society, her remaining children being too young as yet to be her companions.

30 January At night pursued the same train of thinking – found my present situation very different to what it had been ... *[part of next page torn out]* ... patroness or my esteemed benefactor, but now I should think myself at full liberty to consider myself chiefly, for various reasons.

February In [this month] I had an offer from my dear Mrs Upcher to live with her as her sister and friend as long as she lives ... *[part of next page torn out]* ... a tender, obliging and agreeable friend, if I may so express myself to myself. In her, a kind and liberal benefactress. After some consideration, as my time was in my patrimony, I thought it best to write my sentiments to her[1] with candour and precision. There is a species of false delicacy which is injurious to one's self, and unjust towards a friend – I detest it. A letter from Dr Macqueen – he is entirely of my opinion.

20 March Lady H[arriot] told me it was not intended that I should have a *parlour* in Town this year – this little circumstance determined my mind and fixed my conduct. I revolved the whole affair, and considered what I would say on the subject.

28 March Had a conversation with Lord Ilchester on the subject of my leaving his family – I told him my own particular affairs would require my giving up the honour of my charge in his lordship's family. I proposed six months as notice, asked him if he thought *that* a proper one? He was indeed deeply affected – seemed both surprized and shocked. I made no reflection on any person nor circumstance; said it was probable I might live with a friend, but if I was disappointed and returned to the same *line* of *education*, I should trouble his lordship for a recommendation. I then thanked him for *thirteen* years' protection, and *several* years of happiness. The *thanks*, he said, were *due to me* – he took me by the hand and said I had *knock'd him up*, he could not say a word then on the subject, but if it was for my happiness he must acquiesce. At night I reflected on this conversation, was satisfied in my own mind, as I had not said a single word more than I had resolved to do. I had not been induced by any little *female resentments* to hazard or compromise the tranquillity of a family I respected, though I looked upon myself as the victim of circumstances, but I thought I should withdraw with a degree even of dignity. I considered that the three charming little girls whom I had received from their dear mother's hand were now grown up, the youngest near nineteen; I had to the utmost of my power compleated their education, and had tried to supply to them a mother's love. The two eldest were married, the third to be presented this spring. Towards them I had performed the part assigned me. The two dear younger ones are so far advanced in their education as to give more pleasure than trouble to whoever succeeds me in that very important charge. In the afternoon Lady Ilchester invited me to tea, and expressed what she was pleased to term her *sorrow* at my intended departure.

---

[1] Mrs Upcher.

1 April Dear Mrs Strangways paid me a little visit. I mentioned my intention to her – she heard me with tears in her eyes, but said she could not blame me; assured me of her warm endeavours to assist in procuring me a situation. I hinted to her my hopes of being with a friend.

3 April We set off on our journey to London – arrived on the 5th. Found a letter from my dear Mrs Upcher – all settled to my utmost wishes.

6 April Took my place in the stage for next day to go to Hadley, but on my return heard that my dear sister was removed to Knightsbridge – rejoiced at the vicinity.

7 April At my dear brother and sister's – a joyful reception and most happy day.

8 April Still at Knightsbridge with my dear friends, who approve and rejoice at my going to Norfolk. I wrote to Mrs Upcher and told her I accepted of her generous proposition with pleasure and gratitude.

10 April I waited on Lady Harriot Acland. It was a respect due to her to inform her of my change – she had already heard it mentioned in terms of regret by Lady Ilchester. Staid at home all the rest of the week.

15 April My dear Fanny and Mr Richards drank tea with me.

16 April Easter Day – at St James'. Poor old Dr Parker preached – the prayer should have run thus: 'That the words which we have *not heard* may …' Staid [for] the communion – was greatly pleased to see a number of devout communicants – the world is not yet so bad as misanthropists repute it. At my return from church a *rencontre* with P—.[2] In the evening I wrote my journal, reflected on the goodness of Providence: when I left Mrs Ramey in 1782 a home was provided for me to repair instantly to. When I left Swindon I had also a dwelling in readiness for me – there, from January 1784 till now, 1797, my tent has been pitched. I had trusted to its being permanently fixed, but as it is otherwise what a happiness for me to have a friend and home to turn to. My dear Mrs Upcher's affection, friendship and society, with an hundred pounds annually as long as she lives. These are the liberal terms offered me by my true friend. Long may she enjoy the power of being *liberal*! 'Tis a glorious attribute to *give* – Ann Agnes Porter – April 16th 1797.

17 April To-day, a twelvemonth since, my dear Lady Elizabeth married Mr Talbot – she gave me a cast[3] in her carriage to Dr Macqueen,

---

[2] Sic. I have been unable to identify P—.

[3] A lift.

desired me to take her up at my return home. Past a happy evening with Dr and Mrs Macqueen – he the same warm friend as ever, she civil and chatty. Both, indeed, very kind. A Norfolk friend of theirs being present prevented my entering into particular conversation, but the evening past off well notwithstanding. This gentleman their acquaintance was quite a stranger to me. In my way back called upon dear Lady Elizabeth at her cousin Lady Porchester's, who most kindly invited me to see her. Her charming mother Lady Harriot Acland was there also. I spent a nice half hour in their company. Lady Elizabeth brought me home and told me to command her carriage at any time: I asked her to take or send me tomorrow to my sister's. It was a delight to me to see the two charming cousins so happy in the married state – long, long may they continue so!

18 April Our studies in the morning. My dear pupils go on extremely well with their various masters, and at intervals we read history and other improving books. At half past three my dear Lady Elizabeth carried me to my sister's, where I dined and spent the day in a most pleasing manner. A Mr Proctor, an American loyalist, was of our party – an agreeable man. After tea my Fanny sung several sweet songs accompanied by her guitar. It was delightful – her voice would please in a stranger, but from a *sister* each tone sunk into the heart. There was no coach to be had at night, it being Easter Tuesday, so Mr Richards and his friend conducted me home to Burlington Street – a starlight night and their agreeable conversation made the way *short*.

19 April Our studies from eight in the morning till three in the afternoon. After dinner called upon Mr and Mrs Griffith – both out. As I past St Martin's the bell was ringing for prayers. Went in, joined a small congregation of about six people – something remarkably solemn in the service, and devout in the appearance of the assembly. On Sunday a croud of people go from habit; here it appeared an express homage to the deity, unmixed with any other ideas – I never spent half an hour more to my satisfaction. Drank tea with Mr and Mrs Williams. Returned early – letters from Mrs Upcher, Mr Field and Miss Garritt. The former expresses her satisfaction in the thoughts of having me as her inseparable companion – may God Almighty preserve her life and bless our union! Supt on water gruel, then settled my money accounts and wrote my journal. To bed by ten.

20 April Mrs Church drank tea with me. My sister and her pretty little niece Miss Morice called upon me – an agreeable evening.

21 April Good Mrs Pinnock spent the day with me – she was chearful as usual and admired my pretty pupils much. They all paid her great attention – Lord Stavordale drank with her; Lady Charlotte played and sang, and Lady Louisa repeated verses. I saw the dear old lady safe in a hackney coach by nine at night.

22 April   Our studies as usual. I then went to my sister's, where I drank tea and supt. Had a party at whist with Mr Richards, Mr Proctor and Mr Isaac Williams. Two of the gentlemen conducted me home by eleven o'clock. In the morning I had had half an hour with Mrs Goddard – she was surrounded by *six* daughters – a pretty sight. She received me very amiably and invited me to visit her often.

23 April   Sunday: rose at eight, went to church – St Martin's. A most excellent discourse: text 'Be not faithless, but believing'. Called in my way from church at Dr Macqueen's – he from home, but saw his lady. Heard that dear Mrs Upcher was to be there to-day – offered a tea visit. Going thence I saw a poor tar with but one leg: he was talking very chearfully to some people around him and said 'Thank God I can laugh, though I have but one leg, as well as those who have *two*'. To promote his hilarity I gave him sixpence and had a thousand blessings in return. I soon after observed a very different object: a gentleman in mourning was walking *alone* just before me, apparently under great distress of mind. He sighed, he lifted up a hand in token of inward perturbation, and I overheard him say 'Is it indeed possible? Heavens can it be!' Poor gentleman, how I pitied him. While I was thus engaged Mr William Digby overtook me and, rallying me on the seriousness of my air, joined me to Burlington Street. Dined at three with Lord and Lady Ilchester and my dear Lady Harriot – a very agreeable hour. They then went to Richmond. At six Lady Elizabeth Talbot carried me to Dr Macqueen's. In our way one of the horses fell down on his side – some persons gathered round the carriage, others assisted the servants in their endeavours to raise the poor animal. Lady Elizabeth and self much frightened. Upon each door being opened we both jumpt out at the same instant. In about five minutes as all was declared quite safe, we had the courage to resume our seats. Dr and Mrs Macqueen met me in the passage – they had a glimpse of Lady Elizabeth and thought her very handsome. My dear Mrs Upcher received me with a cordial embrace. N.B. as well as can possibly be expected. A Captain Macdonel and a Mr Colombine were of our party – the latter a very amiable young man. As next Wednesday is Mrs Macqueen's rout[4] day, I asked Mrs Upcher to pay a quiet visit with me at my sister's, which she promised. Mrs Macqueen had invited an hundred persons, but did not

---

[4] A large assembly or evening party.

expect above seventy. My friend revolted at the idea of seventy persons in company in her present situation. The carriage took me home again. As the Doctor conducted me to it, he said he wished much for an hour or two's conversation with me, but as I have no parlour this year I do not know how to receive him. N.B. our conversation must be by letter.

24 April Our studies as usual. In the evening my dear pupils went to a ball at the Countess of Warwick's. They both looked beautiful – only in the garden of paradise can there be fairer flowers. My dear sister drank tea with me – she sang, she played and chatted – we were quite happy together. When alone I read half an hour in Tasso – admired these lines upon Tancred's entering the enchanted wood: 'Un non so che, confuso, instilla al core, di pietà, di spavento, di dolore [a certain something, confused, instils into the heart, pity, despair, sadness]'. How can the *Spectator* or any other, Boileau[5] I believe, talk of the 'tinsel *clinquant*'[6] of Tasso – *il est pourtant charmant.* To bed by ten.

25 April Rose at seven; breakfasted at eight, after which my brother called upon me for a party to Greenwich. Went in the stage – a delightful morning and a light heart – the company consisted of my dear Fanny, her husband, Mr Proctor and myself. I enjoyed it amazingly – we visited the Hospital with admiration; we traversed the walks with alacrity and pleasure; we nunched[7] at Greenwich; dined at Knightsbridge; played drafts after dinner, and had on the whole a most charming day: 'Où peut on être mieux qu'au sein de sa famille?'

26 April Our studies as usual. After dinner I carried my dear Mrs Upcher to Knightsbridge – it was a real pleasure to me to introduce my best friends to each other. Mrs Upcher was charmed with my sister, but who would not admire talents, agreeable manners and easy conversation – all of which she possesses, and much more. As for my brother, his modest merits seek the shade, but the more he is known, the better he is liked. He saw my friend and I to our respective homes after a most pleasant evening.

27 April Lady Harriot Strangways, my third dear pupil, was presented at Court. Lady Ilchester, Lady Elizabeth Talbot, and Miss Lily Digby (the Colonel's daughter) accompanied her, They were all most elegantly dressed and looked extremely well indeed. Lady Harriot's dress was a crape white petticoat trimmed with silver flowers, a wreath of pearls in

---

[5] 'Voltaire' crossed out. The reference is to the essayist and critic Nicolas Boileau (1636–1711).

[6] *Clinquant* is the French word for tinsel. Here it refers to a showy style of writing.

[7] Lunched.

her hair, large pearl earrings, and a laylock[8] gown; Lady Elizabeth's
was simple: elegant white and silver. Lady Ilchester, a pale yellow gown
with a white petticoat, large emerald earrings set in diamond; a diamond
feather in her hair of remarkable lustre. They had all feathers. Miss
Digby's dress was laylock and white with bugles[9] – she looked perfectly
delicate and neat, but was eclipsed by the blooming Harriot, the elegant
Eliza and the tall and (in full dress) the graceful-looking Lady Ilchester.
Lord Ilchester was in purple and silver. N.B. he told his lady that had
he not married her three years ago, he must have fallen in love with
her now. Lady Harriot Acland and Lady Mary Talbot came to see them
dressed. Lady Mary and Mr Talbot dined with my pupils and me. All
the men-servants were gone to St James's – Lord Stavordale put the
first dish on the table and helped to wait at dinner. We were very merry
on the occasion – my dear sister was with us, and went with me to drink
tea at Mrs Williams'. Mr Richards joined us. Lady Harriot Strangways
made me a present of a very pretty pair of bracelets – cornelians set
in gold and intermixed with golden links – very pretty indeed.

28 April At our studies – very good and dear children. I walked in
the evening to Mrs Welsh's, who seemed much pleased to see me;
returned home early, settled some accounts; wrote my journal, and to
bed by ten.

29 April Went with Mr Richards to drink tea with Mr and Mrs Griffith.
Introduced my brother to their acquaintance. Spent a most happy
evening – Mrs Griffith seems a very obliging, mild-tempered woman.
Mr Griffith and my brother liked each other much – both sensible and
good. We chatted and played a hand at whist – Mr Richards conducted
me home about eleven at night.

30 April Sunday: to church at St James', and heard the Bishop of
London, Dr Porteus.[10] A charming discourse – the text: 'My house shall
be called the house of prayer for all men'. A most energetick preacher.
N.B. a woman in the pew said he preached *pretty* enough for a *bishop*.
I dined at three with Lord and Lady Ilchester. Lady Mary, her Mr
Talbot, Lady Harriot Strangways, Miss Digby, my two pupils and myself
made up the party. Lord Stavordale went yesterday to school. My dear
Lady Mary looked lovely – her little girls were with her *[a couple of
words cut out here]* children. I drank tea with Mr and Mrs Moser – they

---

[8] Lilac.
[9] Beads.
[10] Beilby Porteus (1731–1809), *Sermons* (1772 and later). Porteus was Bishop of
London from 1787 to 1809.

were rather formal for the first half hour, but gradually unbent during the evening. I think I lost much of their regard because I did not admire Mr Moser's works, and had too much sincerity to conceal my opinion when they put the question close to me. As a man he is valuable – how poor is all comparative praise!

1 May Monday: the day with my pupils. Drank tea with them, which gave them great pleasure.

2 May At Dr Macqueen's. My dear Mrs Upcher kind as usual, and happy to see me. Mrs Macqueen was polite as usual, the Doctor very melancholy – said he had so little pleasure in existence that it was only confidence that God would make him happy in another state that could make this life tolerable. He was ready, he said, to cry out with Hamlet 'How flat, dull etc. is life!'[11] We reasoned with him, we rallied him, but he was too low to be the better for either. When I returned home I revolved his situation and present disposition with surprize, as he seems possessed of every thing that can make life valuable: fine abilities; a most handsome person; a young and rich wife; a beautiful child – healthy and promising to a high degree. There must be something wrong at present either in his health or mind. Shall entreat him to examine into the cause – to probe – to *cure*.

3 May Wednesday: our various masters and studies. In the afternoon made happy by my brother and sister's drinking tea with me. A most happy evening in their company.

4 May I drank tea with Mrs Churchyard: a worthy sensible woman, Lady Harriot Acland's housekeeper. In my return home was overtaken by Mr Richards, who saw me to the door. It was but eight of the clock, so persuaded him to sit an hour with me and eat a bit of bread and cheese. We conversed till ten – he told me he had visited the Bishop of London and also his friend Mr Harper. With the former he was quite delighted: as excellent a man as a preacher – a father of his whole household and a benefactor of the poor. N.B. my brother has some promises from this respectable prelate, which I hope will be accomplished in time – *il faut espérer*. I saw him down-stairs and was called then into the drawing room to see the masks before they set out for their entertainment. Lady Ilchester was in a black domino [a loose cloak worn at masquerades with a small mask over part of the face]; Lady Harriot Strangways and Miss Digby were country girls and looked very

---

[11] William Shakespeare, *Hamlet*, I, ii, 129: 'How weary, stale, flat, and unprofitable, Seem to me all the uses of this world.'

prettily. Mr Neave, Lady Ilchester's brother-in-law, was to be their conductor. Lord Ilchester asked me to sit with them half an hour ... *[part of page cut out].*

5 May Friday: our studies. After dinner Colonel Digby sat an hour with us. Took my two pupils to my sister's on invitation. She entertained them with a dance and musick till the gentlemen came up from dinner to tea: a Mr Harper, a popular preacher, but a noisy unagreeable companion; a French émigré – pensive – gentle and polite, with Mr Proctor and my brother made up our party. My sister acquainted me with a circumstance that surprized me that ... *[last part of this page and most of next cut out].*

6 May Saturday: our studies – nice children. I drank tea with Mr and Mrs Griffith – we played at three-hand cribbage. At ten he saw me home. I told him of my intended change – he was sorry for my pupils' sake to ... *[gap]* . I read a sermon and my Bible; wrote a letter and my journal.

8 May Monday: at Dr Macqueen's. My dear Mrs Upcher all kindness to me as usual. Dr Macqueen walked home with me and acquainted me with the cause of his melancholy – thank God it is of a nature to be removed by contingent circumstances, which I hope in the course of time will happen.

9 May Tuesday: in the morning I went to the bank and purchased a little stock. Returned to dinner – my brother and sister drank tea with me. After tea we went to the Historic Gallery and were much entertained – several pictures by Opie gave us particular pleasure – his Boadicea is a most majestic figure; his Maid of Orléans appears with a fine enthusiasm, while the beauteous Queen Mary previous to her execution is in female softness and patient, suffering a charming contrast to the two Amazonian *heroines*.[12] We had a delightful evening, but the bad weather forced us to part early. I returned home before nine; wrote my journal; practised some musick, and to bed by ten.

10 May Wednesday: N.B. in only one week's time I cannot recollect what happened on that day, but no misfortune thank ...,[13] else would my memory be more retentive.

11 May Thursday: Mrs Churchyard drank tea with me.

12 May Friday: I dined at my brother's. After an agreeable dinner my dear Fanny proposed a trip to the theatre *à l'impromptu*. No sooner said than done – away we went, Mr Richards, Mr Proctor my sister and

---

[12] Robert Bowyer's Historic Gallery was in Pall Mall.
[13] Sic.

I. We went to the pit at Drury Lane – had convenient room and a charming place for seeing and hearing. The play *As You Like It* – liked it much: Mrs Jordan in Rosalind was a most engaging creature; Palmer was Orlando. The entertainments were *The Scots Ghost* and *The Critick*.[14] In a side box perceived my dear pupils with Lady Ilchester – lost a scene in the play by looking at them. Fanny and Mr Richards dropt me in their way home – I supt with Lady Ilchester, Lady Harriot Strangways and Colonel Digby.

13 May Saturday: in the morning our studies – all well. Carried my brother and sister to Mr Griffith's to tea – a most pleasing evening. In some little political dissertation Mr Griffith called me to order. 'I wish' said my sister 'Sir, that some friend of yours would keep her in order for life, for really these single women get so independent that poor married ones have but a poor chance with them. Have you no friend you can recommend her to?' 'He must be a man of ten thousand to whom I would give the authority of a husband over Miss Porter' he politely replied. Good man! I believe he has indeed a great esteem for me, and I am much obliged to him. My brother and sister could not stay, but I remained at supper with them. We played at cribbage – I beat Mrs Griffith; her husband beat me after supper. Upon something that past in conversation he said 'I told it you twelve *years* ago'. 'I thought' said Mrs Griffith 'you had only known Mrs Porter since last year?' 'Do not remind me of that' said he 'for surely we are old acquaintances.' I understood the delicate compliment and was grateful for it, Mrs Griffith seems sweet-tempered, but odd and nervous to a great degree – at times almost to imbecility.

14 May Sunday: at St James's church. A so-so sermon, from I know not who – he had a bad habit of jumping up whenever he wanted to give any extraordinary emphasis, and as he was a little man it appeared the more ludicrous. He wandered from his text – I could scarcely command my attention. Drank tea at my sister's in company with Mr and Mrs Williams.

15 May Monday: I spent the afternoon with dear Mrs Pinnock very happily. She told me all her affairs, dear woman, and it is a great pleasure to try and assist her.

16 May Tuesday: carried my pupils to the Historic Gallery in company

---

[14] The plays performed at Drury Lane on this night were *As You Like It* by William Shakespeare; *The Scotch Ghost* by Arthur Murphy; and *The Critick*, a burlesque by R. B. Sheridan. The actors included Dora Jordan (1761–1816), the mistress of William, Duke of Clarence (later King William IV); and John Palmer (*c.* 1742–98).

with my brother and sister. The optical illusion of Loutherberg's painting of the Fire of London had a very fine effect – the young ladies
were much pleased with the collection of pictures.[15] My brother and
sister drank tea with me – after they were gone I wrote two letters and
my journal. Could not recollect how I had spent the Wednesday, but
now it occurs to me that I dined with Lady Mary and Mr Talbot at
Brumpton – how could I forget such an *event*? She paid me a little visit
to-day – her children are almost well.

17 May Wednesday: at Dr Macqueen's. My dear Mrs Upcher not well
– had caught cold in Westminster Abbey, but she is in good hands to
get soon well again. The Doctor was much pleased at having tickets
for the Princess's marriage.[16] He was obliged to go out in his professional character and his lady was dressing for a rout – in the mean-time
I had a confidential discourse with my dear Mrs Upcher.

18 May Thursday: I dined at Knightsbridge: a charming day – Mr
and Mrs Griffith drank tea and supt with us. While the gentlemen were
engaged together, my sister and I had some conversation with Mrs
Griffith. Her nervous habits have hurt her mind much – she told us
that she loved her *first* husband dearly – she had not, she said, forgotten
him, nor never should. She loved to wear *black*, she said, better than
any other colour. When much pleased with Mr Griffith, she told us,
she called him Thomas. Mr Griffith's name is Joseph – N.B. to ask her
one day what was her first husband's name. Indeed, poor lady her mind
seems a good deal weakened and deranged. I do not now wonder at
Mr Griffith's not talking about his wife or marriage etc. Poor gentleman!
It is no society for him after the labours of his profession, but he seems
of so happy a disposition as to be reconciled to all events. They carried
me home in their way. Memorandum: quite a rake – near twelve o'clock.

19 May Friday: at Mr Moser's. She was chatty, he melancholy. N.B.
one Mr Reeves wrote an address 'To the Common Sense of the People
of England', for which he was prosecuted by the House of Commons.
Mr Moser wrote a vindication of this address.[17] He said the reviewers
had torn him and Mr Reeves in pieces – he aimed at a smile on saying
this, but soon relapsed into his melancholy air – *quelle manie!* How

---

[15] The Alsatian artist Philippe Jacques de Loutherbourg (1740–1812) painted five
large scenes from English history for the Historic Gallery.
[16] Princess Charlotte (the Princess Royal), eldest daughter of George III, married
Frederick, the Hereditary Prince (later King) of Würtemburg, 18 May 1797.
[17] Joseph Moser's *Examination* of the pamphlet entitled *Thoughts on the English
Government* by J. Reeves was published in London in 1796.

happy and estimable he was in his own private character before he wished for *fame* – 'Who strive to grasp her with a touch destroy'.[18] In my return through Parliament Street I stopt at Dr Macqueen's – my dear Mrs Upcher better; Mrs Macqueen at a rout. I played a sober game at whist, and the Doctor saw me home at eleven o'clock. Much discourse in our way concerning my future destination.

20 May Saturday: at home all day. A visit from my dear Lady Mary Talbot in the morning. I gave her my reasons for my intended change – she heard me with a kind interest in my concerns. Her little babes are almost well. My brother and sister drank tea with me – a charming evening.

21 May Sunday – at St James's. A very young gentleman preached – a good discourse and an eloquent one – the text: 'He went away sorrowful'.[19] Lady Elizabeth Talbot called upon me in her carriage and sent me on in it to Little Chelsea. I dined and drank tea with Mr and Mrs Williams – their two children are fine little creatures. She calls the boy, who is remarkably small, 'Prince Pippin', and the tiny thing is the prettiest little creature that can be.[20] I returned in a long coach called the *sociable*[21] – on the whole it did not deserve the name, as several of the company were, like Stephen in the play, rather proud and melancholy in standing *on their gentility*, but one or two more good-humoured chatted till we came opposite St James's Street, where we stopt and I walked home. Kissed my dear children; wrote my journal, and to bed by ten.

22 May Monday: good Mrs Pinnock dined and drank tea with me. Lord Ilchester came in and enquired after her health, which pleased ... *[part of page torn out]* ... 'bless'd with plain reason and with sober sense'.[22]

23 May Tuesday: our studies in the morning. My dear Lady Mary called on me and made me a present of a very fine cotton gown – very pretty, but rather too gay – however I shall wear it with pleasure. Sat with my pupils at dinner, but only ate a potatoe and bread, as I was engaged to dinner at Lady Elizabeth Talbot's for half past five. Went at the appointed hour, but was told she dined out at Brompton – she had forgotten her engagement with me ... *[part of page torn out]* ... returned home *sans diner* – rested myself, then walked to Mrs Griffith's – found her in the *embarras* of a little household employment, but as she

---

[18] Edward Young, *Love of Fame, the Universal Passion*, satire iv, line 252.
[19] *St Matthew*, xix, 21.
[20] Pippin the Short (*c.* 715–68), King of the Franks, was the father of Charlemagne.
[21] An open cart, with rows of seats facing each other.
[22] Alexander Pope, *Epitaph on Mrs Corbet*, line 2.

pressed me to stay [to] tea with much good nature, I staid. Mr Griffith came to tea – we chatted an hour and then he walked with me home – He is a very worthy, sensible man. Mem. not to go there again on a Tuesday, as it is a *busy day* with Mrs Griffith. When I returned I read Tasso; wrote my journal and three notes; said my prayers and went to bed by ten. Lady Harriot rose to-day at two in the afternoon.

24 May Wednesday: Lady Elizabeth came in the morning and, tapping at the door, said she was ashamed to come in and would not see me till I promised *heartily* to forgive her forgetfulness the day before. I made quite light of it seeing her so vexed – she kissed me and exclaimed 'Dear creature!' with a tone of so much affection as would have atoned for a much greater omission. She asked me every day – but every day – to come. I was engaged through the week till Sunday next. My sister drank tea with me, but ... *[part of page torn out]* ... a sort of worldly cleverness but it requires [cha]racter, and his may be, when known, esteemed a very worthy one

26 May Friday: my pupils gave a ball. They behaved very prettily and attentive to their visitors. Some of the young ladies' parents came with them – there was the Duchess of Gordon; Lord and Lady Paulet and the Countess of Leicester; Sir Lionel and Lady Damer; Sir Richard and Lady Neave; Sir John and Lady Caul; Mr and Mrs Mills; Mr and Mrs Holbeck, and many others. My dear sister was invited, and I thought looked very *[some words cut out]* – it did our hearts good to hear the Duchess speak broad Scots. *Ah! c'est un drôle de corps – que celle là.* A grand supper and then the dance was resumed. Sir George Paul came in late, very polite in his attention to me – he was always so – a man of *true* consequence would have been so in any station. The two Mr Talbots and their fair ladies were present, as also Mr and Mrs Neave, Mrs Newbolt, Lady Sheffield, Mr and Mrs Sheffield etc. My sister and I staid to the last and went to bed at two in the morning.

27 May Saturday: my children sound asleep at ten – desired they might not be waked. Walked out with my sister as far as the end of the park in her way home. Returned alone – expected Mrs Welsh, but was disappointed and went early to bed to make amends for the last night's deficiency. About ten she came – received her in bed. Poor lady, she talked a great deal to me about her private affairs – she is not happy: she is going to live at Putney and made me promise to go and see her. If I can, I will. Slept nine hours without waking.

28 May Sunday: at St James's church. A good discourse by Sir Thomas Broughton – some people said he was near eighty, but he spoke in an audible and nervous manner. After church I wrote my journal thus far.

29 May Monday: at Dr Macqueen's – an agreeable evening. Lady Ilchester took me up in her return from Lord Auckland's. Mr Colombine handed me to the carriage. So discomposed at Lady Ilchester's taking the back seat that I forgot to bid Mr Colombine good night – extremely vexed at the omission. Lady Ilchester and Lady Harriot laughed at my uneasiness, but I could not pardon myself.

30 May Tuesday: wrote a line in atonement to Mr Colombine. Went with Mrs Williams to see an acquaintance of hers – did not return till very late; lay at her house.

31 May Wednesday: at Mr Griffith's. A happy evening – again late – he gave Lord Stavordale and me tickets for St Paul's.

1 June Thursday: at St Paul's. The anniversary of the charity children – the grandest spectacle I ever saw: seven thousand children supported by voluntary benevolence – a glorious sight, and affecting beyond description. Dined at my sister's.

2 June Friday: at home all day to repose myself.

3 June Saturday: at home all day. In the evening called upon Mrs Williams and Mr Griffith to take leave; the latter not at home. A visit from my dear Lady Elizabeth Talbot and Lady Harriot Strangways – charming creatures. A gentleman, in praising Lady Elizabeth, said she had more *soul* than any woman he knew.

4 June Whitsunday: rose at seven and breakfasted at eight. Went then to dear old Mrs Pinnock: to Lincoln's Inn chapel with her, then carried her to an hôtel, where we dined and spent some confidential and serene hours. Drank tea with Mrs Moser – when I was very young I mistook her for a friend; find now that she was merely an acquaintance. He was from home, though my farewell visit – I pardon him for the reason and discovery I allude to.

5 June Monday: at home.

6 June Tuesday: at Dr Macqueen's – a tender farewell of Mrs Upcher who goes next Thursday. N.B. Mr Colombine there – thanked me for my note, said it removed some upleasant sensations.

7 June Wednesday: my dear brother and sister drank tea with me.

8 June Thursday: at home. Read Tasso and Thompson's *Seasons* half an hour – delightful poet![23]

---

[23] James Thomson (1700–48). His poem *The Seasons* was first published in the 1720s.

9 June Friday: at Mr Griffith's with my dear Fanny and Mr Richards – a nice party.

10 June Saturday – my dear brother and Fanny drank tea and supt with me. Our farewell was pensive, but we hope soon to meet again.

11 June Sunday: arrived at Sarum.

13 June Tuesday: paid Mr Chubb and took a copy of B—y's letter to Mr Smith.

18 June Sunday: my birth-day – with dear Mrs Peniston I had spent a week.

19 June Monday: reached Melbury House.

26 June The family all returned safe.

2 July Sunday: finished this journal, A. Porter.

13. Letter from Agnes Porter, Melbury, to Lady Mary Talbot, [Penrice Castle], 9 July 1797

My Dear Lady Mary,

I know it always gives you pleasure to hear that your friends here are well; and though several pens may at the same time be employed in saying the same thing, you will accuse none of them whatever of tautology.

Your father looks remarkably well indeed, and has a good appetite and very good spirits. Lady Harriot has quite recovered from her London *veillées*, and never looked better in her life. I will not say that *here* 'she wastes her sweetness on the desert air',[24] yet I could wish she had a few more to admire her. She is quite amiable in every respect, and deserves the utmost partiality that a fond parent could experience. She will, I hope, in due time have the blessing of an affectionate husband, which our sex, both married and single, are apt to name, or esteem tacitly, as the *sumum bonum* [*summum bonum*: supreme good] of wordly happiness. Lady Charlotte is in perfect health and grows very tall, stout and handsome. Lady Louisa has not been quite well, but she is now getting better. I believe she caught cold on the *baking* day – she has been a little feverish, but bids now fair to be quite well in a day or two. We go to Redlynch next Wednesday, and change of air will, I am persuaded, set her quite up again. She looks much as you did from

---

[24] From Thomas Gray, *Elegy Written in a Country Churchyard*, verse 14: 'Full many a flower is born to blush unseen, And waste its sweetness on the desert air.'

twelve to fourteen. I wish she may make as stout a woman – *il faut l'espérer.*

Lord Stavordale returns for the holidays on the 21st. It will give pleasure to all the house to see him return, for he is a universal favourite. Your aunt Strangways was here yesterday – she and all her little ones are well – little Susan is quite recovered. Lady Porchester and her little daughter go on well. I hear that your aunt Lady Susan and Mr O'Brien are in good health.

Two friends of mine, Dr and Mrs McQueen, were at the Princess Royal's marriage: they told me she looked very well satisfied with her lot and that the Prince of Wertemberg, though extremely fat, had a good-humoured, sensible countenance. The Royal Family was affected at the solemnity, even to tears, but that is natural. I have seen the *friends cry* at a marriage before now, have not *you?*

I hope your dear little girls are in perfect health, and that you and Mr Talbot are the same, enjoying the sweets of your garden in more seasonable weather than we can boast of. For three weeks past we have had incessant torrents of rain, and *hollow* blasts of wind, more like the rough November than the usually gentle month of July.

Lady Ilchester is quite well, and the little William has recovered his health entirely. He is so sweet a child that at *last* he makes *even me* love him, *et c'est beaucoup dire.* If you have Swift's works, would you be so kind as [to] copy out for me the poem he wrote on his own death, which he supposes to be canvassed over a pool of quadrille[25] – I should be much obliged to you for it at your leisure.

I paid Mrs Churchyard the half guinea for the pomade. Be so good as [to] add it to our discount, and let me know what remains – I believe only a trifle. Farewell, my ever dear Lady Mary. Yours sincerely, A. A. Porter.

14. Letter from Agnes Porter, Great Yarmouth, to Lady Mary Talbot, Penrice Castle, 20 December [1797]

[The first part of this letter is lost] .... always to church both morning and afternoon, and when any of the gentlemen or merchants are at any time tempted to swear a little, instead of saying 'confound it!' they meekly say 'consider it!' I have remarked this many times. We have some drole originals among them. There is an old rich lawyer of

---

[25] Quadrille is a card-game. The poem referred to is Jonathan Swift's *Verses on the Death of Dr Swift* (1739).

ninety-eight who, whenever he hears a woman's name mentioned, cries
'Cat, cat, cat!' with many sighs of aversion. You will divine he is a
bachelor. We have an old lady who is quite extravagant and luxurious
with regard to herself, yet refuses a grown-up daughter a little pocket-
money, or the least independence in any [thing]. But the bulk of the
town is good. They live to an uncommon age – ninety is very frequent
with them, and a person only seventy must not pretend to any little
indulgencies on account of their time of life. They very often say 'a
young woman of fifty' and 'a girl of six-and-thirty'. I was in company
the other day with six maiden ladies of above sixty. They were much
scandalized at my calling myself *Mrs*, which they took as a reproof to
themselves, and diverted me much by the epithets of 'Miss Babby' and
'Miss Tabby', 'Miss Jenny' and 'Miss Juggy'. Do laugh a little, and mind
the hair which will much oblige my dear Lady Mary's ever affectionate
Ann Agnes Porter.

1798

Agnes probably spent most of 1798 in Great Yarmouth, though she spent a month in the early summer staying with her sister and brother-in-law in Knightsbridge. Agnes was still living with Mrs Upcher in mid October.

15. Letter from Agnes Porter, Great Yarmouth, to Lady Harriot Fox Strangways, 16 January 1798

My Dear Lady Harriot,

I thank you for your most agreeable letter, and desire you will give your sweet sister Mary a kiss for the beautiful lock of hair which it conveyed to me. It occurred to me one day that to have a nice long lock of hair from each of my darling pupils would be a great accession to my felicity. Lady Mary is the first that has granted this wish of my heart, and I know your goodness will induce you to follow her kind example. I shall plait them myself, and then get them fastened in a little golden machine at each end, but I will not quit the sight of the person who does it, lest he should put any deception on me, or commit any mistake. Only think how pretty it will be: *brown, flaxen, auburn.*

Thank my dear Lord Stavordale for his nice letter, but pray tell him that *annecdote* has two *n*'s, and that in the word *piece* the *i* is before the *e*. Remember me to my very dear Lady Louisa; my love to Lady Mary and her stout little loves; and my respectful compliments to your father and Lady Ilchester. It gives me pleasure indeed to hear you have such good accounts from the dear Charlotte who will, I doubt not, repay the pains of absence by the pleasure of her return, and the satisfaction of seeing her in every respect improved.[1] I know her fine abilities will be stimulated to excellence by the various talents of her young companions, while her temper will be smoothed and regulated by the *gentle* discipline

---

[1] Later note: 'Lady Charlotte was at Mrs Devis's school in London'. This was a fashionable girls' school in Queen Square, Bloomsbury.

of a school. She will be an ornament to her own charming family, and a blessing to you all. As to the sweet Louisa, she is almost as perfect as human nature will admit of – what errors she is liable to she has been freely informed of by Po who, indeed, used no ceremony with any one of you in a point so essential to your happiness.

The young women here are beginning to emerge from the ignorance that universally prevailed some years back, yet the sciences and fine arts are by no means in an advanced state. A lady the other night wore miniature bracelets that resembled satyrs more than any thing human, and I was invited to hear a Miss play on the harpsichord, whose mama observed she was now apt to *run away* a *little,* her finger was so rapid, and indeed she not only ran away herself, but was fit to make others do so too, and I would have given a good deal to indulge this propensity. But they are good people: they are happy in domestick life, and the finest gentleman in the town is apparently the most devout. This makes going to church, and a regular life in other respects, quite the fashion. Eleven at night is their latest hour, and their card assemblies begin at six. The women are uncommonly pretty; the men are very plain in general. We have the Forty-Ninth Regiment at present quartered here – a Major St Vincent is one of their commanding officers. They make a fine appearance every day before our windows, being drawn up on the quay.

As Mr Charles Digby did not want a professed governess for his daughter, I am in hopes that Miss Ann Garritt will do very well. She is, I believe, a worthy young woman, very sensible and sweet-tempered.

There is a hint in your letter which gives me extreme gratification – I mean one relative to yourself. You will recollect it – accept my thanks for it. I have lately read *Clara du Plessis or The Emigrants* – it is a beautiful novel. Mrs Robinson's *Pupil of Nature* has been much read: the first volume pleased me much, but the rest I thought bizarre.[2] They say here that Pratt never was in Wales, but I hope it is a mistaken assertion.

God bless you, my dearest Lady Harriot. Believe me ever yours, Ann Agnes Porter.

---

[2] August La Fontaine, *Clara Duplesses and Clairant: or The History of a French Emigrant* (1798); and Mary Robinson, *Walsingham, or The Pupil of Nature: A Domestic Story* (1797).

16. Letter from Agnes Porter, Great Yarmouth, to Lady Mary Talbot, [Penrice Castle], 23 February 1798

My Dearest Lady Mary,

I received your kind letter last night with a mixture of pleasure and pain. To find you are well, and to hear from you, must ever be pleasing; on the other hand to have it confirmed that I am not to see you nor my dearest Lady Harriot, nor the sweet Louisa, nor your dear father, for another long year (if then) sits heavy at my heart. Now that you do not go to London, I will go there on purpose to see my *sister* and *yours*. Dear Lady Charlotte will be glad to see *Po* when she is disappointed in all her other expectations, and I shall look at her with double love as the representative of *all* her family.

My last letter was to Lord Ilchester to request his permission to visit Lady Charlotte and to have her a day with me. I hope he will send me an answer with his own hand. My letter also alluded to a little business concerning the half-year remittance of his promised gift to me during my life of thirty pounds per annum. For these reasons I hope to hear from him.

I thank you for your lock of beautiful hair – it is among my choice treasures. Yourself, my Louisa and sweet Harry have favoured me in this particular, but Lady Elizabeth, Lady Harriot and Lady Charlotte have not yet obliged me. Is not our dear Louisa a most amiable girl? What can be more gentle than her temper, or more insinuating than her manners! Sweet love! I had hoped to see her and *all!* But what we cannot remedy must be supported.

You judged rightly, my dear Lady Mary, that it would have been a most interesting circumstance to me to have witnessed your happiness. Not a foot of your grounds, nor a snowdrop in your garden but would have been dear and lovely in my sight. How precious then to my heart would have been the sight of yourself and little ones! The teething late, I have aways heard reckoned a very favourable circumstance as, should two or three teeth appear at a time, the children are more able to bear it. Your darlings will not be behind hand either in mind or person – there is no fear of either. Your expressing so much concerning the blessings you enjoy gives me real satisfaction. I can build upon your happiness, for its *basis* is virtue and the love of duty. These are permanent foundations, which cannot be shaken – not even by 'the wreck of nature or the clash of worlds'.

I am at present re-perusing Blair's *Sermons* – I generally read one every morning before breakfast, and I hope it tends to strengthen and prepare my mind for the day, whatever various events it might produce.[3] In my opinion they comprehend a compleat system of morality and religion: with my Bible and them I think one need not wish for any other religious instruction. I take an hour also for reading French and Italian, as I would not like to lose either of these languages so far as I possess them.

I am very well, thank God. Mrs Upcher is excessively kind to me: I pass my time with tranquillity, and I hope I fill it up innocently, but I should not think it sufficiently useful if I did not find myself of some consequence to the comfort and happiness of two or three worthy persons – my dear old Mrs Pinnock, Mrs Garritt,[4] and a relation I have in Scotland I have the happiness to assist and be of real utility to *[word illegible]*. And Mrs Upcher is so good as to think that my living with her contributes to her comfort and satisfaction: 'Eternal blessings from the soul ascend, to him who made each being *want* a friend'.[5]

I will write to my dear Lady Louisa next time. Will you meanwhile give her and her nieces half a dozen kisses for me, and believe me ever my own dear Lady Mary's most affectionate Ann Agnes Porter.

You say not a word of our dear Eliza! I hope her health is good. We have had fine weather *here* till *now* – I hope it has been a favourable season with you. God bless you and yours!

17. Agnes Porter, [Great Yarmouth], to Lady Harriot Fox Strangways, [1798]

Many thanks to you, my ever dear Lady Harriot, for your charming letters, and in particular for the happy intelligence you sent me concerning your last little niece Christiana and her sweet mother. Thank heaven they are both doing so well – what a satisfaction it must have been to you to see your dear Mary surrounded by her beloved children! To see maternal affection beam in her lovely eye, with a kind look intervening to her *Ami*[6] and a warm welcome to all her native friends, must have been a delightful sight, even to a stranger. I can therefore both imagine and enjoy your feelings. But in telling me a deal about her, you say nothing of yourself. Do you suppose me, then, to be uninterested in your affairs, or am I left to divination concerning them? Give me but a small thread of intimation, and it will guide me through

---

[3] Hugh Blair (1718–1800), *Sermons* (1777 and later).
[4] This must be Miss Porter's cousin (Miss) Anne Garritt.
[5] S. J. Pratt, *Sympathy*, book ii, lines 239–40.
[6] Lady Mary often referred to her husband as *Mon Ami*.

a labyrinth of conjecture, but even the Highland seers must see some *slight forms* to be able to paint the rest.

I spent a month most agreeably at Knightsbridge. Having had permission from Lady Ilchester through you to call upon your sister, I did myself that pleasure, and had the gratification to find her in perfect health. She was much grown and looked extremely lovely. I hope you will see her this summer – when you do, give my tender love, and assure her it was not from any *deficiency* of affection that I did not visit her again.

You are good indeed to enquire after my friends. My brother and sister are very well – she has had an emigrant in her family for this half year who could not speak a word of English, the consequence of which is that Miss Dalton, Miss Lovedon and Miss Morrice speak French with all the ease and fluency of French women. They could read and understand it before, but this is the grand receipt for acquiring the oral part of it. This French lady is an officer's wife, who served in the Duke of York's regiment – I mean, the *officer* did – his name Valcour. I saw too at my sister's another family that greatly interested me. You have heard me mention Monsieur de Ville Neuve, Commandant de Boulogne during our residence there: his son is now with his lady and family at London, a brave officer; a fine gentleman who had received every advantage of education and married an *heiress*. I saw him and this charming lady full of gratitude towards my sister for a few civilities. I cannot express how much we were both affected at the decline of their prosperity. Another gentleman, Monsieur de Vevrotte, *ci-devant* president of the parliament at Dijon, was of our party also. I had nice practice in the French, and much pleasure from this gentleman's conversation, who had visited most countries in Europe and gathered information where-ever he went. He brought from Lapland a female Laplander with him, whom we have had the pleasure of seeing. She was very composed in her manners; had expressive eyes and a good-humoured countenance; her face was broad at top and pointed extremely towards the chin; her complection sallow; her eyes dark; and her hair beautifully soft and redundant.[7] She was one of the tallest women in her own country, but did not reach above my eyes. She spoke a little French, a little German, and a little English, or rather a mixture of all three. She told us she liked England best, for in her *contree* there was no house, no bread, and no chemise. The greatest difficulty she met with was to learn to sit upon a chair, as in her contree they sit

---

[7] Abundant, flowing.

upon *la* ground. She took a great liking to my sister, and told her at taking leave 'Me tonk you Mawdawm, me love you Mawdawm, and if Monsieur le Président goes away me live with you Mawdawm'. This speech was accompanied by the action of throwing her arms round Fanny's neck and kissing her affectionately. Monsieur de Vevrotte told us she would do the same by the Queen if she saw her and liked her. She has no idea of any inequality of ranks, and in her simple manner does no discredit to the native dignity of a rational being. She might be about four and twenty. In Lapland they are not reckoned grown-up till about that age, and never marry younger.

18. Agnes Porter, Great Yarmouth, to Lady Mary Talbot, Penrice Castle, 7 June 1798

How happy it makes me to hear of my ever dear Lady Mary's health and her family's welfare! I can see you (even at this distance) with the eye of my heart, performing the sweet *office* of a *mother* to your youngest darling, and looking down at her with ineffable tenderness. Now, perhaps, you turn to the eldest with a 'Come here, Mary, *laugh* this minute'. Then comes the dear little Jane, tottling up to mama and lisping out its pretty accents, while you smile around you with all a *mother's* pride and joy. 'This sure is bliss, if bliss on earth there be.'[8] It must undoubtedly be found in the exercise of the most sacred duties of life. These, I doubt not, my dearest love will always discharge in a noble manner. I have always known you from your infancy to cherish the strictest attention to duty, and to entertain the warmest attachment for all that had a natural or acquired right to your affections. With such a bias we can never greatly err. In regard to smaller points, you own good sense which discovers the weakness will also point out the remedy. You may say that *procrastination* is one of your *enemies* – we know it is not a foe to parley with, but to be resisted with vigour and resolution. However this may have affected you in your dealings with others, I see no cause of complaint, but on the contrary am much obliged to you for thinking so frequently of me. I think a few minutes of your useful and precious time a very great favour.

The *encrease* of the family at Melbury House was intimated to me by the dear Louisa.[9] Her health, I hope, will *soon now* be established – she is thirteen this month, sweet creature! It would have been delightful to

---

[8] Alexander Pope, *Eloisa to Abelard*, line 97.
[9] The birth of Lady Mary's half-brother, Giles Fox Strangways.

me to have tended her improvement up to womanhood, but my dear Lord Ilchester's manner altered so much to me that I was afraid I should in time become even an object of his aversion, so from *affection* 'I *tore* myself away'. I never could make my dear Lady Harriot comprehend my feelings or consequent reasonings upon this subject, as with a thousand amiable qualities there is a certain *facility* of nature which makes her adopt a little of any character she is with, unless it were morally evil. She yields to the stream and, I hope, will be the happier for so doing. But had either your turn of mind or Lady Elizabeth's belonged to her, I should not have been by circumstances compelled to remove. Both she and Lady Elizabeth are so kind as to let me hear from them at times. How rejoiced will the charming Charlotte be to see them all again! Dear creature! Nine months has she been separated from all she loves, but I trust it will in the event confirm her happiness by making her sensible that an agreeable home is the greatest blessing in the world.

Now for your query concerning the Laplander. She speaks a little of the French, German and English languages. She always converses in her *own* with her patron, but understands the others tolerably well. She is an interesting creature, all simplicity and candor. After looking around her with an air of sweetness and good nature upon a pretty numerous company, she threw her arms around my sister's neck and said 'Me still love you best Mawdawm'. The last time she was at Mrs Richards', Monsieur de Vevrotte brought her in a carriage in her Lapland dress. It was a robe of deerskin, with a scarlet cap, an Angola ruff, and a very curious belt. If I told you these particulars before, excuse the repetition.

I wish you could procure my Fanny another pupil. You cannot think what an accomplished girl Miss Dalton is likely to prove under her tuition – she speaks French fluently; she draws very prettily; plays well on the harpsichord; and is making a considerable progress on the harp and in Italian. She is mild and good, but not *naturally* very clever. You know I make a distinction between *accomplishments* and *abilities,* which I believe all students do not. My sister possesses both, and it rather vexes me to see all her genius and time employed with such small advantage to herself. One or two more pupils would turn the scale – could not you speak a good word for her upon *my* recommendation?

On the two-pound note there remains due to you eight shillings and sixpence. I can, when you acquaint me with the balance of our account, lay it out for you in any way you please in London. Let me know, and believe me *ever yours* while Ann Agnes Porter.

19. Agnes Porter, Great Yarmouth, to Lady Harriot Fox Strangways, 12 July 1798

My Dear Lady Harriot,

Though I *aimed* at answering your historical queries, and sent you two or three *others* in return, yet I still think myself in your debt for a most agreeable letter which obliged and pleased me at the same time. Receive my best acknowledgement and let us now pass (in spite of distance) *one* happy hour together. Are you well? Do you look rosy, do you go to bed when you go upstairs at night, and are you economical of *time, health* and *money?* 'Pretty little impertinent questions!' you will exclaim, yet pray answer them, and in retaliation ask me whatever you please.

So, my dear Lady Harriot, you betray your indifferent opinion of mankind by the question you put concerning Monsieur le Président and his Laplander. You ask in what capacity she lives with him? My sister made the same enquiry of himself. He replied very seriously that he was a man of honour, and as such could not wish to injure a poor innocent creature who placed entire confidence in him, and who had no friend in this part of the world but himself. That she was in the capacity of a servant: she made his linen; she took care of his apartments; and cooked his dinner for him; that as she was extremely faithful he had in his will left her a maintenance for life in case of his death; that were he only a man of gallantry he would have had a handsomer woman, but as a man of principle he looked upon this poor stranger as his child or ward – *sacred*. My sister told him that he would at any rate rob the poor creature of her happiness, as it was evident she adored him. He smiled and made answer that the Laplanders were a very cold, insensible generation, and their greatest passion seldom rose to more than what we Europeans stiled an inclination or a liking. He begged of her therefore to be quite easy concerning the Laplander's fate. She preferred him to every other person, he believed, but at the same time there was no fear of this preference doing any hurt either to her happiness or virtue. My sister says he ought to marry her – she (the Laplander) has no idea of inequality among mankind: all that she does for him is out of *kindness* not *servility* – her manners are perfectly easy and naturally sweet, as I told you before.

So much for the dear little Laplander, whom I shall never recollect but with interest and pleasure. I am going now to give you an annecdote of a very different nature, and though romantick, *too true*. A gentleman I know, in passing by a solitary cottage, overheard a discourse between a middle-aged woman and a young one. They were in their little garden, and so earnest in what they were talking about that this gentleman was unperceived by either. 'Do not, child, lend an ear to him' said the eldest 'They are all false. If a man swears he will *deceive* – if he *weeps* he will *betray you* – never listen to any of them, as you wish to shun misery'. Upon this, the gentleman went to them and, making a handsome present to the eldest, entreated of her to acquaint him why she entertained so bad an opinion of his sex. With a heavy sigh she informed him of her little melancholy history – when she was about eighteen she lost her parents, and had thoughts of serving in a neighbouring farm, when a young man who had courted her a few weeks offered to marry her. She said she had no objection to him, except that he seemed by his dialect to be above her, and owned that his friends would never consent to his marrying her were they to know it, but he loved her so much he would never forsake her. She loved him and they were married. After two years she proved with child, and he told her he had received letters from his friends, and hoped to reconcile them to his union with her, for which reason they should travel together to his country. They set out on *one* horse. He told her after they had travelled some hours that there was a wood to the right that would by passing through it shorten their journey. She had no objection to any thing he proposed, and entered the wood with him. Here, after some time, he told her that the friend he expected to make up matters between him and his family at home was to meet him in a particular part of the wood; that he would just go on a few yards, and desired she would sit down under a tree and rest herself till he returned. She did so, poor creature, but he was long in coming and, as the evening grew dark, she dared not quit the tree for fear of missing her husband. She remained where she was, half dead with fear, and there she past the night. The next day she filled the wood with her cries and fell into fainting fits. When she recovered, she found her path providentially to a village. She got people to search the wood for her husband, but no-one was to be found: the villain had rode off and abandoned her for ever. It was her poor child, a girl about eighteen or twenty, whom she was tutoring concerning *man*. The gentleman was much affected by her story, which on enquiry he found strictly true. I wish you may not find it tiresome at second hand – let me know your thoughts of it.

I send my dear Lady Louisa a very curious little shoe made, as appears by the work, in *fairy land*. I send her too my love, with thanks for her last letter, which I will answer at large some future opportunity. Pray read the account of the Laplander to her, and tell her Po says she ought to write the word *niece* with the *i* first, the same as in French.

I am, my dear Lady Harriot, your ever affectionate Ann Agnes Porter.

I forgot to tell you that I saw Siddons and Kemble in the play of *The Stranger*. I was at *Wives as they Were* etc., and to compleat all, Lord Ailesbury did my brother and sister the honour of calling on them, and presented us with *four tickets* to the *opera*. We went, and heard Banti in the serious opera of *Cinna*.[10] My sister enjoyed it, but after the first hour I found it powerfully soporifick in its effect upon myself. *Voyez un peu quelle stupidité.*

20. Agnes Porter, Great Yarmouth, [to Lady Mary Talbot], 14 August 1798

By this time I hope my dearest Lady Mary is safely arrived at her dear father's, to her own pleasure and the joy of her friends. O what a delight to see again each other's amiable and beloved countenance! To trace the improvements of time in your three sisters, and to see your own little darlings intermix with so many pretty *uncles and aunts*. I have a thousand thanks to present you and Mr Talbot for your goodness to my sister and her *Caro Sposo*.[11] They were enchanted with the beauties of your place, and most feelingly obliged by your goodness and condescension. They admired your children, and returned home with double pleasure to what they could have had in their excursion had they not seen Penrice Castle. I am in hopes every day of hearing again from Mrs Gumbleton – I hope in God that she and the dear old lady are safe.[12] Two worthy friends of mine, Mr and Mrs Simpson, were forced to flee from Dublin: they locked up their house and, with their only child, were glad to escape with their lives. They reached Conway in North Wales, and from thence they wrote to me. I had no house of my own to ask them to, but I hope the distresses of their unhappy country will soon subside and that it will please almighty God to preserve these kingdoms from our *common enemy*.

Lord Duncan is now at Yarmouth, where he is much beloved. The

---

[10] *The Stranger* by Benjamin Thompson was performed at Drury Lane in April 1798. The only performance of *Wives as they Were, and Maids as the Are* by Elizabeth Inchbald at this time was on 11 April at Covent Garden. Agnes probably saw *Cinna*, an opera by Francesco Bianchi junior, at the King's Opera House, Haymarket, on 17 April. The performers included Brigitta Banti (*c.* 1756–1806), the Italian soprano singer.

[11] Mr and Mrs Richards and Miss Morice were at Penrice from 30 July to 1 August.

[12] Lady Mary's aunt Catherine Gumbleton (*née* Grady) and her widowed mother Mary Grady of Cappercullen, Co. Limerick. There was serious unrest in Ireland in 1798, culminating in the rebellion led by Wolfe Tone in the summer and autumn.

sailors, in particular, idolize him. One of them the other day exclaimed: 'Blessings on Duncan's heart! He calls us sailors his *children*. He *han't* a bit of pride in him, and we could follow that brave heart of oak to the end of the world'. I shall have the pleasure of seeing him to night in the mayor's box at the play of the *Provoked Husband*.[13] The people here are much improved in their exterior within a few years. This extends also to the Corporation, who sometimes laugh at the ignorance of their predecessors, and the other evening I heard an alderman repeat with a good deal of humour an annecdote which he attributed to a Yarmouth mayor of about forty years back who, on looking at the *date* in the Town Hall, and observing *Anno Domini*, said it had in his mind been *Anne* long enough – he should move it to *Georgy Domini*. If this is not an annecdote common in several towns, I hope it will make you and Mr Talbot smile.

I am with much affection yours, Ann Agnes Porter.

21. Agnes Porter, Great Yarmouth, to Lady Harriot Fox Strangways, 14 October 1798

I suppose, my dear Lady Harriot, you have by this time received my few lines of thanks to the ever dear *sisterhood* for their nice present. I now offer them to you in the most affectionate manner for your kindness in thinking of me after so long an absence, yet in idea you must be often near me. I never pass a day without thinking of you all, nor begin one without remembering you in the *most sacred* hour I spend. I hope you are careful of your health, and not *careless* of your heart. Does the *bloom* of early hours paint your cheek? Does the vivacity of a mind at ease sparkle in your eye? Take a glance at your glass before you answer my *impertinent* queries.

As you are so good as to take an interest in the welfare of my friends, I shall now give you some account of them. My dear brother and sister are quite well – their little niece grows a charming girl, with the sweetest temper and warmest heart that can be. She proves very ingenious: at eight years old she reads French and English very prettily; writes well; knows a little Italian; plays remarkably well on the harpsichord; sings; works; and dances as light as a squirrel, and quite as *willingly*. My friend Dr Macqueen has lately got a daughter. Mrs Williams and her *three* children are well. Mr Williams the clergyman had a fourth girl last summer, to whom he asked me to be godmother. Mrs Pinnock has no

---

[13] A play by Colley Cibber.

other complaint but the age of eighty-one years to struggle with, possessing at so advanced an age good spirits, good appetite, and good humour.

I had the satisfaction this summer of seeing Lady Home – she spent six weeks in Yarmouth, and her son a fortnight. He is a remarkably handsome, pleasant young man – full of life and good nature. At first sight, he shook hands with me and hoped I had been well these *twenty years*. After this easy introduction, we were soon well acquainted, and he gave me an account of many persons in the *Land of Cakes*[14] that I rejoiced to hear were well. He told me also how happy his sister Lady Charlotte was in the married state, that her husband Mr Baillie was a charming man, and did so much credit to matrimony that it gave him a desire of following so good an example. This I believe he will very soon do by a marriage with Lady Elizabeth Montague, a daughter of the Duke of Buccleugh's. Lady Charlotte Baillie was delivered last week of a son, so this family is at present well and happy. My dear Mrs Upcher, with her son and daughter, are in perfect health. We visit a little, but our general amusements are of a domestic kind – we work sometimes, and walk out every day. A little music and a great deal of reading fill up the day. Among amusing books, I lately met with *Julia* by Helen Maria Williams, which pleased me much – it is written with the originality of genius.[15] The characters are well-drawn; the situations not exaggerated, yet extremely interesting.

When you write, will you be so good as tell me who *Lord St Helen* was,[16] and what lady it was that Earl of Yarmouth married, said to have a fortune of £100,000, with a sort of a foreign name.[17] I have lately perused Malone's *Shakespeare*.[18] His notes give an insight into the ancient manners that is very amusing. In King Charles I's time the theatre opened at three o'clock. The play began at four and the audience, to entertain themselves till the curtain drew up, would smoke a pipe or play at cards. They had no scenes – the actors never made

---

[14] Scotland.

[15] Helen Maria Williams, *Julia: A Novel* (1790).

[16] Agnes presumably means the diplomat Alleyne Fitzherbert (1753–1839), who was created Baron St Helens in 1791. His house and its contents had been destroyed in 1797, in a fire in which he had himself only narrowly escaped death.

[17] Pencil note: in another hand 'Mlle Fagniani'. She was the heiress Maria Fagniani (d. 1856), the adopted daughter of George Selwyn, a friend of the Fox Strangways family.

[18] Several editions by Edmund Malone of Shakespeare's plays were published, *c*. 1780 and later.

their exit till the drama was finished, but would at their supposed departure seat themselves very quietly in the face of the audience till their part again employed them. The charms of the poet, with now and then a curious annecdote, rewarded me for patiently going through many a tedious comment and tasteless annotation. But it is time to reward your patience by putting an end to this verbose, matter-of-fact epistle from, my dear Lady Harriot, your ever affectionate Ann Agnes Porter.

I will write to my dear Lady Louisa soon. If Lady Elizabeth or Lady Mary be gone, will you please forward my letters to them.

1799

Elizabeth Upcher died in March 1799. No letters or journal have survived from this year, but Agnes was at Penrice Castle with the family of her former pupil, Lady Mary Talbot, by June. Penrice was to be her home for the next six years. From time to time she stayed there with some of the children whilst their parents took the other children to visit friends and relatives elsewhere in Glamorgan, or in England.

1800

22. Agnes Porter, [Penrice Castle], to Lady Mary Talbot, Moreton, Dorset, 23 November [?1800]

My Dear Lady Mary,

I thank God your darlings continue all well, and as good children as ever were known. Miss Talbot is almost always with me, and that by her own choice which pleases me much. Her mind opens daily, which makes a little *intellectual* food both necessary and agreeable. She had observed that Henry Lucas was very stout, so she asked me if boys were stouter than girls. I told her that in general they were so. She immediately inferred that men were stouter than women, and then added 'Why did God make men stouter than women?' I told her one reason was to protect them and to make life more comfortable to them, for if men were not stronger than *we* were, that women would not have such nice houses, nor large ships to sail in, and many other conveniencies that men (being stronger) procured them. She was content with this reasoning, and then said: 'I think, Po, men are very kind to build our houses. What do women do for them?' I told her that women made the *inside* of the house pleasant, and always took care to be good-natured and agreeable in their conversation, to amuse their husbands and papas when they came home fatigued with business. 'So will I, Po. I won't be like *Catharine*.' This was a print of Catharine and Petruchio [from *The Taming of the Shrew*] which I had shewn her, I dare say *three weeks* before – so much for her memory and observation. Our French too goes on very well. I had told her that *beaucoup* was 'very much'. I then asked if she liked bonbons. '*Beaucoup*.' Pictures? '*Beaucoup*.' Papa and mama? 'O *très beaucoup*' said the little love. It must have been a *word monger* indeed that could at that moment have corrected her French.

Tina[1] is the greatest favourite that can be with all that see her, and

---

[1] Christiana Barbara Talbot.

as it never rains but it pours we have had quite an inundation of visitors for the last week. Mrs Collins and daughters, or as Mr King calls them the *Collinas* – indeed, at present there is as little difference between them as in a set of the fowls he alluded to,[2] but time and experience effect great changes. Then we had Mr Collins from Swansea with his daughters, Captain and Mrs King for two or three days, and four officers on Friday. Before they came in such a succession, Miss Talbot and I had called on poor Mrs Green in her little and first widowhood, and asked her to come one day next week to help and *chear* her a little. This we did, not forseeing the run of voluntary visitors that were to insue. The dear little Charlotte is alive and well. I pray God to bless you and them and their good father – amen! A.A.P.

Anna requests Mrs Sheers to give Mrs Longford a guinea for her mother, at Wincanton. Added to my last commission of a gown, I should like a travelling bonnet to suit the pelisse. *Je vous en rends mille grâces.*

---

[2] *Gallina* is Latin for chicken. The word is also used for guinea-fowl.

1801

23. Agnes Porter, [Margam], to Lady Mary Talbot, Llandaff Court, Glamorgan, 20 March 1801

My Dear Lady Mary,

Your darlings continue perfectly well, as I hope you will find them at your return to Margam. There has not been the least trifle the matter with any one of them and they are, as usual, good and happy children. The morning we breakfasted with Dr and Mrs Hunt was spent in high glee. The Doctor had a knee for each of the elders, and an egg between them, while Mrs Hunt secured little Tina. That darling creature has never eaten a bit of orange but what she saved the seeds for you without being reminded by anyone. Miss Talbot brought me her book when we returned from Mrs Hunt's and said very gravely '*Po*, you have not heard me read all this day'. You may be pretty sure that I indulged her. As for Miss Jane, she has a good deal of moderation in this respect, and a little literature goes at present a good way with her. She desired Mary to play with her, saying 'Who will you be Mary?' 'I will be mama.' I asked her what she must do to be like her mama. 'I do not know' said smiling little Jane. Mary then whispered 'Jane, you should *feed* your little child – you know what I mean Jane, *feed* like little Charlotte, you know, before mama went last to England. And, Jane, mama makes cloaths for poor little children.' I asked if they would like mama to *feed* any more dear little children. 'Yes', Jane answered, 'I should like mama to have five more girls.' 'No Jane my dear', whispered little sly Mary 'no more girls for, my dear, the next little girl is to be a boy.' I was much amused with this discourse, which I have given verbatim. Your dear Tina has been a nice child too, sucking her fingers by night excepted. She has slept very sound in the little bed close to yours, which I have slept in. Charlotte is well as possible and pays us frequent visits. Mr Quin goes this afternoon instead of tomorrow morning, but I did not think the difference material. We are to go as far as Cardiff.

God bless you, my dear Lady Mary. I beg my respectful compliments to Mr Talbot, and I am yours affectionately, Ann Agnes Porter.

24. Agnes Porter, Penrice Castle, to Lady Harriot Frampton, Moreton, Dorset, 25 August 1801

My Dear Lady Harriot,
I am greatly obliged to you for the charming description you gave me of my ever beloved Lady Charlotte and Louisa. Had you sent me as particular an account of Lady Harriot, my pleasure would have been compleat. On this point I am left to conjecture, but I flatter myself by the pleasant style of her letter that *all is well.* Lady Mary is going on as well as possible, and she seems very happy in her amiable aunt's society. She too is in perfect health, and desires me to inform you that Lady Frances Morton is now at High Clere, at least she thinks so, but at all rates her letters can be forwarded from thence.

I distributed your kisses among the little loves, remembering your distinction of the birth-day. They are all blooming and lovely as rose-buds, but as I think I sent you a minute account of all of them in my last, *pour cette fois ci, je vous fais grâce.*

I thank you for your researches relative to l'Abbé Saide. How would the gentle spirit of Petrarch revolt at having occasioned so much troublesome enquiry and disappointment to one of his Laura's kind! As for me, I am quite shocked at it, and absolutely resign all hopes, and give up all thoughts of Saide for ever. You, however, persist in desiring me to name a book: I should like *La Chassée* or *Florian* – in French, of course.

I believe I never mentioned a very curious book which I read at Mrs Ramey's, Robert Flemming in AD 1701.[1] By his calculation every pro-phetical year consists of twelve months of thirty days. He makes the seventy weeks or 490 days of Daniel to reach from the Edict of Artaxerxes Longimanus to Our Saviour's sufferings = 490 *prophetical* not *Julian* years. From the Donation of Pipin to Pope Paul I he dates the aera of the papal kindom, which he says will *totally* expire in AD 2000. The French king, he adds, took a sun for his emblem, and for his motto 'Nec pluribus impar',[2] but *before* the year 1794 he will be forced to

---

[1] Robert Fleming, *A Discourse on the Rise and Fall of Papacy* (1701).
[2] No unequal match for several (suns). This was the motto of Louis XIV.

acknowledge that in respect to neighbouring potentates he is even *singulis impar*.[3]

I add a list of my books, as you say you have forgotten them. I hope you will never *forget* my dear Lady Harriot's ever affectionate Ann Agnes Porter.

Shaftesbury's *Letters*; Elesmere's *Sermons*; Newton's *Discourses*; Digby's *Discourses*; Wollaston; Euclid; Saunderson's *Arithmetic*; Nettleton's *Essay*; Sterne's *Journey*; *Amyntor and Theodora*; Charlotte Smith's *Sonnets* and *Ethelinde*; *Henry and Frances*; *Werter*; *Interesting Memoirs*; *Julia Greville*; *Julia de Roubigné*; *Julia*; *Hermin of Una*; Riccoboni's *Works*; *Ophelia*; *Vicenza*; *Sarah M ...*; *Romance of the Forest*; *Ganganelle; l'Isle Inconnue*; *Essai sur le Beau*; *Père de la Rue*; *Journal de Madame de Genlis*; *Les Chevaliers des Cygnes*; *Les Mères Rivales*; *Monsieur Thomas*; *Le Hennade*; *Pastor Fido*; Metastasio; Tasso; Petrarc; *La Bibbia*; Garth's *Dispensary*; Young's *Fame*; Ossian; *Hudibras*; Gaudentio di Lucca; *Pleasures of Hope*; Roscoe's *Nurse*; *Farmer's Boy* (a beautiful poem).[4]

---

[3] No match for one (sun).

[4] The books listed here include: Anthony Ashley Cooper, Earl of Shaftesbury, *Letters* (1721); Sloane Elsmere, *Sermons on Several Important Subjects* (1767); John Newton, *Six Discourses as Intended for the Pulpit* (1760); books on geometry and algebra by Euclid and Nicholas Saunderson; Thomas Nettleton, *A Treatise on Virtue and Happiness* (1729); Laurence Sterne, *A Sentimental Journey* (1768); David Mallet, *Amyntor and Theodora: or The Hermit. A Poem* (1747); Charlotte Smith, *Ethelinde, or The Recluse of the Lake* (1789), and *Sonnets* (1784); Elizabeth Griffith, *A Series of Genuine Letters between Henry and Frances* (1757); Henry Mackenzie, *Julia de Roubigné* (1777); Helen Maria Williams, *Julia: A Novel* (1790); Professor Kramer, *Herman of Unna: A Series of Adventures in the Fifteenth Century* (1794); Sarah Fielding, *The History of Ophelia* (1763); Ann Radcliffe, *The Romance of the Forest* (1791); *Ganganelle* may refer to a work by Pope Clement XIV, Giovanni Ganganelli (1705–73); Madame de Genlis, *Les chevaliers du Cygne* (1795) and *Les mères rivales* (1800); G. B. Guarini, *Il pastor fido* (1590); Sir Samuel Garth, *The Dispensary* (1699); William Roscoe, *The Nurse* (translation of a poem by Luigi Tansillo, published 1798); Samuel Butler, *Hudibras* (1663); Thomas Campbell, *The Pleasures of Hope: A Poem* (1799); Robert Bloomfield, *The Farmer's Boy* (1800). *La Bibbia* is Italian for the Bible.

1802

Agnes spent most of 1802 at Penrice with Thomas and Lady Mary Talbot and their children. In August an old friend, Mrs Simpson, who had recently been widowed, arrived with her son to spend some months in Swansea. In September Agnes's former employer Lord Ilchester died. He had given Agnes an annuity of thirty pounds, but this came to an end with his death. This change in her financial situation was to bring Agnes much anxiety.

Journal, 1802

23 May Sunday: rose at eight. My dear little pupils with me till ten – heard dear little Mary say her prayers, part of the catechism and a hymn. She and my dear Jane read to me. I then amused them with a little history from the Bible – N.B. to make that holy book dear to them from their earliest years. Breakfast a little after ten – Mr Talbot and Lady Mary well, thank God. After breakfast I went up to my own room to write some letters. Received a most obliging one from Lady Ilchester in answer to a favour I had requested of her – she is very good to me indeed, and had used her interest for my friend's son Dr Keir. I wrote immediately to thank her, and informed her that Sir Walter Farqhuar [Farquhar] had obtained a situation for him in the medical line, which I had hopes would suit him. I wrote also to Dr Macqueen and to the Revd Mr Williams. To the first I wished content-ment with his riches; to the second I wished riches to his contentment. Query, which is the happiest man? I then put up my papers and prepared for church. Service was at half past three – Mr Collins' text 'Ask and you shall receive' – a very good and sensible discourse. Mem. he used the word *obediential*. Mr and Mrs King, with Mr Collins, dined with us – a very agreeable evening. Mr King entertained us with some drole annecdotes: a person whom he knew that lived close to the sea, when he advertised his house for sale, said it commanded an extensive view, and possessed an inexhaustible fish-pond. Another person, that

Mrs King had employed to mend a kitchen-jack, was long in sending it home. At last they sent for it, upon which the man assured the servant that the rats had devoured the jack, as it was not to be found. Tea at eight; supper, a cold collation, at ten. I read half an hour, and then to bed. Thank God, a good night's rest.

24 May Monday: a bad morning – did not rise till seven. The five darlings all well. Returned to my books; read till nine; heard the two eldest say their prayers and read. N.B. Miss Talbot begins to improve very much – they are all sweet children. At ten, breakfast. After breakfast a work-party with Lady Mary and Mrs King. Then they walked in the garden and I took a more excursive walk. Delightful weather – the sweet shades of Penrice Castle in full verdure and harmony. In my room two hours – read history and Tasso. Quite pleased to find that charming author has become so easy. Dinner near six o'clock. A very agreeable evening with Mr and Mrs King – a poole at commerce.

27 May Thursday: Mr and Mrs Budgin visited Penrice Castle.

28 May Friday – the party set out to see Worms-head. I was apprehensive of bad weather, so did not choose to go. A very tranquil day at home: music reading and writing, with the company of the dear little children, saved me from *ennui*. At seven the party returned – Mr King told me there was nothing like *pleasuring*. Dear Lady Mary obliged to go to bed directly, wet to the skin; Mrs King quite defeated; Mrs Budgin rather low; and the gentlemen setting the best face on the matter. They went in open carriages, but dined under a tent. I love pleasure, but not when 'The bitter overbalances the sweet'.

29 May Saturday: the visitors took their departure. We past the day *en famille*.

30 May Sunday: a very rainy day. No church. I read in my Bible and Mrs Trimmer's *Comments*.[1] Heard the dear children their prayers and catechism; wrote a long letter to my dear sister Fanny. Mr Collins dined with us – early to bed.

1 June Peace thanksgiving at church.[2]

5 June Saturday: a very happy day with my dear Lady Mary. We walked together in her beautiful garden; we worked and conversed together. A letter from my dear sister Fanny – mutual lamentations, but I hope to make myself a large amends another time.

6 June I wrote to Mr Upcher (the son of my late good friend). I also

---

[1] Sarah Trimmer (1741–1810) was a well-known writer on religion and education.
[2] The Treaty of Amiens, 1802, between Britain and Napoleonic France.

wrote to dear old Mrs Pinnock. I have the great comfort to contribute to *hers*: 'An old friend is like old wine'. To church – Mr Collins preached, as usual, and dined with us.

7 June Mr Talbot and Lady Mary set out on their summer excursion. Their darlings are left under my care, and precious will their darlings be to me! They drank tea with me and were very happy. I shall improve them very much, having leisure and inclination to do so, besides what Mrs Edgeworth[3] styles the 'Resources of property' – no small engine in any government. Monday: I rose at six; saw the children dressed and breakfast; heard then their little prayers, catechism etc. – determined to have them as much with me as possible. Our little studies went off well – they quite happy. I began little dear Mary and Jane to write. N.B. to write slower myself. At eight they went to rest and I read an hour in Mrs Edgeworth's *Education*. Between theory at night and practice all day, I should do *something*. Nature here has done her part – never were there finer creatures.

8 June Tuesday: after our studies we went in the *sociable* and invited Mr and Mrs Collins to come and see us to-morrow. Our airing was very pleasant and the dear children were much amused with it. At our return we had a little collation, then bed.

9 June Wednesday: rain all day – no visiters. We made ourselves happy in our home party. At night I read in the *Annual Register* – a most entertaining book;[4] half an hour in Tasso; my prayers, and to bed at eleven.

10 June Thursday: the weather indifferent but made shift to go out half an hour. The children all well, thank God.

11 June Friday: our various occupations as usual. Little Charlotte told me her mama was gone *a-visicking*. In the evening we went on Kefern Brin, a *high hill* – extremely pleasant. On our return a game at 'puss in a corner', then bed. I wrote, worked and read and thought, from eight to eleven.

12 June Saturday: the day as usual.

13 June Sunday: Trinity Sunday: at church. Mem. sometimes I wish very much to change a word in a sermon – Mr Collins made use of this expression: 'Let not presumption *presume*'. It was, in my opinion, a good sermon. Mr D—, on the text of 'honour all men'[5] advised:

---

[3] The authoress Maria Edgeworth (1768–1849).

[4] *The Annual Register*, a compendium of news and reviews, was first published in 1759.

[5] *The First Epistle General of Peter*, i, 17.

'familiarity with our acquaintance' – it reminded me of a *trite proverb*, yet the discourse was excellent. Mr King dined with me – he was very low, and told me the cause of it. He is an amiable, good-natured man, and Mrs King a very sensible good woman – I love them both. He told me he never saw the children look better – they are rosy cherubs.

14 June Monday: Mrs Collins and two of her daughters dined with me, and her other five children came to tea. Nothing could exceed the pleasure the little ones had in each other's company – we walked, danced, and were most lively companions. At night I enjoyed my book, as usual.

15 June Tuesday: as usual.

16 June Wednesday: a letter from dear Lady Mary dated Gloucester. Memorandum: a week on the road *to me – too long*. We called on Mrs Edwards in the evening.

17 June Thursday: my dear Lady Harriot Frampton's birth day – I remembered it. The loves very good and happy. In the evening an airing on the sands; at night I wrote this journal.

27 June Mr and Mrs King came to visit the dear children and me. We were extremely glad to see them, and they thought the pretty loves much grown and improved.

28 June We walked in the garden immediately after breakfast. In the afternoon we drank tea at Mr Collins'. In the evening Mr and Mrs King and I spent a very social pleasant evening together.

29 June Tuesday: we lost our guests, and both the darlings and I felt a blank in their absence. I amused them as well as I could and had the pleasure of seeing them happy. Our little studies go on – a little reading, writing, work, the maps – flower magazine, etc., and conversation – a mode of teaching I am now more partial to than ever since I read Mrs Edgeworth's work. Mem. I promised Lady Harriot Acland to send her my opinion of this book.

4 July Sunday: Mr Collins preached. He and Mr Watkins dined with me – the conversation after dinner was on sermons: Mr Collins gave a preference to Tillotson, and Mr Watkins to Barrow. Mr Collins observed that Barrow left nothing for any other man to say after him on any subject he investigated. Mr Watkins said that Sherlocke's *Discourse on the Penitent Thief* was superior to any sermon on the subject he had ever seen.[6] At

---

[6] William Sherlock (1641–1707), *Discourses* (many editions published in seventeenth and eighteenth centuries). The other preachers mentioned are John Tillotson (1630–94), Archbishop of Canterbury, and Isaac Barrow (1630–77).

tea the subject still continued on books, but by some strange excursion lighted on novels – Smollet, Le Sage, and Fielding's were praised as giving portraits of life. Mr Collins said he preferred novels in the epistolary style if well written – he quoted my dear Mrs Keir's works as models of excellence – *à propos*, I had a letter from her yesterday. When the two divines were gone I saw my darlings to bed, then I read a sermon by Wheatley;[7] an hour in Mrs Edgeworth; wrote my journal, and then to bed.

7 July Wednesday: a fine day, which is quite a rarity this season. Spent three hours in the garden with the dear children – they, like their mama, have a great taste for flowers and are always pleased to be among them. At our return our studies *par plaisir*. I wrote to Lady Mary a minute account of her darlings. The two Miss Lucas' called on me – literally *to see* one. I had a most pleasant letter from the amiable Mrs Strangways, in which she informed me, or rather confirmed to me, her sister's marriage with the Hon. and Revd Mr Aston Hutchinson Aston, a son of Lord Aston's.

8 July Thursday: the weather so bad I could not let the young ladies bathe – it is rainy, cold and windy. Spent our time very well within-doors – they improve daily and are, I thank God, all well.

30 July Mr and Mrs Collins dined with me.

31 July My dear Lady Mary and Mr Talbot returned safe after having travelled above 800 miles, A joyful meeting with their dear babes – all very happy. Mr Talbot's birth day.

1 August A present from my dear Lady Harriot Acland of a silk shawl for autumn with a nice letter, also a very pretty hussive[8] of Lady Adare's work for me – pleasing remembrances!

10 August I drank tea at Oxwich.

11 August A nice long tête-à-tête with Lady Mary. She gave me the history of her tour – it was very entertaining.

14 August Saturday: Miss Talbot's birth-day – seven years old. The pretty love did no discredit to it. She and her sisters are the sweetest and prettiest children that can be – a beautiful sight to see them all five hanging round their lovely mother, whose chief pleasure is her duty in every character of life. The company at dinner were Mr and Mrs Lucas with their eldest son and daughter, Mr Collins and son, Mr

---

[7] Charles Wheatley, *Fifty Sermons on Several Subjects and Occasions* (1753).

[8] A housewife: a portable case for sewing implements.

King, Major Jones, and Mr Bird. The latter I had never seen before –
N.B. a very agreeable man.

15 August I wrote to good Mr Peele enclosing five pounds for B—y,
and promising, if I lived, to send another such note next March.⁹ I
told him very truly that I could not by pen explain my difficulties in
that quarter. They have been numerous ones and, I suppose, will
continue while she and I live – but our life is not to be strewed with
flowers in every path. I have much, *much* to be thankful for – A. A.
Porter, Penrice Castle, August 15th, 1802.

19 August My dear friend Mrs Simpson, Miss Hoare that was, came
to see me. We had not met for sixteen years. She brought with her a
fine boy, her only child, about twelve years old. She has lost her worthy
husband. Our pleasure was mutual, and we reverted to the days that
are passed and brought many a person and scene to recollection.

20 August A very happy day with my friend – it past with surprizing
velocity. I shewed my dear Mrs Simpson some of the beauties of Penrice
Castle. She is much pleased with the situation, and with the sweet little
girls.

22 August A bad day. Mr Collins dined with us in his way from
church – I introduced my dear Mrs Simpson to him.

23 August Lady Mary and Mr Talbot returned from their visit. They
shewed my dear friend much politeness and requested that she would
favour us with a week of her company. I am much obliged to them,
but every one must like my dear Mrs Simpson – so gentle in her manner,
so sensible and so good, were she not nervous! A happy week with my
friend, and on Monday August 30th I went with her to Swansea and
saw her placed in comfortable apartments for the winter. I shall contrive
to see her, I hope, often. I introduced her to Mr Collins'¹⁰ family at
Swansea. She was invited there for the next day to a card party, and
the Saturday following to another lady's party. I hope she will pass her
time agreeably. I got home by seven, after having spent a most pleasant
day at Swansea.

8 September A most melancholy event was conveyed by letter – the
death of good Lord Ilchester.

10 September Sir John and Lady Sheffield arrived to see their poor
cousin.

12 September Lady Mary rather better.

---

⁹ This may refer to Agnes's sister Betsey.
¹⁰ 'Amiable' crossed out.

17 September She came down stairs pale and thin. The hand of affliction has been heavy upon her, but religious resignation and fortitude support her.

18 September Sir John Sheffield and his lady, with her brother and sister, left Penrice Castle. N.B. I have had letters from Lady Susan O'Brien and Lady Porchester. The dear family as well as can be expected – A.A.P., September 18, 1802.

21 September I left Penrice Castle to spend a day with my dear Mrs Simpson ·at Swansea. We enjoyed each other's company very much indeed – talked of old events, imagined future ones, and the time slipt imperceptibly away. Her pretty boy was our beau: accompanied us in our evening walk and did our little commissions for us. He went to bed early, and my friend and I sat up till eleven. 'O happy state, where hearts each other draw!'

22 September Returned to Penrice Castle with Mr Talbot.

28 September Went to Swansea again to meet my dear brother-in-law Mr Richards. We dined at the Talbot Arms and had a happy day together. My dear Fanny well, thank God. Mr Richards well too. He was invited to Penrice Castle, but declined coming on account of the late melancholy event – his delicate mind revolts at the idea of intrusion. We engaged ourselves in conversing on various subjects that we had a mutual interest in. I sent by him a little present to my dear Fanny that I think she will like, also to their niece Miss Morice. In the afternoon I introduced my brother and my friend Mrs Simpson to each other. We were obliged to part early, that I might get home in good time. I told Mr Richards I would not be another year, if I lived, without seeing him and *our* Fanny. I returned safe, but Park Wood hill is a dreadful one – I walked it.

7 October We went to Margam. I dined with dear Mrs Simpson in our way through Swansea. It will not answer for her to continue there – the place is so extravagantly dear, and the people are rather dissipated. There is too much general acquaintance to admit of any particular society. I was always afraid Swansea would not suit my friend, but by the trial I have had the extreme pleasure of seeing her. I was obliged to leave her very soon. We arrived safe at Margam – the dear children and I. We found their papa and mama there before us. A snug house, small when compared to Penrice, but containing under the name of *cottage* a family of twenty persons.

8 October Dr and Mrs Hunt called upon us in the morning. They both look well – long may they do so! Mr Talbot and Lady Mary dined

10. A page from Agnes Porter's journal, 21–28 September 1802.

with them: I spent the day with my dear little pupils, the evening *sola*. I will not say that 'I am never less alone than when alone', but I would rather be alone *by myself*, than alone *in company*.[11]

9 October The family and I at home.

10 October Sunday: Doctor and Mrs Hunt past the day with us. We

---

[11] 'Numquam minus qual solus', Cicero, *De officiis*, I, ii, 5.

had an excellent sermon from Dr Hunt on the subject of the loaves in the desert.

11 October   A letter from my brother – he reached home safe, and made his little family at Swindon happy by arriving a day before his appointed time. My Fanny is well – *si vale, valeo*,[12] or some such thing I recollect of Mr Griffith's Latin. *A propos*, he now enjoys livings to the value of £500 per annum, the gift of Lord Ilchester. I fear dear Lord Ilchester has forgotten to mention in his will the little annuity he gave me [of thirty pounds per annum].[13] But time will shew – I am resigned, be it as it will! Or rather, as it pleases God! I spent the day with the darlings at Dr Hunt's.

17 October   Sunday: at church – a Welsh sermon etc. alternately. I liked the Welsh singing very much. Dr and Mrs Hunt and Mr Browne, the Member for Dorsetshire, dined and drank tea with us.

20 October   Mr and Mrs Pryce paid a morning visit.

21 October   Half an hour at Dr Hunt's. When I rose to come away Mrs Pryce, who sat next me and who is of a most obliging temper, offered to assist me with my cloak. Her husband made her a sign of disapprobation, and in some confusion she dropt the string and pretended to have her attention called another way. This little incident dwelt on my mind more, perhaps, than it merited. Perhaps after my departure he might hear something said to my advantage, for the next morning, on calling here, his address to me was very polite, but I had not forgotten and answered it with a very reserved silent curtesy. I watched Mrs Pryce's movements, to assist her with her cloak, and on his eying us I said, half smiling, half serious, 'Hail the small courtesies of life, for smooth do they make the road of it!'[14] I looked up at Mr Pryce – he cast his eyes down – I had *my* revenge.

23 October   Letters in the course of this week from Mrs Simpson, Lady Ilchester, and Lady Sheffield. I have heard also from dear Lady Charlotte Strangways, but not from her two *elder sisters*. Lady Ilchester's was a most affecting [and amiable][15] letter. I spent the day at Dr Hunt's, very agreeably.

24 October   At church: Dr Hunt's sermon, on the subject of Naamon, very properly applied.

---

[12] A phrase used at the beginning of a letter: *Si vales, ego valeo* – if you are well, I am also well.

[13] Words in brackets crossed out.

[14] From Laurence Sterne, *A Sentimental Journey* (1768).

[15] Words in brackets crossed out.

25 October　Mr Talbot and Lady Mary went to Dun Raven to visit Mr and Mrs Wyndham, our Member. Spent the day with the darlings.

26 October　We called at Dr Hunt's, and they returned with us and sat half an hour. The children with me till eight; I then amused myself in translating a few pages from *Le Tableau de l'histoire Moderne*,[16] and writing in this journal. It has been very bad weather most of the time we have spent in Margam. I like Penrice Castle better – *tant mieux pour moi.* Memorandum: I have written eleven letters since I came here, and received eight: Mrs Field and good Nanny Longford wrote to me. I thank God I am well, and on the whole comfortable. A letter to-day from my dearest Fanny – they are well.

27 October　The young ladies and I dined at Dr Hunt's. I spent a very agreeable day. We returned at eight o'clock; the darlings went to bed, and I spent the evening as usual – a little work, a little reading … *[rest of page cut out].*

3 November　They had good sport – took the fox. Miss Fanny Collins came to pass some time at the Castle.

7 November　Sunday: at church. I wrote to Lady Ilchester to solicit a favour of Miss Lily Digby, to whom I also wrote – this was to ask her interest with the Queen to procure me to be of St Catharine's Bounty.[17] I have heard nothing of my annuity which Lord Ilchester gave me, and it becomes me to do all I can for myself, and then to be resigned, whatever be the result of my endeavours … *[rest of page cut out]* … I think my right to it is incontestible.

9 November　The hunters went away.

14 November　I had a most kind letter from Lady Ilchester. She told me she had forwarded mine to Miss D[igby] and wished it all possible success. At all rates I am much obliged to Lady Ilchester: she has nothing to do with my annuity – I wish she had. I am afraid that no will is found of Lord Ilchester's.

16 November　I had my own will properly attested by Mr Collins and Miss Fanny Collins. Having suffered so much anxiety lately on account of a will, I resolved that my dear sister Mrs Richards should have nothing to aggravate her affliction when she lost me. I have the greatest esteem for her husband, but were he to die intestate all he has would

---

[16] G. A. de Méhégan, *Tableau de l'histoire moderne* (1766).

[17] Charlotte Elizabeth Digby. I have been unable to identify St Catharine's Bounty, but it may have been connected with the Hospital of St Katharine by the Tower of London, a charity of which Queen Charlotte was patron.

go to his sister's children, and what I left might accidentally go from my own sister. For this reason, I have left it to herself free from the controul of her husband. I have had it written by a lawyer, I have appointed a trustee and had it witnessed as before mentioned, signed and sealed by myself, November 16th, 1802.[18] This is doing my duty, to Heaven I leave the rest. Mem. I had a letter from the maid at Margam with my patten which I had forgotten, in which she styles me her *dutiful friend*. Poor Kitty! I hope I shall always deserve to be reckoned *dutiful* by my inferiors – poor servants in particular. I was much pleased with the appellation.

18 November I wrote in my journal. Studies as well as I can contrive them with my dear little pupils – sometimes in want of what the *Turkish Spy* calls 'the air of the soul' – conversation.[19] Ann Agnes Porter, 1802.

In November Lady Mary and Mr Talbot with her eldest and youngest daughters went to England ... *[next page cut out]*.

---

[18] Agnes remade her will at least once after this: the final version is dated 30 June 1813.

[19] G. P. Marana, *The Eight Volumes of Letters Writ by a Turkish Spy* (1694).

1803

In February 1803 Agnes left Penrice for Swindon, where she was to spend two months with her sister and brother-in-law, Frances and Thomas Richards. On 16 April she returned to Penrice, where she stayed for most of the rest of the year. From mid August until the end of October Agnes was ill at Penrice, suffering from gout and confined to her room for most of the time. Problems with Agnes's annuity continued: Lord Ilchester had apparently intended to leave her a hundred guineas a year for life, but this could not be paid until his heir came of age in 1808. Agnes would therefore need another source of income until then. At the end of November Agnes, together with Thomas and Lady Mary Talbot and their daughter Christiana, left Penrice. The Talbots went to Bath, where Christiana was to have 'an excrescence' removed from her face, and Agnes travelled to Swindon.

Two Months' Excursion, 1803

On Wednesday 9th of February I went to Swansea, dined with dear Mrs Simpson, and set off at eight in the evening in the mail for Bristol. One lady and two gentlemen were my companions. They chose the glasses to be up all night. It was insufferably close, quite a little Calcutta – a room of three feet square only for four persons would be reckoned dreadful, yet many people have no objections to that small space under the name of a carriage. What encreased my regret was its being a bright star-light, which was soon obscured by our breath on the glasses. However, I consoled my self with the thought that none of us could catch cold. The lady was very lively: she prattled and sang pretty little airs alternately, declaring it was very unsociable in any one to wish to sleep. We found it indeed not very practicable. We reached Bristol about twelve the next day. The lady and I dined there. She shewed me a coarse bag of blue cloth as large as a pillow-case, tied round with a piece of tape. She desired me to guess the contents – I told her I could not, to which she gravely replied 'It is my jewels I carry there, I intend to dispose of them in London, as one has very little use for diamonds in Cardigan-shire'. I wished they might reach Town in safety; she replied 'No one would think of valuables being in a coarse blue bag'. I acquiesced. She invited me to visit her in Sloane Street, Kensington, telling me she was niece to Sir Walter Lewis and the Revd Dr Lewis, lately deceased, in Sloane Street. She was a tall, fine woman – not young, but full of juvenile vivacity. She took a kind farewell of me and I proceeded in a stage to Bath, where I was so fortunate as to find another coach just setting out for Marlborough. I arrived there about ten at night – I slept twelve hours very sound at the Marlborough Arms, and the next day, Friday February 12th, took a post chaise twelve miles farther to Swindon, where I found myself in my dear Fanny's arms. Mr Richards and their niece Miss Morris gave me a kind welcome. Happy, thrice happy, was I in their dear society. We breakfasted at nine; dined at three; tea at six, and supper at nine. After breakfast we had generally a work-party of two [or] three hours, then we walked and chatted at pleasure. At nine Miss Morris and my sister's two pupils, Miss Brooke and Miss Gethim, retired and then my brother and sister and self enjoyed the happiness of confidential conversations on our own affairs. Mem. a friend in London sent me a copy of a codicil from Lord Ilchester's will, by which it appeared that he left me an hundred guineas per annum during my life. I gave a thousand blessings to his name – his goodness did not surprize me, but the silence of his executors and agents filled me with deep concern.

13 February I wrote to Colonel Strangways and Lady Harriot Acland. In a few days she sent me word that Colonel S. had submitted several codicils to the opinion of Serjeant Hill, among which my legacy was also, and the Serjeant's opinion was not in my favour. Her ladyship expressed her sorrow on this occasion, adding that if it had depended upon her I might have been as sure of the money as if I already possessed it. I wrote my own statement to Mr Erskine: his opinion was in my favour. I sent copies of these to Lady Harriot Acland: the Colonel and she took these contradictory opinions to Mr Hargrave, who coin-cided with Mr Erskine. Her ladyship wrote me word that the personalty would not be adequate to the legacies, but the business was in train and she hoped in due time I should hear a good account. She assured me that the Colonel was not in the least adverse to my claim, but on the contrary he entertained much esteem for me and wished to satisfy every one to the best of his power. I found this affair a bitter pill to digest, and could not think myself obliged to any one in the family but Lord Ilchester himself, my dear and generous benefactor, to whose intentions I am eternally indebted – he and his first amiable wife. They were my friends indeed, but who remains? Lady Harriot Acland is an angel, but she has been too diffident to be stout in my favour, and all the rest stand neutral. They call it a point in law *[some words cut out here]*. But I will wait in patience till one year is elapsed – I shall then know my dividend.

14 February Mrs Vilett, Mr and Mrs Goodenough and Miss Sanxay called upon me. Mrs Goddard is in London. Mrs Codrington of Overtoun sent to enquire after my health.

15 February We took a very pleasant walk. On passing by some tall elms facing a long gravel walk before Mr Golding's habitation, I was sorry to hear that they were condemned to be cut down as Mr G. did not think them a handsome *tarmination*. I begged to know what was to supply their place, and was informed that a very high wall was in contemplation – O! Plutus![1] O taste!

16 February Mrs Vilett *[some words cut out here]* a few interesting anecdotes. Poor Mrs Radcliffe, the most ingenious writer of *The Castle of Udolpho* etc., etc. is at present confined in a madhouse.[2] She was originally a tayler's daughter: her genius broke through every disadvantage of circumstance, and at last overcame the frail limits of reason – illustriously undone! Mrs West, another charming writer in a different style, was a dairy-man's wife, and used to divide her time between the cheeses and the pen. A lady of rank of Mrs Vilett's acquaintance, who used to look upon Mrs West as a prodigy, frequently invited her to her house and introduced her to many persons of fashion. She frequented them some years before she published her *Tale of the Times*.[3] All her novels are beautiful. When Mrs Vilett was gone my sister entertained me with several other characters, among whom was a Revd Mr Trenchard, a great mimic. He would take people off before their faces, unperceived by themselves, though palpable to every other person. A lady whose husband he had made very free with said to him 'You are indeed, sir, a great and excellent mimic, but there is *one character* you never took off yet'. 'Pray Madam, what?' 'A *good preacher*', replied the lady.

17 February My brother, sister and I spent the day at the Revd Mr Francis, mayor of Marlborough. He and his sister live together, and were both of them intimate companions with my dear Fanny many

---

[1] Plutus was the Greek god of wealth.

[2] Note in another hand: 'I believe not true'. Ann Radcliffe, who wrote *The Mysteries of Udolpho* (1794), was widely (but incorrectly) believed to be in a madhouse at this time.

[3] Jane West, *A Tale of the Times* (1799).

years ago when she resided at Marlborough. They talked over many juvenile parties of pleasure. The two gentlemen seemed to suit each other very much, both sensible men, respectable clergymen and good *loyalists* – Buonaparte was given to the deuce without hesitation, it being agreed his time *here* could be but short. A very agreeable day.

24 February We spent the day with good old Mrs Codrington of Overtoun, who at eighty-six did the honours of her table. We were six in company: her niece and the Revd Mr Evans and *ourselves*. We returned early to Swindon and had a hand at quadrille with the young people at a penny the dozen fish. Sometimes Mr Richards reads to us when we are at work.

26 February We drank tea at Mrs⁴ Sanxay's, who has quite recovered from the most dreadful of all maladies. It was a great pleasure to see this worthy woman again enjoying the comforts of life. We had a hand at penny quadrille. A Mr and Mrs Croudy were of our party – she was a beautiful woman.

4 March Miss⁵ Sanxay drank tea with us – a very happy day in my brother and sister's company. She is one [of] the most charming women I know – amiable in her person, lively in discourse, of the sweetest temper and most benevolent disposition – in music an angel, and clever at every thing. We work, we chat we walk and are happy together. Mr Richards is one of the best and wisest of men – strict in his duties, kind in his sentiments. Mem. I have had several letters: one from Mr Upcher, now a Gentleman Commoner at Cambridge; one from Lady Mary; Mrs Simpson, and Mr Collins of Oxwich.

29 March With a large card party at Mrs Vilett's – a little music, a deal of chat, with a tincture of scandal: Lady Meredith was talked of for being turned out of the Rooms at Bath by the Master of the Ceremonies for having *no* sleeves to her cloaths – the naked elbow appears every where with impunity, but the arm above it is not tolerated as yet. The Bishop of Meath is said to preach against female fashions in dress – he is a popular preacher, but has as yet made no great reform. Then they talked of a marriage and 'What could he see in her?' was repeated by the ladies, while the gentlemen seemed as much at a loss to account for the predilection of the bride – so goes the world: criticising and criticised.

---

⁴ Sic.

⁵ Sic. It seems likely that Miss and Mrs Sanxay are in fact one person. Agnes may be using *Mrs* as a courtesy title for an elderly or middle-aged spinster.

30 March At Mrs Dore's – a very pleasing afternoon. Mrs Sanxay of [the] party. Good Mrs Dore rejoiced so much to see us, and talked of my dear parents and old times with so much kindness that my heart glowed to hear her. A sweet rural cottage in the midst of a garden. We walked home in good spirits, laughing and chatting all the way. One day the same week Miss St John, her brother, and aunt Mrs Collins paid us a morning visit. Lady Bolinbroke was confined at home by her eldest son's illness. This young lady is a most elegant creature, and her aunt a very agreeable woman – she told us that the account given of Buonaparte's rude behaviour to Lord Whitworth was literally true, and when he left our ambassador he slapt the door behind him, and all his mean courtiers laughed at *the wit*.

1 April I took a long walk of three miles, the last up hill, to Overtown and drank tea in a farewell visit to Mrs Calley. In my walk there and back again I viewed my dear father's little white church at Wroughton, and many a tender remembrance crowded into my mind – dear man! I seemed to trace his very footsteps on the road to Overtown – many a time had we walked there together.

2 April Went with Mrs[6] Sanxay and Miss Heath to Mrs Dore's, where we spent an agreeable afternoon and returned by moon-light. My sister very seldom chooses to leave her pupils. My brother had a touch of the influenza. We had a hand at quadrille to close the evening at home.

12 April Took leave of our Swindon acquaintances. My brother and sister made all these calls with me.

13 April They conducted me as far as Marlborough. N.B. all the stages were full – obliged to wait till the next day. My brother and sister left me with their Marlborough friends Mr and Miss Francis – there we three parted. In about an hour I recovered my spirits, and Mr and Miss Francis acted the part of very kind hosts. They invited me to lay there, but I declined their civility. Mr Francis saw me safe to my inn, where the company of the mayor gave me no small importance with the people at the inn. I had an excellent bed, slept four hours, and rose at three to watch [for] the mail myself. I was afraid the servant of the inn might fail me, so I seated myself in the window-seat. It was a beautiful star-light night and I listened with the utmost attention to catch the coach. In half an hour I heard it; I opened my window and enquired if there was room for Bristol. 'Yes' was the welcome answer, on which I told the coach-man I was quite ready and desired him to send some one to light me

---

[6] Altered from 'Miss'.

down-stairs. This was done, and while my trunks were fastening I went into a parlor. A gentleman followed me who, seeing me put on my pelisse, politely offered to assist me, asking me if my way was London. I told him no – it lay towards Bristol. The coach there being announced, he said 'Give me leave, Madam, to *squire* you to the coach', and by the word *squire* I knew him to be Scotch. His civility was not the less agreeable to me for his being my countryman. When in the mail a little merry-looking woman said 'Ma'am, do you know the gentleman that handed you into the coach? His servant tells me he is a major, but be that as it may, he is a *Scotchee* and I hate all *Scotchees*. Once a Scotchee stole my pocket-handkerchief, and I dare say this major might do the same – being as how that one Scotchee is much the same as another'. As I found the talkative lady required little or no answer, I let her go on without interruption. At last a person who was my vis-à-vis[7] said to her 'I hope, Ma'am, you think better of the Irish than you do of the Scotch?' 'La, sir, I never saw an Irish-man – be you one? People calls you *wild Irish*, and I always said as how that if ever I saw an Irish-man I would ask whether they all lives in the woods.' 'Ma'am' replied the Irish gentleman 'the truth is that we do live in the woods, but when we are caught they make us live in houses. I myself was caught about three months ago, and the first thing they did was to cut my wings and my tail that they might squeeze me into cloaths. When we reach the inn, Ma'am, as you may probably think the sight curious, I will shew you my wings now beginning to grow again, and my tail too if you please.' I was much entertained with the Irish-man's humour, and he and I began to talk of Limerick and its environs with much pleasure. He seemed a little of the rattle, but very good- natured. A very elegant-looking man who smiled but said little was our fourth. At breakfast at Bath Mr Stevens, the Irish gentle-man, told me that our fourth fellow-traveller was come to Bath in search of a butler's place, and that he himself should be glad to have so respectable a looking[8] *servant*. I could not but ruminate on the deceit-fulness of appearances. We proceeded to Bristol. I went to the Swansea mail inn, the Bush. It had been gone about five minutes – forced to stay at the Bush till the next day. The house full – only a little dark apartment vacant – glad to have that. Ate my dinner, wrote to my dear Fanny, then drank tea and went to bed. Slept ten hours. Had the mail next day at twelve at noon. Travelled with one English and two Welsh gentlemen: one a banker at Carmarthen, the other an officer returning from the

---

[7] Who sat opposite me.
[8] Sic.

Indies. He had spent a few weeks at London, and repeated the particulars of the late unhappy duel in which Mr Montgomery was killed by Mr Mc-Namara.[9] The banker mentioned Mr Alsett's dreadful failure. The English gentleman was very agreeable in his conversation and polite in his manners – he was so good as to take care of me in the Passage; would not suffer me to be at any expence on the road. Mem. his name is Hawkins and he lives near Neath at the place he inhabits called Something Court – Harford Court, I think.[10] However Dr Hunt can inform me – such a person must be known in their neighbourhood. Arrived at Swansea about five the next morning; went to bed; rose at ten; dressed *smart* and waited upon Mrs Simpson to breakfast. She and her son pretty well. Spent two hours with her very agreeably, and then the phaeton called for me to transport me to Penrice Castle. I reached my present home in two hours and found Lady Mary and Mr Talbot with their five lovely children all well on April 16th, 1803. Finished this little journal April 24th.

23 April Mr and Mrs King left Penrice Castle – I was sorry to see them depart. I took a walk to Oxwich. Good Mr Collins had been ill of the influenza; his second daughter was suffering under it at that time, and his wife was attending her dying mother.

24 April I wrote in this journal. No church etc. – Mr Collins ill; his daughter worse.

25 April Went again to Oxwich – poor Miss Sarah Collins confined to her bed.

26 April Mr Collins of Swansea breakfasted with us – said his niece [was] dangerously ill and he had sent for her mother to attend her.

27 April Poor Miss Sarah Collins died, about eighteen years of age. N.B. only five days ill.

29 April I had a note from Mr Charles Collins 'Dear Madam, your kind message I have delivered to my brother and Mrs Collins, who are both very sensible of your friendly offer, but the torrent of affliction is so great upon them at present that nothing but quiet to give way to it can avail. As soon as ever Mrs Collins can bear the sight of any-one my brother will send his friend Miss Porter a note. I am just going to Swansea, but shall be here again to-morrow. I am, dear Madam, your obliged humble servant, Charles Collins, Oxwich.'

---

[9] Robert Montgomery, a colonel in the ninth Regiment, and son of Sir William Montgomery of Magbiehill, Ayr, was killed in a duel with Captain Macnamara on 6 April 1803.

[10] Later note by Lady Mary Talbot 'Court Herbert'.

30 April Very poorly myself with a considerable portion of the influenza – very low. Wrote some codicils to my will.

2 May I wrote to Mr Wilkes and expressed my great esteem for his conduct. N.B. he has the goodness to pay us a debt contracted by his father to our dear father near thirty years ago. I yesterday sent the moiety of this remittance to my dear sister Fanny. Made the good dairy-maid a present of half a guinea on her intended marriage – a constancy of nine years – both good creatures. Her face, notwithstanding, was full of care, and gave no bad comment in a rural style on Rogers' elegant marriage verses 'To a Friend etc.'[11] Dr and Mrs Hunt left us – *tant pis!* I call this the *Valley of Abyssinia*.

4 May A letter from Mr Collins of Oxwich – Mrs Collins lost her mother last Monday.

5 May I conveyed the Oxwich family to the father, Mr Wells of Penmaen. They were composed, resigned, and bear their affliction as *Christians*.

8 May At church. Mr Edwards did duty for poor Mr Collins. N.B. I walked yesterday and paid Mrs Edwards a morning visit. A letter from my dear Fanny and Mr Richards – they are well, thank God, and are at Clifton Downs for a little amusement, change of air etc.

9 May Lady Mary is to-day so poorly that I suppose she will soon be confined. May the event prove fortunate! Amen. A. A. Porter, Penrice Castle near Swansea, May 9th 1803.

10 May Last night at two o'clock Lady Mary Talbot was safely delivered of a *son*, being her sixth child and *first boy*.

11 May I wrote to [inform] many of Lady Mary's friends [of] the joyful event. Mr King and Mr Charles Collins dined and spent the day with Mr Talbot and me. N.B. I take good care of the darling little girls. I saw Lady Mary at night – wonderfully well, so is babe.

21 May Revd Mr Watkin of Portynon died, leaving seven children and a wife behind him – *sans rien*.

12 June Lady Harriot Frampton paid us a visit *à l'impromptu. Quel plaisir!* Poor Lady Mary having had a relapse, her amiable sister is come to be head nurse herself.

17 June Lady Harriot's birth day.

18 June My own.

20 June Lady Mary much better. Lady Harriot spends the day with

---

[11] Samuel Rogers, *An Epistle to a Friend with Other Poems* (1798).

her, and when she goes to rest, comes down to spend the evening with Mr Talbot and me – a delightful addition to our party.

21 June A letter from my dear Mrs Keir to inform me that her son is appointed to be domestic physician to the Chancellor of Russia, the Russian ambassador's brother, with a salary of 300 [pounds] per annum and liberty to practise. It rejoiced me much to learn that my dear friend's son was so respectably provided for at the age of twenty-two. In time I doubt not he will prove an eminent physician in his own country.

25 June Mrs King favoured us with her company – one day only. She and I always meet with affection and part with regret.

27 June A letter from dear Mr Upcher – a love confidence, a poetical effusion and many kind professions of friendship for myself. Dear youth! I love him for his own sake and for his worthy parents, whom I saw united at the altar twenty-three years ago. This is the only individual left of a happy and numerous family.

1 July Mr Talbot and Lady Harriot Frampton took Lady Mary away for change of air near Swansea. Lady Mary is much better, and I hope in a fair way of recovery to perfect health. We lose her only a week, but my dear Lady Harriot is going home, and leaves us for good – *elle est si bonne, et si charmante que l'on ne sauroit la voir partir sans se plaindre des beaux jours passés.* I was accustomed to her dear society every night till twelve o'clock in my own apartment – how I shall miss her!

2 July With my darling children all day – the little boy thrives much. Wrote to Lady Mary.

3 July A note from Lady Mary. I wrote to dear little *[a word cut out here]*. Mr and Mrs Collins from Oxwich dined with me. The young people came to tea – they begin to recover their spirits and health, which I am truly glad to perceive. We had a very pleasant afternoon. I saw my loves to bed, read in *Public Characters*,[12] and wrote this journal.

9 July Lady Mary and Mr Talbot returned for two [or] three days. Lady Mary much better; Mr T. pretty well.

10 July Mr Collins dined at the Castle.

12 July Lady Mary and Mr Talbot went to Dr Hunt's at Margam to stay a week. They were so good as to offer to convey me to Swansea, but I found a few twinges in my foot, which warned me to stay at home *quiet* in this very hot weather.

---

[12] British *Public Characters* (various editions, 1799–1810).

13 July With two of the little darlings most part of the day. I endeavoured to improve and amuse them as much as I could – I was their mother, tutress and play-fellow by turns. When they went out a-walking with their maids I read, worked or wrote to amuse my self. I felt the pleasure of existence in a peculiar manner, and seemed to derive amusement from resources of my own with extreme satisfaction. But in this delightful season of the year all is beauty and joy:

> When all thy mercies, O my God,
> My ravish'd soul surveys,
> Transported with the view, I'm lost
> In wonder, joy and praise.[13]

14 July With the darlings. I finished *Public Characters* – read some of Francis's *Horace*,[14] and in a French novel called *Camille* by the author of *Laure*.[15] It is written in a masterly manner and interests extremely.

15 July As usual.

17 July At church. Mr Collins spent the day with me and my pretty Christiana – the third daughter and at present my eldest pupil.

18 July I wrote to Mr Upcher – sent him a few verses in return for his poetical communication, and will here transcribe them both:

Mr Upcher's presented to Miss P—r an amiable young lady at Cambridge, who in his opinion resembled a lady he loved:

> Ah think not when you catch my eye,
> So often fondly fix'd on thee,
> For thee my bosom heaves a sigh,
> As if, sweet girl, its deity.
>
> For, know, on earth lives one more dear,
> To whom I vow'd an infant flame,
> And yet 'tis strange, when thou art near,
> My rapture's equal, love the same.
>
> Oh! Say – did some indulgent pow'r
> For Laura's absence, grant thy smiles,
> To cheer the solitary hour,
> It gave thy form which pain beguiles!

---

[13] Joseph Addison, *The Spectator*, no. 453 (slightly misquoted).

[14] Philip Francis (translations of the works of Horace, 1743 and later).

[15] F. Constant de Rebecque wrote *Camille, ou lettres de deux filles de ce siècle* (1785); and *Laure, ou lettres de quelques personnes de Suisse* (1787).

Thou know'st not, canst not, gentle maid,
What thoughts thy form angelic gives,
In thee delusive hope has said,
Though Laura's absent, Laura lives.

Thine are her looks, her modest air,
As hers, thy dimples zephyrs kiss,
And yet, as her, there's none so fair,
And yet, *thy* smile is more than bliss.

Then, sweetly smiling, turn again
For fondly still, I'll gaze on thee.
Ah! Know, no look, no glance is vain,
For still my Laura lives in thee.

Query: does my young friend love one – or both – or neither?
My verses written some years back at Southampton:

As here I solitary stray,
O! Memory, lend thy active pow'rs,
Bright o'er my mind thy tints display,
And give me back my happiest hours!

Let me that blissful time recall
When, shelter'd by paternal care,
A father's tender hand gave all
Which duty asked, or love could share.

While, round the dear domestic hearth
The winter eve flew swift along.
Each youthful bosom prone to mirth,
How gay the story! Sweet the song!

A sister graceful led the dance,
A brother tun'd the lively reed.
Friendship exchang'd the heartfelt glance,
And ev'ry joy, was *joy indeed!*

Mem. I told Mr Upcher I had a sufficient touch of the muse to enjoy his verses with a better relish.

19 July Lady Mary and Mr Talbot returned etc., etc. She is much better, thank God. The six loves all well.[16]

20 July The day at home, as usual. In the evening I wrote this journal; *Horace*; work; and bed at eleven. A.A.P., Penrice Castle, Swansea, July 21st 1803.

---

[16] The word 'six' crossed out.

14 August My dear Miss Talbot's birth day – eight years old. Mem. her dear mother was not so old when I first knew her. Let me see if I can recollect the occurrences since July 21st. Mr Talbot and Lady Mary went to Worms Head; my rheumatism kept me at home. Dr Hunt and Mr Wilbraham Ford came to spend a day or two at the Castle – I entertained them as well as I could. At evening the party returned from Worms Head and we past it very agreeably. Mr Ford's father and mother were our nearest neighbours at Redlynch for some years – their young people used to meet with Lord Ilchester's frequently, and have their dancing-master attend alternately. Mrs Ford was a charming woman – we had a great loss when they left Somersetshire. They had ten fine, good children: Mr Wilbraham is intended for the church, and to fill up some vacant time became a pedestrian traveller. He has walked thus far into Wales and is proceeding south. The next day they returned to Dr Hunt's, and I thought a few lines from me would be acceptable to Mrs Ford to acquaint her with her son's good health and how much he had pleased the Penrice family and her *old*, young, acquaintance Lady Mary. I had an answer from Mrs Ford, in which she expressed much pleasure at my letter, and reverted to *old times* near eighteen years ago in a very pleasing manner. On August 3rd were the Swansea Races – Mr Talbot and Mr Llewellyn were stewards. They gave balls and breakfasts. The Races continued three days – I took care of the darlings at home. In this interval I had a letter from my dear sister Richards, desiring me to leave Wales instantly and take up my abode with them at Swindon, as she is apprehensive of the French where I am. I declined her kind offer – told her I regarded the war as a thunderous bolt, which falls we know not where till the very moment. When I leave my dear Lady Mary I would not do it at a time of apprehended calamity – having shared in her good things, I would not leave her in trouble. But I hope God will preserve us from His scourge, viz. Buonaparte. On August 11th I went to see dear Mrs Simpson. She was rejoiced to see me, and I spent a very agreeable day in her company. Mr King came and saw me, so did Mr Collins and his daughter Fanny. I called upon Mrs Williams and her daughter, also on Mrs *John* Collins – my country-woman, and a very pretty woman she is. Mr Collins' son gained her heart when he pursued his medical studies in Edinburgh.[17] At Swansea I heard of a prosecution against a lady in this county for *defamation*. It will cost her both trouble and money – many persons are summoned as witnesses. 14th August: at church – Mr Collins of Oxwich

---

[17] Dr John Charles Collins (1780–1824), son of Dr Charles Collins of Swansea.

dined with us to help keep the birth day. Many, many, happy ones may the sweet love see! N.B. the eldest of six. A.A.P. 1803.

4 October   Recovering from a very severe fit of the gout – I can just use the fingers of my right hand a little, so will try to recollect my journal, for a little amusement.

15 August   Mr Talbot and Lady Mary went from home, but desired me if her uncle and brother arrived to send an express to them immediately. Mem. I was very poorly indeed.

16 August   Confined to my room.

17 August   Confined to my chair – feet and hands seized by the harpy claws of the gout.

18 August   Worse.

19 August   Worse. To compleat the vexation I could not go down-stairs to receive my dear Harry, Lord Ilchester, and his uncle Colonel Strangways, who arrived early. Sent an express to Lady Mary. In bed all day – much fever – very ill indeed.

20 August   Lady Mary came home. She rejoiced to find her dear brother and uncle. She paid me a visit of condolement.

26 August   Friday: the christening-day. Celebrated, as I heard, with much festivity. Dr and Mrs Hunt, Lord Ilchester, Colonel Strangways and Mr Collins and Mrs Davenport present – an ox roasted for the country people. Poor I in limbo – continued very ill six weeks. Could not turn myself in bed to the right or left – quite stationary where placed, whether in bed or on a chair. Quite a cripple – could not stand, nor move. The first fortnight visited by Dr and Mrs Hunt, by Lady Mary and her dear brother and uncle. Lord Ilchester is one of the most amiable youths in the world. In this period had a conversation with Colonel Strangways respecting my generous benefactor's legacy. Very dissatisfactory – nothing to be paid till the present earl is of age, near five years hence. I asked the Colonel what I was to do in the interval, and added that should I from ill health be obliged to give up my profession and be reduced to want, I thought it would be a reflection on his noble family. He seemed to think what I said was *une façon de parler* – but he knows not me. Constant letters from my ... *[page cut out here]*.

7 October   Finished my journal up to this day. My muscular pain somewhat easier – I can walk a few steps, and scrawl a few lines – A.A.P. *Un triste jour.*[18] October 1803.

---

[18] A sad day. These three words have been crossed out. Does this refer to the death of Agnes's sister Betsey?

16 November Soon after I wrote the above I had a relapse which continued above a fortnight. Quite lame – almost in despair of recovering my limbs. I had Dr Macqueen consulted, who sent me his advice to bathe and rub the afflicted parts in tepid salt water, as also to eat solids and drink a glass or two of sound wine every day. The very next day after I had used this prescription I could walk from my bed across the room – continued to mend, thank God. On the 25th of October my dear sister and Mr Richards came to pay me a visit. O, how the sight of them rejoiced my heart! They spent all their time except when at meals in my apartment. My spirits rose so much that I almost forgot my weakness and pain.

30 October Mr Richards did duty for Mr Collins at Penrice church.

31 October My sister and her worthy husband left Penrice Castle to proceed to Cardiganshire – I was very low after their absence.

1 November I went down-stairs to dinner for the first time. My dear Lady Mary and Mr Talbot all goodness to me.

2 November I resumed my pleasing employment with my darling pupils. I can never be too diligent in my duty, whether I consult conscience or gratitude. My brother and sister think with me that here I may remain with comfort under my dear Lady Mary's roof till my own income becomes due at Lord Ilchester's being of age in 1808. Colonel Strangways promised me that he would recommend it to his nephew to pay me the full annuity mentioned by his dear father, whatever became of the dividends. I hope my health will prove tolerable, that I may exert my self in the improvement of my pupils.

4 November Dr and Mrs Hunt came to spend a few days at Penrice. I esteem her, but I esteem and love him. He has so kind, so benevolent a heart – she is very amiable too.

5 November A letter from my dear Fanny from Worcester – they were to reach home as[19] the next day.

8 November Mr and Mrs King joined our party.

12 November Dr and Mrs Hunt left us. Mr Garthshaw arrived at Penrice.[20] Poor gentleman! He had been married nine years, and was happy in that state except in having no children. His wife this year fell with child and was going on extremely well, when a rash person acquainting her suddenly that her father was that morning dead, whom

---

[19] Sic.

[20] The MP William Garthshore (1764–1806). He never recovered from his wife's death in 1803.

she had seen the day before in perfect health, she was so thunder-struck that she dropt down *dead* herself. Her poor husband, bereaved at once of a much-loved wife and his hopes of children, fell ill of a fever, and remains much impaired in his intellect. He wanders about for a change of objects, and came to Wales. He is quite inoffensive, but evidently *deranged*. N.B. in Parliament, and one of the Lords of the Admiralty. Dear Mrs King adds much to *my* society. Another letter from Dr Macqueen, giving me some kind and judicious rules for my future health.

13 November Miss Jane, my second pupil's, birth-day – seven years old. Heavens bless her!

16 November Worked in our party all the morning, then wrote this journal – Ann Agnes Porter, November 16th, 1803.

28 November Set off on our journey to England – past three days at Dr Hunt's.

1 December Left Margam and reached Newport – lay there.

2 December Friday: breakfasted at New Passage. Proceeded to Bristol, where dear Lady Mary and I parted. Mr Talbot and her ladyship [with Miss Christiana][21] went to Bath; I took a post chaise and went on alone to Mash-Field.[22] It was very dark so I stopt there for the evening – a small place, only one inn in it. Had a comfortable supper and a neat little bed room – slept well, and set out at half past seven the next morning after breakfast. Changed horses at Chippenham and then post to Swindon, where I found my dear Fanny and Mr Richards quite well, and happy to see me. Their family consists of, besides themselves, their nephew and niece, Miss Brook, and two maid-servants – a nice little happy family.

4 December Sunday: too cold for me to venture to church – read a sermon and spent the day comfortably with my good friends.

5 December Several old and new acquaintances came to see me. Miss Sanxay is quite recovered; Dr Vilett and his family well; Mrs Gibson and Mrs Golding are but lately established at Swindon – my sister likes them much.

6 December Very busy at home – with my dear sister's help making up caps and other necessaries. It seems rather a treat for me to be only busied about myself, or enjoying domestic society.

7 December Returned our visits. I called at Swindon House – I did not think it proper to wait till Mrs Goddard called on me. She gave

---

[21] Words in brackets crossed out.

[22] Marshfield, Gloucestershire.

me a very polite reception and told me that as soon as Mr Goddard was better she would pay us a morning visit. N.B. in the course of this month we were invited to card-parties at Mrs Gibson's, Mr Golding's, Dr Vilett's and Miss Sanxay's. We spent a day with Mrs Calley of Overtown. Poor Mrs Codrington lost her eldest daughter;[23] Mr Goodenough was confined by the gout. We spent our Christmas very agreeably and, thank God, I grew stronger in my limbs every day.

---

[23] A monument in Wroughton church records the death of Mary Anne, eldest daughter of William and Mary Codrington, on 7 January 1804 aged twelve years and ten months.

1804

Agnes was with Thomas and Frances Richards in Swindon until the end of February 1804. She then returned to Penrice, where she spent most of the rest of the year. In April Lady Elizabeth Talbot, Lady Mary Talbot's elder sister, married for the second time, at Penrice. In November and December Agnes spent four weeks at the bathing-house in Swansea with six of the Talbot children (including Lady Elizabeth's son Henry), who were recovering from whooping-cough.

Journal, 1804

January 1804 – from memory:

1 January Sunday: at Swindon church with my dear sister. We stayed – the service by Mr Goodenough.

2 January An agreeable day at home. N.B. Mr Richards has the art of saying *multum in parvo* more than any one I know – told him so.

3 January At Mr Golding's. Three tables – a pleasant evening. Mrs Golding is a sweet little woman – chatty yet discreet; good-humoured to a degree; a most excellent mother-in-law to her husband's daughter; remained twenty-five years a widow and late married a Mr Golden – a suitable match in years and fortune.

5 January At Miss Sanxay's – an agreeable party. What a satisfaction to see that worthy woman restored from the most dreadful of maladies to herself and friends. Dr Willis foretold that she would recover which, thank God, proved true.

8 January Sunday: at church. A little walk and a deal of chat with my Fanny.

9 January At Mr Crowdey's. A charming family: nine nice children, with a mother so pretty and young-looking as might pass for an elder sister – three tables. Mem. I beat at whist.

10 January Little Patty and Nancy with us in the morning: two poor little children that my sister is very kind to – indeed Mr Richards and she are a blessing to all the poor within their reach.

11 January Lady Bolinbroke died, universally beloved, admired and regretted.

14 January At Mrs Gibson's. Three card tables – an amiable woman. This week my brother-in-law's nephew, Mr James Morice, was articled as clerk to Mr Crowdey – Mr Richards and he dined at Mr Crowdey's, who termed the occasion of meeting Mr Morice's *wedding-day*.

15 January Sunday: at church ... *[next page cut out]*.

... January   ... to the wenn – it is taking out by caustic.[1]

29 January Sunday: at church.

31 January At Mrs Codrington's – as well as could be expected after the recent loss of a fine child of twelve years old.

1 February At Dr Vilett's. Whist, chat etc., etc. – she is a lovely woman and has got several handsome daughters.

2 February At home with my dear sister. Mem. I have read since I was here Dr Lyttleton [Lyttelton] *On the Articles* and the Bishop of London's lectures.[2] Our amusing reading was *The Infernal Quixote*.[3]

5 February At church.

6 February Spent the day at Mrs Calley's of Overtown – I was always recollecting when there how many happy hours I have spent in the same place with my dearest father and mother. Sweet is their remembrance, may it never 'fade upon my soul'!

7 February At Mr Golden's.

8 February At Mrs Gibson's.

9 February Company at home – four tables. A Mr Tudor from Bath called upon us. Mem. Miss Farmer said it was shocking in Mrs Crowdey not to take her glove off and shew her ring, that she might give the young people a fair chance with so smart a Bath beau as Mr Tudor.

12 February Sunday: at church. An excellent discourse from Mr Goodenough.

13 February At the amiable Mrs Gibson's.

15 February Ash Wednesday – at church.

---

[1] This refers to the Talbots' third daughter, Christiana. She had a disfiguring lump on her face, and this was removed in Bath on 24 January 1804.

[2] Pencil note: '?Porteous'. This was Beilby Porteus (1731–1809).

[3] Charles Lucas, *The Infernal Quixote: A Tale of the Day* (1801).

19 February At church.

21 February A morning visit from Mr and Mrs Goddard – recollected their kindness to my dear parents in old times and felt it with gratitude.

22 February At Mrs Gibson's with a large party.

24 February At Mrs Gibson's by ourselves.

25 February Spent the day at Mr Goddard's – eighteen in company at dinner. In the evening a large party and cards.

26 February At church.

28 February A party at home.

29 February Took leave of my dear friends at Swindon.

1 March Thursday – found my dear Lady Mary, Mr Talbot, her sister and children well. Their house quite full – I could not sleep there.

2 March Journey to the Passage – detained there six hours.[4] At last crossed it in a great boat full of cattle, men, women and children – very disagreeable. It poured rain continually and the boat was too crowded to use umbrellas. Slept at Cardiff.

4 March Stopt at Margam two days with our agreeable friends Dr and Mrs Hunt. Mem. they were displeased at my not having written to them – N.B. never to offend them so again.

7 March Wednesday – reached Penrice Castle, found the other three children quite well.

8 March Lady Elizabeth Talbot and her son, dear little Henry, arrived.

10 March Mr King with us.

11 March Sunday: Mr Collins with us.

12 March My dear pupils with me at their studies as usual – very happy to be again of some utility in life.

14 March I wrote to my dear sister and Mrs Williams. The morning as usual – an agreeable evening. Mr Talbot read to us Moritz, *Travels in England* – they are uncommonly simple and amusing.[5]

18 March Sunday: Mr Collins dined with us. I still am afraid of mounting the church hill and encountering the keen wind – read a sermon at home.

21 March Captain Richard Jones spent the day with us. Mem. Lady

---

[4] There were two ferries across the river Severn at this date: the Old Passage at Aust, near the site of the first Severn Bridge; and the New Passage, a mile and a half further down the river.

[5] C. P. Moritz, *Travels, Chiefly on Foot, Through Several Parts of England, in 1782* (1st English edn, 1795).

Elizabeth says it is not *tonnish* [6] to say *Captain* or *Major* – nothing under a General. This prevails so much that Captain Fielding calls himself *Mr* Fielding in a note left at the Admiralty. They asked him if he was ashamed of his profession. I suspect this Mr Fielding to be an admirer of Lady E.'s, but time will shew.

22 March The two Mr Collins' dined at the Castle. Lady E. had a cold. In the evening an agreeable conversation with my dear Lady Mary, who gave me several particulars relative to her cousin Mr and Mrs William Digby.

24 March I go on as usual with the dear children. They come to me at half-past seven, stay near three hours, then I breakfast with their papa and mama. I then am by myself till one o'clock – I walk, work, read and write at pleasure. I again meet my pupils at their dinner and my nunch at one, and they stay with me till half-past four. I then dress for dinner at five. The children come in at desert, and continue in company till eight. I then very often see the two elder young ladies put to bed, and after that return below stairs to the drawing-room till ten. Then to bed. I endeavour to be as useful as possible to my dear pupils, and may God bless them here and for ever, amen. A. A. Porter, Penrice Castle, Swansea, March 24th, 1804.

30 March I changed a Bible with Lady Elizabeth Talbot, and gave her an Italian in a small type for an English Bible, a large quarto.

10 April Dr and Mrs Hunt, with Mr Wrixton, Mr Treherne, Mr Jenkins and Mr Morgan came to Penrice Castle – a very agreeable day. At night, cards. Mr W. very polite to me in those small attentions which are so pleasing.

11 April A hunting party – Mr Lucas and Mr Thomas joined them. At night cards – Pope Joan.[7]

13 April I wrote to my friend Mr Wilkes at Nevis, W. Indies.

14 April All the party went away except dear Dr and Mrs Hunt – an agreeable evening in their company. N.B. always spend the day with my pupils.

15 April At church. Dr Hunt preached – Mr Collins not yet well.

16 April Captain Richard Jones past the day with us.

17 April Dr and Mrs Hunt left us.

18 April I presented my *Walker's Dictionary* to the new library at

---

[6] Not fashionable; not 'the done thing'.
[7] A card-game.

Swansea.[8] At night amused my self with the *Sentimental Journal*.[9] Mr and Mrs King spent a few days with us. They went away on April 30.

19 April Captain Fielding, an acquaintance of Lady Elizabeth Talbot's, came to visit at Penrice Castle.

22 April They were married at Penrice Church by the Revd Mr Pritchard. Witnesses: Mr Talbot, Lady Mary, and me. About this time eight years ago she was married to poor Captain Talbot. Mem. she has been four years a widow – I wish her and her present husband all happiness. They set out soon after the ceremony, leaving little Henry Talbot with us.

30 April Mr and Mrs Llewellyn and Miss Adams came on a visit. Within the course of a few weeks there has been a succession of company at the Castle: Dr and Mrs Hunt, Mr and Mrs King, Mr Wrixton, Mr Jenkins, Mr Treherne and Mr Morgan on a hunting party – and now since they went Mr and Mrs Llewellyn of Pantligare and the very agreeable Miss Adams. I had last week a pleasing letter from my friend Mrs Keir – her son is physician to the Lord Chancellor of Russia and likes his situation much. Mem. she advises me when my annuity becomes due to go and reside in Scotland. Letters from my dear friends at Swindon – all well, thank God. Long may they be so! A. A. P., May 6th, 1804, Penrice Castle.

4 May Mr and Mrs Lewellin of Pentligare came to spend a few days. They two went on the 7th, but left the amiable Miss Adams behind with us – a great accession to the domestic party.

10 May Master Talbot's birth-day – one year old. The party: Miss Adams, Dr Hunt, Messrs Collins and Messieurs Lucas. N.B. my darlings have begun to dance – a master comes every Tuesday.

12 May I spent the day at Mr Collins of Oxwich – met there Mrs McFarquhar, a Scots lady, mother to Mrs John Collins – a very agreeable woman.

13 May Mr and Mrs Pritchard dined at the Castle.

14 May Dr Hunt went, and conducted Miss Adams to Pentligare. I was sorry to see them go – Dr Hunt is an old friend. Miss Adams is a very attaching character – her motto might be a *violet* with 'il faut me chercher – çela vaut bien la peine'.

---

[8] The Glamorgan Library, formed 1804. Dictionaries by John Walker were published in the 1770s and later.

[9] Sic. Does Agnes mean *A Sentimental Journey* by Laurence Sterne (1768), or *The Sentimental Magazine* (London, 1773–75)?

15 May My dear Lady Mary and Mr T. went to Margam – they left me three darlings.

20 May At church. Wrote to my dear sister Fanny. Mr and Mrs Collins, with their friend Mr Johns, dined and drank tea with me. I made the visit as agreeable as I could to them, and found myself in that lively chearful humour in which, if one ever pleases, one must please. *C'est selon* – with some people you find yourself in a good light; with others you are cast in the shade. I had last week a note from Mrs King. Mem. my late reading has been *Lady Mary Wortley Montagu's Letters* published by the Marquis of Bute[10] – a charming correspondence on her side, but I do not give up my ever-dear Madame Sévigné.[11] *Arabian Nights* in French; *History of the French Consulate and Buonaparte*; *Countess of Castle Howel,* a pretty novel; *Chaucer's Life* – a charming book; Dr Fordyce's *Sermons*;[12] Florian's *Estelle*. Thus comfortable and unconcerned 'I find hours, days and years glide fast away'.[13] A.A.P., May 20th, 1804, Penrice Castle. N.B. a letter from my dear Lady Mary, as also from the gentlemen of the library committee to thank me for my book.

28 May So cold as to be obliged to have a fire to make my self and the darlings comfortable.

3 June Mr and Mrs Collins dined with me – a very pleasant day.

12 June A happy evening with my dear Lady Mary.

19 June Mr Joseph Green came to spend a few days at the Castle – a very agreeable sensible man he is.[14]

22 June Mr King with us – *toujours gai.*

25 June We had a charming day at Worms Head. It is about six miles off – a rock of a very singular form. It is said to be Gibraltar Rock in miniature. The scenery is wild and grand. We pitched our tent at pleasure where the prospect was most varied and extensive – we dined with appetite on a cold collation and then wandered about as fancy enclined us – I suppose I walked at least five miles. Our party consisted of Mr Talbot and Lady Mary, Mr and Mrs Collins of Oxwich, their daughters and myself.

---

[10] Later note: 'Her son-in-law'. Numerous editions of the letters of Lady Mary Wortley Montagu were published from 1763 on.

[11] Numerous editions of the letters of Madame de Sévigné were published from 1726 on.

[12] James Fordyce, *Sermons* (1755).

[13] Alexander Pope, *Ode on Solitude*, line 10.

[14] Pencil note: 'Mr Green was living at Fairy Hill'.

30 June A letter from my old friend Dr Macqueen.

9 July Mr King and Colonel Booth past the day at Penrice Castle.

11 July Mr Talbot and Lady Mary went to the Races at Swansea. N.B. Mr Talbot gave the plate, fifty pounds.[15] He also subscribed towards a new assembly room £200 – very generous! In their absence one of my great entertainments was *Cowper's Life* by Haley – his poem of *Mary* moved me to tears.[16] *O! L'aimable homme! Quel tendre coeur!*

14 July Lady Mary and Mr Talbot returned home. All their darlings well, thank God.

[At this point Agnes quotes William Cowper's poem 'To Mary', and says that it was addressed to Mrs Unwin at the age of seventy, when Cowper was about sixty.[17]]

[Of William Cowper and Mrs Unwin:] Theirs had been a friendship of thirty years standing, as virtuous as constant. She had nursed him in his cruel *maladies*. He was the most grateful of men – and she, in my opinion, a happy woman in possessing such a friend. A.A.P., July 16th, 1804, Penrice Castle, Wales.

22 July Dear young Lord Ilchester came to Penrice Castle, to the great joy of his sister Lady Mary and myself. I have not forgot the love I bore him in his infancy and childhood. He is a sweet youth of seventeen – manly and elegant, rather reserved in his manner, but perfectly obliging. He is going on a tour through Wales, with Mr Selwyn, an Oxonian also – a few years older than Lord Ilchester.

23 July Mrs Edwin came to pay a visit at the Castle – N.B. a widow for the third time, seems an agreeable woman in company.

24 July Mr Quin[18] came for a few hours only. He appears greatly improved – was on his way from Swansea to Ireland. Mem. three years since he was here before. Mr and Mrs Hurst came to Penrice, she is a pretty woman. At night we had a party at commerce – Lord Ilchester reminded me of my weekly parties at Mr Jenkins', where I used sometimes as a great favour to take him with me. Mr Selwyn seems a very amiable young man – I rejoice at dear Lord Ilchester's having so pleasing a companion.

---

[15] A prize (probably of silver) worth £50.

[16] William Hayley, *The Life and Posthumous Writings of W. Cowper* (1803–4).

[17] See *The New Oxford Book of Eighteenth-Century Verse*, ed. Roger Lonsdale (Oxford, 1984), pp. 612–14. Agnes omits the verse starting 'And then I feel that still I hold'.

[18] Pencil note: 'Wyndham'.

25 July Mr and Mrs Price joined the party, and their niece (Miss Richards). I wrote the other day to Lady Ilchester.

26 July An agreeable day – Lord Ilchester revives his old acquaintance with me daily. Cards in the evening.

29 July At church – Mr Collins dined with us. Dear Lord Ilchester and Mr Selwyn took their leave – their vacation is to be spent in Wales on a tour. Mr Selwyn seems well informed and very sweet-tempered. A letter from my dear Lady Harriot Frampton – mem. she desires me to send her the particulars of Michael Angelo's antique seal – gained this information from Mr Selwyn, wrote to Lady Harriot the particulars. Mr and Mrs Hurst returned home.

31 July Mr Talbot's birth-day – *fifty seven.* Mr Collins and his three eldest daughters joined the festal party.

1 August Mr and Mrs Price went away.

2 August Mrs Edwin departed. Mem. *rouge* – £1600 per annum – *too little – obliged to be an œconomist* – what will this world come to? A letter from Lady Ilchester – she is appointed lady of the bed-chamber to the Queen – unsolicited – £500 per annum. A very kind letter, ditto from Lady Harriot Frampton.

3 August The evening with my dear Lady Mary and Mr Talbot – the dear children well, thank God, and making daily improvement in person and mind. A.A.P., August 4th, 1804. N.B. my dear Fanny and Mr Richards have left Swindon and are removed to Fairford, Gloucestershire. As usual I hear from, and write to, them often.

14 August Miss Talbot's birth-day – nine years. Mr Collins and his family dined at the Castle. In the evening the pretty love, as a treat, sat up to supper with her papa and mamma and me. Her pretty eyes glistened with pleasure at this indulgence, while we observed her with an united interest – I have seldom past a more agreeable evening. When I came up to my room I reverted to the years that were past, in which I had seen the dear mother at a still earlier age and assisted in keeping her birth-day, and her amiable sisters.

24 August I spent the day at Oxwich.

27 August I drank tea with Mr and Mrs Edwards. A long letter from my dear sister Fanny – she and her worthy husband like their situation at Fairford very much.

29 August Lady Mary and Mr Talbot went to Margam with their little nephew and three of their daughters for change of air in the whooping cough – the little boy and the two elder sisters are left with me.

30 August Rose at seven, visited the nursery, heard my dear pupils say their prayers and catechism. After breakfast they read and wrote letters in their best hand to their friends at Margam. They supt at five, then walked till seven, then again with me till bed-time. Mem. I saw them to bed and sat some time with them. At night *sola* – amused myself with a little botany; half an hour with *Herman of Unna*, and wrote this journal.

1 September All the night I dreamt of good Mr Peele. I thought he was dying and said to me 'Do not be sorry, consider I am above eighty years of age'. When I awoke I thought of this and recollected his many virtues and kind friendship towards myself and my dear father.

2 September Went to church. At my return found a letter from Miss Tayler, Mr Peele's niece, as he was too ill to write himself. 'But what' added she 'can we expect at my uncle's advanced age of *eighty-three*?' I fear indeed no recovery here.

4 September Mr Talbot came from Margam to pass a day with his children – Lady Mary is too *heavy* for unnecessary journeys.

15 September The family returned home. Four of these dear children have the whooping cough – all but the two eldest, who had it when infants.

20 September Mr Talbot was so good as to give me a drive in the phaeton to Swansea, where I provided myself in *winter* shoes and stockings and sat an hour with Mrs Collins and daughter. Dined with Mr Talbot and his agent Mr Llewellyn and we got home before dark to dear Lady Mary.

28 September Mr Wyndham, our Member,[19] and Mr King came to spend a day or two at Penrice Castle. Mem. I beat them at night at Pope Joan.

30 September They returned.

1 October Dr and Mrs Hunt with their sister, Mrs D. Hunt, Mr Prynn their nephew, and his pretty bride, came on a visit. They spent a [week] at Penrice to our general satisfaction. Mem. Mrs Prynn, except in dress, is quite a pretty Quaker – she is by all accounts a very worthy young woman, and much beloved by her new relations. My good luck continued: I beat them all at Pope [Joan].

8 October Our visiters left Penrice. The dear children have had a fever, but thank God are now nearly well again. It was putrid: I helpt to nurse, but no one caught it – it was the three eldest children that

---

[19] Of Parliament.

had the fever.[20] We sent the others away as soon as possible. My dear Fanny and Mr Richards are well – I had a letter from Mrs Simpson. Mr King has had a slight attack of the gout. My dear Lady Mary is as well as possible in her situation, the little whoopers are better. A.A.P., October 13th, 1804.

21 October   Mr Haverfield came to Penrice Castle. I observed more attention and cordiality in his manner of speaking to me than I had ever before remarked, but when he told me that an old acquaintance of mine had desired to be kindly remembered to me I soon comprehended that his sister-in-law, formerly Mrs Calley of Burderop, my dear father's neighbour and our obliging acquaintance, had spoken favourably of me to Mr Haverfield. Many a happy day have I spent in her house near Swindon, where we then young people were invited to her parties, balls etc. A Mr Poyntz, uncle as I heard to the Duchess of Devonshire, was at the last dance I saw there. He danced with every female in the room, yet had hunted that day from four in the morning. I have since been told that he keeps a most minute journal of his time, which he reads to his particular friends. A daily journal I should feel laborious, but now and then to 'crop the flowrets dropt by time' I think very pleasing. Mr Haverfield spent three days with us. I sent a few lines by him to Mrs Haverfield.

27 October   I wrote over a page or two *fair* from my own translation of two epochs from Le Chevalier Méhégan's *Tableau de l'Histoire Moderne*. At night Mr Talbot read us an act of a new play called *Almahide*. The author gave a very ingenious and critical dissertation upon tragedy, after which he published his *Almahide* so stupid that we could not go on with it.[21] In his expressions he makes use of the words 'thankless thanks' and tears that 'only laugh' – how surprizing the difference between criticism and performance! Let this be a caution to me *touchant mon tableau!*

28 October   At church – dear Lady Mary continues well, and the dear children are all recovered, thank God. October 28th, 1804.

29 October   Dr Hunt came to pay a friendly visit at Penrice Castle. At night an agreeable game at cribbage – Mr Talbot and Lady Mary, Doctor Hunt and I.

---

[20] 'Putrid fever' was a term used for typhus, which was frequently fatal. It seems likely that the Talbot children were suffering from some less serious infection.

[21] Benjamin Heath Malkin, *Almahide and Hamlet: A Tragedy* (1804).

30 October Mr Collins joined the dinner party. At night cribbage again.

31 October Dr Hunt returned home. At noon I received the melancholy intelligence of the death of my worthy friend the Revd Mr Peele, at the age of eighty-three. He has closed his earthly existence full of good works, as of days. I have lost a respected friend, and the world an excellent man. Dear man! How kind he was to me! Alas! How ill can we spare a true friend. A.A.P., October 31st, 1804.

16 November About November 10th Lady Elizabeth Feilding came to the Castle. Went with six children for change of air to them after the whooping cough and fevers, as also to clear Penrice Castle of those who had been ill before the little stranger should appear.[22]

17 November A most bleak situation: no trees, no houses. Close on the sea; the *dwelling* poor; windows ill-fastened; the bed curtains shaking with the wind; the sea roaring with 'hollow blasts'. But we must hope it will be salutary.

18 November My dear Mrs King came and took me in her carriage to Swansea church, after which we called on some acquaintances. I had many invitations, but declined them as the children were not to go to Swansea, so I resolved to go no where except to Marino, and church. Mr Talbot wrote me word that Lady Mary was that day safely delivered of a daughter – her seventh child. Both well as could be expected.

19 November Company all the morning – Mr King and Mr Collins our *daily* visiters. My darlings and I prosecute their studies when we can, but already find that the vicinity of a town is not favourable to attention.

20 November I spent the day with Mr and Mrs King, who sent their carriage for me. The company were Mr and Mrs Mansel Philips; Captain Jones; the Portreeve Mr Jeffries; Monsieur Séjan, and Mrs King's niece, with Miss Fanny Treherne and me. Mrs King always studies to make her house agreeable to her guests: she gives herself up to them entirely and has that serene and disengaged manner which contributes so much to social happiness.

21 November Mr Talbot came to spend the day with his children and me. All goes on well at Penrice Castle – a very stout babe.

2 December At church. Mr Jones, an Irish gentleman, preached. A

---

[22] They went to the bathing-house on the edge of the burrows, an area of sand-dunes to the west of Swansea.

most excellent discourse – text 'Keep the commandments'.[23] After church a little tour with Mrs King.

5 December   Monsieur Séjan dined with me. He is a very worthy man, and suffers for conscience sake. He was almoner to the sisters of Louis Seize, and might have his church again in Paris, would he acknowledge the usurper.

7 December   Mr Talbot and Lady Elizabeth dined with us at the bathing hôtel – all goes on as it should do at Penrice.

9 December   Mrs King was so good as to spend the day with me and my half dozen, including Lady Elizabeth's son Henry Talbot. I had an agreeable hour with her after the children went to bed – she told me the wind never blew, but she thought of me – not words, of course – Mrs King is *truly sincere – simplement simple.*

11 December   Dr Hunt called on us.

13 December   We returned home after a month's absence. The children's health and mine quite good, thank God. We found dear Lady Mary and her last child as we could wish. At the bathing house our morning visiters were: Miss Collins, aunt, nieces and cousins (seven); three Mrs Collins, three Messieurs (six); two Miss Williams and a friend (three); Mr and Mrs King, Dr Hunt (three); Mr and Mrs Page, Captain New (three); Dr and Mrs Hobbes, Mr Thomas (three); Mr Treherne, Monsieur Séjan, Miss Bassett (three); Mrs Llewellyn, Miss Adams (two). In all thirty-two persons who called frequently, at least many of them. My mornings were taken up, and my evenings were spent in solitude. *A qui mieux, mieux.*

16 December   Lady Elizabeth left us. She is a charming companion where-ever she goes or stays. At church and heard good Mr Collins. He told me he did not like to preach at Swansea church, as he heard the ladies there praise their preachers in terms he could not aspire to. One was 'the sweetest preacher'; the other 'a divine creature', and so on.

23 December   At church. Dreadful cold weather – Lady Mary could not venture out. The children all well, thank God, and we go on as well as we can, my pupils and I, considering the number of young children that attend our studies.

31 December   Dr and Mrs Hunt with Mr Price came to Penrice Castle – very agreeable visiters.

---

[23] *Ecclesiastes*, xii, 13.

1805

Agnes was away from Penrice from mid-February to mid-May 1805. During this time she spent two weeks with friends in London, after which she set off for Edinburgh, where she stayed for a month, visiting relations and old friends. On her way back to Penrice she spent a month at Fairford in Gloucestershire, where Thomas and Frances Richards were now living. Agnes spent the rest of the year at Penrice, apart from a journey at the end of September to the Passage over the River Severn, to collect Lady Mary Talbot's two youngest sisters, and accompany them back to Gower.

Journal, 1805

1 January The day as usual. At night a pool at commerce. N.B. a very happy week in their society.

5 January Dr Hunt and Mr Price went.

6 January At church.

7 January Mrs Hunt went.

9 January I meditated a journey to Scotland, which I hope I shall *realize*. Duty to a near relation and the pleasure of visiting some long-absent friends will be my *motives*. N.B. a kind letter from my dear Fanny – all there well thank God. I hope to see them before three months pass, and also I hope to see many other persons dear to me – A.A.P.

20 January A letter from my dear Mrs Keir to desire I would make her house my home while at Edinburgh. How happy it will make me to see my dear old aunt! To embrace my dear Mrs Keir, with whom I have corresponded since I was thirteen; to visit my dear Mrs Alexander – Miss Mitchel that was, with whom I formed a tender friendship in my juvenile days at Yarmouth! To see again Lady Home and the Hirsel – to call on Mrs Watkin who has so long forgotten me. To see my native country! The house my dear parents inhabited! *O, quel plaisir!*

21 January Not well. God forbid I should have the gout just now! *Nous verrons.*

30 January I wrote to my sister Fanny to offer her a meeting at Bath. N.B. they could not come to Bath, but invited me to their new abode at Fairford as soon as I could go to them. I shall take them in my return home after my expedition to the Land of Cakes.

On the 21st of this month the two Miss Collins of Swansea visited Penrice: they are most amiable young women. On the 31st came dear Doctor and Mrs Hunt.

1 February The anniversary of my dear Lady Mary Talbot's wedding day, kept with much festivity. She and her seven charming children all well – would to God that Mr Talbot was the same, but his health is very precarious. Mem. Lady Mary has written to my friend Dr Macqueen for his advice – may a blessing accompany it!

4 February The two Miss Bassets, daughters to the rector of Swansea, were sent for to Penrice Castle – very fine young women. N.B. I made my will lately.

5 February I settled to commence my journey with Mrs Frances Collins and her nephew on the 18th of this month so far as Bristol – am invited to sleep at Mr Collins of Swansea, that I may be ready to start early the next morning. I look for much pleasure in my intended excursion if it please God it takes place. A.A.P. February 7th, 1805.

11 February My dear Lady Mary's birthday.

16 February I went to Swansea, spent two days very agreeably at Mr Collins. His daughters are very agreeable girls; he is very sensible and Mrs Collins very obliging. A large party the first evening: a Captain Jones, a great talker. Mem. he had the vile Buonaparte's picture in the lid of his snuff box.

17 February At church at Swansea. Mr Basset the rector preached. Spoke loud – appeared to have all his teeth, though near eighty years of age. His eldest daughter a very graceful young woman – both of them very good-natured.

18 February Set off on my expedition with Mrs Frances Collins and her nephew – an agreeable journey. We lay at the Passage. We parted at Bristol, where I took coach on the 19th and reached London on the 20th. On the road from Bath a very whimsical fellow-traveller. He had only to whisper the Master of the Ceremonies a word in the ear to dance with the beauties of the ball – but the mamas became afraid of his accomplishments, and that he would make too strong an impression on their daughters' hearts. The young ladies wept at his departure, and the London fair-ones fainted in his arms. While abroad generals had consulted him relative to their military movements, and on shipboard admirals, by taking his advice in their naval manœuvres, won several engagements. We lost this great personage upon our arrival in London who, calling for a hack, ordered it to *Finsbury Square*. I found my dear Mrs Williams and her family well.

22 February　Called at Dr Macqueen's, who had been consulted upon Mr Talbot's illness. A long conversation with this good old friend, who engaged me to dinner on the following Tuesday.

23 February　A large card party at Mrs Williams'. A very agreeable hand at whist, and a pleasant evening.

24 February　At St Martin's church, then past the day at Dr Macqueen's. He himself friendly and agreeable; his son a charming boy about thirteen; his lady *as usual.*

25 February　Drank tea and supt at Burlington Street with my dear Lady Charlotte Strangways and Mrs Campbell. Lady Harriot Frampton was there too, and a delightful evening I had in their company. Lady Ilchester and Lady Louisa were at the grande fête at Windsor. Lady Charlotte was confined to the house from the consequence of a fall in dancing, and Lady Harriot *avoit faite une fausse couche* [had had a miscarriage].

26 February　Spent the day with my dear Mrs Pinnock, very comfortably – we talked over the days of yore. Mem. her dream.

27 February　At home with my dear Mrs Williams – a very agreeable day. We had a long conversation relative to her eldest daughter, whom she intends for the line of education – I promised very sincerely to assist her to the utmost of my power, on condition that she was duly qualified.

28 February　At Burlington Street. Lady Ilchester pretty well; Lady Charlotte better. Dear young Lord Ilchester quite well – mem. he handed me to the carriage with the same politeness as if I had been a countess. They all rejoiced to see their old friend Po. Lady Louisa is quite a beauty. Mrs Campbell is appointed sub-governess to the Princess Charlotte of Wales. At my return to the Strand found dear Mr Upcher. He drank tea and supt with us. He reminds me much of his father in some respects, but he has better abilities with a more liberal education. May he prove as worthy as his parents!

1 March　At Mr Walsh's who is married to Mrs Williams' sister. A dinner of fourteen in company; tea and cards. Mrs Walsh is much improved since her marriage – talks with more ease, and seems to feel herself of more importance. My partner at whist was a lawyer – I strove to do my best. In the morning we saw the Welsh procession and heard a discourse at St Martin's church from Dr Fisher, Bishop of Exeter.

2 March Saw *Roscius*. A delightful boy – quite great in *Norval*.[1] Mr John Home saw him act it in Edinburgh and said he had never seen it performed so much to his own satisfaction. He is indeed a phenomenon in his line, and not yet fifteen years of age! Scots music filled up the intervals between the acts – 'Tweed-Side', 'Low Down in the Broom', 'Sae merry as we Twa hae been', and 'O! Dear Lassie Loves beguiling'. Sweetly did they suit the entertainment of the evening.

3 March Spent the day at Mr Joseph Green's; went with his family to the *Foundlings*, saw the children at their dinner.[2] Charming music at their chapel and an excellent discourse. Mr Green has four fine children, all grown up, and looks himself like an elder brother of his family. Mrs Green is much better.

4 March At home with my dear Mrs Williams.

5 March Mr Williams conducted me to the Saracen's Head whence I set off on my northern journey. Travelled all day and all night. N.B. the travellers were hums-drums.

6 March Travelled again all the day and arrived at York about ten at night. Out of forty hours I had been thirty-seven in motion – rejoiced to throw myself on the bed – quite a luxury to sleep with my cloaths off. Slept very sound. Thank God, quite well. Had taken leave of my humdrum friends.

7 March At York all day to rest myself. Walked out and saw the minstrel[3] – a glorious building. The man who shewed it asked me if I had ever seen the cathedral at Salisbury. Upon my saying 'Yes' he replied 'It is a very pretty thing, Madam'. I returned to the inn and wrote to my sister and Lady Mary Talbot. N.B. the milliner – post office – letter.

8 March Journey – pretty girl – officer – city lady.

9 March Arrived at dear Edinburgh where I first drew breath – stopt

---

[1] The actor William Henry Bettey (1791–1874) was known as the 'Young Roscius'. Norval was a character in the play *Douglas* by John Home, which was performed at the Drury Lane on this night, together with *The Devil to Pay* by Charles Coffey.

[2] The Foundling Hospital (in Guilford Street from 1754) was founded by Captain Thomas Coram in 1739. Sunday services in the chapel were open to the general public.

[3] Sic. Agnes means York Minster.

at the hôtel thinking it too late to disturb Mrs Keir, it being near twelve at night. I slept sound after my very long expedition.

10 March I went at eight o'clock to George Street, No. 10, where I met with a most pleasing and cordial reception from Mrs Keir, my dear relation and thirty-year correspondent. We met indeed with joy after a separation of twenty-one years, in which time her youngest child, then unborn, is become a fine young woman. The elder son is a physician at the Court of Russia, the second is a surgeon and fixed in Edinburgh. A delightful morning. In the afternoon I accompanied Mrs Keir to St Andrew's chapel[4] – a very good discourse extemporary. No organ, but the most pleasing vocal music by the congregation. They sang in parts; singing employed half the time of worship. They prayed standing, and sat while they sang. The Lord's Prayer was said *alone* – a pause before and after it had a great effect. Mem. the Lord's Prayer was not repeated. The minister wore a band like our clergymen, and had also a sort of gown resembling that of our church-wardens. They are much softened in the Presbyterian church and seem to assimilate more with us. There are six episcopal chapels now in Edinburgh, and the people of the different churches intermarry and seem to be equally free from bigotry. Tea and supper at Mrs Keith's, my dear friend's sister – a charming family, an elegant house and every thing suitable to its exterior.

11 March Went to my aunt's and spent the day at her bed-side. Dear woman, she has but a short time in all likelihood to spend here. Be it my part to contribute to her comfort to the best of my power.

12 March Went with Mr MacLaurin and bought every thing I thought my aunt wanted, of cloaths, provisions etc. Her husband's carelessness and pride have reduced them to poverty, and been the cause of alienating both from their respective and respectable relations. But my aunt is a worthy woman and Mr MacLaurin has been a kind husband to her, both during her health and sickness. N.B. she is eighteen years older than her husband, yet was it a match of love on both sides. At night Mrs Keith's lovely family joined the party at Mrs Keir's – a charming evening: good sense and chearfulness distinguish my dear country-women.

12 March[5] Miss Patoun came to visit me as a relation. She informed me that our grandmothers had been first cousins. She was very obliging, but had too great a desire to shine in conversation – at least I thought

---

[4] St Andrew's church in George Street. It was designed by Major Andrew Frazer of the Royal Engineers, 1782–84.

[5] Sic.

so, and Mrs Keir, when Miss Patoun was gone, confirmed my opinion but added that she was a worthy woman. A charming day at Mrs Keith's.

13 March We spent the day at Mrs Major Balfour's, my dear mother's cousin. There were in company herself, her daughter Mrs Biggar, her grandson, and Miss Louisa Balfour her niece – a very fine young lady. At night she dressed for Mrs Duff's assembly, so I saw her handsome figure to advantage. Mrs Keir, with her son and daughters were in company – a most charming day – refreshing to my heart to see so many dear relations, and gratifying to my pride to see them move in so respectable a sphere. Mrs Major Balfour's brother-in-law, the *General*, is now in London. His wife was an Ogilvie and a near relation of my dear mother's.

14 March The Miss Lowes, two very agreeable ladies, spent the day with us at Mrs Keir's. The eldest is a very sensible woman indeed; the second is very good also, but has a touch of flirtation in her character. Very entertaining in their anecdotes. Mem. the song 'She play'd the town'.

15 March At my aunt's. She is very weak – she rambles a little in mind, but sees and hears remarkably well for her age. After having slumbered a little she awoke suddenly and said 'Nannie, I shall see your *dear father* before you will'. May we both see him!

16 March Drank tea and supt at Miss Menie Cant's. She was my dear mother's relation, and sister to Mrs Keir's mother. There were eight sisters of them. All handsome women – cotemporaries with my dear mother. Four of them were married: Mrs Rae, Mrs Balfour, Mrs Hay and Mrs Orr. Of these only Mrs Orr remains; of the single ones only Miss Menie. She talked of my mother and their juvenile days, and was very kind to me. Mrs Graham, her niece, lives with her. N.B. in Scotland an old relation is seldom ever left *solitary, whether rich or poor* – a sense of domestic duty is very prevalent.

17 March At St Andrew's church, then with my aunt all the day. Were I independant, I would remain with her the rest of her days – *mais, c'est impossible*.

18 March Mr Ogilvie, my mother's nearest relation, came to see me. A very charming man – our meeting gave us pleasure. We reminded each other of an appointment to dance together at Carlisle House assembly many years ago, but the vessel he was to go in to the Indies sailed that very day. He told me he was now married and had a good wife, and a fine family with an easy fortune; that he had purchased a good estate in the neighbourhood of his elder brother called *Chester*, to which he was then going. Should time permit, he invited me to visit Chester. His brother and family are well; his sister, Mrs *General* Balfour, died in the Indies. He said she was an excellent creature and an irreparable loss to her husband and family.

19 March Company at Mrs Keir's in morning. Visits: Mrs Crawford, Mrs Scott of Moncrief, Mrs Major Drummond, and Miss Patoun. I dined at Doctor Duncan's, brother-in-law to Mrs John Collins junior of Swansea. Her sister Mrs Duncan a handsome, sensible woman. Their mother Mrs McFarquhar, Miss McFarquhar, Miss Duncan, and Mr Howel, a Welsh student, were our party. We talked of Swansea acquaintances etc. At night my dear Mrs Keir called upon me and took me home.

20 March A morning visit to Miss Keith of Ravelston. Her brother possesses a good collection of paintings, which she obligingly shewed me. Mem. a charming portrait of Queen Mary's, copied from an original at Lord Moreton's. We paid several other morning visits, to Mrs Orr, Mrs Balfour, and Mrs Elliot – the latter well acquainted with my dearest parents. She was a daughter of Sir James Elphinstone's, and married Doctor Elliot my mother's cousin. My father united them, and three months after preached Dr Elliot's funeral sermon. The widow bought the house, that she might never be obliged to quit it. For fifty years she never could mention her husband's name, but now she loves to talk of him as of one she is soon to meet. A charming woman – reads, thinks, and expresses herself with the utmost precision, both of words and ideas, at eighty-seven years of age. Very kind to me. N.B. her discourse about Mr Barkley.

21 March With my aunt and Mr MacLaurin all the day. He kind and attentive to his wife, but in other matters rather inconsistent. I helped to nurse and comfort my dear aunt.

22 March A morning visit to Miss Patoun. In the evening went with my friends to Mrs Davison's: a very fine woman, and an excellent mother to ten children. Her daughters are accomplished; her sons are studious – all *good*. She is a lovely woman, and it is a fine sight to see her with her eight daughters around her. She regretted Mr Davison's absence.

23 March In the morning saw Mrs Scott of Moncrief's very curious works: shell-work; embroidery; paper raised to imitate seals in *relievo* – very ingenious indeed, and herself so neat, so prim, and so quiet as to be quite a curiosity too. My dear Mrs Keir and I proceeded in a carriage to St Bernard's well, one of the sweetest spots I ever saw. A Roman temple is erected near the fountain, with the goddess of health pointing to the spring. We then proceeded to Leith; walked on the pier some time and admired the lovely scenery. In our return we visited the glass manufactory – N.B. a chandelier valued at 500 guineas. To compleat our pleasure Mrs Keir and I, with her son and daughter, dined and spent the day at the Miss Lowes. The party were, beside ourselves, Mr and Mrs Scott of Moncrief, Mr and Mrs Gibson. N.B. she is niece to the celebrated Dr Blair,[6] and he claimed acquaintance with me on my father's account who was, he said, his particular intimate and one of the worthiest of men. 'Besides which' he added 'he was a good musician and many a happy hour have we played our violins together.' Mr Gibson was my partner at whist, my assistant at table, and saw me down *many* stairs to a chair that waited for me. Miss Preston, a niece of Sir Robert Preston's, sang most sweetly: Italian and Scots songs. It has been a most happy day indeed, and my dear friends and I chatted over the occurrences of it at our return till two o'clock in the morning.

24 March At church twice. Drank tea at Mrs Doctor Elliot's – a very superiour woman. We supt at Mrs Orr's – her three daughters agreeable, particularly Louisa. The mother shewed us a present sent her by her son, Colonel Orr in the East Indies – he has made a large fortune and is married to General Sidenham's daughter. He is probably fixed abroad for life, but never forgets his duty and affection towards his mother and sisters. The ring might be valued at about seventy pounds: the old lady said she was too old to wear it and it was too fine for her daughters, so she would leave it to her daughter-in-law Mrs Orr as she thought she had the best right to it. To this her daughters never made the least objection – I am proud of my country-women. The youngest Miss Lowes, on being asked to which country she gave a preference, made answer: 'The English ladies are more elegant and more accomplished, but we are more lively and sensible' – and I think she might have added '*more dutiful*'. Miss Patoun of our party. Mr Cornelius Elliot, brother of Mrs Major Balfour's, and of course our relation, paid me a morning visit between churches. He was very chatty and told me the establishment of all his family: his eldest daughter was married to Colonel Dallas – a very rich man; his second was a widow; his youngest was married to Sir James or John Carmichael; and both his sons had died in the service of their country. He promised to meet me next day at his sister's.

25 March Dined at Mrs Major Balfour's – a sweet woman. Saw there Mrs Colonel Dallas; Mr and Mrs Ross of Rossie; Miss Elliot, a rich and beautiful heiress whose father, Mrs Balfour's other brother, died in his

---

[6] Dr Hugh Blair (1718–1800) was a well-known preacher and lecturer in Edinburgh.

way home through London, so never returned to his child or native country. Mr Cornelius Elliot, Mr Russel, Mrs Biggar and son of the party – a very agreeable day. At night I had a chair and met my dear Mrs Keir at Mr Keith's of Ravelstone. Nine in company – an elegant entertainment.

26 March The day at my dear aunt's. Mr MacLaurin saw me home. N.B. a most particular conversation – *[word illegible]* lady – friendship etc. I found company at Mrs Keir's: her sister Mrs Keith and family; Mrs Major Drummond; Mr Keith of Ravelstone; Mr Creech the editor of the *Mirrour*;[7] Miss Patoun. Mem. Mr Creeches anecdote of Mr ?Craigy of ?moony-shine, two bottles of brandy, river, moon, wood, wig, hat etc – never to be forgotten – a rival to *Gilpin* in wit and humour.[8]

27 March Walked with my dear friend on the Calton Hill. Went also up the Castle Hill – viewed the castle with admiration. Then we proceeded to Holy-Rood House – walked in the picture gallery; saw Mary's apartments, the coverlet she worked, the bed she lay in, the table and secretaire she used, the little room where she was at supper with her maids and Rizio, the back door and narrow stairs where the murderers entered, etc. A fine copy of a picture of her when at Paris was brought by le Prince D'Artois to the palace. N.B. I saw the altar where the French princes had *messe* performed at one end of the gallery, also the rooms they inhabited which had been modernized, that is spoiled, for their accommodation. Two old nobles requested leave to remain at Holy-Rood House, which request was granted. Called to take leave of Mrs Doctor Elliot. Mrs Major Balfour called upon me – she had not walked so far, she told me, for years. Mr Howel paid me a visit and desired me to inform Mr Collins' family at Swansea that he should return to Wales for good next June. At night company at my dear Mrs Keir's – the lady and daughters of Lord Woodhouselee. N.B. Mr Tytler, author of many excellent papers in the *Mirror*; Miss Patoun; Mrs and Miss Orrs. They took a kind leave of me.

28 March The morning with my aunt. Settled every thing with Mrs Keir for her comfort – left money in Mrs Keir's hands, who promised to visit my aunt once a week. My dear aunt wept at our parting. My heart too felt a knell – had I been independant I would not have left her, dear woman. I parted with my most amiable friend Mrs Keir and her lovely Isabella the same evening. 'We shall meet again' said my

---

[7] *The Mirror* was a periodical paper, published in Edinburgh by William Creech, 1779–80.

[8] This probably refers to William Cowper's poem *John Gilpin* (first published 1782).

dear Mrs Keir as she embraced me – yes, we shall meet. Lay at the hôtel.

29 March Reached Newcastle. In the coach a communicative Scots man; a conceited English man, and a *mad* German with a sulky-looking, silent young man that I privately gave the name to of 'Simon Pure'.[9]

30 March The maid forgot to call me according to her promise – the coach went without me. N.B. they carried away my trunks – sadly vexed. He I had called 'Simon Pure' begged me not to hurry myself, and then represented the hardship of the case with so much good sense and benevolence towards me that the landlady promised to [do] all in her power to compromise [settle] the matter – I was to pass the day without expence, and be sent to York the next morning with a letter to the people to whose house my trunks had been sent. This amiably settled, my obliging fellow-traveller took his leave and left me for the time averse to Lavater and all his tribe.[10] The German returned and drank tea with me in the evening, giving me to understand that he was to be of my party to York the next day. He told me that he had injured his brain by a fall from an open carriage, that his health was now better, and he was travelling in pursuit of happiness, that he had passed through France, Spain and Scotland, but with no success. He believed he should return to England again. I went up to bed very early – had a fine night's rest.

31 March Was not sorry to leave Newcastle the next morning. A decent farmer and the German, who talked a great deal and looked at times very wild. His notions of marriage, his proposals to a young woman's father, the farmer's opinion of the same. Arrived late at York; had my trunks.

1 April Staid at York all day. Wrote to my sister, to Lady Mary Talbot and Mrs Keir. Walked to the Post Office with my letters.

3 April At Mr Williams'. His house full of company.

4 April Went to Mr and Mrs Joseph Green's – made the twentieth person at table. N.B. the generality of the company very witty upon Scotland – its poverty; its cookery; its customs etc. – one wondered to see me so plump after having been three weeks in Edinburgh; another asked me if I had seen such a sight as roast beef, etc. Mr Green himself a pleasing man, but his *rich* visiters intolerably vulgar – I laughed and

[9] Simon Pure was a character in the play *A Bold Stroke for a Wife* (1718) by Susannah Centlivre.
[10] John Caspar Lavater, the German author (see below, p. 355).

took all their *smart* sayings as wit. One of them hoped he had not *hurt* me – poor souls!

5 April Spent the day with my dear Mrs Pinnock. She is wonderfully well, considering her great age – eighty-seven.

25. Letter from Agnes Porter, 18 Guilford Street, London, to Lady Mary Talbot, Penrice Castle, 5 April 1805

My Dear Lady Mary,

I received your letter safe, as also its contents: £30 draft. I went immediately to Parliament Street, but Dr Macqueen was at his country house. If he does not return to-morrow I will write to him. I called at Burlington Street, and signified that I had a corner of a trunk for your commissions. Lady Ilchester was at Court, but I saw your dear brother with your two sisters. Lady Charlotte is better, and Lady Louisa is in perfect health and compleat beauty. Lord Ilchester and little Giles were also quite well. I did not see Mrs Campbell.

I wrote to you again from York on my return, and put the letter into the post with my own hand. I will remember the commissions for my dear little loves, and will only remain a fortnight at Fairford: out of the time I have been absent thirteen days were employed in the mere act of travelling 1000 miles. I met with some delicious fellow-travellers, and have committed all the circumstances to memory for your amusement when we meet. I heard a great deal in Edinburgh of the author of *Modern Philosophers* – it is a Miss Hamilton, who has also written on education.[11] The latter work induced Lord Lucan to offer her by letter the care of his unfortunate children, with a carte blanche as to terms. She declined the situation, but his lordship came post to Edinburgh to prevail on her acceptance of his proposal. His daughter, a fine young lady, made use of entreaties and caresses for the same purpose, and Miss Hamilton accompanied them back. Her celebrity is great in Edinburgh, and her character is so highly estimated that every-one says it stands too high for calumny's envenomed arrows ever to reach.

I dined here yesterday with twenty in company. As they found I was but just returned from Scotland the general topic was the poverty of the country; the greediness and nationality of the Scotch; their wretched houses; poor entertainments, etc. I ventured to hint that the houses of the New Town were beautiful; that the public edifices were grand; the

---

[11] This was Elizabeth Hamilton (1758–1816), whose wrote *Memoirs of Modern Philosophers* (1800).

country was improving; they had *enough* at their tables, with an easy flow of conversation after dinner to assist digestion – but I was looked upon as a most partial observer, and forced to content myself with drawing a secret comparison not much in their favour. But all this *entre nous*.

Mr and Mrs Green have been very kind indeed. They desire their best compliments.

I am my dear Lady Mary's most obliged Ann Agnes Porter.

My respects to Mr Talbot.

Journal, 1805

6 April At Mrs Green's.

7 April Went with them again to the Foundling Hospital. A most charming place: the children, the music, the preacher – all interesting. N.B. the *unhappy fair*[12] who sat next me.

8 April Did some stock business – Mr Green so good as to go with me.

9 April Returned to Mr Williams.

11 April Went with Mrs Williams to Hammersmith to see her daughter at her boarding school – a very good house and agreeable mistress of it – Mrs Dunlop. Saw the young ladies dance – about sixty, and not a whisper past between them – all silent. Miss Williams grows a very pleasing girl in her person – she is about thirteen, has a remarkably fine complection, with light hair and fine blue eyes. We dined next door at the Revd Mr Turner's, where Mrs Williams' only son is at school – returned in good time to our evening hand at cards.

12 April An agreeable day with my dear Mrs Williams. Dr Macqueen called upon me to take leave – his lady is, it seems, no friend to society, and neither makes her own acquaintances nor his welcome – *tant pis pour le mari!* But he wished for riches – *et le voilà riche*. He told me with a sigh that wealth did not confer happiness.

15 April Left my good London friends and set out for my still dearer friends at Fairford. Left London at six o'clock – travelled all night.

16 April Reached Fairford about six in the morning. My Fanny's arms open to receive me; a most kind welcome from Mr Richards and his niece Miss Morice; breakfast ready set – a delicious meal; then my sister insisted on my going to bed; did so and slept till two o'clock, then

---

[12] Sic.

dressed for dinner. A most happy party – my brother and sister in good health, thank God. Their nephew goes on well at Mr Crowdy's of Swindon, lawyer, and their niece is a lovely amiable girl of fifteen. Miss Brooke is much the same, poor girl, and their new child, Miss Edwards, is a sweet girl. She was daughter to the late rector of Fairford, who left his affairs in great disorder. Mr Richards and Mr Keeble,[13] another worthy clergyman, undertook to settle them and assist the widow and children. They did so, and Mr and Mrs Richards have taken this dear little girl to educate her. They are both very fond of her, and my sister gives her the name of her 'dear sparkle'.

17 April Mrs Keble, Mrs Edwards and Mrs Darby called upon us. In the afternoon my sister and family drank tea at Mrs Darby's. She is a pleasing woman, and has been in Scotland – knew Mr and Mrs Scott of Moncrief, and Major Hay our relation – was there when the accounts came of his death. He was killed in an engagement where he was next in command to Sir Ralph Abercrombie.[14] His last words were 'Abercrombie, remember my wife and children!' N.B. Mrs Major Hay has an annuity of £500 from [the] government and fifty pounds per annum for each of her children.

18 April We drank tea at the Revd Mr Keble's. A charming family of five children. The eldest son is, at thirteen, a prodigy of learning – can repeat fifty or sixty verses in any part of Homer, and when he translates can repeat either the sense or the words of the original with pleasure and exactness. Mr Richards told me this circumstance.

19 April Walked about Fairford. A very pretty little town, but the church is most curious. It was built on purpose to put in very fine painted glass windows, a prize from the Spaniards in Henry VIIth reign.[15]

21 April At church. A most excellent discourse from Mr Richards: 'Work out your salvation etc., etc.' Every word had weight. His church was quite full, for he is equally beloved and respected by his parish. In the afternoon again at church. Dined late and spent the evening in

---

[13] Sic. This was the Revd John Keble (1745–1835), vicar of Coln St Aldwyn, who lived in Fairford. His eldest son was John Keble (1792–1866), a founder of the Oxford Movement.

[14] General Sir Ralph Abercromby (1734–1801) led the landing of the British troops at the Helder on 27 August 1797. The aim of the expedition was to capture the remains of the Dutch fleet, which had been defeated at Camperdown.

[15] This is incorrect. The early Tudor glass at Fairford is thought to have been painted under the direction of Bernard Flower, the king's glazier.

friendly conversation; prayers early and to bed at ten. N.B. we rise at six; breakfast at eight; dine at three; and sup at half past eight; prayers half-past nine, and to bed at ten. This is the life of the people of Fairford. It is needless to add they are diligent, good and happy.

22 April   Drank tea at Mr Wane's.

23 April   Mr Edwards, surgeon, and his wife, with Miss Oldesworth drank tea with us.

24 April   Mr Carter and Mrs Darby made our party at tea and whist – an agreeable evening.

26 April   Drank tea at Mrs Luckman's.

3 May   Mr Morice came to see us. He likes his profession and the family he is in very much.

4 May   We walked to see the paper mill: the young Mr Kebles, Mr and Miss Morice, Miss Edwards and I.[16] We took Mr Barker's place in our way – extremely pleasant and in high cultivation. The paper mill a most curious process – returned with good appetite to dinner, after a walk of five miles.

5 May   At church. A long conversation with my dear Fanny, on many subjects.

6 May   An agreeable day at home. Miss Morice entertained me with a very fine lesson. She plays extremely well and draws very prettily. She is a very fine young woman indeed, and does great credit to my sister's education of her. N.B. an excellent workwoman.

7 May   *Twelve* at our dinner party, comprehending *toute la jeunesse de Fairford*. To tea Mr and the Mrs Kebles, Mrs Luckman, and Mr -[17], a young gentleman at Mr Edwards', whose name I forget. A little dance in the evening – very nice dancers indeed. My dear sister was quite in her element to see the children so happy.

8 May   A letter informed me of the death of Miss Matilda Church of Yarmouth. She has had the kindness to leave me a hundred pounds. I read this instance of her goodness with tears, while my friends rejoiced at my legacy.

9 May   Drank tea at the agreeable Mrs Darby's. A table at whist: Mr Carter and Mrs Darby; my sister and I. Mem. what I think of Mr Carter.

10 May   At home: a nice walk and tête-à-tête with my dear sister.

---

[16] The paper mills were at Quenington, near Fairford. Pigot and Co.'s *National Commercial Directory* of 1830 lists (p. 139) Joshua Carby Radway, paper maker, Quenington mill. Fairford Park belonged to John Raymond Barker.

[17] Sic.

11 May Ditto.

12 May At church morning and afternoon – an agreeable day.

13 May A tender farewell of my dear sister and her circle. Mr Richards saw me to the stage – a clergyman and an officer in my party. The two gentlemen soon began to tell where they had been – the officer was just from London, the clergyman had been in Kent. He mentioned Canterbury cathedral and said the man who shewed it seemed to think the chair of the saint was the thing most worthy notice: 'Here Sir', said he 'sat Thomas à Becket'. 'And here' interrupted the clergyman, seating himself, 'sits Thomas A. Becket again.' 'That is really my name' added he, and the man looked as if Thomas had left his shrine he was so much surprized. This led to his predecessor's character etc., some historical remarks – a very agreeable journey to Bristol in their company. From Bristol to Swansea with a Captain W. Dobbin, His Majesty's Pioneer ?Act in Milford. N.B. he gave me his address with an invitation to see his wife, should I ever travel that way – *I never will.*

15 May Reached Swansea about five in the morning – went to bed and slept till ten. Breakfast. Mr King, Colonel Price and Miss Basset paid me a visit. The carriage came, which conveyed me to Penrice Castle by dinner. Found Mr Talbot rather better; Lady Mary and her lovely children all well – a kind reception. Penrice Castle *beautiful.*

17 May Mr King spent the day with us – a nice *billet* from Mrs King: she is well.

18 May Dined at Mr Collins, Oxwich.

27 May Colonel Price spent the day with us.

28 May Drank tea at Mrs Edwards.

30 May Dear Nanny Longford came to spend a few days – rejoiced to see her.

Finished this journal, Ann Agnes Porter, Penrice Castle, June 3rd, 1805.

I have had a letter from my sister – they are all well. A letter from Mrs Keir – my aunt is better. My pupils improve and are charming creatures. Heavens bless them!

5 June A most charming evening with such a concert of birds! How charming!

1806

No journal or letters have survived from the period between June 1805 and November 1806, but the diaries and letters of the Talbots give some information on Agnes's movements during this time. In October 1806 Agnes left her position at Penrice: her advancing age and often poor health meant that she found her responsibilities there too heavy. She went instead to live with her sister and brother-in-law in Fairford.

26. Letter from Agnes Porter, Fairford, to Lady Mary Talbot, Penrice Castle, 22 November 1806

My Dear Lady Mary,
I received both your letters. The *former* conveys an indelible obligation upon me, *never, never,* to be forgotten.[1] I shall only add on that subject that there is no reason for you to entertain the smallest uneasiness on my account. I shall do very well, my dear Lady Mary, with due œconomy till Lord Ilchester comes of age, and after that period, should he be *regular* in the remittance of what your good father left me, I shall then be in affluence for my situation in life, and enabled also to do a *little good* to others.

I hope Miss Pryor and Miss Elborough will prove worthy of their employment in your family. I hope my dear Lady Elizabeth will not leave Penrice Castle for some time to come, and I hope Dr and Mrs Hunt will soon be your visitors. These hopes and wishes being expressed, I pass on to another part of your letter, namely Betsy Glover. She was most attentive indeed, and went as far as she could with me, to Chepstow. She was both so very kind and so very clever in her attentions to me that I missed her a little too much during the rest of my journey. She told me that the captain of a London trader had made her an offer of marriage, but she had not made up her mind to it as

---

[1] The Talbots gave Agnes a leaving present of 200 guineas [£210].

yet, but chose to consider the subject well on her children's account. This I commend her for, but advised her not to encourage *dangling*.

I bore the travelling much better than I expected to do. My brother and sister are extremely kind to me, and under their roof I may (if it is not my own fault) lead a life of 'piety and peace'. Mr Richards *composes* two excellent sermons every week, which he preaches on Sunday. The saints' days are kept, and there is a sacrament every month. At nine in the evening he reads prayers to his family, and at ten we go to bed.

Reading in a religious book the other day, I met with a quotation that pleased me uncommonly. It alluded to our redemption:

> Love so transcendent, so divine,
> Description makes it less.
> Tis what I know but can't define,
> Tis ... I feel but can't express.

I should like to know the author. I think he contradicts *by proof* Dr Johnson's assertion relative to sacred poetry.

My love attend my darling pupils of the two generations. God bless them all! Tell dear Mr Talbot that I thank him for his last most obliging letter to his and your ever affectionate servant, Ann Agnes Porter.

I beg my kind remembrance to Mr and Mrs Collins of Oxwich etc.

Will my dear Miss Talbot be so good as write out Mrs Hunt's receipt for tooth powder – I forgot it. Are the loves all quite well? *Et vous, ma très chère Lady Mary – se va t'il bien?*

Pray, what was it that Mr John Collins gave his little boy for the water in his head? I have some idea it was *antimony*.

27. Letter from Agnes Porter, Fairford, to Lady Mary Talbot, Penrice Castle, 11 December 1806

My Dearest Lady Mary,

I know your goodness so well that I think you will like to know how I am, and how I go on in the new scenery around me. Barring my accident, my health is good and I every day endeavour to preserve it by air and exercise: I go out when not another soul in the house would stir. One day they find it too sharp; another day the air is close; a third it looks gloomy; and a fourth the wind is troublesome. I mind none of those particulars but, wrapping my self well up, I sally forth. It has been a great comfort to me to find that it was possible to remove myself through a long journey, for this gives me hopes that I shall be able to see you and Mr Talbot and your loves again, and that were you in Bath or London, and that one of your governesses chanced to go, I could try my best to supply for a few weeks their temporary absence. This gives me great satisfaction, even in idea, for I had harboured an opinion that my accident would force me, like a log of wood, to remain where ever I fell. But thank God I have great mercies to be thankful for, nor is it among the least that I have a probability of seeing your dear faces again.

My brother and sister are exceedingly kind indeed: I am very comfortably situated under their roof and made by them a welcome guest till your brother's being of age shall put it in my power to make an agreement more consonant to their circumstances, and my own feelings.

You would smile to see me, my dear Lady Mary, who used to shrink so from the least particle of humidity, now mounted upon high pattens which do not preserve me from the mud, wading half a mile through the dirtiest streets to pay an afternoon visit, and return home at night with no other light than a lantern. In April, if it please God, I propose going to Town for about three months. My chief employment there will be to examine into the progress my god-daughter has made in her education, and improve her so far as I am able.

I beg my love to your circle, my best respects included to Mr Talbot, kind compliments to Mr Collins and his family. Where are Dr and Mrs Hunt? Where are Mr and Mrs King? Is Miss Adams married? Are your dear sisters all well? And how are you, my own dear Lady Mary? God bless you all! Ever yours, Ann Agnes Porter.

Mr Drummond wrote me word that before he could transfer my money into my own name he must send a power for Mr Talbot to sign – I have not heard since.

1807

Agnes appears to have spent most of 1807 in Fairford, apart from a trip to London in July and August.

28. Letter from Agnes Porter, [Fairford], to Lady Mary Talbot, Penrice Castle, 3 March 1807

My Dearest Lady Mary,

I received your letter of the 9th of last month, and cannot give you sufficient thanks for your goodness in writing to me in the throng of your nearest friends, and in the midst of what you always have, various occupations. I rejoice at your welfare, and that of *our* lovely and good children. I was indeed surprized at the progress the dear little Charlotte has made in writing. It was so much admired here that I had need of all my veracity to make it believed that the writer was not more than just seven. My dear Christiana, too, sent me a nice letter; I shall write to her and her sister Charlotte soon. I am indebted also to my good little friends Miss Talbot and Miss Jane for two very agreeable letters, for which I return them my best thanks along with my constant love. Tell Miss Jane that the enigma will be discovered by the proper arrangement of four letters, *viz.* E.O.L.V.

I hope poor Davis has been found,[1] and is better. I often think of Miss Adams and puzzle my head to find out the *intended*. I have heard a report that Mr J. Lucas is soon to be married, but I trust it is to some other lady, yet Hymen and Cupid play sad tricks sometimes, and often occasion a losing game to both parties.

I have lately read a book which I think merits a place in your cabinet. It is the *Antediluvian World* by James Parkinson-Hoxton and is, notwithstanding its title, a subject quite in your way.[2] I am going to London

---

[1] Note in another hand: 'A [bailiff] he threw himself over the cliff'.
[2] James Parkinson, *Organic Remains of a Former World* (1804).

in about three weeks: will you favour me with something or other to do for you and Mr Talbot, to whom I beg my affectionate and grateful respects. Will you send me instructions relative to my box of prints? I owe Lady Charlotte several of them. Will you be so good as send me word where I may see Lady Harriot Acland or any other near connection of yours. Is there any chance of your being in London during the three months I shall be there? My chief errand is on my god-daughter's account. I want to examine her progress in education and lend a hand, for three months, towards it. I find but few occasions of being useful now, and am desirous to grasp at the *little* in my power.

God bless my dearest Lady Mary with his blessings both *here* and *ever*! A.A.P.

29. Letter from Agnes Porter, Fairford, to Lady Harriot Frampton, Moreton, 14 March 1807

You cannot think, my dear Lady Harriot, how vexed I am at not being able to send you the particulars of *Marie Bauvin*. I have written to several historical friends, but had the shabby satisfaction of hearing they knew no more of the fair lady than I did. As I have not Roscoe's *Leo*, would you be so good as transcribe the lines that relate to her with the *page, volume* etc., etc.[3] Perhaps I may yet pop upon it. It may be that we might both know her by her title, though we forget her name.

I hope your dear little ones are well – whenever you favour me with a few lines be sure to give me some details of them. You and yours are dear to me, and it will be quite an indulgence to hear of your pretty prattlers and your own health.

I have been lately delighted with Roscoe's *Lorenzo del'Medici*.[4] It is an elegant performance indeed, and gives me the highest opinion of the writer's abilities. Do you know I am going to Town at Easter, or rather just after it? Will you make me happy by giving me some little commission to do for you when there. I shall be at my old *nid*, No. 11 Strand[5] ... *[part of next page torn].*

... twenty persons to dinner – it was a most acceptable addition to the entertainment.

My sister and Mr Richards present their respectful remembrance. As

---

[3] William Roscoe, *The Life and Pontificate of Leo the Tenth* (1805).

[4] William Roscoe, *The Life of Lorenzo de Medici, called the Magnificent* (1795).

[5] This was the house of Agnes's friend Evan Williams.

for me I am, while I exist, my dear Lady Harriot's affectionate and obliged Ann Agnes Porter.

My letters come free if enclosed to Mr Windham, Downing Street, Westminster, with an A. under the outer seal.

30. Letter from Agnes Porter, London, to Lady Harriot Frampton, [Moreton], 7 July 1807

My Dear Lady Harriot,

I hope you and all yours are well. You may suppose I have not forgotten your Marie Baudin: on the contrary she has been an object of my peculiar research, among my literary friends and my *émigré* acquaintances. I have tormented them incessantly about *Marie Baudin*. Not contented with this, I hied to a fashionable jeweller's, bought a gold-pin which I wanted not, and then humbly besought them to throw a little more light over a certain inestimable jewel called the *Baudine* Diamond. They shook their wise heads, and I mine, and so 'we parted as we met first', and I returned home melancholy. 'This will never do', thought I, 'this plaguey *Marie Baudin* will not suffer me to rest till I do homage to her memory, which in my present state of darkness is impracticable.' In despair I snatched a pen and gave vent to my perturbed emotions on paper: this I addressed to an oracle of the muses ycleped[6] *Roscoe*. From him I have just received an answer, and from this answer I learn that there was no such divinity as *Marie Baudin*. O! Thou Harriot! But that *Gaudin* was the proper appellation. Mr Roscoe derived his information from Amelot on the authority of Fabroni.[7] He thinks it not improbable that she may appear among *les Dames Galantes de Brantôme*,[8] but promises me, at a more leisure season, to make farther inquiries and write to me again. If he does, I will not fail to communicate them to my dear Lady Harriot.

When I saw your sisters they looked lovely; when I heard from dear Lady Mary, she was well. God bless you and your house! I am your affectionate and obliged Ann Agnes Porter.

I return to Fairford next Monday, viz. June 13th.[9] I have had the very great pleasure of seeing Lady Susan and Mr O'Brien. I fear I shall

---

[6] Called.

[7] Probably A. N. Amelot de la Houssaie; and Angelo Fabroni (numerous works on history and biography published, 1770s and later).

[8] Pierre de Bourdeille, Seigneur de Brantôme, *Vies des dames galantes* (1660s).

[9] Sic, but should presumably be July.

not see my dear Lady Elizabeth – I was in great hopes she would have visited London.

31. Letter from Agnes Porter, [London], to Lady Mary Talbot, Penrice Castle, 13 July 1807

[*At top of page in a different hand:* 4th July 1807, received of a lady anonymous, a five pound Bank of England note, for which I return sincere thanks for myself and family, Geo. Robt. Kirke.]

My Dearest Lady Mary,
Since my last to you I have made several inquiries concerning Mr Kirke. Mr Maud, a navy agent, a relation of Mr Amyot's, at his request procured some account of him from the captain with whom Mr Kirke had sailed. They reported him to be a worthy gentleman. From Mr Long's I went to Mr Brook's of Paternoster Row, to whom Mr Kirke is at present a reader. Mr Brooke had known him but six weeks: so far as he knew him he gave him a good character, said he appeared willing to be employed and had been regular and attentive in the transactions between them. He believed him to be good-natured to a degree of quixotism, as his care of the cabin boy proved, whom he had raised to be a midshipman and provided for accordingly, but who, like himself had lost all by the shipwreck. This boy with another, the wife's son by a former husband, he Mr K. had bound apprentice to this Mr Brooke. That he did church duty whenever he could procure it, and that the Revd Mr Parker, Well Street, Cripplegate, had employed him on Sundays for many years and allowed of a reference for Mr K.'s character. I next saw Mr Kirke, who appeared to me a man of slender capacity but of very gentle, good humoured, countenance – his manners very tolerable. He gave me to understand he was in debt, that his daughter was still a great expence to him, that he should be happy to obtain a curacy in London, which place he could by no means leave – he seemed very grateful to Mr Talbot's bounty and yours. Let me know if I have done right.
    Ever yours, Po.

32. Letter from Agnes Porter, Fairford, to Lady Harriot Frampton, Moreton, Dorset, 24 August 1807

My Dear Lady Harriot,
I shall with pleasure take your advice relative to my picture, in waiting till Christmas, and in the mean time have got one more raffler in Mr

Richards, whose name you will be so good as add to our list, as also your sister's, Lady E. Feilding, whom I believe I mentioned before. We have now to return your ladyship our thanks for the intended present of game next week, but we request the favour of you to transfer it to a friend of ours in London to whom we have been a good deal indebted for many civilities. I know your kindness, or I would not take so great a liberty.

I make no doubt that your darling boys are every thing you should wish them to be. I think you would approve of Mrs Hamilton's work on the subject of education: she begins with infancy and handles her subject in a masterly manner – I wish every mother of young children to read her system. As Locke[10] has unfolded the human mind, she shews a method of bringing the faculties to perfection. I dislike nothing in the whole book but the author's dislike of dolls, which I think may be made useful, as well as amusing where little girls are concerned. In the first faculty which she wishes to be cultivated, the perception, I think Lady Mary's practice keeps pace with Miss Hamilton's theory.

Receive our best acknowledgements, and believe me ever yours, A. A. Porter.

If you are so good as to send the game to our friend, the address is: Mr Amyot, No. 21 Downing Street, Westminster.

33. Letter from Agnes Porter, Fairford, to Lady Mary Talbot, Penrice Castle, 22 October 1807

My Dear Lady Mary,
I received your favour, and rejoice to find that you and your pretty ones are all so well. I think Mr Christopher begins betimes to be a literary character – I suppose dear Christiana will be happy to assist him in learning to write. Little Isabella, I suppose, prattles away as well as any of them. My dear Miss Talbot is, I know, a most amiable pupil, and I hope poor Miss Smyth will recover and be enabled again to resume her important charge. Was she the *person* recommended by Mrs Trimmer?[11] In the absence of any tutress, it is not your children who are losers, but yourself. You have so much patience and intelligence that they cannot fail to improve, but then the fatigue might be too exhausting both for your health and spirits.

---

[10] The philosopher John Locke (1632–1704).
[11] The well-known writer Sarah Trimmer (1741–1810), who acted as an unofficial employment exchange for governesses.

I am quite pleased to tell you that at last I have got a harper's direction. He will be very willing to attend Mr Talbot's family, but there are two musicians of them, who always travel in company: Thomas Ricards, Llanidloes, *musician*; Mr Blaney, harper, Newtown, Montgomeryshire. It will give Mr Talbot amusement of an evening to hear sweet music, and be at the same time an enlivening circumstance to his light-hearted and light-footed tribe.

I have not yet had Miss Talbot's epistle – my best love to her and Miss Jane and my other darlings.

It is a satisfaction to me that you approve of the destination of your bounty, to a clergyman's family, and still more, from his being son to my good Mrs Pinnock. He has two daughters and four sons. One of the boys he wishes much to gain admittance for, into Christ's Hospital; another he would educate for the church, could he afford it. I am at present trying to do all I can for them.

Je vous salue ma très chère, Po.

1808

In 1808 Agnes was still living in Fairford, but she spent a part of the months of August and September at Penrice with five of the Talbot children, whilst Thomas and Lady Mary Talbot were at Margam with the other two children. Agnes then spent a week at the Fox Strangways family's old home, Redlynch in Somerset, whilst her financial affairs were sorted out, following the third Earl of Ilchester's Coming of Age. By the end of September Agnes was back in Fairford.

34. Letter from Agnes Porter, [Penrice Castle], to Lady Mary Talbot, Margam, 17 August 1808

My Dear Lady Mary,
Your darlings are as well as when you left them and all very happy and good. Miss Talbot was a little in the *penseroso* style, but I sent her a little backwards and forwards, with a message *here* and an errand *there*, till I found she was better, and then we sat down to read in her *new* book of Goldsmith's poems, and his *Haunch of Venison*,[1] by giving a hearty laugh, set all to rights again. I then glanced at her being one of the next party to Margam, and observed what a satisfaction it was to see one's dear friends well enough to take a little excursion and to entertain hopes it would do them good, and so make them all *still better*. We then went a little deeper into our studies; a French irregular verb and a pretty long sum closed our labours for the morning. I then had the two little ones to join our party till dinner was ready. Miss Ellinor and Mr Christopher were with Miss Raines and very good children. They all ate a *hearty* dinner, and are all as well as *heart* could wish.

To conclude in the *same style*, I am, my dearest Lady Mary, *heartily* yours, Ann A. Porter.

---

[1] *The Haunch of Venison*, a poem by Oliver Goldsmith (1728–74).

I beg my love to dear Mr Talbot and to dear Doctor and Mrs Hunt.

35. Letter from Agnes Porter, [Penrice Castle], to Lady Mary Talbot, Margam, Wednesday Evening, 17 August 1808

My Dear Lady Mary

I wrote a few lines to you to-day by the post, lest you should send to Swansea for letters. The loves are all well and the best children in the world. Little Emma only observed that 'Mamma was gone to Wansea'. She visited Miss Raines last night from six to past seven, and joined a full party with me this morning. She had a very good night and is as well to-day as can possibly be. Miss Isabella is quite well too: taking care of the main chance, she sticks 'devoutly to her beef and pudding'. Miss Ellinor is as well as when you saw her and a very good child when *duly* amused. When Miss Talbot's studies were over they all came to us up-stairs, and after writing letters through their sister Mary's pen, they flocked around me to look at some prints in the *History of England*. These gave general satisfaction, and a very particular one to dear little Christopher. He listened most attentively to the account I gave of each, and upon coming to Alfred's print he said 'Po, I do *so* love Alfred!' He has been an exceeding good child indeed. He is at present with Miss Raines, who is much better than she was and as attentive to the darlings as can possibly be.

I hope Mr Talbot and your other Margam loves are well. With kindest remembrances to them, and best compliments to Dr and Mrs Hunt, as also to Mrs Dodd Hunt I am etc., etc., Po.

36. Letter from Agnes Porter, [Penrice Castle], to Lady Mary Talbot, Margam, 24 August 1808

My Dear Lady Mary,

Miss Raines is now as well again as when you went. She and Mr Christopher are gone a pretty little quiet walk into the garden; the other darlings are at play in my room, and I believe before the post goes there is but time to tell you how very well and very good they all are. Miss Talbot, after reading her English and French, had her choice of writing from the *Roman History*, or of writing to mamma or her sisters. She chose to write to Miss Jane because she had written to you last. She looks charmingly to-day. Yesterday she had a little head-ach, and to-day her nose bled, since which she is perfectly well. Miss Ellinor continues, as I think, to gain strength; Miss Isabella is as stout as the Welsh kids, and as active too. The little one is quite well, and as lively as possible. She was much admired by Mr Collins' friends who, as soon as they saw her, exclaimed 'What a beautiful little creature that is! What eyes!' etc., etc. Mr Christopher looks very well – the same sober-minded young gentleman as usual. On looking out of my window he said 'I am glad, Po, that those *cruel men* have not cleaned away your swallows – they have cleaned away the rest'.

I shall gladly defer my going till the seventh instead of the 30 current, and am, my dear Lady Mary, your own Po.

Excuse a few shakings, quakings, blots etc., etc.

37. Letter from Agnes Porter, Fairford, to Lady Mary Talbot, Penrice Castle, 27 September 1808

My Dearest Lady Mary,

I had your favour in due course of post and thank you for it. I hope I shall see the words *very* well, instead of *pretty*, when next you write, and that you will send me a particular account of each darling child. I am quite comforted when I think of your aunt Lady Harriot Acland's being with you, when society so pleasing to every one must be doubly so to you, and I hope and trust that when she quits the Castle, another of your numerous tribe will visit you. Have the goodness to let me know what ever contributes to your happiness as it passes, my own dear and ever-beloved Lady Mary, whom heavens bless!

I slept six nights at Redlynch waiting for Mr Field to settle his account with me: it was done entirely to my satisfaction, both on my own account, and from the interest I must ever take in your brother's noble conduct, exclusive of *self* advantages. Mr Charles Digby called on me before he went to Melbury and most obligingly offered the use of his carriage. I went once in it to Bruton. Mrs Digby sent her children to pay me a little visit and said she would have called on me herself, had she not been indisposed with her usual complaint in the face. I did not call on her as *she* was indisposed, and *I* a stranger.

With good Longford and his wife, I had full satisfaction in talking of your dear family – it was a pleasure to me to see such faithful servants of your house. I then went to Shepton Mallet, and Mr Moore on the Tuesday morning went with me to Bath, and just as the chaise reached the White Hart the mail arrived. It was to stop only five minutes, so I was forced to give Mrs Sandford's letter to Mr Moore's care for her brother, and had it not in my power to give it myself as I had voluntarily promised, which vexed me, nor yet to see Miss Bere, which I regretted.

However it was convenient for me to pop into the mail, and I reached my dear brother and sister about six the same day. They and their niece and nephew rejoiced to see me, and I was glad to find them all in good health.

Mr John Collins[2] called last Thursday, and Mr Richards invited him to spend the interval of his time here between this and the 10th of October when he returns to Oxford. We expect him to-morrow. I am sure Mr Richards will be happy to give any hint for his improvement.

I beg my love and respects where so justly due – I embrace the darlings and am *ever yours*, Ann Agnes Porter.

One of my fellow travellers feared she would be in only at the *teel* of the Bristol fair – and said the *meeds* of the inns were very *rummiss*.

38. Letter from Agnes Porter, Fairford, to Lady Harriot Frampton, Moreton, Dorset, 2 October 1808

My Dear Lady Harriot,
I am afraid a letter I wrote from Bristol has miscarried. In it I acquainted your ladyship that a draft for the picture money would be as good a method of conveyance as any other. It may, if you please, be drawn payable at sight, twenty days after date. I am much obliged to you for the trouble you took concerning the raffle, and I should have been well pleased had the prize been your own.

I hope your darling children are well, and that Mr Frampton and his *Cara Sposa* enjoy perfect health. I left your dear sister Lady Mary pretty well, her children improving in health, and Mr Talbot better than I thought him two years ago. I felt a severe pang at leaving Lady Mary: it was the *tax* upon affection, and the pleasure I had experienced in her family, but I trust we shall meet again. All of you, my other dear pupils are happily situated, but she, sweet creature is an exile from her country and her nearest friends. Her aunt's visit and the seeing her brother William gave her high satisfaction. I hope she will frequently receive such pleasing and enlivening society.

When you write be so good as give me some particulars of your health and happiness, which will ever interest my dear Lady Harriot's very affectionate Ann Agnes Porter.

My brother and sister present their best compliments.

---

[2] Son of Revd John Collins of Oxwich (q.v.).

39. Letter from Agnes Porter, Fairford, to Lady Mary Talbot, Penrice Castle, 4 October [1808]

My Dearest Lady Mary,

I hope you and all the darlings are well – that is, in the way of getting better. Does Miss Jane bear the change of season without its causing any effect on her breathing? How are my dear little Charlot's spirits? And does my little Ellinor encrease in plumpness? How is the precious young *gŵrr*,[3] stout Isabella, and the darling Emma? Does my sweet Mary think I have forgotten her? 'Ah! No, my love, no!' Pray tell her I bought a very pretty little ruler for her at Bristol, so her commission is executed already. I will not fail to do the others when I visit the grand city, and should any thing else occur as an object of purchase I hope they will let me know between this and Easter. Did they continue bathing? How has it agreed with them? *A propos* to bathing, a lady went from this neighbourhood last summer to Swansea, and she took it into her wise pericranium[4] that if bathing was beneficial once a day, three times bathing in the day would do three times the good. She pursued this plan for some weeks and returned here in a very bad way.

My brother and sister had lately a visit from Dr Smith. He told us he had once a living in Cornwall, but the poor people were so superstitious as to give him a dislike to the place. A person came for him one day to baptize a child, saying it was very ill. As they proceeded to the cottage he said 'Come, come, Doctor, make haste, as I do not choose my child to grow a pudsey'. They had had a full persuasion that children who died before baptism were changed into young fairies – *pudseys*. There was no reasoning with them, Dr Smith said, on this subject. He does not talk any more of giving up his living of Fairf[ord]. [Should] he do so, it would be no loss to ... *[page torn here]* but I fear a very great one to ... people. He is so judicious ... his pastoral charge, and so truly charitable to the poor of every ... I have known many a worthy clerg[yman] – I never yet knew his equal.

How is my dear Lady Harriot Acland? I fear she will soon depart from Penrice Castle. If I did but know how to take such a liberty as to entreat her to drop me a few lines, I would gladly do it – just to say how you look, my dearest Lady Mary, and how your rose-buds are. I am distressed to think how much Mrs Raines' calamity[5] will affect you.

---

[3] *Gŵr* – the Welsh for man. Thomas Mansel Talbot used this word to refer to his male heir.

[4] Brain.

[5] Note in pencil: 'The death of her eldest daughter, Miss Smith'.

Yet were she to take her surviving daughter[6] to England with her, it might be all for the best.

My sister is quite persuaded that Miss Beach caught infection from Mrs Wheeler, before she began to spit.[7] I know you will ascribe what I say to the true motive, my warm affection to yourself and family.

Ever yours, Ann A. Porter

I beg my kind compliments to Mr and Mrs Collins of Oxwich. I will write to them when we have seen her[8] son – he should be with us to-day.

40. Letter from Agnes Porter, Fairford, to Lady Mary Talbot, Penrice Castle, 16 November 1808

My Dearest Lady Mary,

Your letter was like a refreshing shower to a thirsty land, and I thank you cordially for it. It delights me to hear that nothing material is the matter with any of you, and that my lovely Ellinor is growing plump again. You do not mention the *gŵrr yvank* [young man] nor Isabella, nor that 'beam of light' Emma; but I take it for granted they are all well. I hope you received mine of October 4th: I entertained some hopes of having a few lines from Lady Harriot Acland to tell me how you looked etc., etc., but being disappointed, and feeling the penalty of *hope delayed*, I was just going to write again to you when I was made happy by your dear epistle.

I hope Miss Talbot liked her little ruler which I sent by Mr J. Collins, as likewise a little knife to Miss Ellinor. The pruning knives for the other darlings I defer procuring till I go to London. It was such indifferent weather when Mr Collins went that Mr Richards asked him to drop a [line] to inform us how he past the water, but this he failed doing, *malgré sa promesse.* He is good in the main, I believe, and good-natured, but thoughtless to a degree – at least I fear so.

I have not read *Newton's Life* yet – when-ever it falls in my way I will certainly do it. *Marmion* has charmed me with his magic spell, his splendid descriptions and tender thoughts:[9]

---

[6] Note in pencil: 'Miss Raines'.

[7] Mrs Wheeler was employed as a governess by the Hicks Beaches. She died of consumption. See Trevor Lummis and Jan Marsh, *The Woman's Domain* (London, 1990), p. 100.

[8] Sic.

[9] Sir Walter Scott, *Marmion* (1808).

> When musing on companions gone,
> We doubly feel ourselves alone;
> Something, my friend, we yet may gain,
> There is a pleasure in this pain:
> It soothes the love of lonely rest,
> Deep in each gentler heart impress'd.

Letters from the Mountains, too, are beautiful.[10] I past over those in which she mentions her three children's death as being *too affecting.* There [is] also a small book published by [a member of] the Bowdler family, entitled *Fragments by a Young Lady lately Deceased.*[11] This young person was such a phaenomenon as appears perhaps but once in the course of centuries. Her name began with an S and her home was Piercefield, which her father left about the year 1793, as I think, on account of his bankruptcy, in which was involved another respectable gentleman from merely having lent his name to the firm. I dare say Mrs Hunt knows all about this Mr S. and family.[12]

I think the picture you possess must be quite a treasure. I am very glad you visited the theatre with your two sweet companions – my love to them all, and kind compliments to the friends that are now your guests. *Dieu vous bénisse,* Po.

I am well, so are my good friends here. We unite in most respectful remembrance.

---

[10] Anne Grant, *Letters from the Mountains* (1807).

[11] Henrietta Maria Bowdler, *Fragments in Prose and Verse: By a Young Lady, Lately Deceased* (1808).

[12] Added in ink, in another hand 'Smith of Piercefield'.

1809

Agnes spent the first part of 1809 in Fairford, but by the beginning of June she was back at Penrice, where she stayed until the second half of July, whilst Thomas and Lady Mary Talbot were in Wiltshire and Gloucestershire with three of their daughters. By September Agnes was at Scratby Hall, near Great Yarmouth in Norfolk, one of the homes of her old friend the dowager Countess of Home.

41. Letter from Agnes Porter, Fairford, to Lady Mary Talbot, Penrice Castle, 5 January[1] 1809

Though I wrote lately in so verbose a manner, it seems to me as if I had not half answered my dear Lady Mary's last favour, so I shall even trouble her again with half an hour's chat and my repeated wishes for her health and happiness.

Your discrimination between the effects of mental and bodily pain appeared to me a very just one. We can indeed enlarge upon the last, when it has ceased, with a degree of pleasure, while only mentioning our mental distress shall make a new and painful impression on the heart. This, if attended to, will prevent our conversing even with our nearest friends upon subjects that admit not of their consolations, but the observation ought to carry us a step farther and prevent our communing with *ourselves* on past calamities. That power of abstraction which providence has given to all, and most largely to the strongest minds, should be used for our comfort and applied to from a principle of duty, as from the *present* blessings we ought to derive our happiness, and a sense of [what] we possess will promote in us *chearfulness* and gratitude.

The *first* of *February*[2] was kept by us, and your health drank in a

---

[1] Sic, but should probably be February.
[2] Pencil note: 'Mama's wedding day'.

bottle of Mr Richards' *holiday-wine*. Mr Talbot is one of his very first favourites – he says he is certain that Mr Talbot is a *real British gentleman*, and that his heart is the seat of honour. You may suppose that Mr R. and I have no difference on this subject.

Mr M. Beach and his bride[3] have Williamstrip to themselves. Mrs Hicks Beach left it just a few hours before their arrival. The father is in London. Mr Loveden tells us that he himself has had the 'Devil to pay'. He invited an old acquaintance, a Captain Wicks, to live in his neighbourhood, and he would build him a house. The house was begun, and while it was building the bean[4] was made an inmate of Buscot Park, and all went on well 'Till little cupid took his stand upon Miss Loveden's future land', or at least what £2000 per annum might purchase. *She* told her father, who chased the *inamorata* instantly, and says he was originally a footman. This is talked of all over the country and gives great amusement to his acquaintances.

Ever yours A. A. P.

P.S. My love to my darlings. Heaven bless their sweet faces and may I again see them! By Mr Talbot's bounty I am a *journey in pocket* for some future day.

42. Letter from Agnes Porter, Fairford, to Lady Mary Talbot, The Close, Salisbury, 16 March 1809

My Dearest Lady Mary,

Words cannot express the pleasure your letter gave me. 'Your Ellinor surprisingly better; your Jane stout, and dear little Charry in the way of being better' – bravo! Such intelligence is reviving indeed, and many thanks for your most kind communications. Lady Harriot too, with you to augment and share your comforts; your brother expected – and such a trio! Dear to *your* heart must such a meeting be, and dear to theirs. Heaven bless the party!

I hope Mr Talbot is quite recovered from his bowel complaint – I beg my love and respects to him.

I do not wonder you should be shocked by the late dereliction of some fashionable people. The good make less noise, but no doubt their numbers greatly preponderate, and in that confidence I shall venture

---

[3] Pencil note: 'Miss Mount'. Michael (1780–1815), son of Michael and Henrietta Maria Hicks Beach, married on 26 January 1809 Caroline Jane, daughter of William Mount of Wasing Place, Berkshire.

[4] The young man.

to visit London. Mr Richards tells me he is persuaded that in proportion to numbers there are as many virtuous and excellent persons among the nobility as in any other rank of life, but that when any of them swerves, he or she becomes the *city on the hill*. I give him (whose own morals are so pure) great credit for this candid opinion of his superiours. He cannot bear any *levelling*, and feels quite hurt that the *son* of his sovereign[5] should now stand in so awkward a point of view. If you have time for light reading I would venture to mention *Geraldine*, and Mrs Grant's *Memoirs of an American Lady*.[6] The former must be perused *quite through* to be judged, and the latter, though neither historical nor strictly speaking *memoirs*, is yet pleasing. I think the French term *souvenirs* would have suited it exactly: easy, agreeable and, as far as it goes, *interesting*.

It is a great comfort to me to think that such a sensible chearful woman as Mrs Edwards is now with your absent darlings. My love to the dear creatures that are with you – I hope Miss Jane my old friend, Charry my old companion, and Miss Ellinor my sweet little *new friend*, will all give me some commissions to do for them in Town.

Farewell my dear Lady Mary. Ever yours, Po.

43. Letter from Agnes Porter, Fairford, to Lady Mary Talbot, The Close, Salisbury, 18 March 1809

My Dear Lady Mary,
When I last past through Bristol I saw at the Bush Inn a person who told me he had been a footman of your dear mother's. He wished to go to service again in the capacity of a footman, and requested me to mention him to the ladies of your family. His name is Abram Ansom, to be heard of at the *Bush*, Bristol. I hope I mentioned him before, but if not I thought it right to repair my breach of promise, or rather forgetfulness, as soon as I could. In this interim of nineteen years he was in several places, and for two years at Mrs Davenport's.

Does Miss Bere return with you? If not, perhaps she and I could contrive to travel together from Bristol to Penrice Castle – but this as you think best. I have been as gay as a lark, though not so melodious, ever since I had your welcome letter. I trust all continues to go on well, and that dear Mr Talbot's bowel complaint has left him.

---

[5] Pencil note: 'The Duke of York'.
[6] Probably *Geraldina: A Novel, Founded on a Recent Event* (1798); and Anne Grant, *Memoirs of an American Lady* (1808).

My love to your darlings. Heavens bless them and you prays your affectionate and ever obliged Ann Agnes Porter.

There is a young woman now leaving my sister who has been with her eight years, of whom she has a good opinion as an honest, trusty servant. It is her own choice to go *pour voir le monde*. She washes and irons well: a pretty good work-woman at her needle, tho' not quick at it – between twenty and thirty – young enough to improve.

44. Letter from Agnes Porter, Fairford, to Lady Mary Talbot, The Close, Salisbury, 16 May 1809

My Dear Lady Mary,

I am happy at the idea of being useful to you *any-where*, and shall be ready to set off for Penrice Castle as soon as I hear again from you. I rejoice at the amendment of your little darling and trust this fine weather and her native air will quite set her up again. It will be a mutual pleasure to your dear little Mary and me to see each other. I know she has warm feelings for an *old friend*. You, I hope will take precious care of your own health, as a duty of the *first magnitude*. But I know ease of mind is half in half. May this blessing be your own in its fullest extent! Have you had time to read *Coelebs*?[7] I think you would approve of a great part of it. *A propos* to reading, a little boy was studying history, whose papa accustomed him to explain any particular words he met with, so, coming to the account of the Independents in Cromwell's time, he stopt and, after a little pause, said 'Independents, papa, are I suppose persons who cannot be depended on'. It was 'hitting the nail'.

I beg my love and respects to dear Mr Talbot. I look forward to a trimming from him at cribbage. Remember me to my own three darling friends with you – Charry will *crowd* you in the carriage, being so plump.

You understand me, my dear Lady Mary, that you have only in your next to *issue forth your mandate* to your ever affectionate Ann Agnes Porter.

I had yours this morning of the 13th.

45. Letter from Agnes Porter, [Penrice Castle], to Lady Mary Talbot, The Close, Salisbury, 1 June 1809

My Dear Lady Mary,

Yesterday I had the satisfaction to find your children in *perfect* health

---

[7] Hannah More, *Cœlebs in Search of a Wife* (1808).

– you never saw any thing look more blooming. The sweet rose-bud Emma is most beautiful, and as to spirit and activity she seems to keep her own among them very well. Miss Isabella is a picture for stoutness: she bustles about and sings her little song with great glee. I think Mr Christopher is much grown since I saw him, and much improved. He and I are already so gracious that he took me by the hand to shew me his ship *Nelson*, and told me several of the technical terms. He likewise informed me that Mr Edwards and he had taken a large perch that weighed so much etc. Nothing can be happier than they are, and Mr and Mrs Edwards are quite fond of them. Your dear Mary is grown so like yourself that I was surprized when she met me. Her nose now assumes a certain dignity, and every other feature is much embellished. Her figure, in my opinion, wants only a straight neck to be a very fine one. She was rejoiced to see me, sweet love! I like very much to lay in her room – we can make such good use of the morning. She awoke at seven after a profound sleep. I desired her to *do so, and so*, just as I used to do, and found her equally docile. She read in the Bible, did a sum, wrote three lines very slow in a copy book, and wrote a little French from *my English*. 'Ma chère Po, je suis bien …[8] de vous voir. J'aime beaucoup de faire mes études.' I told her I was sure I expressed her sentiments: she told me yes, I did. Then I informed her that the word she had omitted was *aisé*, and the *de* was too much. I rubbed the lines out and she wrote them again quite correct and currently. After breakfast Mrs Edwards, Miss Talbot and I had a little work party at hemming, in which I strove to do my best, but I was *outlined* all to nothing.

Dear Doctor Hunt is here but goes to-day. We are going to make a large play party as the weather will not permit any amusement out of doors. At last I got a place in the Oxford mail last Monday, left Bristol the next day, and reached Penrice Castle yesterday. I hope all is well with you.

Ever yours, Ann Agnes Porter.

46. Letter from Agnes Porter, Penrice Castle, to Lady Mary Talbot, The Close, Salisbury, 11 June 1809

My Dear Lady Mary,
Your children here are extremely well, and I hope you can say the same with regard to your darlings at Salisbury. The weather, I fear,

---

[8] Sic.

has been rather unfavourable for you and them, but this circumstance cannot be of long continuance at this time of the year, viz. June 11th. Miss Isabella was soon well after she took the grain of calumel – she is to-day both stout and lively. Dear Christopher looks charmingly, and between Mrs Edwards and me he fares very well I can assure you. The little *star* is as bright as ever, and dispenses her beams amongst us, though not on all alike. She was playing yesterday with a ball, and as she ran after it she kept saying to herself '*Dood Mrs Tollins* to give me a ball, dood Mrs Tollins – very *dood indeed*'. Pray take the accents along with you. Miss Talbot is exceedingly good and diligent – this morning she said her catechism and read the psalms, collect and epistle etc. with great attention. When this was done she took her *Sacra Privata*[9] and read in it of her own accord. I then proposed the *active* duty of visiting and amusing brother and sisters, which we did most willingly together. They are all of them very fond of Mr and Mrs Edwards.

Farewell my ever dear Lady Mary, *dearer* than tongue can tell or pen express to your own *old* Po.

47. Letter from Agnes Porter, [Penrice Castle], to Lady Mary Talbot, The Close, Salisbury, 17 June 1809

My Dear Lady Mary,

Your darlings here continue perfectly well, for which we can never be too thankful. They go out whenever the weather permits, and the sea-side is the usual place of resort, as nothing can exceed the glee with which they pick up shells and perform their various evolutions on the sands. We are just returned from a most pleasant airing – I mean the little ones, Susan[10] and I. Miss Emma sang all the way back, and Miss Isabella was busily employed in cleaning and counting her marine treasures. Mr Christopher observed yesterday that his mamma had been gone near four months. 'How do you know, my dear?' 'Why, Po, she went in February – and March one; April two; May three; and June four. She went on a Saturday.' I asked Miss Talbot if she would like to set off with me for Salisbury? Her answer was that she should like to go, if she *even went alone*. So you may guess how much you are wished for – but I must remark *en passant* that this longing has no injurious

---

[9] At Penrice there is a book with this title, subtitled *The Private Meditations and Prayers of the Right Revd Thomas Wilson, DD* (1804). Inside is an inscription in ink: 'Mary Thereza Talbot, August 14th 1808'.

[10] Pencil note: 'Nurse'.

effect either on the health or spirits, for you never saw *your* Mary look better than she now does. She is a *true Mary* – reckoning from Mrs Grady, the fourth I have known, and I shall only add: '*There be few such Maries.*'

I hope all you love are well in your quarter. Will you recall to their remembrance your ever affectionate Ann Agnes Porter.

Susan is now well again.

48. Letter from Agnes Porter, Penrice Castle, to Lady Mary Talbot, The Close, Salisbury, 21 June 1809

My Dear Lady Mary,

Miss Talbot and Mrs Edwards are just returned with a merry little party of bathers who look most charmingly after their immersion. This was their *first day* of bathing, and I hear a good account of their behaviour. Mrs Edwards desired Mr Christopher to lay down for an hour; the two little darlings are enjoying their roast mutton and green-peas, and dear Miss Talbot is now at the other end of the table, elbow on lap and head in hand, considering a sum done in the rule of three, which she intends to prove by practice. Plaguey Po, in spite of this abstracted occupation, comes in with a 'Hold up your head my dear'. I stopt writing just now to look at the sums, which were quite right. She is looking most blooming, but I will say no more now, that your pleasure may be the greater at your meeting.

Mr Christopher had great amusement yesterday in being with Mr Edwards an-angling. Miss Talbot, Mrs E. and I were there too and had the pleasure of seeing five perch taken before we left the new walk. The dear boy was quite delighted at eve[ry] capture, and enjoyed the triumph of his own nature in the subjection of inferior beings. Dr Hobbes, chancing to be this way, was much pleased with the appearance of each of them. I wish, poor man, that he was as well himself, but his heavy eye and purple cheek always give me the idea of distemper.

Shall I see *you* looking well, my dear Lady Mary? I hope in God I shall, with your other rose-buds. I trust I shall soon see them, by a *compleat* union, add '*sweetness to the sweet*'.[11]

All here join in love to their *papa* and *you* and *sisters*. I am ever yours, A.A. Porter.

---

[11] William Shakespeare, *Hamlet*, V, i, 265: 'Sweets to the sweet'.

49. Letter from Agnes Porter, [Penrice Castle], to Lady Mary Talbot, The Close, Salisbury, 6 July 1809

My Dearest Lady Mary,

I hope your darling[12] goes on well at Salisbury, and that the other precious loves are in perfect health. I cannot express to you how lovely your rose-buds look that bloom in Penrice Castle. *Morning Star* shines most auspiciously.[13] To-day, in returning from the sea-side, she asked her sister Isabella for a shell, who gravely replied 'I picked them up for myself and not for you'. On this repartie I made no remark, only told them of a little girl who asked one sister for a bonbon, who told her she had got them for herself and not for *her*. The little girl then turned to her other sister, who replied 'Yes my dear, you shall have one of mine and welcome'. I asked them whether Jenny or Betsey was the best little girl, and before any one could answer, Emma exclaimed 'O! Betsey was the dood dirl'. Miss Isabella was of the same opinion and added 'I will give Emma a shell when we get home', and she performed her word. Mr Christopher, on being asked the other day what flower he destined for his Mamma, made answer 'I will give her *all*'. Miss Talbot is very good and diligent. It makes me happy to think that I am of real *use* to her. I can observe at times that she is rather enclined to be *mother-sick*, and I cannot wonder at it. Her health continues perfect, and I flatter myself that between *hook* and *crook* I have flattened her back. Do not fail to praise her when you see her for holding up her head. It is of great consequence to her shape.

Miss Raines spent two or three days here lately, which gave great pleasure to your Mary.

God bless you, my dear Lady Mary, prays yours affectionately, Ann Agnes Porter.

50. Letter from Agnes Porter, [Penrice Castle], to Lady Mary Talbot, 'at M. H. Beaches Esqr., Williamstrip, Fairford, Gloucs.',[14] 16 July 1809

My Dear Lady Mary,

We received your letter last night, giving hopes of your reaching home next, or rather this, week. After an ague, change of air proves generally

---

[12] Pencil note: 'Ellinor'. She was seriously ill, and had been taken to Salisbury to see Dr Fowler.

[13] 'Morning Star' was the youngest daughter, Emma.

[14] 'Close, Salisbury' crossed out.

beneficial, and I have no doubt that dear Miss Jane will find it so; and as to your little Ellinor, her native air will, I fervently hope, restore her to health. It is much milder than Salisbury, and therefore likely to prove more salutary for this darling of the heart. I do indeed take a real concern in your disappointments, having many reasons exclusive of personal ones to wish for you here, yet none of them so important as the delight it would give my dearest Lady Mary to see her loves again. But if weighty reasons detain you, the same good sense which gives them the balance will induce you to acquiesce in your disappointments a little longer. Well do I know that it is neither for your pleasure nor Mr Talbot's that you are absent from Penrice.

Thinking you on the wing, I have not written so frequently of late, but beside dispatching epistles to each of the *Salisbury* Miss Talbots I have written to you at least once a week. So the darling Henry wished to come with you – dear child, I wish he could! Your loves here continue in perfect health, thank God.

If you write to Miss Bere, will you be so good as to tell her a letter came for her directed here yesterday. I mention this that she may not be uneasy about not hearing from her friends.

It is time for me to go to the *Alpean church.*[15] Mr Christopher accompanies us. I repeat to my dear Lady Mary that all her children are quite well. God bless her and them, amen! Po.

51. Letter from Agnes Porter, Penrice Castle, to Lady Mary Talbot, 'at M. H. Beaches Esqr., Williamstrip, Fairford, Gloucs.',[16] 20 July 1809

My Dear Lady Mary,
I hope the extracting of your little darling's teeth will prove indeed a *radical* cure, and that you will soon be reunited to all your precious children. In the mean time you have reason to feel yourself happy in the discharge of your maternal duties, and in the prospect of their sweetest reward, their future virtue and felicity. It is impossible to be better than all your loves are here, and it is the greatest comfort to see them so stout, blooming and happy. *Morning Star* sparkles with encreasing lustre; Miss Isabella is a nice child in her way; Mr Christopher grows to the eye – on hearing just now to whom I was writing he said 'Tell mamma that I desire she will come home to-morrow. I will write

---

[15] Penrice church. Reaching it from Penrice Castle involves climbing a steep hill.
[16] 'Close, Salisbury' crossed out.

to her by and by when I am with Mrs Edwards'. Miss Talbot is now writing to her mamma, but perhaps it may not be ready to go with Po's to-day. She has been very diligent at her studies and has done a great deal in these few weeks past. We take time, however, for exercise, and for her amusement Po tries to walk and talk as if she were *quinze ans*. My best performances are, however, but a poor substitute for the pleasures she looks forward to, and which I hope she will soon enjoy. There is a letter for you superscribed 'Oxford' in your brother's hand. It seems to have something more *weighty than paper* – should I send it you?

All here unite in love to their dear papa and mamma and sisters three, Ellinor, Charlotte and *Euclida Jenny*.

Farewell, my dearest Lady Mary, Po.

52. Letter from Agnes Porter, Scratby Hall, Norfolk, to Lady Mary Talbot, [Penrice Castle], 17 September 1809

My Dear Lady Mary,

How I rejoiced to see your hand-writing and to find that your sweet little invalid is better as to her cough – surely a most important circumstance. Do you think that milk might not be tried in small quantities two or three times in the day as I described it, warm from the cow, and shaken in a bottle till it have particles of butter as large as pins' heads? I hear it is so extremely nourishing!

I hope Lady Charlotte, when at Bristol, will proceed to Penrice for your enjoyment and her own compleat recovery. If Lady Louisa travels, it should be soon. I am charmed with the idea of your seeing both your amiable sisters in so short a time! How they will be delighted with your lovely and good children! My kindest remembrance to the two dear elders, whose studies with you give me great satisfaction, as I regard improvement to be a matter of course. I hope dear little Charlotte *makes merry* at dancing, playing, dolls etc. If she reads too much she will be called a book-worm – that will never do. I suppose that dear Christopher, Isabella and Emma are making a progress in their studies with mamma and Miss Bere – Po sends her love to them. I hope, my dearest Lady Mary, you are pretty well yourself, and that you value your health as a 'jewel of the soul'. Indeed, while we remain here the health of the body and that of the soul have a most intimate connection together.

I will now, as you desire, give you a sketch of my Norfolk prospects. I have a wide and unbroken view of the greenest pastures, filled with fat cattle; the richest fields of corn, and turneps. The horizon is bounded by wood at a distance, which gently rises all around and forms an ornamental border to the scenery. The house is plain and neat to a degree. The rooms are large and light. Every apartment is stucco and of only two colours, blue and green. The hall which is oval and central to the lower rooms, is of a pale yellow – but the beauty of the house is a turret on the top of it, giving from the windows an extensive view of the ocean. So full and so grand a prospect one seldom meets with – some hundreds of vessels: men-of-war and merchantmen give it an endless and most pleasing variety. But I do not mount the turret *every day*, and the *flats* are *flat* indeed. Were these confined to the terrestrial only it would not matter so much – but the rational objects seem to me *flat* also – but this is a little secret I keep snug between my dear Lady Mary and her ever affectionate Po.

53. Letter from Agnes Porter, Scratby Hall, Norfolk, to Lady Mary Talbot, Penrice Castle, 6 October 1809

My Dearest Lady Mary,
Your letters are indeed *refreshing* to me beyond description, and to hear that your lovely children are well. Six out of *seven*, is to me delightful. I suppose as to your dear Ellinor, *that is a case of time*, but in the meanwhile her being free from pain is a most consolatory circumstance.[17]

I rejoice at Lady Charlotte's intended visit to you – I trust you will both enjoy it to the utmost, and that her health will improve in the salubrious air of Gower. I do not like those Cheltenham waters – they seem to require both advice, preparation, and caution.

When you write to Lady Elizabeth, will you request her to remember (along with Mr Talbot's watch) to send the parcel I left for Mr Griffith Llewellyn, which I shall be much obliged to you if you will mention to him that he may not purchase the books before my little present arrives: it is Joyce's *Arithmetic* – two volumes[18] – and when it comes will you be so kind as to take off the paper which, as well as I can recollect, indicates *the price*.

Is Mrs Hunt getting better? Madame Puirvaux's society must be an agreeable acquisition to the young ladies, who I hope talk *responsively*

---

[17] The Talbots' third daughter, Christiana, had died in 1808. Ellinor, the fifth daughter, died in 1810.
[18] Jeremiah Joyce, *A System of Practical Arithmetic* (1808).

to her in her own charming language. Et Miss Bere comment se porte elle? Parle t'elle *un peu, tant soit peu* françois? Je l'espère.

The weather here has changed for the better within these few days. I hope it is improved likewise in your quarter, for all your sakes, but in particular for sweet Ellinor's. I suppose she wears her flannel petticoat next her skin, and never goes out but when the air is perfectly dry.

I thank you, my dear Lady Mary, for enquiring after Mrs Ramey. She enjoys wonderful health. At the age of eighty-four she is erect, walks well, converses with ease and chearfulness, and gives her attention to nothing but what is likely to contribute to her own satisfaction. Her daughter Lady Home is by far the oldest woman of the two. There is a Scots lady at present on a visit at Scratby Hall – a very pleasing, I might add almost a necessary, circumstance for me. Do you recollect the s[tor]y of Cowdeneughs? Lady Home's, that is Lord Home's cousin, came to inherit the estate of Cowdeneughs some years ago. The dwelling was antique, and had subterraneous vaults under it to a great extent. The gentleman was of an inquisitive cast of mind, and frequently wandered under ground. In a *paved* cellar he observed one of the stones to project a little, as he thought, above the others: he moved it, and found a box of antediluvian appearance under the stone. Upon exam- ining the contents, a number of jewels were found all set in ivory – rings, necklaces, ornaments for the hair etc. There was a bunch of rubies of great value, for a head dress, still set in ivory. The lady of the mansion new set most of them, reserving only a sample of this curious treasure. Having introduced a subject worthy of *Aladin's pen*, I leave my dear Lady Mary to its contemplation, and am ever hers *while* Ann Agnes Porter.

My love to *our* darlings – *Dieu les bénisse!*

54. Letter from Agnes Porter, Scratby Hall, Norfolk, to Lady Harriot Frampton, Moreton, near Dorchester, Dorset, 25 November 1809

My Dear Lady Harriot,

Will you favour me with a line or two, to inform me how you do, and how your children are? It would give me great pleasure to hear of your continued welfare since I heard from, and of, you last. It would also oblige me much if you would acquaint me how Lord Ilchester's leg is, and whether there be hopes of an entire cure. I would have written to you when I left Lady Mary if I could have given you a good account of the sweet Ellinor, but alas! I fear a tender mother's heart must bleed again. Yet my last accounts were more favourable.

I have been these three months past in Norfolk, on a visit at the Dowager Lady Home's. It was a curious retrospect to me to look around me on the same scenes I frequented thirty years ago. The infants I knew have reached maturity, the young people *that were* are now become middle-aged, and the old that remain, are on the verge of *futurity*. I find them still the same unlearned, uninformed race – at least all I am local with. I enquired at a bookseller's for French books: 'Have you any?' 'No Madam, except French grammars, Madam, we have one or two of them.' 'Any Italian book by a lucky chance?' 'Italian Madam?' with an exclamatory tone of voice. 'No, no, we don't deal in them there.' They are languages quite unknown, as far as I can perceive. In English I have feasted upon *Cumberland's Life*; Helen Maria's *French Revolution;* Hannah More's *Hints for the Education of a Princess*.[19] The latter work I found both elegant and interesting – it is I think her most polished composition as to style, and the matter of it, or rather the spirit I should say, soars to immortality. *Cœlebs* and *Celia* I like very well, particularly the lady – I think she is likely to do more good than the prim bachelor.[20] From a bachelor I shall lead you to an old maid – one that has loved you and yours since she was a young one. That same antique person is well, but thinks that flats and sharps of Norfolk will send her, by the medium of easterly winds, in another month to London. Shall I have a chance of seeing you there?

I am, my dear Lady Harriot, yours affectionately, Ann A. Porter.

---

[19] Andrew Henderson, *The Life of William Augustus, Duke of Cumberland* (1766); Helen Maria Williams, *Letters on the French Revolution* (1791); and Hannah More, *Hints towards Forming the Character of a Young Princess* (1805).

[20] I have not been able to identify *Celia*. The book to which Agnes refers could be (anon.), *The Unfortunate Lovers: Or the Genuine Distress of Damon and Celia, in a Series of Letters* (London, 1772). Or does Agnes mean Fanny Burney's *Cecilia* (1782)?

1810

Agnes left Scratby Hall in May 1810, and she then returned to Fairford. She spent most of the rest of 1810 at Fairford, apart from six weeks or so in September and October, when she stayed with some of the Talbot children at Malvern.

55. Letter from Agnes Porter, Scratby Hall, Norfolk, to Lady Mary Talbot, Clifton, Bristol, 9 February 1810

My Dearest Lady Mary,

How are you and how are all you love? Have you the whole of your family or only a part with you at Clifton? Does dear Mr Talbot continue better? And how is Lady Charlotte? When you are a little at leisure I shall be happy to catch at a few lines from your dear hand, and I thank you for having written to me so often as you have done. Your heart and mine have a point of union which is strong and lasting as life. Without words we understand each other, and no distance can prevent our sympathies. Let me know how Christopher's cold is, and whether your little Charlotte improves as much by change of air as she did last year.

Now I know your goodness will make you want to hear a little about me. I am in very tolerable health, having never been ill but from mental uneasiness. As to my plans, it is most probable that I shall remain in Norfolk till May. I shall then, if it please God, go to London to transact a little business, after which I shall be ready to take my summer flight, and shall hope to find you in the shades of Penrice. How must you delight to see that charming place after some months' absence! Sure, no-one has a sweeter home, a kinder husband, more amiable sisters or lovelier children (person and mind) than you have. How I rejoice in your various blessings and regard them as the intimations of what you are to possess in a still better country, where there shall be no aching void in the *breast* 'but all be full, possessing, and possess'd'.[1] But to

---

[1] Alexander Pope, *Eloisa to Abelard*, line 93.

descend to very common prose, I must beg the favour of you to do a small commission for me when you chance to make purchases in the gown way, to buy one for me such as you would think fit for morning wear. I have had a deal of good out of those you chose for me but the *yellow stripe* begins to call out [for] a successor.

I think you would like Mrs Hamilton's *Cottage of Glenburney*, and Mrs Edgeworth's *Tales of Fashionable Life*. Bigland's *Essays* lately fell in my way – I thought them good and sensible. Aikin and Barbauld's *Essays* I liked much. Kotzebue's *Exile* I have reperused with very great interest, and if you do not recollect it perfectly I think it would fix your attention on extraneous subjects.[2] I am convinced that the power of abstraction is one of the most useful the mind possesses, but this is a subject fitter for the pen of your *Salisbury*, amiably philosophical, physician,[3] than of my dearest Lady Mary's affectionate Po.

A young clergyman was doing duty in this neighbourhood lately for the first time he had officiated. After prayers a farmer stood up and said in a loud voice 'Very well read! Very pretty for the first time indeed! And young man – we excuse the sarment'.[4]

56. Letter from Agnes Porter, [Scratby Hall, Norfolk], to Lady Mary Talbot, Post Office, Salisbury, 22 March 1810

Do you know, my dear Lady Mary, that when I am inclined to feel *easterly* I take a letter or two of yours to read, and never fail to pronounce them a sovereign cordial for my spirits. The interest they express for my comfort makes me kind to my self. I can promise you to wear the shawl you recommend, and I now take my pen with this ample sheet of paper, on purpose to let you know how I am and what I am doing. My health is very tolerable, I take daily walks, I have made shift to get through the winter in this dreary spot, and look forward to a change in May with much satisfaction. Lady Home wished me to remain here till then, and urged it so much that I could not decline her invitation. It is nearly a year since I saw my brother and sister – we look forward to a meeting in May with great and, I believe, equal ardour. He, poor

---

[2] Elizabeth Hamilton, *The Cottagers of Glenburnie* (1808); Maria Edgeworth, *Tales of Fashionable Life* (1809); John Bigland, *Essays on Various Subjects* (1805); John Aikin and Anna Lætitia Barbauld, *Miscellaneous Pieces in Prose* (1773); A. F. F. von Kotzebue, *The Most Remarkable Year in the Life of Augustus von Kotzebue* (1802).

[3] See Dr Richard Fowler.

[4] The sermon.

man, has been extremely ill indeed, but thanks to Dr Macqueen he is now convalescent. He understood the case better at a distance than all the Fairford medical men who were close by. Such a superiority does science confer, when grounded on a good understanding. I cannot help being of opinion that science itself is not useful to a naturally weak intellect, for the *base* must be suitable in all instances to the super-structure. *A propos* to learning and learned men, I must congratulate you on your present vicinity to Dr Fowler. I am pleased to hear that he and Mrs Fowler are well, knowing as I do your regard and high esteem for both.

I know you will like to hear the welfare of my friends. Mrs Keir's son, after having apparently been at the point of death these four years, is now suddenly recovering from his illness. Poor woman, she has watched by his bedside all this time, and never expected to see him rise from it more. Her joy is very great, and I hope it will be lasting. Mrs Williams was too ill to receive me at Christmas, else I had thoughts of leaving Norfolk, but she is now better. My other friends, Dr Macqueen etc., are all well. What a melancholy affair was poor Mr Eden's disappearance and death! How much more difficult must it be to bear such sudden blows than any calamity of which we have warnings? In the case of those unfortunate parents, I can see only religion and abstraction of mind to enable them to bear up with decency and fortitude. Surely there is no property of the mind more useful than *that* of abstracting itself from a disquieting subject and fixing on a pleasant one! It is at once to be wise, grateful and happy! It is to act like you, my dearest love, whose duty is your polar star, and to whom the precious objects of your affection give *present exertions* and *future* tranquility. I rejoice at the Salisbury air's proving so beneficial to your children and am, with kind love to yourself, Mr Talbot and the darlings, ever yours, Ann Agnes Porter.

Should the time of my being in London agree with dear Miss Talbot's transit, I shall be most happy to convey her to you – I could do that *first*, and return to accomplish my London business.

What a pleasure for you to see two such Harriots as your aunt and sister! I beg my respectful remembrance to both.

The Refusal is very interesting, by Mrs West. Andrew's *Anecdotes of Illustrious Persons* are well spoken of. *The Cottage of Glenburney* may be of great local utility.[5]

---

[5] Jane West, *The Refusal* (1810); J. P. Andrews, *Anecdotes &c., Ancient and Modern* (1789).

57. Letter from Agnes Porter, Scratby Hall, Norfolk, to Lady Mary Talbot, Post Office, Salisbury, 28 April 1810

My Dearest Lady Mary,

How is it with you and with those you love? I should be very glad to know how Colonel Strangways and Lady Elizabeth do, for they haunt me in my sleep. If I make you smile at me, *tant mieux*. Among some pleasing realities, I heard a long time ago that your aunt Lady Harriot Acland was to visit you, and that your dear little Mary was returned to your party.[6] I hope all goes on to your wish relative to your dear boy and sweet little Emma. If you are well too, how happy will it be for your darlings! I quite rejoice to think that Mr Talbot is so much better. Pray give Po's respects and love to him.

I have fixed the day for my departure hence: on May 8th. I propose vesting a day on the journey, and by the 10th shall be, if it please God, in London, No. 11 [Strand]. I only propose remaining there one week, but you will let me know if I can be of the least use to you. After the 20th I shall be at Fairford, and there I long to be – a year is so long an absence from friends – that it is absolutely *un siècle*.

I have been reading two charming books – Mrs Carter's *Memoirs*, and *Anecdotes of Distinguished Persons*.[7] The first is interesting both to the head and heart, and the second is uncommonly entertaining – an anecdote of Lorenzo di Medici struck me much: a few hours before his death he shut his eyes, and upon his wife's asking why, he replied 'That I may see the better'. This seemed to me quite characteristic of his profound and energetic mind. Is it not a fine anecdote? When I wrote to Miss Talbot I was not sure of Lord Lansdowne's address, but I make no doubt the letter went safe. At present I am with one or other of your family every night. I hope, as Lovegold says, to touch – in time, instead of these shadowy satisfactions.

I shall rejoice to say farewell to Norfolk. You never saw a less agreeable prospect than now tires the eye, in looking around, of your ever affectionate Ann Agnes Porter.

---

[6] Pencil note: 'She had been in London with Aunt Louisa'.

[7] Revd Montagu Pennington (ed.), *Memoirs of the Life of Mrs Elizabeth Carter* (1807); William Seward, *Anecdotes of Some Distinguished Persons* (1795–97).

58. Letter from Agnes Porter, Fairford, to Lady Mary Talbot, Post Office, Salisbury, 12 June 1810

My Dearest Lady Mary,

How are you and how are your children? God almighty grant you may be able to answer me to our wishes. I thought I should never be competent again to travelling – I was so very ill in London with my *very bad* cold. I made shift to creep to Old Burlington Street, to New Burlington, and to Sackville Street. I did not see Lady Lansdowne, nor hear from her in return to a note, and I was too poorly to make repeated attempts. On the road I entirely recovered from the oppression on my breathing, and I am now (weakness excepted) quite well again. The sight of my dear brother and sister did me so much good as I cannot express. We had been *so long* apart that our meeting went far beyond pleasure, and my health has rapidly amended ever since I joined their affectionate party.

My sister wishes much to commence a new plan with regard to young people, which some of her friends think would be likely to meet success. Her plan is to receive children whose friends have not determined on their own views for them; or who have not been able to fix them to their own wishes – for instance, I will suppose the relations are on the look-out for a governess at home: my sister would like to receive them till a proper person presented herself. I will suppose that a rich young lady had lost her mother: my sister would willingly take care of her till the friends had fixed their plans, for a longer or shorter period – even to a few weeks. She seems to think that her scheme would be a useful one to many persons. You will understand me, though I cannot say I have been very luminous on this subject. I propose writing to Lady Harriot Frampton too, being also assured of her benevolence towards us.

God bless you, my ever dear Lady Mary. I came here only last Friday, Po.

59. Letter from Agnes Porter, Fairford, to Lady Mary Talbot, Penrice Castle, 13 August [1810]

My Dearest Lady Mary,

In writing to you yesterday, I was so entirely in my mind transported to your habitation, and its environs that I forgot to mention a circumstance in this neighbourhood which gave me great pleasure. I have seen Mrs Beach and her little Jane and all her family. She invited me by a note to accompany my brother and sister to spend the day there. We accordingly went, and she was so good as to receive me, not like a stranger, but as if I had been an old acquaintance – so kind in her manner and conversation. I am to thank you, my dear Lady Mary, for this pleasure. I think the place very beautiful. We past a very agreeable day indeed. Little Miss Jane is a very good, nice child, but in spirits far below par – so gentle as to lead to timidity, so humble as to make one fear a future deficiency of self-confidence, and of consequent exertions. But you know how much I prefer, in children's culture, the want of a pruning knife to a barrenness of fruits. Mrs Beach and I had some talk together on the subject of systems. We neither of us thought that Miss Hamilton understood the best purposes of a doll, but in other matters we gave her great credit.[8] Indeed, I cannot express how much I admire her work – her passing in review the rational qualities of the mind: perception, attention, conception, judgement, taste and imagination, abstraction, reflection, with their appropriate methods of improvement, charmed me. It was a fine theory (in which my dear Lady Mary's being a practitioner rendered it doubly interesting to me). Lord Lucan has, I hear, lost this worthy assistant by bringing home a kept mistress. Sad doings in London!

God bless you all at Penrice (where there are no such doings). Ever yours, A. A. Porter.

60. Letter from Agnes Porter, [Great Malvern], to Lady Mary Talbot, 4 September 1810

My Dear Lady Mary,

I am not afraid of tiring you with repetitions of your dear children's welfare – they are indeed blooming as the rose, and even the little Charlotte is both active and stout, *for her*. Their appetite is very good, their exercise is daily, and their minds are good and affectionate as you would wish. We revolve gradually into some of our old habits, and yesterday I proposed an hour's reading, which was readily acceded to. Our subject was Charles V, and the place in the history was his rash invasion of Francis.[9] They gave their opinion on the subject as we went on: Miss Jane observed that it was very *obstinate* in him not to take advice from his old experienced officers; Miss Talbot said he should have considered it well before he entered an enemy's country – that he was very rash and presumptuous. 'He was so, indeed' interrupted Charlotte 'but the reason was that he was *intoxicated* by *prosperity*.'

---

[8] The writer on education, Elizabeth Hamilton.

[9] William Robertson, *The History of the Reign of the Emperor Charles V* (1769).

I recollected that the historian had made the same remark, but how clever in a child of ten years of age to apply it so very properly. Miss Jane finds herself forced to lend her attention, as I frequently ask her the impertinent questions of 'Who was this person? What was his motive? How did it succeed?' And so on. Her delight is Shakespear, which I cruelly tore from her bosom in bed this morning, telling her that Shakespear loved *rising* early. The time we spend together passes very happily, but I will say no more lest I make you envy my happiness. How I rejoice to hear that dear Mr Talbot is better, and your darling little ones gaining in strength!

The church here is under repair in the side-aisle, but as I heard there was service performed every Sunday I supposed it was not thought in a dangerous state, so I went. The clergyman is a Dr Greaves and officiates very decently. His sermon was on numbering our days. In the latter part of it, on applying the heart unto wisdom, he said: 'The affections are the wings of the soul, and we must be careful to disengage them from those *clammy* sweets which might impede their flight to the heavenly regions'. I thought this idea had something new in it, but great part of the discourse was from an excellent essay of Dr Johnson's on the lapse of time.

I left my dear Fanny and her good partner well. He possesses but one measure for time – the gospel. Farewell for the present, my ever dear Lady Mary. All here send their love, Po.

61. Letter from Agnes Porter, Great Malvern, to Lady Harriot Frampton, Moreton, Dorset, 8 September 1810

I think, my dear Lady Harriot, it will give you pleasure to hear that your benevolent wishes towards my sister and my self have been successful. Do you recollect sending me a paragraph from the news-paper relative to two young ladies? These young ladies are now under my sister's care, and while they continue with her they encrease her income £400 per annum. This emolument is of use to her, and both she and I entertain hopes that these young persons will be essentially benefitted by her care and attention towards them. She desired me to present her grateful sentiments to you on this subject. We both thank you for your promptitude of doing good to others. These ladies came only last week to Fairford. Their name is Gough – they have no mother, and their father's attention seems more animated towards *hounds* than *daughters*. *Ah! Que c'est là un drôle de corps!* I have been here a week, but my dear Lady Mary is not yet come. I have had, however, the pleasure of seeing

Lady Charlotte and Mrs Campbell, and the happiness of believing myself of some use to your three amiable nieces, Mary, Jane and Charlotte. The youngest has a decided inclination for literature which merits the greatest cultivation. The elder has a great resemblance to her excellent mother, being discreet and sensible beyond her years. As for Jane, she is a compound *at present* of whim, indolence and genius: 'Honest as light, transparent even as day, tender as buds, and lavish as the spring'.[10] She has hitherto made very little progress in what is called *learning*. I should particularly wish to have her taught drawing and music – I think I know where she would improve very much, could her mamma part with her.

Will you favour me with a few lines at your leisure, and ever believe me yours most affectionately, Ann Agnes Porter.

I am at present reading *Corinne*. It is *too* beautiful – it absorbs too much.[11]

62. Letter from Agnes Porter, Great Malvern, to Lady Mary Talbot, Williamstrip, Gloucestershire, Tuesday Morning, 11 September 1810

My Dear Lady Mary,

After three hours *good* studies, your darlings have just left me, and I have half an hour before dinner to give to my pen and you.

I am somewhat perplexed at the idea of your sending your other three before you come yourself. What will you do in the absence of all your little darlings? Mr Talbot and you will pine very much on losing their prattle – I hope indeed you will hasten after them, and that the imposing hand of business will not detain you long. You will be delighted to see how well they look: the two *seniors* beautifully healthy and the dear little Charlotte is extremely well. I make her my walking companion, as my walks and hours just suit her. While I take the *lower* path of the hills she skips about and runs up every eminence that looks inviting. I suppose she goes three times my road over without being fatigued. Miss Talbot and I read Goldoni together and practise music according to Hüllmandel's method every day.[12] I used to pay great attention to his mode of teaching and his opinions, which I flatter

---

[10] William Shenstone, *Elegies Written on Many Different Occasions*, elegy xi, line 43.

[11] Madame de Staël, *Corinne, ou l'Italie* (1807).

[12] Carlo Goldoni (1707–93), the playwright; and Nicolas Joseph Hüllmandel, the music teacher.

myself may now be useful to her. She reminds me of your self in many of her ways – almost every day she brings me a little nosegay with a 'There Po' and a look that makes it a valuable gift. I try to make the dear Jane attentive: amiable she must ever be. I still think you one of the happiest mothers in the world: these precious girls are a heart's treasure. From the *first*, I thought of giving them three months of my time, a fortnight of which is elapsed, but you will regulate this little matter to your own conveniency. They will want another volume of *Charles*. Miss Charlotte continues her critical remarks. She said to-day: 'I really think Francis might know the emperor by this time better than to put any confidence in a man who has deceived him over and over again. How silly Francis is!'

   Farewell, my dear Lady Mary. Ever yours, Ann Agnes Porter.

63. Letter from Agnes Porter, Great Malvern, to Lady Mary Talbot, Penrice Castle, 21 September 1810

My Dear Lady Mary,
I think it will be comfortable for you and Mr Talbot to *find* a letter at Penrice, especially as I have nothing but what is pleasant to communicate. Little Emma is quite as well as when you left her – we think her eyes are rather better. Sukey[13] took her on the hills after breakfast and had the ablutions of the well. She is now with me while her maid is doing a few jobs, and is drawing circles round a halfpenny. I am now to draw *Hannah*, and then I shall go on again. When Miss Bere and I looked at them last night I was much pleased to see her feel their breast and heads as you do. 'J'aime à voir ces petits attentions qui décèlent le coeur.' They had a very good night. From ten to twelve Miss Jane and Miss Charlotte were at their studies with Po, and very attentive they both were. Miss Jane was a good deal interested in Fiesco's conspiracy, and dear little Charlotte was much pleased with her favourite Andrew Doria's escape. They wrote English and read French. Miss Jane practised her music as soon as breakfast was over, and very nicely indeed. Miss Charlotte as usual is as good as old gold. They are now, with the other darlings, gone to the wells with Miss Bere, who appears to me old enough to be *careful*, and young enough to be *playful*. Miss Jane complained that was not a walk sufficiently long for her, so there past something of an agreement for a very elevated excursion for to-morrow. Christopher is a darling boy – so sweetly sedate and sensible.

---

[13] See Susan Tatham.

Miss Isabella goes on very stoutly and on the whole is very good. Emma is now gone to her dinner – I told her who I was writing to and asked her what she said to mamma? Her answer was '*Good mamma*'. As I was not quite sure of her meaning I said 'Who is good?' 'Mamma' was her dear little answer.

A letter came to you, and another to Mrs Campbell, which I directed respectively. I hope Mrs Hunt was pretty well, and that poor Mr King was composed. Your darlings here send love to you and their papa and to their dear sister, to whom I beg you will also remember my dear Lady Mary's ever affectionate Po.

64. Letter from Agnes Porter, Great Malvern, to Lady Mary Talbot, Penrice Castle, Sunday 23 September 1810

My Dear Lady Mary,
Your children, I thank God, are *at least* as well as when you left them, and as happy as they can be in your absence. Little Christopher is really extremely well in health, and is one of the best children I ever knew. I think indeed that he is all the tenderest parents could wish for at his age. Miss Emma, that darling star, sparkles yet in the better part, her intelligence, and as to her looks they are much mended in my opinion by her eyes being better. The ears I think are not so much enflamed as they were; she eats heartily, sleeps soundly, and plays as well as any of the party. Miss Isabella coughs a little, but they tell me it is no more than it was before you went, and is caused by a slight cold. Miss Charlotte looks nicely and Miss Jane does not pine. I have nothing but good to say of them all as a set of the dearest and best children in the world. To-day I told Miss Bere that she and I would take church in turn, so she went and we at home read in the Bible and said catechism. I asked Miss Jane if she chose to hear it? 'No' she answered, she chose to say it too. In the course of it I stopped to ask a few questions: I asked Master Talbot what was meant by being said to be 'Born in sin' – he immediately answered 'Since Adam's fall'. Our chapters were one in Proverbs, and then Miss Jane chose to read the twenty-fifth of St Matthew, and their explications of the seven virgins etc. were very satisfactory. I cannot say as much for the weather, which was foggy and rainy all yesterday and to-day, so I proposed while I was writing to you up-stairs that they should have a most pleasant game at romps below, with Janet or Susan to guard the dear little Emma and promote the general exercise. I have the pleasure to hear 'king call' and 'pretty miss are you at home?' go on to admiration. This is to last an hour, and

then they lose their present auxiliary to make way for Miss Bere and me. She is not yet returned from church, but soon will come. It has poured torrents to-day; last evening we had a storm – thunder etc. I hope the weather is auspicious where you are, and that every other good attends you.

My respectful love to dear Mr Talbot, Po.

65. Letter from Agnes Porter, [Great Malvern], to Lady Mary Talbot, Penrice Castle, 26 September [1810]

My Dear Lady Mary,
Your little darling goes on improving very much indeed: her ears are less inflamed, her eyes begin to recover their brightness, and her general health is encreasing. Accept a few minutes while disagreeables are performing in a morning, she scarcely ever cries. She eats hearty, her bowels are quite regular and well, and she is as blythe as a lark. Miss Jane is perfectly well, and very diligent, *for her*. We get three good hours together every morning, and dear little Charlotte is never behind hand – she is extremely well. Isabella and Christopher have both a touch of cold, but hitherto it seems of no consequence. We did not observe it in the dear, good, little boy till yesterday, but as it was a very fine day he went out as usual. I hope next time I write to be able to tell you that it is quite gone. I hope my dear Miss Talbot is quite well and has derived pleasure from her visit to her *native home*. If I send but a short letter now, it will be in time for the post to-day, Wednesday 26th. Were I to write you a long one after breakfast it would not go till Friday.

I am my, dearest Lady Mary, ever yours, Po.

Remember me respectfully to dear Mr Talbot. A thousand loves to him and you and sister from your jewels.

66. Letter from Agnes Porter, Great Malvern, to Lady Mary Talbot, Penrice Castle, 30 September 1810

My Dear Lady Mary,
Your children are all well and have been in the air as much as possible. They daily mount the hills, and are much out in the garden when it is dry weather, but when it has been wet I object to their playing in the garden as they are apt to sit down on the damp ground which I am fearful might give colds. I think the last little cold Christopher had was gained by that circumstance. At times he coughs a little, and so

does Isabella, but it is very trifling. He is sometimes a little languid, and I think with him there might be such a thing as *over-exercise*, but of this you will be the best judge when you come. He is in the mean time *made* to take some repose and goes on very well both in mind and person. Little Emma improves every day in health and looks; Charlotte and Isabella are stout, and Miss Jane needs no improvement in the article of health. I have insisted on some hours industry and she is very good indeed – I have persuaded her to write some letters in her best hand-writing – to Miss Raines, as you desired her, and to Mrs Fowler. They will be rather surprized with these *comparatively* copper-plates. Miss Talbot's letter sent yesterday as *ad libitum*, unseen but by the dear little careless writer.

Some passages in your last kind letter, my dear Lady Mary, go home to the heart. I understand both you and them. Afflictions which in general are regarded as common events in life, have been to you most poignant cause of sorrow. You have with-held all exterior signs of woe, and the impressions are the deeper. As you have never frittered your feelings away on trivial matters, they are the more condensed and heavier where there is real cause. But you have such *treasures* left – you have such *Christian consolation*, and such natural fortitude, that *time* and *pursued occupations*, and various scenes, will perform their due effect on your heart and understanding.

All their loves attend you, ever yours, Po.

67. Letter from Agnes Porter, Great Malvern, to Lady Harriot Frampton, Moreton, Dorset, 1 October 1810

My Dear Lady Harriot,
I know it will give you pleasure, in your sister's absence, to hear how her children are, and the more as I have a very good account to give you. Little Emma is very considerably better: her eyes are nearly well and her face is regaining its roundness and beauty. Christopher is gaining strength: his appetite and spirits are very good. Isabella is the same stout, good-humoured, sensible child as when you saw her. Miss Charlotte is well and a remarkable clever child *at her studies*. Her love of literature is already both strong, and decided; her memory is excellent, and she uses Dr Johnson's art to improve it – 'the art of attention'. As for Miss Jane, she is in perfect health, blooming as a rose, blythe as a lark, and 'as careless of to-morrow's fare' either in a personal or a mental view. I endeavour, while I am with her, to fix her mind as much as I can to some improving objects, and from the sweetness of

her temper she complies, rather than from any *self-gratification*. History, French and music, English, of course, we daily *labour* at. With good natural abilities she is not likely to acquire any depth of science, having but little diligence – notwithstanding this, she is a both lovely and beloved young creature: kind, sweet-tempered, and open as the light. Miss Talbot is with her mamma in Wales. I was happy it was so settled, as she would be a pleasing companion to your dear sister. I hope Mrs Frampton and your darlings are well.

I am my dear Lady Harriot's very affectionate and obedient servant, Ann Agnes Porter.

I hope your aunts Lady Susan and Lady Harriot are well. Offer them my kind and respectful remembrance.

68. Letter from Agnes Porter, Great Malvern, to Lady Mary Talbot, Revd Dr Hunt's, Tynycaeau, Margam, 7 October 1810

My Dear Lady Mary,
Your letter dated the 4th we received on the 6th, so I think it did come more expeditiously. I suppose you are now with dear Mrs Hunt and shall direct accordingly. I am in hopes you will find all your darlings here quite as well as when you left them. You know they had little coughs, Isabella and Emma, but the latter is on the whole so much stronger, and so generally amended in her habit, that Sukey makes but little account of the little cough, only all possible care is taken to prevent the increase of it. Little Star had her flannels put on the very first chilly day, last Thursday, and Miss Isabella has on the stockings to-day, of which she is not a little proud. Dear Christopher is at present with me, in the midst of an engagement between the French and English fleets. 'Po, look at the smoke, is it not very well done? So thick, thick that they cannot see one another!' 'I wonder who will win the battle, my dear Christopher.' 'O! Po, you know that the English will gain the battle, because they are the best sailors.' He reasons (pretty little fellow) very logically, does he not? We take care that he does not walk too much at a time, but of late I have preferred short walks to their remaining long in the garden, as the fogs have been so heavy as to wet the ground long after mid-day, and they are apt to sit down on the grass which is by far too damp for them. I find him much improved both in his health and spirits. Miss Charlotte is charmingly; her sister Jane is the picture of health and good humour. Miss Jane, Miss Bere and I were at church this morning – there came on a mist and rain so

the children did not go out. Mr Darke dined with us yesterday – he made us promise to inform him when Mr Talbot and you returned. He was much pleased with Mr Christopher, looks and all.

Pray give my respectful compliments to Dr and Mrs Hunt. I hope Mr Talbot and you know me to be your ever grateful and affectionate Ann Agnes Porter.

69. Letter from Agnes Porter, Great Malvern, to Lady Mary Talbot, 14 October 1810

My Dear Lady Mary,

Your letter *without date* reached us yesterday. Your loves are all quite as well as when I wrote last. Miss Jane's little swelling in the arm went off again in three days, and she alledges her perfect health as a sound and sufficient reason against the swallowing senna or any other nauseous draught whatsoever. Miss Charlotte (except *once* a headach) has never had the smallest complaint – she is in charming health. Christopher's little cough does not encrease, and Isabella's is better. They had both taken the composition you mention before you wrote. Though Miss Bere makes no fuss about them, I observe that she is very watchful over health, and the maids are very careful. As for Po, you know her of old to be a fidgetty wretch, and the *trop* is much more likely to be her fault than the *trop peu* in *these matters*.

We have had some very pleasant days since I complained to you of the fogs. The worst of it is the frequency of the east and north-east winds, which feeling in my own breast I am apt to dread for the darlings, but thank God, their strength augments and they will, I trust, with due care be able to brave the seasons.

Dear little Christopher is at present absorbed in a book of geography. I shall make him look about him by telling him whom I am writing to – his answer is 'I wish mama to write to me again', and this said, not *comme tout le monde*, but with an expression on the word *wish*, and a certain look, that says more than words. How expressive is that language in all who possess a heart! As well as I recollect Madame Genlis lays her emphasis on *tones* – they indeed, when involuntary, express much, but I think a single look still sinks deeper in the heart. Isabella is a very stout little maiden, and Miss Bere is making both her and Miss Charlotte very expert at their needles, but this to remain a *profound secret* in order to cause you an agreeable surprize. Your Morning Star is resuming her lustre and will, I trust, shed cheering rays on your future life.

I admire your idea of the *individuality* of friends and the consequent discrimination in friendship. *I am persuaded* there are many persons to whom *friends* are as the leaves on trees: let them but succeed each other and blossom, the *identity* is nothing. Much good may this do all such easy *persons*, says your ever affectionate Po.

It has been observed by Miss Jane that you have not answered her letter. *Elle est de toute beauté.*

1811

In 1811 Agnes was at Penrice from mid-February until the end of June. In July she spent a few days in Dorset, visiting the O'Briens at Stinsford and her former pupil Lady Harriot Frampton and her family at Moreton. Agnes then went to London before returning to her sister and brother-in-law's house at Fairford.

70. Letter from Agnes Porter, [Penrice Castle], to Lady Mary Talbot, Moreton, Dorset, 20–22 May 1811

My Dear Lady Mary,

To-day being very fine, I took the two little darlings and Sukey an-airing. The senior ladies preferred a long walk with Miss Bere, so we were all out at the same time, though not together. The little loves were as happy as possible, looking upon it as a great treat to go out in the carriage and to have both Sukie and Po. We were speaking of the wind when little Emma said 'The wind is behind us for I see the grass fall down before – the wind sweeps it down'. Is not that a true mother's own child? Not five years old, and to make such acute remarks! Sweet love! She is indeed a jewel of the first water. We met Mr Williams[1] on the road, who gave me a letter, which said letter to our great joy was from you. At dinner I said: 'My dear Emma, what had Po on the road?' 'A letter from mamma.' 'What did mamma say?' 'That Kit and Charry were very well, they ride their cousin's pony and Kit was to go next day to school.' There was a general inquiry what day that was, but I could not inform them, for mamma had *not dated her letter*. Thus far from us, Monday 20th.

The music was very attentively executed, and every *chromatique* in Miss Talbot's lesson was exactly echoed by Miss Isabella – *sotto voce*, thinking she was not heard. Mr Williams was so much pleased with her

---

[1] Later note: 'Music master'.

that he said he should like much to have her for a pupil. I replied it must be for a very few minutes, he said that would be sufficient at one time. I promised to mention this to you, and ask your approbation – she has certainly a fine ear, and beginning so young, would give her a chance for voluble fingers. To-day Mr Hart was here. It chances to be very favourable weather for dancing. The Miss Collins with their mamma and Mr John were of the party. Mrs Collins told me that two *Mr Parsons* were fishing who would be glad to join in the country dance if agreeable; I answered *sans façon* that it would *not be proper* – they are good people but have very little diffidence or judgement in these matters. I hope you think I did right. We meet on the Tuesdays, but I am rather shy of promoting visits on other days, thinking it rather time lost. We settle that and all other matters very well – how happy I am that my being here just now contributes to your ease of mind! For esteem and *gratitude* bind me. Ever yours, Ann Agnes Porter

71. Letter from Agnes Porter, Penrice Castle, to Lady Mary Talbot, Moreton, Dorset, 24 May 1811

My Dear Lady Mary,
Upon repeating to you that all are well, I am not in the least afraid of your exclaiming 'Pho! This is the old story! Is there nothing new to tell me?' For well do I know that neither wit nor invention could furnish you with such agreeable information as contained in these few words, 'All are well'. The weather has been on the whole so rainy and unfavourable that I am really sometimes surprized at their continued good health, and my own great happiness and good fortune, in having them continue so well. Yesterday afternoon proved remarkably fine, so the two elder ladies took a long walk with Miss Bere. They went to Oxwich, and Miss Bere told me that Miss Talbot invited the family party to hold themselves disengaged any where else but at Penrice Castle for the 5th of June, a day she intended to celebrate. I was pleased to hear that she took so much in hand of her own accord, and no doubt we shall pink ourselves out to do honour to her loyalty. Mr Llewellyn[2] has been here these few days: I dropt a line by him to Mrs Hunt, to inform her how well the darlings were. Miss Isabella said 'Po tell Mrs Hunt that I love her *very much indeed*'. 'For what reason do you love Mrs Hunt, my dear?' 'Po, she shewed me all her fine things: pretty little carriages, and cats that cried because their *tabby* friend was dead.' She has a grateful heart

---

[2] Later note: 'Griffith Llewellyn, agent'.

within her dear little breast as can be. Morning Star is as bright as ever
– *c'est tout dire*. When it is fine over-head I take them a little airing in
the carriage – no one else chuses to go, but Sukie and Po make out
their *partie quarrée* [foursome].

My kind love to dear little Charry and best respects to Mr Talbot
from his and your affectionate and obliged Ann Agnes Porter.

Mrs Sheares begs her duty to you.

72. Letter from Agnes Porter, Penrice Castle, to Lady Mary Talbot, Moreton, Dorset, Sunday 26 May 1811

My Dear Lady Mary,

All here continue as well as we could wish. Within these few days the
weather is improved, so the little ones are more frequently taken out,
to be *hardened* to the air as much as possible. Yet we are careful not to
over do, nor to run any hazards. To-day is very fine, and at this moment
every one is enjoying it out of doors but Po, who thinks the afternoon's
walk up the hill to church will sufficiently exert her *corporeal* faculties.
You would not soon divine what has lately occupied my *mental*: a most
attentive perusal of Sir George Paul's work on the regulations etc. of
prisons.[3] I would style him, as he does Howard,[4] a 'hero of humanity',
and think what the former wished to have done, it was Sir George's
destiny to execute. No one can read the book without entertaining the
highest opinion both of the head and heart of the writer, and I read
it with great interest both in the subject and the pen.

Miss Talbot's health and spirits are both excellent. She was rather
low after you went, but now, though she ardently wishes your return,
all is well again. Miss Jane is perfectly well, and very good indeed. Miss
Isabella is making a daily progress in the arts and sciences, and Miss
Emma is just this instant returned from a ride on Donky and a walk
in the wood. She ran into my room to shew me the colombines she
had gathered: 'Hush, Po and Sukie till I speak. See Po, I gathered
these pretty colombines my own self in the wood. Did not I, Sukie?'
'Yes my dear, you did, and very *ullegant* they are.' Both Sukie and I
agree in one story, that this lovely darling is *quite well*. How are you
my dear Lady Mary? *Et l'estomac, va t'il bien? Je l'espère de tout mon coeur,*
A. A. Porter.

---

[3] Sir G. O. Paul, *Considerations on the Defects of Prisons, and their Present System of
Regulation* (1784).

[4] The prison reformer John Howard (*c.* 1726–90).

73. Letter from Agnes Porter, Penrice Castle, to Lady Mary Talbot, Moreton, Dorset, 30 May 1811

My Dear Lady Mary,

I think you have great reason to make your mind easy with regard to dear little Christopher, who begins school with peculiar circumstances of advantage and *agrément*.[5] To have his dear parents so near him, and to return home with them in a few weeks, must be gratifying indeed both to the dear boy and you. You will be enabled to judge by this means both of his health and happiness: as to his progressive improvement, that is a point beyond doubt. I hope dear Charry reads French and touches an instrument every day – under her mother and aunt she ought to do great things.

Dr Hobbes came yesterday to visit poor Mrs George who is, he apprehends, dropsical. He was very much pleased with the very healthy appearance of your four daughters: he thinks Isabella rather thinner but says she looks clear and well. Little Emma was quite in her element jumping round and round his chair, playing bo-peep and so on. He was quite delighted with her – would she go with him to Swansea? 'No, certainly not.' He then enlarged on fine dolls, tarts, jellies, little coaches: her resolution began to waver, and after a few seconds of deep thinking, she said she would get sister Mary to write for her and ask mamma's leave, but in case mamma consented she must take Sukie too, and Miss Bere and Po should come too. She then enquired whether he had frocks and night caps for her, and little red shoes. She mentioned every comfort and pleasure she is accustomed to enjoy, and well would it be for many of her sex if they exercised a proportionable degree of foresight and caution before entering into any lasting contract.

Miss Talbot is now in the garden; Miss Jane on horse-back, at eight Thursday morning, fair settled weather for the present. The little ones are dressing, Miss Bere practising. At nine we read Mrs Trimmer. Yesterday it rained a great deal – we snap at an hour of dry weather.

I repeat, all are well and that I am always yours affectionately, A. A. Porter.

---

[5] C. R. M. Talbot went to the Revd Mr Bowle's school at Wimborne, Dorset, for the first time in May 1811.

74. Letter from Agnes Porter, Penrice Castle, to Lady Mary Talbot, Moreton, Dorset, 1 June 1811

My Dear Lady Mary,

I go on in a regular way of writing to you, though I make no doubt you have frequent letters from your own dear girls. I hear sometimes of their writing, but I do not even send a message, wishing their epistles to be not only sent at their own times, but to contain only their own spontaneous dictates. They continue all well, thank God, and I think they are all very happy. Po's indulgence is tempered by Miss Bere's *solidity*, so we do passing well. When the little ones are out we do our morning studies all together. In our history of Europe Miss Bere makes one of the readers, and as she reads very correctly she is an acquisition to the party. This morning, after Miss Talbot had read Italian, I opened the book at a chance place, and said 'Now my dear! Take your slate and write a few lines from my reading to you!' 'O! Po, I know I cannot write Italian'. 'Try, you had several lessons of a master in London, and some months at Great Malvern and here together, you have read it with me. Try if you cannot perform as much as I wish you to do!' She then accordingly wrote about seven or eight lines from Goldoni, to my reading, and there was only one word *(peggiore)* that had a mistake in it. I saw the dear creature smile with *tacit* satisfaction. Miss Jane then offered to write French in the same method, and she is improved a good deal. As we dine at two, I left them near one and just met Miss Isabella coming in at the window-door. Sukie and Pet Lamb were gone up two pair of stairs before her. She went into her nursery to put her flowers in water I told her I must go up, but asked if she could open that stiff door herself? 'No Po, you must leave it open.' 'And were it to shut accidentally, what would you do?' 'I would wait till Sukie came back.' 'How would you amuse yourself?' 'I would settle my flowers and rummage my play things. But, Po, you may shut the window before you go, that the wind may not bang the door to when you are gone.' Very good reasoning! Emma is beauteous as a rose-bud – the darling of all that behold her. As for *me* she could draw me by a single hair to the *Indies*.[6]

Farewell, my own *ever dear*! Po.

---

[6] Alexander Pope, *The Rape of the Lock*, ii, line 27. 'And beauty draws us with a single hair'.

75. Letter from Agnes Porter, [Penrice Castle], to Lady Mary Talbot, Moreton, Dorset, 6 June 1811

My Dear Lady Mary,

Yesterday was Miss Talbot's grand gala. *Present*: the Miss Lucas's, the Miss Collins, Mrs Collins and Mr and Mrs Edwards. The number in all (reckoning Mr John Collins) was fifteen. Tea at six, and the ball commenced at a little after eight and finished a quarter past ten. Then some refreshments were *offered*, and received *most heartily*. The dancers retired at eleven, and I remained with Mr and Mrs Edwards till twelve. Miss Talbot gave a general invitation to stay all night which I perceived was a very agreeable circumstance to the party, as it rained a torrent and the winds sounded tremendous after the soft, feet-inspiring tones of Mr James George's violin. I whispered to-day in Miss Jane's ear that the visit would suffice for this time, as music, French, Italian etc., etc. must of course be at a stand. Mrs Collins and her family have such little idea of education that they would think a pause of three months was only a *comma*. Mrs Collins asked me if she might send Miss Anne likewise on Mondays to attend music. I said I thought we had better wait till Lady Mary returned, and endeavoured to make her comprehend that dancing was a very different matter, but that in music, with only one master, no young person could have an hour out of his time but as deducted from the practice of the others, and that these young ladies, with Miss Bere, fully employed the allotted time. The dear woman looked, I thought, a little vexed and I believe your own darlings thought it a little cross in Po, but I am callous to these sort of things. They have now had an amusement much to their taste, and most amiably they behaved to all their party. The Miss Lucas's seemed much happier and danced better in their mamma's absence, which I was very sorry to observe, as a mother must make some sad mistake whose presence does not add to the hilarity of her children.

Miss Talbot and Miss Bere are now doing the honours of the garden. The younger Miss Lucas's and the two darlings are at play around me, keeping house and school, at which the *youngest* preside with all confidence and *allowance*. Miss Jane is shewing the *Antiquities of Pozzuoli and Baja* to Miss Caroline and Matilda, who are waiting for their carriage.[7] As for *Po*, you will *see* what she has been doing, and I trust *feel* that she is yours most affectionately.

---

[7] The book was probably *Le antichità di Pozzuoli, Baja e Cuma, incise in rame e pubblicate da F. Morghen* (Naples, 1768). Thomas Mansel Talbot may have bought it in Italy, during his Grand Tour.

76. Letter from Agnes Porter, Penrice Castle, to Lady Mary Talbot, Moreton, Dorset, 9 June 1811

My Dear Lady Mary,

I wish you joy of your new nephew[8] – I hope the dear mother continues well. I suppose it was the rainy weather that gave Miss Talbot a touch of the tooth-ach, but it is now quite gone. Miss Jane too said she had a little head-ach, for which Miss Bere prescribed a dose of salts, and we hear no more of it. They are both looking very well indeed, and I only mention the above slight aches from the *old way* of telling you every particular relative to them, however minute. Miss Isabella looks in my opinion better than when you left her, and as for Emma she is charming. After a little story about a patient child, to which she listened with the greatest attention, she said 'I know, Po, what one should be'. 'What, my love?' '*Patient*, Po. And I know another thing they should do – tell the truth – you know, like the man who lost his ?axe – that story you told me when Miss Anne Basset was here' – at least *three months* ago.

Your garden looks beautiful. When the weather permits I go to it, and examine the flowers to the best of my ability. I was much pleased yesterday with the balsams: Mr Ace told me they were pretty well, he could not say that he had much reason to complain of them. This I interpretted into their being very fine. The lychnadeas [lychnidea or phlox] make a serene appearance; the roses are beginning to bloom. The kitchen-garden has been the most injured by the weather. The young ladies walk whenever they can – I generally know when Miss Talbot comes from the garden by the gift of a nice little nosegay, which I either receive [or] find. She was much enter[tained] yesterday by an act of Molière. We left off *Les Journées Amusantes* after a story or two. The style is stiff and rather pedantic, so I cater for them. I shall not be obliged to leave them till the 25th, but I hope you will return ere that – at any rate they will not be long in seeing you after I am gone.

I had a few lines from Dr Hunt yesterday – he and Mrs Hunt are pretty well, but she expects to hear every day of the death of a near relation, otherways Dr Hunt would come to see your darlings. They unite in love to their papa and mamma and *Charry*.

I am, dear Lady Mary, most truly yours, Ann Agnes Porter.

---

[8] Note in ink: 'Charlton Frampton'. This was William Charlton, son of James and Lady Harriot Frampton, born 4 June 1811.

77. Letter from Agnes Porter, Bristol, to Lady Mary Talbot, Penrice Castle, 4 July 1811

My Dearest Lady Mary,

I have been writing to Miss Bere about her brother's box and it appears like a heresy against the friendship I bear you to write to any other on your side of the water, and not to you. This feeling of mine will cost you postage and the trouble of reading this scrawl written with an *unwritable* pen and *substantial* ink.

I reached Mrs Hunt's Thursday night and found her up and wonderfully well. We spent two happy days together. I saw Margam church and admired Mr Talbot's magnificent spirit. On Monday morning I popt into the Prince Regent's coach as it past by Mrs Hunt's door. I am sorry to remark that His Royal Highness had not a sound bottom, for the lower part of the coach was like a sieve, having round holes all over it, and I was afraid to lean my feet *at full* for fear of destroying the foundation. At Cowbridge I perceived Mr Price's carriage, with coachman *and footman*: the first for utility, the second to do me honour in the opinion of all observers. Nothing could be kinder than dear Mrs Price.[9] Mr Price was quite polite and hospitable; Miss Richards[10] so goodnatured and obliging! Indeed, only a line *from yourself* could requite their kindness. I feel that my writing would be inadequate, but that a few lines from your hand would leave them my debtors. Am I not very bold to trouble you with my *obligations*?

I had an unpleasant voyage – *Old Passage*. Two of my fellow travellers from Cardiff inveighed against that town all the way, but as we past through Newport the wife exclaimed: 'La! Husband, I wish we had come here to spend our three weeks instead of going to Cardiff. Do you see, there's a sadler, and here is a grocer. Why, Newport must be quite a *polite* place.'

Will you ask if my letter to Mr King was sent, which Mr Hart *did not carry*. I saw nothing of him at Swansea. My love to Mr Talbot and darlings. I am ever your own Po.

---

[9] Note in ink: 'At Llandough Castle'.
[10] Later note: 'Afterwards Mrs J. Homfray'.

78. Letter from Agnes Porter, Moreton, Dorset, to Lady Mary Talbot, Penrice Castle, 11 July 1811

My Dear Lady Mary,

I received your kind letter at Stinsford and request that you will make my most grateful acknowledgements to Mr Talbot. His goodness and yours have always covered my heart with benefits, and it feels happy in a sense of obligation to such generous minds. Heaven bless you both!

I think it would be a most happy circumstance to Mrs Lucas and family were their acquaintance at Penrice Castle to encrease, for the truth and vivacity of your young people might have some effect on the mind and manners of her children, while a little change, in going sometimes there, might serve for a half hour's amusement.

Your letter gave me a nice idea of your general welfare: it ran in that *cheary* and *chearing* strain that convinced me, without naming particulars, that all was well. Dear Mr Talbot in tolerable health considering the hot weather; your two eldest hopes in a blooming and vigorous state; little Charlotte still *round-faced*; Christopher daily better; Isabella hearty; and Morning Star as bright as usual – all this I divined from your letter, and it was delightful to me so to translate it. Yet on this subject the *text* can never be too plain, nor too often repeated.

I left Lady Susan O'Brien very well indeed, and Mr O'Brien pretty well. Lady Adare came there the same day I did – I had not seen her for twenty-one years and was struck at the great difference that grief, more than time, had wrought on her. She very soon renewed her acquaintance with me with all her wonted sweetness and condescension, and we had many conversations relative to the repository and Poppy.[11] Lady Susan was so good as to take me out, very pleasant walks and airings. I left them yesterday, and am now under (I do believe) one of the happiest roofs in the world. Your dear sister soon remembered me again: she says my voice is quite natural to her, and possessing, as she does, the Strangways memory, we chatter away on the days that are past, of which she claims to recall the minutest circumstances.

I proceed to London next Monday, *s'il plaît au bon Dieu*. Ever yours, Ann Agnes Porter.

---

[11] Pencil note: 'Her favourite maid'.

79. Letter from Agnes Porter, Fairford, to Lady Mary Talbot, Penrice Castle, 22 October 1811

My Dear Lady Mary,

It rejoiced my heart to hear that your dear little boy continues so well. I hope sweet Emma blooms and strengthens to your wish. If they all remain well at this season of the year it will give reasonable hope of their health in future. When you do write, you cannot give me a higher treat than to enlarge upon this subject generally and individually. I read over their beloved names as misers do the inscription of their treasures and, like them, longing for a nearer view.

It gives me great satisfaction to know that Lady Elizabeth is with you, but pray tell her she is an indolent fair one, for not having written to Po. We have had a month of delightful weather, which would animate any set of people but the *dullinas* of Fairford.[12] I really do not think that there is a ray of chearfulness out of our own little dwelling. It seems a strange assertion, but I really fear it is too true – however I make it a rule to visit our neighbours now and then, and take *le monde comme il va*.

Your *Frederic of Prussia*[13] has entertained me much: it is a wonderful character, which left its own peculiar impression and never ceased to aim at encreasing singularity. *Laura*,[14] too, has interested me much in a very different way – I should like to find out who the author is. Mrs Grant's *Highlands* is a book well spoken of – have you read it?

In your next, tell me how dear Mr Talbot does and who is his evening party at cribbage. You were right as to the portrait and painter. As you had done me the honour to take my profile, I thought [I] might take the liberty of sending it to you, and the young artist planned and urged the mode of sending it, from the overflowings of youthful confidence. She will do her best to profit by the remarks you so kindly make on her performance.

Will Lady Elizabeth or you send me information in the following particulars, at your leisure: is Sir James Kerr Innis, Duke of Roxborough? What is Lord Palmerston's family name? Who is Lord Callidon? Our *Red Book* is antique, and here we have neither living oracle nor chronicle.

Farewell my dearest Lady Mary, *Dieu vous bénisse!* Ann Agnes Porter.

---

[12] *Dullinas* may be an allusion to *gallinas*: chickens or guinea fowl in Latin.

[13] Pencil note: 'Probably Thiebault's *Memoirs of the Court of Berlin*'. This was D. Thiebault, *Original Anecdotes of Frederick the Second, King of Prussia* (1805).

[14] Note in ink: '*Laure de ?Germaden*'.

I enjoy the idea of your historical games. I have done another pair of repository garters. Shall I send them to you in a frank to Mr Wyndham?[15]

80. Letter from Agnes Porter, Fairford, to Lady Mary Talbot, [Melbury], 27 November 1811

My Dear Lady Mary,
Your last gratified my longings to hear from you and leaves me, as your letters generally do, both pleased and *indebted*. But, as some one observes that 'a grateful mind stands at once indebted and discharged', I flatter my self that the love I bear you smoothes or cancels every *other inequality* in our epistolary intercourse. How I rejoice that you see your sisters face to face! That your son is well again, and the rest of your darlings so comfortable! It pleases me greatly to hear that your three elder daughters are with you, as they are standard dishes of a most delectable flavour to such a mother's taste. Heaven bless them with a continuance of their blessings, and you with a continued sense and thankfulness! Miss Charlotte's health will, I trust, improve as usual by change of air. If you would only lend her to me for *three* months, I would bring her back to you with care and gratitude. Have I not some little property in the children of my ever-beloved child, my own sweet Mary!

How is dear Mr Talbot? Does he agree with change of scene? Does he … *[part of page torn]* … you both joy … sister Charlotte's … a pet at Penrice … Ladyship her *Caro* … Lady Ilchester had the goodness to inform me of that joyful event – I hope she received my acknowledgements. I wish she would do me the honour to wear the garters I send with this, but if not they may go to Lady Adair's repository. I have just finished Mrs Grant's *Highlanders*. I love both her and them. Her wish of having … *[torn]*.

My love to my dear young friends, with thanks to Miss Jane for her very nice letter. I am, my dearest Lady Mary, yours, Ann Agnes Porter.
Is Lady Elizabeth with you?

---

[15] The repository may have been a charity bazaar of some kind. Thomas Wyndham of Dunraven was MP for the county of Glamorgan; letters could be sent to him without payment.

81. Letter from Agnes Porter, Fairford, to Lady Mary Talbot, 7 December 1811

My Dear Lady Mary,

I must trouble you once more before you cross the Channel: to mention two young women whom I wish to assist, and to beg your kind interest to accomplish it. The one is Miss Elbury[16] who, having kept her brother's house for two or three years, wishes now to return to the more pleasing care of instructing *little* children. I wish in your way home that you would have the goodness to name her to Dr and Mrs Hunt: among their numerous acquaintance something eligible might occur for her. The other *younger* person is a poor cottager's daughter – her parents have six children; the father and mother are both sickly, which has kept the two elder girls hitherto at home, but now, their health being better, they and the daughters wish to part for their mutual good. They are, as far as we hear and can discover, industrious sober people, and the young woman I like much. She can handle her needle uncommonly well for a cottager, and seems to me both willing and apt to learn. Perhaps under a clever nursery-maid or house-maid she might soon be taught the business of either, and I believe her to be very innocent and sweet-tempered. You know, my dear Lady Mary, I always trouble you when I wish to be of use to my fellow creature, at least when the affair is above my scope.

I hope indeed that you will have a merry Christmas with all your rose-buds blooming around you. I should like to hear in particular how Mr Talbot and Mr Christopher bear their journey and how they both are. I have been reading *Says I to my Self* – how do you like it? I have been told that the writer is Mr Nares, who married a daughter of the Duke of Marlborough's.[17] Did they ever forgive the marriage?

I have quite enjoyed your excursion here and shall also rejoice to hear that you are snugly seated by your own happy fire-side with the loves in reunion bustling about you. May your sisters experience such maternal felicity as you do! I cannot wish it more.

Farewell my ever dear Lady Mary! Your Po. Love, compliments, etc., etc.

---

[16] Pencil note: 'Elborough'.

[17] Edward Nares, *I Says, Says I: A Novel* (1812).

1812

During the first half of 1812 Agnes left Fairford, which had been her home for five years. In April she visited her pupils' old home at Redlynch in Somerset, and she was at Stinsford again for a few days in May and June. She may have visited London in July, but most of the rest of the year was spent in the small Somerset town of Bruton, near Redlynch, where she stayed with her old friends Mrs and Miss Lloyd.

82. Letter from Agnes Porter, Fairford, to Charlotte Talbot, 9 February 1812

My Dear Miss Charlotte,

I wish you joy on your *twelfth* birth-day, and hope you will see many as happy as the last. I think your doll's gown must be extremely pretty by your description, and what a darling little thing must your cottage be! These beauties, with many more, I shall expect to see when I next pay a visit to your dear mamma, so pray take due care of them. I wish I could, in the mean time, transport you here to see some of the beauties of Fairford. There is a little dog you would like, and a tabby puss that you would admire: just such a one as *Miss Baillie's* – you recollect hers, I am persuaded. Besides these, my sister has four beautiful pigeons that inhabit the *upper* apartment, whom we visit and feed. The captain of this winged party is of the *carrier* kind – a large, full-plumaged, ample-chested bird. He moves about majestically, swelling his golden crest, and claims the homage of his courtiers and the love of his spectators. A little robin, too, comes every day to ask benevolence – and the sparrows, a bold set, come by dozens to catch at whatever they can. All this is very amusing, you will say, and may well be very improving also, but as you love to *think* I leave this point to your consideration.

Farewell, my dear child. I see you remember Po, who used to love you so truly. You recollect, in mamma's absence, being one of her pets, and sitting on a little stool by my side. I am making something for your mamma that she will be surprized when she sees. Tell her so, with my respectful compliments to her and your good papa.

My love to your sisters; my kind remembrance to Mr Collins' *tribe* and to Miss Bere. I am, my dear child, yours affectionately, Ann Agnes Porter.

83. Letter from Agnes Porter, Bruton, to Lady Mary Talbot, 25 April 1812

My Dear Lady Mary,

If you are still at Penrice Castle, and my going for dear Christopher would be convenient for you, I would go for him at *any time, to or from* any place. I know not how I mentioned my intentions for next June and July, but certainly I could have no engagement that would not be superceded by the desire, and the *duty*, of being useful in any circumstance to you and dear Mr Talbot.

You have not treated me with the names of all your darlings: next time give me a trait of each, particularly if we do not meet this year. What you say of your *garden* affects me much, but we must not think too deeply – there would be an end of all exertion, and consequently of every comfort both personal and social, were we to be too much impressed by the feelings you allude to. On the contrary, let us enjoy what at present is ours, and not regret that those who come after us may have in their own estimation superiour enjoyments.

When I saw dear Redlynch I thought of that angel your mother – but she was transplanted to a fairer clime, and her successors leave her late abode because they prefer another, and it is a *voluntary* departure. After a few tears, my regrets became *selfish*: I looked at the place she called *Mrs Porter's Walk*, and which she said would long retain the appellation. I thought of the goodness that gave me thus a kind of nominal property in what was hers; I thought what a friend I had lost! But much remains to everyone, and to enjoy is to obey. Last winter I was one day thinking of you and how much you disliked to work for yourself. 'All that love her' thought I 'should do something for her.' I wish I could work her a tippet – but I never did work muslin – is it *impossible* for me to learn? I will try, however, so I set about it *straight*, asked half a dozen questions of muslin workers and began daily practice. The precious fruits of these labours I sent last week, or rather the other day, by Mr Moore, in a small box to Bristol, to be thence forwarded to you at Penrice Castle. There was with it a little *repository* net bag, and some music which I shall play next time I see your darlings. Be so good as to lay it carefully by for me, not for its intrinsic worth, but for the agreeable magnitude of the notes.

I have seen your uncle the *Colonel* in perfect health; I have seen your cousin the *Cannon*[1] in ditto. Mrs Charles Digby senior was so obliging as to call on me here with her daughter, grandson and Mr Dampier. This procured me a visit from Mrs Admiral Goldsborough and the other ladies of Bruton ... *[letter ends here].*

84. Letter from Agnes Porter, Bruton, to Lady Mary Talbot, Cheltenham, 21 May 1812

My Dearest Lady Mary,

I think it will give you pleasure to hear how well your brother looks, and how well he is. On Friday last his lordship and Lady Ilchester past through Bruton in some little morning airing or visit; the next day he did me the honour to call on me and sat half an hour. You will guess whether I rejoiced to see him. He had that clear animated complection which indicates health, and that happy expression of countenance which reveals that all is contentment within. He was so very good as to say he should be glad to see me at Melbury, and added with a smile 'No time like the present'. Sometime or other after I have chanced to see the new Lady Ilchester I think I will indulge my self with a few days, *where* I spent several happy years.

I hope you are well and Mr Talbot not worse – and your darlings *better*. I think of you every day. Heavens bless you!

I propose being here till the beginning of July; I then am to pay Dr Macqueen a visit at his earnest invitation and shall be a few days in Town for my own little *interests*. As it is no longer convenient for my brother and sister to have me continue at their house as their inmate, I could wish to set up my little tent at Bruton, which I like very much on several accounts – it quite suits me. I am trying to find a situation to return to. Mrs Lloyd is so old that she thinks me rather a dissipated person for going out twice a week to tea, although I return to her supper hour at nine. She says were Mrs Porter not of so rambling a disposition she should like to have her – *ainsi va le monde* to the *singleton tribe*, of which an unworthy member is your affectionate Po.

---

[1] Sic.

85. Letter from Agnes Porter, Bruton, to Lady Mary Talbot, Great Malvern, 22 September 1812

My Dear Lady Mary,

I had a letter from Mrs Giles dated only *Lisnabrin Fallow*.[2] I took it into my head that this was not a sufficient direction, so thought I would send it to you to address properly and to forward. When this was done, it seemed to me a strange thing to send you double postage, and taking my chance of Lord Lansdowne's being still at Malvern I directed the packet to him. I make no doubt that Lady Lansdowne will forward her aunt's letter where ever they are, but if they be gone from Malvern my intended 'How do ye do' might not so soon reach my dear Lady Mary.

I hope Mr Talbot and your darlings are all well. A day or two after I had your last letter Lord and Lady Ilchester were at Redlynch. They invited me to breakfast, so I had the pleasure of seeing your *new* sister, and a very amiable woman she seems. Lady George Murray is such a person as one seldom meets with, and her children surrounded her in a most pleasant manner. Mr and Mrs Selwyn asked me if I knew whether they might flatter themselves with the hopes of seeing you next October, and yesterday Mr Selwyn called on me and said he hoped Lady Mary would pay them a visit next month at Kilmington. I have told you their wishes, which is all I can do for them.

I am very well and very comfortable at Bruton. Mrs Lloyd, poor woman, is grown very much attached to me – her daughter is one of the best creatures in the world. I wrote to Mr Green's step-daughter relative to the hundred pounds. She is now Duchess of Roxburghe. She sent me a polite sensible letter, and promised to repay the money. A few weeks after, His Grace sent me a draft upon Coutts for the hundred pounds. The satisfaction of their liberal conduct is much damped by an abusive letter from Mr Green, saying the prints had paid me and if I do not refund the money instantly he threatens me with the utmost vengeance of the law. Mr Richards desired I would send him an exact account of all the monies I had received for the prints, and the years since I lent the money, and he offers to deal with Mr Green in my stead which is a great relief to me but I never thought he could have been so cruel and ungrateful.

Farewell my dearest Lady Mary. Yours, Po.

---

[2] Pencil note: 'Aunt Kitty'. This was Catherine (*née* Grady), whose third husband was Walter Giles of Lisnabrien Lodge, County Cork

86. Letter from Agnes Porter, Bruton, to Lady Mary Talbot, 7 November 1812

I thank you, my dear Lady Mary, for your travelling narrative. They were so interesting to me that I have laid the letters by to read as a cordial to my spirits whenever they are a tone too low. With regard to our not meeting so soon as I expected, I shall have recourse to that good old proverb 'The worse luck *now* etc., etc.'[3] When I have the happiness to see you I shall hope to be indulged with a sight of your *manufactory* journals.[4] I think it must have been delightful to you to make so much of your time under the name of amusement, and to see your darling girls enjoy and investigate what they saw with all the hilarity of youth and the quickness of *improved* rationality. You have endeavoured to enlighten and to strengthen their minds ever since they began to reason or perceive; you *now* reap the fruits of your maternal labours.

I send you by this conveyance a purse of my netting which, I hope, will prove quite the thing. I send with it a bag of Mrs Peniston junior's painting that she gave me, as I wish you to see her colours, which are so prepared as to last a long time. I saw a screen which she told me had been painted nine years, that was as fresh as if it had been finished but a few days. She makes and sells these colours, and keeps a small school at Salisbury to assist her husband in maintaining their good mother and five fine children. I send my dear Mr Talbot a pair of spectacles, and if they suit his sight how pleased I shall be! I add some *patterns* just received from Sarum which, as you will see by the letter, are to be returned by me.

I send the *parcel* of *letters* you said you would receive – the two journals, I think, will perhaps amuse you, and are peculiar in the circumstance of adverting to the education both of the *mother* and *her children*. Miss Jane will like a peep at them.

My love to dear Miss Talbot and all your other darlings. Ever yours, Po.

---

[3] 'The worse luck now, the better another time'.
[4] Pencil note: 'A visit to Birmingham'.

1812 Bruton Nov'r 7

I thank you my Dear Lady Mary
for your travelling Narrative. They
were so interesting to me that I have
laid the Letters by to read as a cordial
to my spirits whenever they are a
Tone too low. — With regard to our
not meeting so soon as I expected,
I shall have recourse to that good
old Proverb the worse luck now &c
When I have the happiness to see
you I shall hope to be indulged
with a Sight of your Mannfactory
a visit to Birmingham
Journals. I think it must have
been delightful to you to make

11. A page from a letter, Agnes Porter, Bruton to Lady Mary Talbot,
7 November 1812.

1813

In 1813 Agnes was still living at Bruton, though by November she had moved into lodgings with the Revd William Cosens, the headmaster of the King's School, and his family. In June she visited Fairford, and wrote of plans to visit Norfolk and London, and then to return to Fairford before travelling to Penrice. She certainly spent some time at Penrice with her recently-widowed former pupil, Lady Mary Talbot, before returning to Bruton in October.

87. Letter from Agnes Porter, Bruton, to Charlotte Talbot, The Crescent, Clifton, 19 January 1813

My Dear Miss Charlotte,

Be so good as cut out the above-written letters and give them to your little sisters with my love. It was very good in you to remember me in your mirth on Twelfth-night. I have made some young people happy by letting them have a part in your kind present of the plum cake, which was the nicest I ever tasted. As to my name of Miss *Tinder-Heart*, were I to see any of *you* it would prove in some respect a true appellation: it would catch flame as easily as tinder, but a flame both bright and permanent.

In answer to your question, I can acquaint you that I have some very pleasing young friends in Bruton. Miss Letitia Goldesbrough is a very sensible, good young lady. She frequently declines going to a gay juvenile party to stay at home alone with the old admiral, her father, to play cribbage with him for his amusement. The next young lady I shall introduce you to is *her* cousin, Miss Mary Goldesbrough, who is very pretty and good-natured, and so charming a musician that she has melody in her throat and harmony at her finger-ends. She is indeed compleat mistress of her instrument, and gives high gratification to her hearers. The third young person is a young poetess, not yet eleven. I saw her compose this charade, which I give to you to find out:

My first within the human form you'll find,
My next I trust is ever in your mind,
My *whole* denominates a simple flower
Search for it, bards, in yonder fragrant bower. [Heartsease]

She is Dr Sampson's granddaughter. Mr Cosen's family are charming young people – I shall tell you about them at some future time and, I trust, *de vive voix. Adieu, ma très chère, et bonne amie. Je suis votre affectionnée* Ann Agnes Porter.

Give my love to our dear Miss Bere, and tell her I wrote to her a day or two ago.

88. Letter from Agnes Porter, [Bruton], to Lady Mary Talbot, Deans Leaze, Blandford, 20 January 1813

I have to thank you, my dear Lady Mary, for a large portion of a most delicious Twelfth-cake which was sent to me by your order, and could you but have seen the number of happy faces the division of it caused, you would think I had reason indeed to thank you as the *prime mover* of all this festivity. It was accompanied by two nice letters from Miss Charlotte and Isabella. Little Morning Star sent me a landscape of her performance. You may suppose I was not tardy in answering their letters – I directed them [to] No. 6, Crescent, Clifton, Bristol. I hope this was right, but as I added Mr Talbot's name, no doubt the epistles reached them.

When you return to Clifton, be so good as send me Mrs Peniston's patterns, as she makes use of them to procure orders for the trimmings of gowns. A lady opened a Salisbury ball in one of these dresses lately, but ornaments might suit a Salisbury ball that would not be proper for one of your party.

Will you give my love *à mes ci-devants élèves*, to Mr Talbot, and to Lord Ilchester with respectful compliments to his lady. Tell Lady Elizabeth that, as she is to me a Mirrour of the Times,[1] I request the favour of her to inform me where all the branches of the Royal Family of Bourbon now are, including that of Orléans.

Tell my dear Lady Harriot Frampton that I rejoice to hear of her child's recovery. Nanny Longford gives me a most pleasing account of her. Will you inform Lady Charlotte that my heart feels a tender interest in her situation? I shall soon hope to hear of her *happy hour*. When

---

[1] This may refer to *The Mirror of the Times*, which was published weekly from *c.* 1796 to 1823.

you write to Lady Lansdowne, will you mention me to her, and will you excuse all these egotisms *de ma part?* I have lately been reading a history of London, published in 1804, which I like much, and I have derived great pleasure from Mr Johnes of Havod's *Lord Joinville*.[2] His style appears to me characteristic of the original writer and the times, while his researches are curious and scientific.

Kiss your two *great* darlings for me – I have heard of them from Mrs Longford.

My brother and sister are, I hear, well. She tells me of a little pupil she hopes to have, and then adds 'I will not give you her name nor any particulars, as a dear friend of yours will soon *de vive voix* inform you of all that relates to it'. I am puzzling my brains to think who this may be – can you resolve me? All I can know is that *you are the friend I wish to see*, but the rest does not coincide.

Mrs Keir's son and child escaped from Moscow. Farewell! God bless you! Ever yours, Po.

89. Letter from Agnes Porter, Fairford, to Lady Mary Talbot, Penrice Castle, 7 June 1813

My Dear Lady Mary,

Your letter, the transcript of your mind, affords me the most solid satisfaction. Happy are those who can bear afflictions in such a manner! For their sorrows shall be turned into joy, and their temporal grief promote their eternal felicity. You have, indeed, every reason to rest satisfied in the recollection of Mr Talbot's virtues, and the consciousness of having performed so great a duty by him ever since your marriage. May his children inherit his benevolence and unblemished honour, and take a pattern from their dear mother, both in connubial and maternal duties!

I have not heard from Dr Hunt, but be dear Mr Talbot's legacy what it may, it will be both an *honour* and a blessing to me to be remembered by him, and I shall hope to receive it through *your own hands*. Miss Bere was so good as to drop me a few lines once or twice, but I had been a fortnight without hearing of you since I wrote. I thank you again for writing to me so soon – what a delight it is to hear that the children are all well! What pleasure will it give me to see again your dear faces – ye darlings of the heart!

I am to be at Mr Upcher's about the 6th of July to stay three weeks,

---

[2] Thomas Johnes (trans. and ed.), *Memoirs of John, Lord de Joinville* (1807).

at which time I think they leave home. I am to pass a week with my cousin Amyot in Town;[3] a fortnight at Dr Macqueen's; take Fairford in my return for a few days, and then, with your permission, I shall proceed to Penrice Castle. I shall bring you an account of all my friends, because I know you are so kind as to take some interest in those I love.

In a letter I sent about a month ago I told you I was ten pounds in your debt on the money you sent Mr Cosens – please to remember it, and let me know whether you have any commissions for London. In my way to Norfolk I only pass through it, but towards the end of July I shall be there for a week.

Farewell, my dearest Lady Mary. My brother and sister join in respectful compliments. I am your ever affectionate Po.

90. Letter from Agnes Porter, Bruton, to William Henry Fox Talbot, Harrow School, 20 October 1813[4]

Caro Signore,

Ho ricevuto la sua lettera e le sono molto contenta [I have received your letter, and I am very pleased with it]. I wrote to your mamma from Shepton Mallet as I told you I would, and informed her that I had some hopes of soon hearing of your safe journey to London by your own hand. You may recollect that I wrote three or four letters from Bristol. Miss Shakespear sent me a very agreeable epistle from Lidley. She will be detained there longer than she thought by her younger sisters having the meazles.

I found my acquaintances at Bruton all well, and very glad to see me again. I was asked last night to a little party to meet Mrs Charles Digby senior, who used to live at Kilminton – perhaps you do not recollect her, but it makes my heart beat quick to see any connection of your family. When you grow older you will experience these sensations, till when *vive l'allégresse!*

I had a charming letter from your dear mother – she was on the wing for Bowood. All at Penrice were well, *Dieu merci!*

Accept my best wishes for your true happiness. May you improve daily in virtue, understanding and health! I am, dear Mr Henry, yours sincerely, Ann Agnes Porter.

---

[3] Probably Thomas Amyot (q.v.).
[4] Wiltshire Record Office, Lacock Abbey, 2664, Box of miscellaneous correspondence, Feilding-Strangways-Talbot.

91. Letter from Agnes Porter, Bruton, to Lady Mary Talbot, Penrice Castle, 6 November 1813

My Dear Lady Mary,

How happy it makes me to hear that you and your beloved family are so well! It was indeed a most agreeable history that you sent me, and your domestic party is interesting to me in all they do, even down to the oysters. Sweet creatures! I can figure their engaging alacrity in every movement, and their kindness in every word. You possess, as you ought to do, their entire confidence, and heart-rooted love. I wonder not that where they are, a magic spell should fix you with them, or that even the rocks in winter should have power to please, but be not *locally* attached to *them*, whatever you may be to the animated beings that surround you! There is a melancholy in being much attracted by any peculiar place that creeps upon the mind, lessening its functions by narrowing its sphere of activity. You will give a natural gratification to your young people by a little change of scene, and make your dear friends on this side of the water happy by the sight of you and your darlings.

Do you know, I have had a visit from good Dr Hunt, which rejoiced me much, both on his own account and his connection with Penrice Castle. I thought he was looking very well, but he was on his way to Wells, and in a great hurry. However, I had seen him, and that was a real pleasure.

I hear that your brother Lord Ilchester is perfectly well. They are now at Redlynch. He called at Mrs Lloyd's cottage door, and on not finding me there was so good as to leave word that he would certainly see me before he quitted Redlynch – so I live in hopes. Mrs Cosens has a good fire lighted in the *best room*, which I scarcely ever leave farther than a walk before the door, for fear I should miss the sight of his dear countenance. Should Lady Harriot come, I have another chance. Lord Ilchester left a letter for me, which I was surprized to see directed to Melbury, a liberty I never suffered any of my friends to use. This letter was in an unknown hand, but began familiarly *My Dear Agnes* – went on in a style that was Hebrew to me, and ended with 'I shall write to you soon again, and am in the meantime, and while I live, my dear love, your affectionate husband, Thomas Porter'. All that vexes me in it is that it should be addressed to me at the Earl of Ilchester – freed by, and superscribed, *Darby*. I hope this adventure will make you *smile*.

Pray tell my dear Miss Talbot that my answer to her *Amate mi* [do you love me]? is *Sempre* [always]. '*Manco male*' is a pure Italian phrase that can scarcely be translated, but it means 'It might have been worse' or 'it is well it is no worse'. In French 'Il a cela de bon'. I am glad the Italian is not neglected. My love too, to dear Miss Jane, Charry, Isabella, and Bijou, and to Mr Christopher when you write – dear boy! Mr Henry wrote to me – you may be sure I was not long in answering his letter.

My sister told me in her last that Mr Gough had sent them a basket of game, with inquiries after their health and a good account of his daughters. I believe Mr Richards has, under providence, laid a better basis for their duty and forbearance than they ever had before, and I hope their patience will in time make the father more kind.

I am very *tolerably* well, very *tolerably* comfortable – and whatever I am, always yours, Po.

1814

Agnes was seriously ill during the winter of 1813 to 1814. Her last letter to Lady Mary Talbot was written in January 1814, when Agnes seemed to be recovering, but she died at Bruton less than a month after the letter was written. She was buried the Lloyd family's plot in Bruton churchyard on 21 February 1814.

92. Letter from Agnes Porter, Bruton, to Lady Mary Talbot, Penrice Castle, 26 January 1814[1]

My Dear Lady Mary,

I last night received your kind letter enclosing a twenty-pound bank-note, for which I am both *indebted* and obliged. I am much better than I was when I wrote to you. I hope my epistle was *compos*, but I would not answer for it. However, there are [some] persons you may write to in every disposition, and in every *indisposition*, of the heart – very few, I grant you.

I thank you for your home intelligence. Lady E. Feilding had the goodness to drop me a line the very day that Lord and Lady Ilchester had a daughter. It was kind indeed of her. I have been four weeks in my room, went down yesterday for the first time to tea. Mr Cosens and family are extremely good-natured to me – he is much improved in his *temper* since his fever and has, I believe, a worthy humane heart. He has been catering for the poor, to procure them coals. The roads were blocked up, and this useful article has totally failed the poor for three days. A subscription has been made, forty men set to work in the roads to open the way for the *colliers*, and yesterday coals, bought at eighteen pence the bushel, was[2] sold to them at the rate of one shilling. Mr Cosens and his man measured them out. A crowd of 200 people

---

[1] Note in ink: 'The last I ever received'.
[2] Sic.

surrounded them, and were quite rejoiced at the idea of a little sparkling fire. They had lived on bread and butter. The gentlemen here say it shall never happen again. The frost and snow have lasted three weeks. I am pinched to a *thread-paper*.[3]

I am delighted with dear Miss Talbot's perseverance, because it is so closely connected with fortitude of mind. I send Miss Jane a poetical effusion for her amusement, and I send love and respects to dear Penrice Castle and its still dearer inmates, Po.

In bed: sick, feverish. First multiplication table *backward*, and then moaned out these lines:

> As here I sick and pensive lay,
> Oh! Memory lend thy active powers;
> Bright o'er my mind thy tints display,
> And give me back my earliest hours.
>
> Let me the blissful time recall,
> When, shelter'd by parental care,
> A mother's tender hand gave all
> [Which dut]y asked, or love could share.
>
> As round the dear domestic hearth
> The winter-eve flew swift along;
> Each youthful bosom prone to mirth,
> How gay the story! Blithe the song.
>
> A sister, graceful, led the dance,
> A brother tun'd the rural reed;
> Friendship exchang'd the heart-felt glance,
> And ev'ry joy, was joy – indeed!

I could not *démêler* whether I composed this now or had done it before.[4]

---

[3] A strip of paper used to hold skeins of thread. Used figuratively to describe extreme thinness.

[4] See 18 July 1803 for another version of this poem.

After Agnes's death, her friend Lucy Lloyd wrote to Lady Mary Talbot's sister

93. Letter from Lucy Lloyd, Bruton, to Lady Harriot Frampton, Moreton, Dorset, 24 March 1814

Honoured Madam,

I received this day your ladyship's kind favor, and take the earliest opportunity of sending you my most grateful thanks for your valuable gift, though by me unmerited. It was a great consolation to me that I had it in my power to administer to the ease and comfort of my dear and lamented friend, though far short of what her sisterly kindness and attachment to me deserved. She *sleeps* in the little spot of ground appropriated for our burying place and near my dear sister as possible – they *lov'd each other well*. I will take care of the book till I can safely send it to your ladyship, and I have enclos'd a few lines which I found of dear Mrs Porter's – if not her *own* composition, I know they were her *own sentiments,* and therefore I am sure you will be pleas'd with them.

My mother begs to send you her humble duty, and she shall never forget the good and worthy family she so many years has known and to whom she has been so much oblig'd. She is very weak but retains her faculties wonderfully at the great age of ninety-four.

Again repeating my most grateful acknowledgements for your great kindness I am your ladyship's most obedient humble servant, Lucy Lloyd.

P.S. Good Mrs Porter left me in her will forty pounds – it was originally fifty, but she, dear kind friend as she was, gave me ten while she liv'd as she thought it might be useful.

Biographical Notes

Note: (DNB) indicates that there is an entry relating to the person concerned in the *Dictionary of National Biography*.

Acland, Elizabeth Kitty (1772–1813). Only surviving child of John Dyke Acland and his wife Lady Harriot (*née* Fox Strangways). In April 1796 she married Henry George, Lord Porchester, later second Earl of Carnarvon.

Acland, Lady Harriot (1750–1815). Born Christiana Henrietta Caroline Fox Strangways, third surviving daughter of the first Earl of Ilchester. In 1771 she married John Dyke Acland of Pixton Park, near Dulverton, Somerset. In 1776 she accompanied her soldier husband when he was sent with his regiment to Canada. Lady Harriot was a famous heroine in her day, having rescued her wounded husband after the second battle of Saratoga in 1777. The Aclands had five children, but only one survived to adulthood. This was Elizabeth Kitty (q.v.). (DNB)

Adams, Miss. *See* **Llewelyn, Mr John.**

Adare, Lady (1755–1814). She was Frances Muriel Fox Strangways, youngest daughter of the first Earl of Ilchester. In 1777 she married Valentine Richard Quin of Adare, County Limerick. In 1793 Lady Frances Quin left her husband and returned to England. Valentine Quin, who became Baron Adare in 1800 and remarried in 1816, was created first Earl of Dunraven in 1822, and died in 1824.

Ailesbury, Lord. Thomas Brudenell Bruce (1729–1814), created first Earl of Ailesbury in 1776. He lived at Tottenham House in Savernake Forest, Wiltshire.

Alexander, Mrs. An old friend of Agnes from her 'juvenile days' in Great Yarmouth. Born Miss Mitchell, she married Mr Alexander, 12 August 1790. She appears to have been living in Scotland in 1805.

Amyot, Mrs. First cousin of Agnes Porter. She was born Susannah Garritt, daughter of Thomas Garritt of Norwich, hot-presser, and his wife Susannah (*née* Porter). Susannah Garritt married Peter Amyot of Norwich (died 1799), a watch- and clock-maker of Huguenot extraction, at Norwich St Edmund, 1773. The Amyots had several children, including Thomas Amyot (1775–1850), who was articled to an attorney in Norwich, but later moved to London. He was appointed private secretary to the Whig MP for Norwich, William Windham, when the latter became war and colonial minister in 1806. Thomas Amyot held several valuable appointments in the colonial department before retiring to concentrate on antiquarian studies. (DNB, Thomas Amyot)

Aston, Hon. and Revd Mr Walter Aston Hutchinson (1769–1845). He married Elizabeth, daughter of the Revd Nathan Haines, D.D., on 14 June 1802.

Auckland, Lord. William Eden, first Baron Auckland (1744–1814). His elder son,

William (1782–1810) was drowned in the Thames in January 1810. The younger son, George Eden (1784–1849), later second Baron and first Earl of Auckland, was a great friend of the younger members of the Fox Strangways family. He was Governor-General of India, 1835–41. (DNB, William and George Eden)

Balfour, Mrs Major. Cousin of Agnes Porter's mother, whom Agnes saw in Edinburgh in 1805. She was Jean, daughter of William Elliot of Wolfelee, Roxburghshire. She married Captain (later Major, in the 1st Regiment of Foot) Henry Balfour in Edinburgh in 1765. Had a daughter, Mrs Biggar.

Banti, Signora Brigitta (née Giorgi) (*c*. 1756–1806). An Italian soprano singer, whom Agnes saw in 1798.

Bassett, Mr and Misses. Miles Bassett (*c*. 1731–1813) matriculated at Christ Church, Oxford, 1752, B.A. 1756, and was vicar of Swansea from 1757 to 1813. His daughters, Anne and Ellinor, were regular visitors to Penrice in the early 1800s.

Beach, Mr and Mrs. Michael Hicks Beach (1760–1830) and his wife Henrietta Maria (1760–1837), who married in 1779. Mrs Beach, a first cousin of Thomas Mansel Talbot, was the daughter and eventual heiress of William Beach of Fittleton and Keevil, Wiltshire, who bought Netheravon House, Wiltshire, *c*. 1772, and Williamstrip Park, near Fairford, Gloucestershire, in 1788–90. The Beaches' children included two sons: Michael (1780–1815) and William (1783–1856); and four daughters: Henrietta Maria (*c*. 1785–1808), Ann (*c*. 1786–1802), Jane (*c*. 1787–96) and Jane Martha (born 1801). Jane Martha was the only daughter to survive to adulthood: she married Edward William St John of Ashe Park, Hampshire, in 1848. Agnes's sister Frances Richards (q.v.) may have been governess to the eldest daughters before her marriage.

Bensley. An actor whom Agnes saw in London in 1791. He was Robert Bensley (*c*. 1738–1817). (DNB)

Bere, Miss. Mary Bere was a governess at Penrice, 1809–14. In December 1814 she married Robert Bower in Winchester.

Bird, Mr. Probably John Bird (1761–1840), clerk to the first Marquess of Bute.

Bolingbroke, Lady. Charlotte (died 1804), daughter of the Revd Thomas Collins of Winchester, and wife of George Richard St John, third Viscount Bolingbroke, of Lydiard Tregoze, Wiltshire. She lived apart from her husband, who married his mistress six months after Charlotte's death.

Booth, Colonel. Lieutenant Colonel William Booth (died 1826) of the Corps of Engineers. A talented artist, he was a friend of Edward King of Marino (q.v.).

Browne, Mr. Francis John Browne (1754–1833) of Frampton, Dorset, MP for Dorset, 1784–1806. A friend of the Talbots.

Calley, Mrs [Anne]. Anne Calley (*c*. 1719–1812) of Overtown House, Wroughton, Wiltshire. An old friend of Agnes's parents. She was the daughter of Robert Codrington and widow of Oliver Calley (1710–74), uncle of Thomas Browne Calley of Burderop Park, Wiltshire.

Calley, Mrs [Elizabeth]. Elizabeth (*c*. 1755–1812), widow of Thomas Browne Calley (1752–91) of Burderop Park, Wiltshire. She married secondly, in 1795, Thomas Haverfield of Hampton Court. The 1808 edition of *Paterson's Roads* lists Thomas Haverfield Esq. at Burderop House.

Campbell, Mrs. Alicia Campbell (1768–1829), widow of Major William Campbell of the 24th Regiment of Foot (died 1796). She was a great friend of the Fox Strangways family. In 1805 she was appointed sub-governess to Princess Charlotte, the daughter of the Prince of Wales (later George IV).

Cant, Miss Menie. Daughter (probably Williamina, born 1725) of Ludowick Cant of Thurston, East Lothian, and Elizabeth (*née* Muirhead). A relation of Agnes Porter's mother. Agnes saw her in Edinburgh in 1805, when her niece Mrs Graham was living with her.

Church, Miss Matilda (1736–1805). An old friend, and distant relation, of Agnes in Great Yarmouth. Daughter of Richard Church and Elizabeth (*née* Barker). In 1796 she was living in Yarmouth with her mother, who died in 1800 aged ninety-one. When Matilda Church died she left Agnes £100.

Codrington, Mrs. Mary Codrington (*c.* 1765–1838) of Wroughton, Wiltshire, an acquaintance of Agnes and her sister. She born Mary Palmer Lewsley, and married William Codrington of Wootton Bassett and Wroughton (1753–1802), nephew of Anne Calley of Overtown House (q.v.). Old Mrs Codrington of Overtown (born *c.* 1717) may have been Mary Codrington's mother-in-law, Mary, *née* Stretton.

Collins, Dr Charles (*c.* 1743–1817). A prominent Swansea surgeon, who was doctor to the Talbot family at Penrice. Brother of Revd John Collins (q.v.). Dr Collins married Ann (died 1825), and they had children John Charles (1780–1824; became a doctor and married Elizabeth McFarquhar in Edinburgh in 1803); Charles James; Fanny and Anne.

Collins, Revd John (*c.* 1740–1830). An old friend of Thomas Mansel Talbot. Rector of Oxwich, near Penrice Castle, from 1772 to 1830. In 1781 he married Ann, daughter of Robert Wells, the rector of Ilston and Penmaen in Gower. The Collinses, who lived at Oxwich rectory, had ten children: Ann (1782–94), John (1783–1854), Judith (1784–1840), Sarah (1785–1803), William (1787–98), Frances (born 1788), Anstance (born 1791), Robert (born 1793), Charles (1796–1862) and Ann (born 1798). The eldest son, John, matriculated at Jesus College, Oxford, in 1802, and graduated B.A. in 1805 and M.A. in 1808. He visited the Richardses in Fairford in 1808.

Cosens, Mr. The Revd William Cosens (*c.* 1762–1831) of Bruton, Somerset. He was admitted to St John's College, Cambridge, in 1779, then moved to Oxford, where he matriculated at St Mary Hall in 1782, but did not graduate. A clergyman, he was headmaster of the King's School, Bruton, 1799–1826. The school did not exactly flourish during this period: in 1811 there was just one scholar. Cosens was perpetual curate of Bruton 1800–1, minister 1801–31. In 1790 he married Eleanor Hyde Hutching Champion at Ipplepen, Devon. Their children included two sons, Edward Hyde (born *c.* 1793) and Rayner (born *c.* 1806). Agnes spent the last months of her life at the home of Mr and Mrs Cosens in Bruton.

Coxe, Mr. William Coxe (1747–1828). An author and traveller, whose *Travels* in Poland, Russia, Sweden, Denmark and Switzerland were published in 1784, 1789 and 1790. (DNB)

Creech, Mr. William Creech (1745–1815), the publisher of the *Mirror* and the *Lounger*, and a founder of the Speculative Society. (DNB)

Crowdy/Crowdy, Mr and Mrs. *See* **Morice, James.**

Dade, Mr and Miss. Agnes met them in Yarmouth in 1796. He was the Revd Charles Robert Dade (*c.* 1763–1820), who matriculated at Caius College, Cambridge, in 1781. He was minister at St George's Chapel in Yarmouth, 1791–1813, and rector of Denver, Norfolk, 1801–20. Miss Dade, who may have been his sister, was a companion to Mrs Ramey (q.v.) in 1796. In her will (written 1809) Abigail Ramey left £500 to 'Miss Margaret Dade who now lives with me' (NRO, ANW 1811/158).

Damer, Mr and Mrs L. Lionel Damer (1748–1807), youngest son of Joseph Damer, first Earl of Dorchester, and his wife Williamsa (*née* Janssen).

Darke, Mr. The Revd Richard Darke (*c*. 1771–1830) was rector of Grafton Flyford, Worcestershire, 1797–1830. His father, John Darke of Bredon, Worcestershire, was an old acquaintance of the Talbots.

Davis, Mr. Mark Davis (*c*. 1755–1832) of Turnworth and Holnest, Dorset, a friend of the O'Briens.

Digby, Mr Charles (1743–1810). The Revd Charles Digby, M.A., canon of Wells. A first cousin of the second Earl of Ilchester. In 1775 he married Priscilla Mellier. Their only surviving child, Mary Charlotte Digby, married the Revd John Dampier in 1810.

Digby, Mr Charles (1775–1841). Nephew of the second Earl of Ilchester, eldest son of Colonel Stephen Digby and his wife Lady Lucy (*née* Fox Strangways). He matriculated at Christ Church, Oxford, in 1793 and entered the church. He married *c*. 1800 Mary, daughter of the Hon. Hugh Somerville, by whom he had several children. Charles Digby was a canon of Windsor from 1808.

Digby, Charlotte Elizabeth (Lilley) (1778–1820). Daughter of Colonel Stephen and Lady Lucy Digby. In 1803 she married her cousin the Revd William Digby.

Digby, Elizabeth Juliana (Julia) (died 1807). Cousin of the second Earl of Ilchester, daughter of the Very Revd William Digby, Dean of Durham. She was a maid of honour to Queen Charlotte in 1790. On 18 February 1794 she married Sir John Henry Newbolt.

Digby, Frances Caroline (Caroline) (1772–1835). Sister of Elizabeth Juliana Digby (q.v.). On 13 June 1791 she married Thomas Neave, later second Baronet.

Digby, Maria (1771–1842). *See* **Fox Strangways, Maria, Countess of Ilchester.**

Digby, Admiral Robert (1732–1815). Of Minterne, Dorset. He was a brother of Colonel Stephen Digby, and a first cousin of the second Earl of Ilchester. His wife was Eleanor (*née* Elliot), widow of James Jauncey of New York. (DNB)

Digby, Colonel Stephen (1742–1800). A first cousin of the second Earl of Ilchester whose sister, Lady Lucy Fox Strangways (died 1787) was Colonel Digby's first wife. In 1790 he married, as his second wife, Charlotte Margaret, daughter of Sir Robert Gunning, fourth Baronet, of Horton, Northamptonshire. Colonel Digby was vice-chamberlain to Queen Charlotte from 1783 to 1792, and held the post of Deputy Ranger, and then Ranger and Keeper, of Richmond Park from 1792 to 1800. He was a friend of Fanny Burney, who was employed in the royal household as a keeper of the robes to the Queen, from 1786 to 1791.

Digby, Mr William. Probably the Revd William Digby (1774–1848), second son of the Very Revd William Digby, Dean of Durham. His second wife (married 1803) was his cousin, Charlotte Elizabeth Digby.

Digby, Mrs William (died 1798). Charlotte (*née* Cox), widow of the Very Revd William Digby, Dean of Durham, mother of William, Julia, Caroline and Maria Digby (q.v.). In 1791–92 she was living at Hawley, Hampshire.

Duncan, Lord. Admiral Adam Duncan (1731–1804), who commanded the North Sea fleet, which was based in Great Yarmouth, 1797–1801. In 1797 Admiral Duncan was created Baron Duncan of Lundie and Viscount Duncan of Camperdown, following a successful engagement against the Dutch fleet. (DNB)

Dyke, Mrs. The Dykes, who lived at Syrencot House, Wiltshire, were friends of Agnes Porter's sister Frances Richards. William Dyke (*c*. 1745–1818) and his wife Elizabeth had five daughters: Caroline (*c*. 1776–1818), Elizabeth Martha (died 1791), Arabella (died 1800), Sarah Maria (died 1805) and Frances (died 1806). Of these, only Caroline married (in 1803, the Revd James Williams of Matherne, Monmouthshire). It is possible that Frances Richards was governess to the daughters before moving to the Beaches, whose house at Netheravon is only a mile or two from Syrencot.

Eden, Mr. *See* **Auckland, Lord**.

Edgeworth, Mr. Abbé Henri Essex Edgeworth de Firmont (1745–1807), an Irish priest who was was confessor to Louis XVI. (DNB)

Edwards, Miss. Pupil of Frances Richards in 1805. She was daughter of the Revd James Edwards, vicar of Fairford from 1785 until his death in 1804.

Edwards, Revd James and Mrs. James Edwards (*c.* 1746–1834) was rector of Reynoldston, near Penrice Castle, 1796–1834. He married Sarah Lay, *c.* 1800. The Edwardses lived at Brynfield in Reynoldston and were regular visitors to Penrice in the early nineteenth century.

Edwin, Mrs. Mrs Charlotte Edwin (*c.* 1738–1816), step-mother and mother-in-law of Thomas Wyndham of Dunraven (q.v.). She was an old friend of Thomas Mansel Talbot.

Elborough, Miss. Governess at Penrice, 1806–7.

Elliot, Mrs (born *c.* 1718). Agnes visited her in Edinburgh in 1805, when she was aged eighty-seven. She was Helen, daughter of Sir John Elphinstone of Craighouse and Logie. She married Dr Thomas Elliot, FRCPE (1725–51), a cousin of Agnes's mother. The marriage ceremony was performed in 1751 by Agnes's father, but Dr Elliot died later in the same year.

Elliot, Mr Cornelius (1733–1821). Son of William Elliot of Wolfelee, Roxburghshire (1688–1768). Cornelius Elliot was a relative of Agnes Porter, and half-brother of Mrs Major Balfour (q.v.). Agnes saw him in Edinburgh in 1805. He married Margaret Rannie in Edinburgh in 1765. They had two sons, who died in the service of their country before 1805. Their eldest daughter, Mary (1767–1814), married Colonel (later General Sir Thomas) Dallas in 1793; the second daughter was a widow in 1805; the third daughter, Janet Hyndford (died 1825), married first in 1799 Sir John Gibson Carmichael, sixth Baronet, of Stirling (1773–1805), and secondly, in 1806, John, twelfth Baron Elphinstone.

D'Eon, La Chevalière. The 'Chevalière' d'Eon was actually a man: Charles Geneviève d'Eon de Beaumont (1728–1810). In his youth, he was a member of Louis XV's secret service, and he was granted a pension of 12,000 livres in 1766. He lived in London from 1775 and always wore female dress during the rest of his life. A skilled swordsman, he made a living by giving fencing displays. Not surprisingly, d'Eon's contemporaries were unsure of his sex during his lifetime, but an examination of his body after his death proved that he was a man. (DNB)

Fagniani, Mlle. Maria Fagniani (died 1856), adopted daughter of George Selwyn, a friend of the Fox Strangways family. In 1798 she married Francis Seymour, Earl of Yarmouth and later third Marquess of Hertford. Both Selwyn and the Duke of Queensberry claimed to be Mlle Fagniani's father, and both left large sums of money to her when they died. (DNB, George Augustus Selwyn)

Farquhar, Sir Walter (1738–1819). Physician to the Prince of Wales, created a Baronet in 1796. A fashionable doctor who was consulted by the Fox Strangways family. (DNB)

Faulconberg, Lord. Major Henry Belasye, second Earl Fauconberg of Newborough, Viscount Fauconberg of Henknowle (1743–1802), who married (5 January 1791) Jane, eldest daughter of John Cheshyre of Bennington, Hertfordshire.

Feilding. Captain. *See* **Fox Strangways, Elizabeth Theresa**.

Fennel. Agnes saw him in London in 1791. He was James Fennel (1766–1816), an actor and dramatist. (DNB)

Field, Mr and Mrs. John Field was Lord Ilchester's estate steward at Melbury.

Fielding. *See* Feilding.

Floy[d]er, Mr. The Revd William Floyer (*c*. 1746–1819), vicar of Stinsford, Dorset, and a friend of the O'Briens.

Ford, Mr and Mrs. From about 1777 to 1785 John and Margaret Ford and their ten children lived at Hadspen House at Pitcombe, about three miles from Redlynch. They later settled in Bath, where John Ford was still living, aged seventy-three, in 1822. One of their sons, Richard Wilbraham Ford (1781–1862), was admitted to King's College, Cambridge, in 1799. He visited Penrice in 1803, shortly before being ordained as a deacon. He became a priest in 1805.

Fowler, Dr Richard (1765–1863). He was physician to the General Infirmary in Salisbury from 1796 to 1841. He also had an extensive private practice, and was consulted by the Talbots and their relatives. His wife, whom he married in 1805, was Ann, daughter of William Bowles of Heale House, Wiltshire. (DNB)

Fox, Mr Charles. The Whig politician Charles James Fox (1749–1807). He was a first cousin of the second Earl of Ilchester. (DNB)

Fox Strangways, Revd Charles Redlynch (1761–1836). Third son of the first Earl of Ilchester. He went into the church and was rector of Maiden Newton, Dorset, from 1787, and of Brimpton, Somerset, from 1788. From 1811–36 he was rector of Kilmington, Somerset. He married Jane, daughter of Revd Dr Haines in 1787, and they had six sons and two daughters.

Fox Strangways, Charlotte Anne (1784–1826). Fourth daughter of the second Earl of Ilchester. She married, in 1810, Sir Charles Lemon, second Baronet, of Carclew, Cornwall.

Fox Strangways, Christiana Caroline Henrietta. *See* **Acland, Lady Harriot.**

Fox Strangways, Elizabeth, first Countess of Ilchester (1723–92). Elizabeth Strangways Horner, the heiress of the Melbury estate, who married Stephen Fox (later first Earl of Ilchester) in 1736.

Fox Strangways, Elizabeth Theresa (1773–1846). Eldest daughter of the second Earl of Ilchester. She married first in 1796 William Davenport Talbot (1763–1800) of Lacock, Wiltshire, by whom she had a son William Henry Fox Talbot (q.v.); and second in 1804 Captain Charles Feilding (1780–1837).

Fox Strangways, Frances Muriel. *See* **Adare, Lady.**

Fox Strangways, Giles Digby Robert (1798–1827). Second son of the second Earl of Ilchester by his second wife.

Fox Strangways, Harriot (1778–1844). Third daughter of the second Earl of Ilchester. She married, in 1799, James Frampton of Moreton, Dorset.

Fox Strangways, Henry Stephen (1787–1858). Only surviving son of the second Earl of Ilchester by his first wife. Known as Lord Stavordale until his father's death in 1802, when he became the third Earl of Ilchester. He married, in 1812, Caroline Leonora Murray.

Fox Strangways, Henry Thomas, second Earl of Ilchester (1747–1802). Eldest son of the first Earl of Ilchester. He married first in 1772 Mary Theresa (*c*. 1755–90), daughter of Standish Grady of Cappercullen, County Limerick. Lord Ilchester's second wife, whom he married in 1794, was his cousin Maria Digby (q.v.).

Fox Strangways, John George Charles Fox Strangways (1803–59). Third son of the second Earl of Ilchester by his second wife.

Fox Strangways, Louisa Emma (1785–1851). Fifth daughter of the second Earl of Ilchester. She married, in 1808, Henry Petty, later third Marquess of Lansdowne.
Fox Strangways, Lucy (1748–87). Second surviving daughter of the first Earl of Ilchester. She married Colonel Stephen Digby (q.v.).
Fox Strangways, Maria, Countess of Ilchester (1771–1842). Daughter of the Very Revd William Digby, Dean of Durham, and the second wife of the second Earl of Ilchester (married 1794).
Fox Strangways, Mary Lucy (1776–1855). Second daughter of the second Earl of Ilchester. She married first, in 1794, Thomas Mansel Talbot (1747–1813) of Penrice and Margam, Glamorgan; and secondly, in 1815, Sir Christopher Cole (1770–1836).
Fox Strangways, Colonel Stephen Strangways Digby (1751–1836). Second son of the first Earl of Ilchester. He died unmarried.
Fox Strangways, Susanna Caroline (1790–92). Sixth daughter of the second Earl of Ilchester.
Fox Strangways, Susanna Sarah Louisa. *See* **O'Brien, Lady Susan**.
Fox Strangways, William Thomas Horner (1795–1865). Eldest son of the second Earl of Ilchester by his second wife. He became the fourth Earl of Ilchester on the death of his half-brother in 1858.
Frampton, Lady Harriot. *See* **Fox Strangways, Harriot**.
Francis, Revd Mr and Miss. He was Charles Francis (born *c.* 1751), son of William Francis of Marlborough, and he matriculated at Brasenose College, Oxford, in 1768. He became rector of Mildenhall, Wiltshire, in 1788, and of Collingbourne Ducis, also in Wiltshire, later in the same year. Charles Francis was mayor of Marlborough in 1779, 1784, 1794 and 1803. He and his sister were 'intimate companions' of Frances Porter when she lived in Marlborough. Agnes saw Mr and Miss Francis in Marlborough 1803.
Garrick. David Garrick (1717–79), the most famous actor of his day. (DNB)
Garrett. *See* **Garritt**.
Garritt or Garrett, Miss Ann (born *c.* 1767). First cousin of Agnes Porter. Her mother was Susannah Porter (1726–88), the only surviving sister of Agnes's father, who married Thomas Garritt (*c.* 1729–97) of Norwich, hot-presser, at St Peter Mancroft, Norwich, 1750. Thomas and Susannah Garritt had several daughters, including Charlotte; Susannah, who married Peter Amyot; and Ann, who may have become a governess. In 1813, when she was mentioned in Agnes's will, Ann Garritt was of Chequer Square, Bury St Edmunds.
Garthshaw, Mr. William Garthshore (1764–1806). He was MP for Launceston 1795–96, and for Weymouth, 1796–1806. A Lord of the Admiralty, 1801–4, Garthshore never recovered from his wife's death in 1803. (DNB)
Genlis, Madame de (1746–1830). Stéphanie Felicité, Madame de Genlis, was a lady-in-waiting to the Duchess of Chartres and governess to her children, including the future monarch Louis Philippe. She was also the mistress of her pupils' father, Louis Philippe, the Duke of Chartres and then of Orléans. The Duke was a Jacobin who took the name Philippe Egalité at the time of the French Revolution and was executed in 1793. Madame de Genlis, whom Horace Walpole called 'the scribbling trollop', was 'a woman of encyclopaedic information ... with a mania for instructing others'. She was a well-known authoress in her day. In England, Madame de Genlis was accompanied by her 'pupils' Adèle, Pamela and Harriot. Adèle was the legitimate daughter of the Duke of Orléans. Pamela's birth and parentage are somewhat obscure, but contemporaries believed that she was the illegitimate daughter of

Madame de Genlis and the Duke of Orléans. In December 1792 she married Lord
Edward Fitzgerald, the Irish republican leader. Harriot (or Henriette) de Sercey
was a niece of Madame de Genlis.

George, James (1764–1841). Of Nicholaston Hall, Gower. He was employed by
the Talbots for almost sixty years, latterly as a bailiff.

Giles, Mrs. *See* **Quin, Mrs.**

Goddard, Mr and Mrs. From *c*. 1782–84 Agnes was governess to the daughters
of Ambrose Goddard, of Swindon House, near Swindon (*c*. 1727–1815) and his
wife Sarah, only daughter and heiress of the Revd Thomas Williams of Pilroath,
Carmarthenshire. Ambrose Goddard was MP for Wiltshire, 1777–1806. The Goddards, who married in 1776, had sons Thomas (1777–1814), Ambrose (1779–1854),
Richard (1787–1844) and Henry (born 1789, died young); and daughters Ann
(married 1803 Sir Thomas Buckler Lethbridge, Bart, of Sandhill Park, Somerset,
and died 1857), Elizabeth (died unmarried 1797), Sarah, Lucy (died unmarried
1800), Emma (born 1787, twin with Richard, died unmarried 1802), Priscilla (died
unmarried 1805) and Margaret (died unmarried 1799). In 1797 Agnes saw Mrs
Goddard, with six daughters, in London.

Goldesbrough, Admiral Thomas and Miss Letitia. John Goldesbrough was incumbent at Bruton, 1743–68. His son Thomas (born *c*. 1747) entered the navy
and became an admiral: Letitia Frances, daughter of Thomas and Letitia Goldesbrough, was baptised at St Mary's church, Bruton, in 1796. Admiral Goldesbrough's
brother John (born *c*. 1745) entered the church and was also of Bruton. He may
have been the father of Mary Goldesbrough, who is also mentioned by Agnes.

Goodenough, Mr and Mrs. Acquaintances of Agnes in Swindon. They were the
Revd Edmund Goodenough (*c*. 1744–1807), vicar of Swindon from 1790, and his
wife Ann Juliana.

Grady, Mr and Mrs. Standish Grady of Cappercullen, County Limerick (died *c*.
1795) and his wife Mary (*née* Hungerford; she died 1808). They were the parents
of the second Countess of Ilchester.

Grady, Revd Thomas (died *c*. 1825). A brother of the second Countess of Ilchester.

Green, Mr and Mrs Joseph. Joseph Green was a Londoner who rented Fairyhill,
a house near Penrice Castle, from the Lucas family of Stouthall in the early
nineteenth century. In 1805, when Agnes stayed with Mr Green and his wife Eleanor
at their London house in Guilford Street, they had four children, all of whom were
grown up. Joseph Green was killed in a road accident in London in 1809.

Green, Mr. An old friend of Agnes in London who helped her to publish her book
of stories in 1791. He was Valentine Green (1739–1813), a well-known print
merchant and mezzotint engraver, of Berners Street (off Oxford Street). He was
extremely successful until the 1790s, when a disastrous enterprise involving the
publication of prints from the pictures in the Düsseldorf Gallery (which was bombed
and destroyed by the French in 1798) led to his financial ruin. Friends assisted
him by securing his appointment as Keeper of the British Institution on its
foundation in 1805, at an annual salary of £150. He was also an antiquarian, being
a Fellow of the Society of Antiquaries and of the Royal Society. Valentine Green's
wife, whom Agnes had known, was dead by 1790. By 1792 he was living with (but
probably not married to) Mary, the widow of Benjamin Charlewood of Windlesham,
Surrey. Valentine Green's son, Rupert Green (1768–1804), who was in partnership
with his father *c*. 1785–98, married Susannah Slade on 26 June 1790. Valentine
Green's 'step-daughter' Harriet Charlewood (1777–1855), married the fifth Duke

of Roxburghe in 1807, eight days after the death of the seventy-year-old Duke's first wife. (DNB)

Griffith, Revd Mr Joseph. Tutor to Lord Stavordale in 1796. Lived in London, where Agnes visited him in 1796 and 1797.

Gumbleton, Mrs. *See* **Quin, Mrs.**

Gunning, Miss. Elizabeth Gunning (1769–1823), the only daughter and heiress of General John Gunning. She carried on simultaneous flirtations with her cousin the Marquess of Lorne and with the Marquess of Blandford. This led to a widely publicised scandal in 1791. (DNB)

Hamilton, Miss. Elizabeth Hamilton (1758–1816). A popular authoress. She wrote *Memoirs of Modern Philosophers* (1800) and *The Cottagers of Glenburnie* (1808) and several books on education. She was governess to the children of the second Earl Lucan from for six months in 1804–5, after which she wrote one of her best-known books, *Letters Addressed to the Daughter of a Nobleman on the Formation of Religious and Moral Principle* (1806). (DNB)

Haverfield, Mr. *See* **Calley, Mrs [Elizabeth]**.

Hay, Mrs Major. Agnes Porter's relation Mary Cant married William Hay of Crawfordton. Their second son, Lieutenant Colonel Lewis Hay, married Barbara, daughter of John Craigie of Glendoick, Perthshire, in 1784, and was killed at the landing of the British troops at the Helder on 27 August 1799, under the command of Sir Ralph Abercromby.

Hayes, Mrs (died 1791). Probably Anne Hays, who was Lord Ilchester's housekeeper in the 1780s.

Helmandel, Monsieur. *See* **Hüllmandel.**

Herschel, William (1738–1822). The famous astronomer, who discovered the planet Uranus in 1781. He was created a Knight of the Royal Hanoverian Guelphic Order in 1816.

Hoare, Master. He was Henry (1784–1836), only son of Sir Richard Colt Hoare of Stourhead (q.v.).

Hoare, Sir Richard. Sir Richard Colt Hoare, second Baronet (1758–1838) of Stourhead, Wiltshire, a friend of the Fox Strangways family. In 1783 he married Hester, daughter of William Henry, first Lord Lyttelton. She died in 1785. (DNB)

Hobbs, Dr Thomas (*c.* 1757–1820). A prominent Swansea surgeon, regularly consulted by the Talbots at Penrice Castle.

Home, Lady (1747–1814). Abigail Browne, daughter of John and Abigail Ramey of Great Yarmouth (q.v.), married Alexander, ninth Earl of Home, in 1768. They had a son, Alexander (1769–1841), later tenth Earl of Home, and a daughter Charlotte (*c.* 1773–1866), who married the Venerable Charles Baillie Hamilton.

Hookham, Mr. Involved in the publication of Agnes's book in 1792. The *Universal British Directory* of 1790 lists Thomas Hookham, bookseller, 145 New Bond Street, London.

Hüllmandel, Monsieur. Probably Nicolas Joseph Hüllmandel (1751–1823). A native of Strasbourg, he was a pupil of C. P. E. Bach. He settled in London in 1771 as a virtuoso and music teacher, and wrote and published keyboard sonatas and musical exercises.

Hunt, Mrs D. Anna (*née* Nettleship), the second wife of Doddington Hunt (*c.* 1744–1803). They married in 1797. Anna was the sister of Catherine Nettleship, wife of Doddington's younger brother, the Revd John Hunt (q.v.). Doddington Hunt's first wife (married 1771) was Elizabeth, daughter and heiress of William Prynne of

Charlton Park, Gloucestershire. Their son, William Hunt Prynne, inherited Charlton Park on his father's death.

Hunt, Revd Dr John (*c.* 1748–1816). An old friend of Thomas Mansel Talbot. He was the younger son of Doddington Hunt of Compton Pauncefoot in Somerset, and matriculated at Corpus Christi College, Oxford, in 1763. He was vicar of Pitcombe in Somerset, near Redlynch, before Talbot presented him to the living of Margam in 1794. Dr Hunt married Catherine Nettleship (*c.* 1744–1813), in 1794. The Hunts lived at Tynycaeau in the parish of Margam. Dr Hunt was one of the executors of Agnes's will.

Hurst, Mr and Mrs. Herbert Hurst (*c.* 1765–1822) of Gabalfa and Dinas Powis, Glamorgan, and his wife Mary Ann (*née* Wrixon).

Ilchester, Dowager Lady. *See* **Fox Strangways, Elizabeth, first Countess of Ilchester.**

Ilchester, Earls of. *See* **Fox Strangways**.

Jeffries, Mr. William Jeffreys was portreeve (mayor) of Swansea in 1804.

Jenkins, Mr and Mrs. The Revd William Jenkins (? born *c.* 1748) was rector of Melbury Sampford, Dorset, from 1780–1822, and of Abbotsbury from 1786. Probably son of John Jenkins of Chetnole, Dorset, and matriculated at Corpus Christi College, Oxford, in 1767.

Jones, Captain Richard. Calvert Richard Jones (1764–1847) of Veranda, Swansea.

Jordan, Mrs. Dora Jordan (1761–1816), a famous actress and the mistress of William, Duke of Clarence (later King William IV). (DNB)

Keble, Revd John (1745–1835). He was for fifty-two years the vicar of Coln St Aldwyn, Gloucestershire, but lived in Fairford. He and his wife had five surviving children. The eldest son, John Keble (1792–1866), whom Agnes described as a prodigy in 1805, went on to become a founder of the Oxford Movement. (DNB, John Keble, junior)

Keir, Mrs Elizabeth (died 1834). Relative of Agnes's mother. Of 10 George Street, Edinburgh, in 1805, when Agnes stayed with her. Daughter of James Rae, an Edinburgh surgeon, and Isobel, daughter of Ludovick Cant of Thurston, East Lothian. Elizabeth Rae married Dr William Keir in London in 1779. He was a physician at St Thomas's Hospital in the 1780s. They had two sons: one son, James (born *c.* 1780), was a doctor in Edinburgh and Moscow. Also a daughter Isabella, who was unmarried in 1828.

Keir, Mrs Susannah Harvey (1747–1802). Born Susannah Harvey, married James Keir, chemist (1735–1820), in 1770. Susannah was an authoress, and apparently a friend of Agnes, though mentioned only in 1790 and 1802. (DNB, James Keir)

Keith, Mr and Miss, of Ravelston. He was Alexander Keith of Ravelston, Edinburgh, and Dunottar, Kincardine, who died in 1819. He was an antiquarian and friend of Sir Walter Scott.

Keith, Mrs Marianne. Sister of Mrs Elizabeth Keir (q.v.). She married Mr William Keith, 'accomptant', in Edinburgh in 1779. Still alive in 1805, when Agnes saw her in Edinburgh.

Kemble. An actor whom Agnes saw in London in 1791. He was John Philip Kemble (1757–1823), who belonged to a well-known family of actors, and was a brother of Mrs Siddons. (DNB)

King, Mr Edward (1750–1819). An old friend of Thomas Mansel Talbot. He lived at Marino, an octagonal villa which was built in 1783 to the design of the Swansea architect William Jernegan. It now forms the administrative block of the University College of Swansea. King was appointed Deputy Comptroller of Customs in the port of Swansea in 1786, and was Collector of Customs from 1810–15. He married Jane (died 1810), sister of the prominent Radical Robert Morris (1743–93), and of John Morris of Clasemont and Sketty Park (1745–1819), who was created a baronet in 1806.

Kirke, Mr. The Revd George Robert Kirke, aged twenty-four, was admitted to Magdalene College, Cambridge, in 1786.

Lansdowne, Lord and Lady. *See* **Fox Strangways, Louisa Emma**.

Lewis. An actor, whom Agnes saw in London in 1791. He was William Thomas Lewis (*c*. 1748–1811), known as 'Gentleman Lewis', famous mainly for his comic roles. (DNB)

Llewellyn, Mr. Griffith Llewellyn (1767–1822) of Baglan, Glamorgan, steward of the Margam estate, 1798–1822.

Llewelyn, Mr John (1756–1817). Of Ynisygerwn near Neath. He inherited the Penllergaer estate *c*. 1790 and was sheriff of Glamorgan in 1792. He married but had no children by his wife. His illegitimate daughter and eventual heiress, Mary Adams (1776–1865), lived with the Llewelyns. In 1807 Mary Adams married Lewis Weston Dillwyn (1778–1855). The Llewelyns and the Dillwyns were close friends of the Talbots, and the families visited each other regularly. John Dillwyn Llewelyn, the eldest son of Lewis Weston Dillwyn, married Emma, the youngest daughter of Thomas Mansel Talbot, in 1833.

Lloyd, Mrs and Misses. Friends of Agnes Porter in Bruton. John Lloyd (died 1774) and Hannah Johnson married at Bruton in 1751. They had two daughters: Mary, born 1752, who married Edward Moore of Shepton Mallet in 1794 and died in 1811; and Lucy, born 1755, who nursed Agnes in her last illness. Mrs Hannah Lloyd, who may have been a housekeeper at Stourhead, died aged ninety-eight in 1817. Lucy died in 1835.

Longford, Mrs (Nanny Longford). Joan, wife of Richard Longford, gamekeeper at Redlynch. She was a nurse to Lord Ilchester's family for many years, and later acted as a maternity nurse for Mary Talbot at Penrice.

Loveden, Mr Edward Loveden (1750–1822). Born Edward Loveden Townsend. He was of Buscot Park, Berkshire, and a friend of Michael Hicks Beach. Loveden had several children by his first wife, Margaret, daughter and heiress of Lewis Pryse of Gogerddan, Cardiganshire, who died in 1784. A daughter, probably the youngest, Jane Elizabeth (1783–1855), was a pupil of Frances Richards in 1794.

Lucan, Lord. Richard Bingham, second Earl of Lucan (1764–1839). He and his wife separated in 1804.

Lucas family. Of Stouthall in Gower, a mile or two from Penrice. Friends of the Talbots. John Lucas of Stouthall (1759–1831) married Catherine Powell (1761–1841) in 1778. They had three sons: John Nicholas (*c*. 1784–1863), George (*c*. 1786–99), Henry (1797–*c*. 1870); and four daughters: Mary Catherine, Caroline, Harriet and Matilda.

McFarquhar, Mrs. *See* **Collins, Dr Charles**.

McNamara, Mr. *See* **Montgomery, Mr**.

Macqueen, Dr Malcolm (*c*. 1750–1829). An old friend of Agnes Porter. He graduated MD at Edinburgh in 1777, and was a physician in Great Yarmouth in 1778. A friend of the Rameys and Upchers, he subsequently lived in Norwich, and then in Bedfordshire and London. In 1791 he married an heiress, Mariana, only daughter of Thomas Potter Esq. of Harley Street, London. Their son, Thomas Potter Macqueen (1792–1854) was a politician and a coloniser of New South Wales.

Mansfield, Lord. David Murray, second Earl of Mansfield (1727–96), who died 1 September 1796. (DNB)

Masterman, Mr. Lord Ilchester's estate steward.

Montgomery, Mr. Robert Montgomery, a colonel in the ninth Regiment, and son of Sir William Montgomery of Magbiehill, Ayr, was killed in a duel with Captain Macnamara on 6 April 1803.

Morgan, Mr. A hunting companion of Thomas Mansel Talbot. Possibly Edward (*c.* 1759–1832), son of Edward Morgan of Aberdare, Glamorgan, who matriculated at Jesus College, Oxford, in 1776, aged seventeen. He later entered the church.

Morice, Mr James (1786–1848). Nephew of Revd Thomas Richards (q.v.). He and his sister Mary Morice (1790–1866) spent a good deal of time in the Richards household. In 1804 James Morice was articled to an attorney, Mr (James) Crowdey of Highworth and Swindon. Mary Morice inherited Thomas Richards's property when he died in 1852.

Morton, Lady Frances. Lady Frances Herbert (died 1830), only daughter of the first Earl of Carnarvon and sister-in-law of Kitty Acland (q.v.), who married Thomas Reynolds Moreton, later first Earl of Ducie, in 1797.

Moser, Mr Joseph (1748–1819). He and his wife were old friends of Agnes. He was of Swiss extraction and was an artist, author and magistrate. His wife, whom he married in 1780, was Elizabeth Julia, daughter of Peter Liege, an eminent London surgeon. Agnes's friendship with Mrs Moser probably dated from before 1780. In the 1790s the Mosers lived in Little Smith Street, Westminster. (DNB)

Murray, Lady George (1765–1844). Lady George Murray (*née* Anne Charlotte Grant) was the widow of Rt Hon. and Rt Revd Lord George Murray, Bishop of St David's, and mother-in-law of Lady Mary's brother Henry Stephen, 3rd Earl of Ilchester (who married Caroline Leonora Murray in February 1812). Lord Ilchester's friend Townshend Selwyn (q.v.) married Caroline Leonora's sister, Charlotte Murray, in June 1812. There were eight other children, including Edward (born 1798) and Henry (born 1800). (DNB, George Murray)

Nares, Mr. Lady Charlotte Spencer, daughter of the fourth Duke of Marlborough, married in 1797 the Revd Edward Nares, D.D. (1762–1841), Professor of Modern History and Languages at the University of Oxford. (DNB)

Neave, Mrs. *See* **Digby, Frances Caroline.**

Newbolt, Mrs. *See* **Digby, Elizabeth Juliana.**

O'Brien, Lady Susan (1743–1827). She was born Susanna Sarah Louisa Fox Strangways, eldest daughter of the first Earl of Ilchester. A headstrong and determined young lady, she fell in love with a successful young professional actor of humble origins, William O'Brien (*c.* 1738–1815), whom she met when they both took part in amateur theatricals at her uncle's home, Holland House in London. William O'Brien and Lady Susan Fox Strangways married in 1764, without the knowledge of the bride's parents, who were horrified but could do nothing as Susan was twenty-one. Lord Holland gave the young couple an allowance and they were packed off to America in the autumn of 1764. They returned to England in 1771 and were eventually reconciled with Lady Susan's family. From 1774 they lived in the old manor house at Stinsford near Dorchester, which belonged to Lady Ilchester, from where they paid regular visits to Melbury and Redlynch. The O'Briens had no children of their own, but were very popular with the younger members of the Fox Strangways family. (DNB, William O'Brien)

Ogilvie, Mr. Thomas Elliot Ogilvie (1751–1831), Agnes Porter's mother's 'nearest relation'. Son of William Ogilvie of Hartwoodmyres, Selkirkshire, chamberlain to the Duke of Buccleugh, and Elizabeth, daughter of William Elliot of Wolfelee, Roxburghshire (sister of Dr Thomas Elliot, q.v.). Thomas Elliot Ogilvie joined the Madras Civil Service, and made a fortune which enabled him to buy the estate of Chesters in 1787. In 1782 he married Hannah, daughter of Robert Dashwood, and widow of Dr Gilbert Pasley. Thomas Elliot Ogilvie's sister Jean married General William Balfour in 1786.

Orr, Mrs. A relation of Agnes's mother, living in Edinburgh in 1805. She was Elizabeth, daughter of Ludowick Cant, and married Alexander Orr of Waterside (1725–74), Writer to the Signet, in 1761. The Orrs had a son, Alexander, born 1764; and three daughters, Elizabeth (born 1762), Agnes (born 1767), and Lewisa (born 1769).

Palmer. An actor, whom Agnes saw in London in 1797. He was John Palmer (*c.* 1742–1798). (DNB)

Parker, Dr. The Revd William Parker, DD (1714–1802). He was rector of St James, Westminster, from 1763 to 1802. (DNB)

Patoun, Miss. A first cousin of Agnes's (maternal) grandmother, Agnes saw her in Edinburgh in 1805. Possibly Marion (1752–1840), daughter of Robert Patoun, Minister of the Gospel at Haddington.

Paul, Sir George. Sir George Onesiphorus Paul (1746–1820), third Baronet, of Rodborough, Gloucestershire, was a friend of the Fox Strangways family. He was a landowner, philanthropist and prison reformer. (DNB)

Pearson, Mr. A first cousin of the first Countess of Ilchester. Thomas Horner Pearson (*c.* 1752–1832), matriculated at Wadham College, Oxford, in 1768. He was rector of Podimore Milton, Somerset, from 1776, and vicar of Queen Camel from 1785. His mother, Edith Horner, was Lady Ilchester's aunt.

Peele, Revd John (*c.* 1721–1804). An old friend of the Porter family. He was the son of John Peele of Norwich and Mary, the sister of Nathaniel Symonds of Great Yarmouth (husband of Agnes's great-aunt, Elizabeth Porter). John Peele matriculated at Pembroke College, Cambridge, in 1737. He was vicar of Tilney All Saints, Norfolk, 1749–1805, but lived in Norwich, where he was 'upper minister' at the church of St Peter Mancroft from *c.* 1766 until his death.

Philips, Mr and Mrs Mansel. Richard Mansel Philips (1769–1844) lived at Sketty Hall near Swansea. He was High Sheriff of Glamorgan in 1802 and mayor of Swansea in 1837. His wife, whom he married in 1797, was Caroline (died 1850), daughter of B. Bond Hopkins, MP.

Pinnock, Mrs (*c.* 1717 to *c.* 1805) An old friend of Agnes, who sent money to her from time to time. Last mentioned in 1805, when she was eighty-seven and living in London. In 1807 Agnes was trying to help her son, a clergyman with two sons and four daughters.

Pope, Miss. Jane Pope (1742–1818), an actress. (DNB)

Porchester, Lady. *See* **Acland, Elizabeth Kitty**.

Porter, Mrs Elizabeth (*c.* 1724–94). Agnes's mother. A Scotswoman: maiden name unknown, but probably Elliot or Ogilvie. By 1791 she was living in Salisbury. Buried at Wroughton, Wiltshire, with her husband.

Porter, Elizabeth (Betsey). Agnes's sister. She is only mentioned by name 1791–92, but a reference in August 1802 suggests that she may still have been alive then. She may have died in 1803.

Porter, Frances (Fanny). *See* **Richards, Revd Thomas and Mrs**.

Poyntz, Mr. Uncle of the Duchess of Devonshire: Agnes met him at Burderop Park, Wiltshire. Georgiana, wife of the fifth Duke of Devonshire, was a daughter of John, first Earl Spencer, and his wife Margaret Georgiana, daughter of Stephen Poyntz (1685–1750) of Midgham, Berkshire, an eminent diplomat. Stephen Poyntz had two sons, either of whom could have been Agnes's acquaintance: William Poyntz (*c*. 1733–1809), of Midgham, and Charles Poyntz (*c*. 1735–1809), prebendary of Llandaff and Durham, and rector of North Creake, Norfolk, 1760–1809.

Price, Mr and Mrs. Friends of the Talbot family in Glamorgan. John Price (*c*. 1751–1818) and his wife Jane, daughter of Peter Birt of Wenvoe Castle, Glamorgan, married in 1776. They leased Llandaff Court from Thomas Mathews from 1787, and then rented Llandough Castle, which belonged to Thomas Mansel Talbot, from *c*. 1803. Mrs Price's sister Mary Birt, married John Richards of the Corner House, Cardiff, and their only daughter Ann Maria ('Miss Richards') married John Homfray of Penllyn Castle, Glamorgan, in 1819.

Pritchard. Hannah Pritchard (1711–68) was an actress, who played with David Garrick. Her daughter, Miss Pritchard, was also an actress. (DNB)

Pritchard, Revd Mr and Mrs. Agnes met them at Penrice in 1804. He was Richard Pritchard (*c*. 1757–1850), rector of Port-Eynon in Gower 1803–50.

Quin, Mrs. Born Catherine (Kitty) Grady, sister of the second Countess of Ilchester. She married first in 1784 the Revd John Quin, younger brother of Sir Valentine Richard Quin of Adare, County Limerick. John Quin died in 1789. In 1792 his widow married George Gumbleton of Castle Richards, County Cork. Her third husband was Walter Giles of Lisnabrien Lodge, County Cork, later of Coolnagour, County Waterford. Mrs Giles died *c*. 1831.

Quin, Mr. Windham Henry Quin (1782–1850), later second Earl of Dunraven. Elder son of Lady Adare (q.v.), and a first cousin of Lady Mary Fox Strangways. In 1810 he married Caroline, daughter and heiress of Thomas Wyndham of Dunraven (q.v.).

Raines, Miss. Emily Raines, governess at Penrice 1807–8. Sister (or half-sister) of Miss Smyth (q.v.).

Ramey, Mrs (*c*. 1726–1811). She was Abigail, daughter and coheiress of William Browne. She married John Ramey (*c*. 1719–94) of Yarmouth, a lawyer, and mayor of Yarmouth in 1760 and 1773. The Rameys lived at Scratby Hall (q.v.), and they also had a house in Yarmouth. They had a son, John Ramey (*c*. 1753–98), who was disinherited: he suffered from a brain fever whilst a student at Pembroke Hall, Cambridge, and was subsequently thought incapable of conducting his own affairs. The Rameys also had two daughters and eventual coheiresses: Lady Home (q.v.) and Mrs Upcher (q.v.). Agnes lived with the Rameys for some time before 1782.

Ramey, Mrs Joseph. Elizabeth, widow of Joseph Ramey (*c*. 1721–94) of Yarmouth, a surgeon and Collector of Customs.

Richards, Revd Thomas and Mrs. The Revd Thomas Richards (1762–1852) was born at Hyssington, Montgomery, and attended Shrewsbury School, 1776–80. In 1780 he matriculated at Magdalen College, Oxford. Ordained deacon 1784, and priest 1785. Awarded degree of Bachelor of Law, 1786. In 1792 he married Agnes's sister, Frances (*c*. 1764–1823) at Netheravon, Wiltshire. She may have been a governess to the daughters of the Hicks Beach family there. Curate at Hatherop, Gloucestershire (near to the Hicks Beach house at Williamstrip), *c*. 1787–1792. By 1794 the Richardses were living at Hadley, Middlesex, but in 1797 they moved to Knightsbridge. By 1802 they were living in Swindon, Wiltshire. From 1804–19

Thomas Richards was curate at Fairford, Gloucestershire. He was also master of Farmor's School there from 1814 (or earlier) to 1819. After 1819 the Richardses moved to Aberystwyth – Thomas Richards had inherited the Carrog estate, at Llanddeiniol, ten miles south of Aberystwyth. Frances Richards took pupils after her marriage, including her husband's niece Mary Morice and at least one Beach daughter. She and her husband were both buried at Llanddeiniol, Cardiganshire.

Roscius. William Henry Betty (1791–1874), known as the Young Roscius. He began his acting career in 1803 and was extremely successful until 1808 when he went up to Cambridge. (DNB)

Roxburghe, Duke of. Sir James Innes Kerr, fifth Duke of Roxburghe (1736–1814). His second wife (married 1807) was Harriet Charlewood, 'step-daughter' of Agnes's friend Valentine Green. (DNB)

St Asaph, Lady. The first wife of George, Viscount St Asaph (1760–1830), later third Earl of Ashburnham. She died on 9 April 1791.

Sampson, Mr. The family doctor at Redlynch. He was Thomas Sampson, surgeon and apothecary, who married Nanny Robins at Bruton in 1770. Several children were baptised at Bruton, 1772–87.

Séjan, Monsieur. Abbé Albert Séjan was an *émigré* French priest who was in Swansea *c*. 1799–1814.

Selwyn, Mr. He was Townshend Selwyn (*c*. 1783–1853), who matriculated at Christ Church, Oxford, in 1800, and was a close friend of the third Earl of Ilchester. Townshend Selwyn was eventually ordained. He became vicar of Milton Clevedon, Somerset, in 1811, and was rector of Kilmington, 1837–53 (both places are near Redlynch). He married Charlotte Sophia Murray, the sister of the third Countess of Ilchester, in 1812. The Selwyns were living at Kilmington in 1812: Townshend may have been acting as curate there for the rector, the Revd Charles Redlynch Fox Strangways.

Shakespear, Miss. Mary Ann Shakespear, daughter of John Shakespear and Mary (*née* Davenport) was a cousin of the Talbots. In 1813 she was living as a companion to her unmarried aunt Barbara Davenport.

Sheers, Mrs. Edith Shears or Sheers, who was lady's maid to Lady Mary Talbot from 1794 to 1813 (or later).

Sheffield, Lady. Charlotte Sophia (died 1835), daughter of the Very Revd William Digby, Dean of Durham. In 1784 she married Sir John Sheffield, second Baronet (died 1815).

Siddons, Mrs. Sarah Siddons (1755–1831), the well-known actress. (DNB)

Smith, Dr. John Smith or Smyth (*c*. 1744–1809). Matriculated at Pembroke College, Oxford, 1761. Prebendary of Gloucester Cathedral, 1768–1809, vicar of Fairford 1804–9.

Smith, Revd Sydney (1771–1845). Later famous as a preacher, essayist, social commentator and witty conversationalist, he was curate at Netheravon, Wiltshire, from 1794 to 1796, and was employed as a tutor to the sons of Michael and Henrietta Maria Hicks Beach (q.v.) from 1798 to 1803. Sydney Smith met Agnes when he visited Penrice in 1799. (DNB)

Smyth, Miss. Miss Smyth was a governess at Penrice, 1807–8. She was probably consumptive, and died in April 1808. She may be the Miss Charlot [sic] Smith who was buried at St Mary's, Swansea, on 29 April 1808, aged thirty-three.

Stavordale, Lord. *See* **Fox Strangways, Henry Stephen**.

Strangways, Mr and Mrs Charles. *See* **Fox Strangways, Charles Redlynch**.

Strangways, Colonel. *See* **Fox Strangways, Colonel Stephen Strangways Digby.**
Sukey. *See* **Tatham, Susan.**
Syndercombe, Miss. A school-friend of Harriot Fox Strangways. She was probably a daughter of the Revd Gregory Syndercombe, rector of Symondsbury, Dorset.
Talbot, Charlotte Louisa (1800–80). Fourth daughter of Thomas and Lady Mary Talbot. Married in 1830 Revd John Montgomery Traherne of Coedarhydyglyn, Glamorgan (no children).
Talbot, Christiana Barbara (1798–1808). Third daughter of Thomas and Lady Mary Talbot.
Talbot, Christopher Rice Mansel (1803–90). Only son of Thomas and Lady Mary Talbot. Married in 1835 Lady Charlotte Jane Butler, daughter of Richard Butler, first Earl of Glengall, of Caher Castle, County Tipperary (four children).
Talbot, Lady Elizabeth. *See* **Fox Strangways, Elizabeth Theresa**.
Talbot, Ellinor Sybella (1801–10). Fifth daughter of Thomas and Lady Mary Talbot.
Talbot, Emma Thomasina (1806–81). Seventh daughter of Thomas and Lady Mary Talbot. Married in 1833 John Dillwyn Llewelyn of Penllergaer, Glamorgan (six children).
Talbot, Henry. He was William Henry Fox Talbot (1800–77), only son of William Davenport Talbot of Lacock (q.v.) and Lady Elizabeth Fox Strangways (q.v.). He spent much of his childhood with his cousins at Penrice, and was later to become famous as a photographic pioneer.
Talbot, Isabella Catherine (1804–74). Sixth daughter of Thomas and Lady Mary Talbot. Married in 1830 Richard Franklen of Clemenstone, Glamorgan (seven children).
Talbot, Jane Harriot (1796–1874). Second daughter of Thomas and Lady Mary Talbot. Married in 1821 John Nicholl of Merthyr Mawr, Glamorgan (ten children).
Talbot, Lady Mary. *See* **Fox Strangways, Mary Lucy**.
Talbot, Mary Theresa (1795–1861). Eldest daughter of Thomas and Lady Mary Talbot. She died unmarried.
Talbot, Thomas Mansel (1747–1813). He inherited the estates of Penrice and Margam, Glamorgan, from his father in 1758. He matriculated at Oriel College, Oxford, in 1764. He married Lady Mary Lucy Fox Strangways (q.v.), second daughter of the second Earl of Ilchester, in 1794.
Talbot, William Davenport (1763–1800). Of Lacock, Wiltshire. A first cousin of Thomas Mansel Talbot, he married Elizabeth Theresa Fox Strangways in 1796.
Tatham, Susan (Sukey). Nurse to the Talbot children at Penrice for nearly thirty years. She was born Susan Tatham, *c.* 1782, and probably went to Penrice in 1804. In 1811 Sukey married David Jones, the Talbots' postilion, at Penrice. She died in 1832 and was buried in Penrice churchyard, where the Talbots erected a stone in her memory.
Treherne, Mr. A hunting companion of Thomas Mansel Talbot. He was Llewellyn Traherne (1766–1841) of Coedarhydyglyn, St Hilary and Castellau, Glamorgan. His son, John Montgomery Traherne, was to marry Charlotte Louisa Talbot in 1830. A daughter, Charlotte Frances (Fanny), died unmarried in 1852.
Treherne, Miss Fanny. *See* **Treherne, Mr.**
Trimmer, Mrs. Sarah Trimmer (1741–1810), a well-known writer on education and religion, who 'became known as an unofficial employment exchange for young governesses'. (DNB)

Tytler, Mr. *See* **Woodhouselee, Lord**.

Upcher, Mr and Mrs. Elizabeth (1750–1799), daughter and coheiress of John Ramey of Great Yarmouth (*see* Ramey, Mrs) married Peter Upcher of Sudbury, Suffolk in 1777. He died in 1796. The Upchers had two sons who died young: Robert (killed in a riding accident in 1795) and Ramey, who died of smallpox in 1797. Two daughters, Harriet and Augusta Abigail, died in 1794 and 1800 respectively. The only surviving son, Abbot Upcher (1784–1819), the builder of Sheringham Hall, Norfolk, married the Hon. Charlotte Wilson, daughter of the Revd Henry Wilson of Kirby Cane, Norfolk (later Lord Berners), in 1809.

Vilett, Dr and Mrs. Acquaintances of Agnes in Swindon. He was the Revd Thomas Goddard Vilett (*c*. 1751–1817). Dr Vilett belonged to an old Swindon family, and was related to the Goddards and the Calleys (q.v.).

Watkins, Revd Mr. The Revd William Watkins (*c*. 1747–1803), rector, was buried at Port-Eynon on 7 June 1803. Agnes gives the date of his death as 21 May, but this appears to be wrong, as his monument in Port-Eynon church says that he died 28 May.

Whit[w]ick, Mr. *See* **Wightwick, Revd Walter**.

Whynfield, Lady Charlotte. *See* **Wingfield, Lady Charlotte**.

Wightwick, Revd Walter (*c*. 1728–1807). Of Somerton, Somerset. A friend of the Fox Strangways family. He was rector of Chiselborough and Middle Chinnock, Somerset. He had a daughter, Mary Theresa, who was born *c*. 1781.

Williams, Mr and Mrs. Friends of Agnes in London. He was probably Evan Williams, who is listed as a bookseller and stationer in the Strand, 1789–1826. From 1789 to 1799 Thomas Williams, who may have been Evan's brother, is listed too. In 1814 Evan Williams of 11 Strand, bookseller, swore an affidavit concerning Agnes's will. Another brother may have been the Revd David Williams, whose daughters Elizabeth and Mary Elizabeth were baptised at Wroughton, Wiltshire, in 1790 and 1792. The older daughter died of whooping cough in 1791 and the mother, Mary, was buried at Wroughton in 1792 aged thirty-three.

Wingfield, Lady Charlotte. Charlotte Maria (died 1807), daughter of Henry, seventh Baron and first Earl Digby, who married William Wingfield Baker, MP, on 22 July 1796.

Woodhouselee, Lord. Alexander Fraser Tytler, Lord Woodhouselee (1747–1813). He contributed to the *Mirror*, 1779–80, and to the *Lounger*, 1785–86. (DNB)

Wrixton, Mr. A hunting companion of Thomas Mansel Talbot. Probably Robert Wrixon of Corntown, Llandaff, and Penarth, Glamorgan (born *c*. 1769).

Wyndham, Mr and Mrs. Thomas Wyndham of Dunraven (*c*. 1763–1814) was an old friend of the Talbots. He was MP for Glamorgan, 1789–1814. His wife was Anna Maria Charlotte, daughter of Thomas Ashby of Isleworth, Middlesex.

Places

A guide to some of the smaller and less easily-identifiable places mentioned in the text. This list does not include the better-known towns and villages.

Abbotsbury, Dorset. A small village on the coast between Weymouth and Bridport. The first Countess of Ilchester build a summer residence there, known as Abbotsbury Castle.

Amesbury, Wiltshire. A village eight miles north of Salisbury. There were nuns at the priory there from the tenth century until the Dissolution. The priory was succeeded by a house known as Amesbury Abbey. This was occupied for a few years after the French Revolution by a group of *émigrée* nuns from Louvain in Flanders.

Burlington Street, London. 31 Old Burlington Street was the London residence of the Fox Strangways family.

Cappercullen, County Limerick. In the parish of Abington, about eight miles east of Limerick. The house stood in the grounds of what is now Glenstal Castle. Cappercullen was the home of the Grady family (parents of the second Countess of Ilchester) from *c.* 1760–70 to the early nineteenth century.

Discove House, Somerset. Near Redlynch, the house was used by the first Countess of Ilchester in the latter part of the eighteenth century.

Dunraven Castle, Glamorgan. The medieval castle of the Butler family, rebuilt 1802–6, it was demolished in 1962. The home of Thomas Mansel Talbot's friend Thomas Wyndham (*c.* 1763–1814), MP for the county of Glamorgan, 1789–1814.

Hadley, Middlesex. On the borders of Middlesex and Hertfordshire, between Barnet and Potters Bar. Thomas and Frances Richards lived there *c.* 1794–97.

Highclere, Hampshire. A large country house, seat of the Earls of Carnarvon.

Historic Gallery. Probably Robert Bowyer's Historic Gallery in Pall Mall, London.

Kilmington, Somerset. A village on the Wiltshire-Somerset border, about five miles from Redlynch. The living was usually held by a relative or friend of the Earl of Ilchester, who was the patron.

Llandaff Court, Glamorgan. A large Georgian house, built by Admiral Thomas Mathews, *c.* 1745. After 1787 it was rented by Mr and Mrs John Price (q.v.) and then from *c.* 1801 by John Richards (*c.* 1768–1819), a member of a leading Cardiff gentry family, who married Catherine Diana Jones of Fonmon, Glamorgan.

Maiden Newton, Dorset. Eight miles north west of Dorchester and about six miles from Melbury. The Reverend Charles Redlynch Fox Strangways was rector there from 1787.

Margam, Glamorgan. Three to four miles south east of the modern town of Port Talbot. The Cistercian abbey was bought in 1536 by Sir Rice Mansel. It was the main seat of the Mansels and then the Talbots until the mid eighteenth century. The old house was demolished between 1789 and 1793 by Thomas Mansel Talbot, and was replaced in the 1830s by a new house, designed for C. R. M. Talbot by Thomas Hopper.

Marino, Glamorgan. An octagonal villa, built in 1783 to the design of the Swansea architect William Jernegan for Edward King (q.v.). The house was subsequently added to and was later known as Singleton Abbey. It now forms the administrative block of the University College of Swansea.

Melbury House, Dorset. In the parish of Melbury Sampford, twelve miles north west of Dorchester. The principal residence of the Fox Strangways family. The house, which belongs to a descendant of the second Earl of Ilchester, is not open to the public.

Moreton, Dorset. About seven miles east of Dorchester. Moreton House was built in 1744 for James Frampton. His son, also James Frampton, married Harriot Fox Strangways (q.v.) in 1799.

Old Passage. The old ferry across the river Severn at Aust, near the site of the first Severn Bridge. The New Passage was a mile and a half further down the river.

Orphan Asylum. This was the Foundling Hospital in Guilford Street. It was established by a royal charter granted in 1739 to Captain Thomas Coram, and the building in Guilford Street was opened in 1754. There was a chapel, with Sunday services open to the general public. Handel was a generous benefactor: he donated a organ to the chapel and left the score of his *Messiah* to the hospital.

Oxwich, Glamorgan. A village on the coast of Gower, a mile or two from Penrice Castle. The Revd John Collins (q.v.) and his family lived at the rectory.

Passage. *See* **Old Passage.**

Penrice Castle, Glamorgan. On the Gower peninsula, about twelve miles west of Swansea. The Georgian villa was designed by Anthony Keck and built for Thomas Mansel Talbot, 1773–76. The grounds and gardens, designed by William Emes, were first laid out *c.* 1776–79. Penrice was the main residence of the Talbot family until Margam Castle was built in the 1830s. The house still belongs to a descendant of Thomas Mansel Talbot. It is not open to the public.

Redlynch House, Somerset. A seat of the Earls of Ilchester, near Bruton. It was the home of the second Earl of Ilchester and his family, *c.* 1775–92.

Scratby Hall, Norfolk. In the parish of Ormesby St Margaret, about five miles north of Yarmouth. Home of the Ramey family (q.v.) from the mid eighteenth century. Sold by Lady Charlotte Hamilton, the granddaughter of John and Abigail Ramey *c.* 1823, and rebuilt in the mid nineteenth century.

Shakespeare Gallery. Alderman John Boydell's Shakespeare Gallery was in Pall Mall. It contained illustrations of scenes from Shakespeare, specially commissioned from the best-known artists of the day. The gallery was opened *c.* 1789, its contents being dispersed after Boydell's death in 1804.

Stinsford House, Dorset. Two to three miles east of Dorchester. Home of William and Lady Susan O'Brien (q.v.).

Syrencot House, Wiltshire. An early Georgian house in the parish of Figheldean, near Netheravon and about twelve miles north of Salisbury. The home of the Dyke family (q.v.).

Williamstrip Park, Gloucestershire. A Georgian house in the parish of Coln St Aldwyn, near Fairford. One of the homes of the Hicks Beaches.

Wroughton, Wiltshire. A village two to three miles south of Swindon. Francis Porter, Agnes's father, was vicar there 1778–82.

Agnes Porter and the Theatre

Theatrical Performances Attended by Agnes Porter

13 March 1788, Covent Garden: *The Belle's Stratagem*. By Hannah Cowley. First performed (at Covent Garden) 1780.

7 March 1791, Little Theatre, Haymarket: *The Busy Body*. By Susannah Centlivre. First performed 1709. Also *The Advertisement: or A New Way to Get a Husband*. By James Fennell. (*The Advertisement* was a farce, and this appears to have been the only eighteenth-century performance.)

28 March 1791, Drury Lane: *Othello*. By William Shakespeare. The 'entertainment' was *The Deaf Lover*, a farce by Frederick Pilon. First performed 1779.

29 October 1796, Drury Lane: *The Grecian Daughter*. By Arthur Murphy. First performed 1772. Also *The Scotch Ghost, or Little Fanny's Love*, a ballet by Giacomo Gentili, first performed 1796.

12 May 1797, Drury Lane: *As You Like It*. By William Shakespeare. Also *The Scotch Ghost* (see 29 October 1796), and *The Critick* a burlesque by R. B. Sheridan, first performed 1779.

April 1798, Drury Lane: *The Stranger*. By Benjamin Thompson. First performed 24 March 1798.

11 April 1798, Covent Garden (the only performance of this play at this time): *Wives as They Were, and Maids as They Are*. By Elizabeth Inchbald. First performed 1797.

?17 April 1798. King's Opera House, Haymarket: *Cinna*. An opera by Francesco Bianchi junior 'musician and composer'. First performed 1798.

14 August 1798, Great Yarmouth: *The Provoked Husband: or A Journey to London*. By Colley Cibber. First performed 1728.

2 March 1805, Drury Lane: *Douglas*. A play by John Home. First performed 1757. Also *The Devil to Pay*, a farce by Charles Coffey. First performed 1731.

Agnes Porter's Books

Books Owned or Mentioned by Agnes Porter

Addison, Joseph, *Cato: A Tragedy* (1713, numerous later edns).

Aikin, John and Barbauld, Anna Lætitia, *Miscellaneous Pieces in Prose* (1st edn, London, 1773; numerous later edns).

Amelot de la Houssaie, Abraham Nicolas, The *Annals* and *History* of *Tacitus* (French translation, 1st edn, The Hague, 1692; 1st English edn, 1698).

Andrews, James Pettit, *Anecdotes &c., Ancient and Modern* (1789, various later edns).

Ariosto, Ludovico (1474–1533), *Orlando Furioso* (many edns).

Barbauld, Anna Lætitia. *See* Aikin.

Bigland, John, *Essays on Various Subjects* (Doncaster, 1805).

Blair, Hugh (a well-known preacher and lecturer in Edinburgh; numerous edns of his sermons, published 1777 and later, in Scotland, England and on the Continent).

Bloomfield, Robert, *The Farmer's Boy* (poem, 1800, numerous later edns).

Boileau, Nicolas (essayist and critic; numerous edns of his works published 1670s and later).

Bowdler, Henrietta Maria, *Fragments in Prose and Verse: By a Young Lady, Lately Deceased* [i.e. Elizabeth Smith] (1808, several later edns).

Brantôme, Pierre de Bourdeille, Seigneur de, *Vies des dames galantes* (1660s and later edns).

Burney, Frances (Fanny), *Evelina* (1778, numerous later edns).

Butler, Samuel, *Hudibras* (1663, numerous later edns).

Campbell, Thomas, *The Pleasures of Hope: A Poem* (Edinburgh, 1799, and other edns).

Carle, Thomas, *The History of the Life of James, Duke of Ormond* (London, 1736).

Claris de Florian, John Peter, *Estelle, pastorale* (1790, several later edns, in French and English).

——, *Rosalba; Nouvelle Sicilienne* (A Sicilian Novel), (translation by William B. Hewetson published London, 1786).

——, *The Adventures of Numa Pompilius* (an English edn of this book, in eight volumes, was published in London in 1788).

Constant de Rebecque, François, *Camille, ou lettres de deux filles de ce siècle* (1785).

——, *Laure, ou lettres de quelques personnes de Suisse* (1787).

Cornaro, Luigi, *Discourses on a Sober and Temperate Life* (published in Italian, *c.* 1627 on; several edns in English, *c.* 1634 and later).

Cowper, William, *The Task* (numerous edns of this poem, 1785 and later; also many other poems).

Coxe, Sir Richard, *Hibernia Anglicana: or The History of Ireland* (London, 1689).

Crabbe, George, *The Village* (first published 1783).

Dryden, John (unspecified works).

Edgeworth, Maria, *Tales of Fashionable Life* (1809, several later edns).

Edgeworth, Maria and Edgeworth, Richard Lovel, *Practical Education* (London, 1798).

Elsmere, Sloane, *Sermons on Several Important Subjects* (London, 1767).

Euclid (numerous edns of his works on geometry published from the sixteenth century on).

Fielding, Sarah, *The History of Ophelia* (London, 1760).

Fleming, Robert, *A Discourse on the Rise and Fall of Papacy* (1st edn, London, 1701; several edns in 1790s).

Fordyce, James, (sermons published 1755 on, including *Sermons to Young Women*, London, 1766).

Francis, Philip (translator of the works of Horace: 1743, numerous later edns).

Garth, Sir Samuel, *The Dispensary* (poem, 1699, and later edns).

Gaudentio di Lucca (pseudonym), *The Memoirs of Signor Gaudentio di Lucca* (account of the discovery of an 'unknown country' in Africa, supposedly copied from a manuscript in St Mark's library, Venice. Probably an original work by Simon Berington. Various edns, 1737 on).

Genlis, Stéphanie Felicité, Madame de, *Adèle et Théodore, or Letters on Education* (translated from the French, published in 3 vols in London, 1783-88).

——, *Leçons d'une gouvernante à ses élèves* (1st edn Paris, 1791; also published in English as *Lessons of a Governess to her Pupils* (London, 1792).

——, *Les chevaliers du cygne, ou la cour de Charlemagne* (1795 and later).

——, *Les mères rivales* (1800 and later).

Goethe, Johann Wolfgang von, *The Sorrows of Werter* (English translation published 1779; many later edns).

Goldoni, Carlo (Italian dramatist, numerous plays, *c.* 1750 and later).

Goldsmith, Oliver (numerous edns of his works, 1760s on).

Gordon, Alexander, *The History of Peter the Great, Emperor of Russia* (Aberdeen, 1755).

Grant, Anne, *Letters from the Mountains* (London, 1807).

——, *Memoirs of an American Lady* (1808, various later edns).

——, *The Highlanders* (poem, 2nd edn, London, 1808).

Griffith, Elizabeth, *A Series of Genuine Letters between Henry and Frances* (1757, numerous later edns).

Guarini, Giovanni Battista, *Il Pastor Fido* (*c.* 1590; many later edns in Italian, English and other languages).

Hamilton, Elizabeth, *Letters on Education* (1801, various later edns). (She also wrote other books on education.)

——, *Memoirs of Modern Philosophers* (3 vols, Bath, 1800).

——, *The Cottagers of Glenburnie: A Tale for the Farmer's Ingle-Nook* (Edinburgh, 1808).

Harte, Walter, *The History of the Life of Gustavus Adolphus, King of Sweden* (London, 1759).

Hayley, William, *The Life and Posthumous Writings of W. Cowper* (Chichester, 1803–4).

Henderson, Andrew, *The Life of William Augustus, Duke of Cumberland* (London, 1766). (This is probably the work mentioned.)

Hume, David, *The History of England* (1754, numerous later edns).

Hurdis, James, *Adriano or the First of June: A Poem* (1st edn, London, 1790).

Johnes, Thomas (trans. and ed.), *Memoirs of John, Lord de Joinville* (Hafod, 1807).

Johnson, Samuel, *The Prince of Abissinia: A Tale [Rasselas]* (1759, numerous later edns). (Also numerous collected edns of his works, 1780s on.)

Jonson, Ben, *Volpone* (1607, numerous later edns of this play).

Joyce, Jeremiah, *A System of Practical Arithmetic* (London, 1808).

Keir, Susannah Harvey, *Interesting Memoirs: By a Lady* (2nd edn, Edinburgh, 1785).

Kotzebue, August Friedrich Ferdinand von, *The Most Remarkable Year in the Life of Augustus von Kotzebue, Containing an Account of his Exile into Siberia* (English edn, London, 1802).

Kramer, Professor, *Herman of Unna: A Series of Adventures in the Fifteenth Century* (published in German, 1794).

La Fontaine, August, *Clara Duplesses and Clairant: or The History of a French Emigrant* (London, 1798).

Lavater, Johann Caspar (numerous works on religion, education and physiognomy, 1770s and later).

Le Prince de Beaumont, Jeanne Marie, *Letters of Madame du Montier* (1756, various later edns).

Le Sage, Alain René, *Histoire de Gil Blas de Santillane* (various edns, 3rd edn Rouen, 1721–24. Also an English translation by Tobias Smollett, first published 1750).

Locke, John (numerous works on philosophy, 1686 and later).

Lucas, Charles, *The Infernal Quixote: A Tale of the Day* (London, 1801).

Mackenzie, Henry, *Julia de Roubigné* (Edinburgh, 1777).

Malkin, Benjamin Heath, *Almahide and Hamlet: A Tragedy* (a play, published London, 1804).

Mallet, David, *Amyntor and Theodora: or The Hermit. A Poem* (London, 1747).

Malone, Edmund (various edns of Shakespeare's plays, *c.* 1780 on).

Marana, Giovanni Paolo, *The Eight Volumes of Letters Writ by a Turkish Spy* (1694, numerous later edns).

Marivaux, Pierre Carlet de Chamblain de, *La vie de Marianne* (1730s, numerous later edns in English and French).

Massillon, Jean Baptiste de, Bishop of Clermont (*c.* 1750, numerous later edns of his sermons).

Méhégan, Guillaume Alexandre de, *Tableau de l'histoire moderne* (1st edn Paris, 1766; several later edns).

Metastasio, Pietro Antonio Domenico Bonaventura (poet and dramatist: numerous edns of his works, *c.* 1730 on).

Moir, John, *Sermons on Some of the Most Useful and Interesting Subjects in Religion and Life* (London, 1784).

Molière, Jean Baptiste de, *Le malade imaginaire* (numerous edns of this play, 1670s on).

Montagu, Lady Mary Wortley (numerous edns of her letters published 1763 on).

Montaigne, Michel de (numerous edns of his essays, sixteenth century on).

More, Hannah, *Cœlebs in Search of a Wife* (1808, several later edns).

——, *Essays on Various Subjects, Principally Designed for Young Ladies* (1st edn London, 1777, also published Cork, 1778).

——, *Hints towards Forming the Character of a Young Princess* (1805 and later).

Moritz, Carl Philipp, *Travels, Chiefly on Foot, through Several Parts of England, in 1782* (1st English edn, translated from German 'by a lady' was published in London in 1795).

Moser, Joseph, *The Adventures of Timothy Twig Esq., in a Series of Political Epistles* (London, 1794).

——, *Turkish Tales* (London, 1794).

Nares, Revd Edward, *I Says, Says I: A Novel* (1812. He also wrote *Thinks-I-to-Myself*, first published 1811).

Nettleton, Thomas, *A Treatise on Virtue and Happiness* (1729 and later edns).

Newton, John, *Six Discourses as Intended for the Pulpit* (London, 1760).

Ossian, *Poems* ('translated', but actually composed by James Macpherson, 1762, numerous later edns).

Parkinson, James F. G. S., *Organic Remains of a Former World* (London, 1804–11).

Paul, Sir George O., *Considerations on the Defects of Prisons, and their Present System of Regulation* (London, 1784).

Pennington, Revd Montagu (ed.), *Memoirs of the Life of Mrs Elizabeth Carter* (London, 1807).

Poisson de Gomez, Madeleine A., *Les journées amusantes* (Paris, 1722 and later).

Pope, Alexander (numerous essays, poems and other works published 1709 on).

Porteus, Beilby, Bishop of London, *Sermons* (1772 and later edns).

Pratt, Samuel Jackson, *Sympathy: A Poem* (1780 and later edns).

Radcliffe, Ann, *The Mysteries of Udolpho* (London, 1794, and later edns).

——, *The Romance of the Forest* (1791 and later edns).

Riccoboni, Marie-Jeanne, *Lettres de Milady Juliette Catesby, à Milady Henriette Campley, son Amie* (a novel, 2nd edn Amsterdam, 1759. English translation, 2nd edn, 1760).

——, *Lettres de Mistriss Fanni Butlerd à Milord Charles Alfred, duc de Caitombridge* (Paris, 1759, and later edns).

(Also 8-volume edn of Riccoboni's works published Paris, 1786, in French.)

Robertson, William, *The History of the Reign of the Emperor Charles V* (1769, numerous later edns).

Robinson, Mary, *Walsingham, or The Pupil of Nature: A Domestic Story* (London, 1797).

Rogers, Samuel, *An Epistle to a Friend with Other Poems* (London, 1798).

Rolli, Paul Antonio, *Alessandro* (a drama in verse, London, 1726).

Roscoe, William, *The Life and Pontificate of Leo the Tenth* (Liverpool, 1805, and later edns).

——, *The Life of Lorenzo de Medici, Called the Magnificent* (Liverpool, 1795, and later edns).

——, *The Nurse. See* Tansillo, Luigi .

Saint-Pierre, Jacques Henri Bernardin de, *Paul et Virginie* (1788, numerous later edns).

Saunderson, Professor Nicholas (several works on algebra, 1740 and later).

Scott, Sir Walter, *Marmion* (first published Edinburgh, 1808).

Sévigné, Marie, Marquise de (Madame de Sévigné), *Letters* (1726, numerous
later edns).
Seward, William, *Anecdotes of Some Distinguished Persons* (London, 1795–97).
Shaftesbury, Anthony Ashley Cooper, Earl of, *Letters* (London, 1721, various
later edns).
Shakespeare, William (various works). Agnes may have used an edition by
Edmund Malone (q.v.)
Shenstone, William (numerous edns of his poems, 1737 on).
Sherlock, Revd William, Dean of St Paul's (various *Discourses* published in the
late seventeenth and eighteenth centuries).
Smith, Charlotte, *Ethelinde: or The Recluse of the Lake* (1789, several later edns).
——, *Sonnets* (1784, various later edns).
Staël-Holstein, Anne Louise Germaine, Baroness de (Madame de Staël),
Corinne, ou l'Italie (1807, numerous later edns in French and English).
Sterne, Laurence *A Sentimental Journey through France and Italy* (1768, various
later edns).
Sully, Maximilian de Béthune, Duc de, *Memoirs* (various edns, *c.* 1640 on).
Swift, Jonathan, *Verses on the Death of Dr Swift* (London, 1739).
Tansillo, Luigi, *The Nurse* (a poem translated from the Italian by William
Roscoe, 1798, various later edns).
Tasso, Torquato (1544–95) (numerous edns of his works in the original Italian
and in translation in the seventeenth and eighteenth centuries).
Thiebault, Dieudonné, *Original Anecdotes of Frederick the Second, King of Prussia*
(translated from the French: 3 vols, London, 1805).
Thomson, James, *The Seasons* (numerous edns of this poem published, 1720s
on).
Trimmer, Sarah (numerous works on religion, history and education, 1780s on).
Voltaire, François-Marie Arouet de, *Zaïre* (a play, first published 1733).
Walker, John (eminent English philologist; dictionaries published 1770s on).
Watson, Robert, *The History of the Reign of Philip II, King of Spain* (1777, various
later edns).
Watts, Isaac, *Against Idleness and Mischief* (poem first published 1715).
West, Jane, *A Tale of the Times* (1st edn London, 1799).
——, *The Refusal* (London, 1810).
Wheatley, Charles, *Fifty Sermons on Several Subjects and Occasions* (London 1753).
Williams, Helen Maria, *Julia: A Novel* (London, 1790).
——, *Letters on the French Revolution* (Boston, 1791, and later edns).
——, *Poems* (London, 1786).
Wilson, Revd Thomas, *Sacra Privata: The Private Meditations and Prayers of the
Right Revd Thomas Wilson, DD* (Bath, 1804).
Young, Edward, *Love of Fame, the Universal Passion* (1728, numerous later edns).
Zimmerman, Johann Georg (unspecified work).

Anonymous or Several Authors

Annual Register (started by R. Dodsley and published 1759 on).
British Public Characters (various edns, 1799–1810).
Geraldina: A Novel, Founded on a Recent Event (London, 1798).

The Correspondents: An Original Novel in a Series of Letters (possibly by Miss Berry, 1st edn 1775).

The Lounger, by H. Mackenzie and others (a periodical paper published by W. Creech in Edinburgh, 1785).

The Microcosm: A Periodical Work by Gregory Griffin of the College of Eton (written by George Canning, John Smith, Robert Smith and John Hookham Frere). (Windsor, 1787, also later edns).

The Mirror, by H. Mackenzie and others (a periodical paper published by W. Creech in Edinburgh, 1779–80).

The Spectator, by J. Addison, Sir R. Steele and others (periodical published 1711–14, with many later edns).

The Whole Duty of Man ... with Private Devotions (various edns in the seventeenth and eighteenth centuries).

Bibliography

Acland, Anne, *A Devon Family: The Story of the Aclands* (London and Chichester, 1981).

Bell, Alan, *Sydney Smith* (Oxford, 1980).

Benger, Miss [Elizabeth Ogilvy], *Memoirs of the Late Mrs Elizabeth Hamilton* (London, 1818).

Bindman, David, *The Shadow of the Guillotine: Britain and the French Revolution* (London, 1989).

Boorman, David, *The Brighton of Wales: Swansea as a Fashionable Seaside Resort, c. 1780–c. 1830* (Swansea, 1986).

Borer, Mary Cathcart, *Willingly to School: A History of Women's Education* (London, 1976).

Borsay, Peter, *The English Urban Renaissance* (Oxford, 1989).

Brewer, John, *The Pleasures of the Imagination* (London, 1997).

Collins, Irene, *Jane Austen and the Clergy* (London and Rio Grande, Ohio, 1993).

Collinson, Revd John, *The History and Antiquities of the County of Somerset* (3 vols, Bath, 1791).

Cox, Cynthia, *The Enigma of the Age: The Strange Story of the Chevalier d'Eon* (London, 1966).

Davidoff, Leonore, and Hall, Catherine, *Family Fortunes: Men and Women of the English Middle Class, 1780–1850* (London, 1987).

Davies, T. G., 'Lewis Weston Dillwyn and his Doctors', *Morgannwg*, 32 (1988), pp. 70–89.

Denny, Barbara, *Chelsea Past* (London, 1996).

Dictionary of National Biography (London, 1885–1900).

Evans, Eric L., *The Forging of the Modern State* (London, 1996).

Foster, Joseph, *Alumni Oxonienses, 1715–1786* (London and Oxford, 1887–88).

Furbank, P. N., Owens, W. R., and Coulson, A. J. (eds), Daniel Defoe, *A Tour Through the Whole Island of Great Britain* (London, 1991).

Gardiner, Dorothy, *English Girlhood at School* (Oxford, 1929).

Gentleman's Magazine (London, 1731 on).

Greig, James (ed.), *The Farington Diary* (Joseph Farington, RA, 1793–1821) (8 vols, London, 1922–28).

Hall, Edward (ed.), *Miss Weeton's Journal of a Governess* (new edn, Newton Abbot, Devon, 1969).

Harvey, Sir Paul, and Heseltine, J. E. (eds), *Oxford Companion to French Literature* (Oxford, 1959).

Hemlow, Joyce et al. (eds), *The Journals and Letters of Fanny Burney (Madame d'Arblay)* (12 vols, Oxford, 1972–84).

Hicks Beach, Mrs William, *A Cotswold Family* (London, 1909).

Honan, Park, *Jane Austen: Her Life* (London, 1987).

Howe, Bea, *A Galaxy of Governesses* (London, 1954).

Hufton, Olwen, *The Prospect Before Her* (London, 1995).

Hughes, Kathryn, *The Victorian Governess* (London and Rio Grande, Ohio, 1993).

Hutchins, John, *The History and Antiquities of the County of Dorset* (4 vols, 3rd edn, London, 1861–74).

Kamm, Josephine, *Hope Deferred: Girls' Education in English History* (London, 1965).

Kinross, John, *Fishguard Fiasco* (Tenby, 1974).

Le Faye, Deirdre (ed.), *Jane Austen's Letters* (paperback edn, Oxford, 1997).

Lewis, Samuel, *A Topographical Dictionary of England* (London, 1831).

Lonsdale, Roger (ed.), *Eighteenth-Century Women Poets* (Oxford, 1989).

Lucas, R. L. T., *A Gower Family: The Lucases of Stouthall and Rhosili Rectory* (Lewes, 1986).

Lummis, Trevor, and Marsh, Jan, *The Woman's Domain* (London, 1990).

Malkin, Benjamin Heath, *The Scenery, Antiquities and Biography of South Wales* (2nd edn, London, 1807).

Martin, Joanna, *Henry and the Fairy Palace: Fox Talbot and Glamorgan* (Aberystwyth, 1993).

Martin, Joanna (ed.), *The Penrice Letters, 1768–1795* (Cardiff and Swansea, 1993).

Mundy, Harriot Georgiana (ed.), *The Journal of Mary Frampton* (London, 1885).

Palmer, C. J., *The Perlustration of Great Yarmouth* (3 vols, Great Yarmouth, 1872-75).

Phillips, Patricia, *The Scientific Lady* (London, 1990).

Pollock, L. A., 'Teach Her to Live Under Obedience: The Making of Women in the Upper Ranks of Early Modern England', *Continuity and Change*, 4 (1989), pp. 231–58.

Renton, Alice, *Tyrant or Victim? A History of the British Governess* (London, 1991).

Sale, Geoffrey, *Four Hundred Years of a School: A Short History of King's School, Bruton* (Dorchester, 1950).

Schama, Simon, *Citizens: A Chronicle of the French Revolution* (London, 1989).

Scheider, Benn Ross Jr, *Index to The London Stage, 1660–1800* (Illinois, 1979).

Skrine, Henry, *Two Successive Tours Throughout the Whole of Wales* (London, 1798).

Smith, Nowell C. (ed.), *The Letters of Sydney Smith* (Oxford, 1953).

Smith, Sydney, *The Works of the Revd Sydney Smith* (3 vols, 2nd edn, London, 1840).

Stone, Lawrence, *The Family, Sex and Marriage in England, 1500–1800* (London, 1977).

Thorne, R. G., *The House of Commons, 1790–1820* (London, 1986).

Tillyard, Stella, *Citizen Lord: Edward Fitzgerald, 1763–98* (London, 1997).

Venn, J. and J., *Alumni Cantabrigienses*, ii, *1757–1900* (Cambridge, 1940–53).

Vicinus, M. (ed.), *Suffer and Be Still* (Bloomington, Indiana, 1972).

Virgin, Peter, *Sydney Smith* (London, 1994).

Wallis, P. J. and R. V., *Eighteenth-Century Medics* (Newcastle-upon-Tyne, 1988).

West, Katharine, *A Chapter of Governesses* (London, 1949).

Williams, Glanmor, *Swansea: An Illustrated History* (Swansea, 1990).

Index

(references to plates are in bold)